The State of the Parties

People, Passions, and Power

Social Movements, Interest Organizations, and the Political Process
John C. Green, Series Editor

Titles in the Series

Forthcoming

The State of the Parties

The Changing Role of Contemporary American Politics

FIFTH EDITION

Edited by John C. Green
and Daniel J. Coffey

ROWMAN & LITTLEFIELD PUBLISHERS, INC.
Lanham • Boulder • New York • Toronto • Oxford

ROWMAN & LITTLEFIELD PUBLISHERS, INC.

Published in the United States of America
by Rowman & Littlefield Publishers, Inc.
A wholly owned subsidary of The Rowman & Littlefield Publishing Group, Inc.
4501 Forbes Boulevard, Suite 200, Lanham, Maryland 20706
www.rowmanlittlefield.com

PO Box 317
Oxford
OX2 9RU, UK

Copyright © 2007 by Rowman & Littlefield Publishers, Inc.

All rights reserved. No part of this publication may be reproduced,
stored in a retrieval system, or transmitted in any form or by any
means, electronic, mechanical, photocopying, recording, or otherwise,
without the prior permission of the publisher.

British Library Cataloguing in Publication Information Available

Library of Congress Cataloging-in-Publication Data

The state of the parties : the changing role of contemporary American politics / edited by
John C. Green and Daniel J. Coffey.—5th ed.
    p.   cm.
Includes bibliographical references and index.
ISBN-13: 978-0-7425-5321-7 (cloth : alk. paper)
ISBN-10: 0-7425-5321-3 (cloth : alk. paper)
ISBN-13: 978-0-7425-5322-4 (pbk. : alk. paper)
ISBN-10: 0-7425-5322-1 (pbk. : alk. paper)
    1. Political parties—United States.   I. Green, John Clifford, 1953–
II. Coffey, Daniel J., 1975–
JK2261.S824 2006
324.273—dc22   2006007292

Printed in the United States of America

©™ The paper used in this publication meets the minimum requirements of American
National Standard for Information Sciences—Permanence of Paper for Printed Library
Materials, ANSI/NISO Z39.48-1992.

Contents

Tables and Figures

Tables

Figures

7.2   Colorado Republican and Democratic Parties, Total
      Contributions, 2000–2004   126
7.3   Florida Republican and Democratic Parties, Total
      Expenditures, 2000–2004   128
7.4   Colorado Republican and Democratic Parties, Total
      Expenditures, 2000–2004   130
14.1 The Dynamic of Third Parties   232
14.2 Two-Dimensional Map of 1992 Candidates and Parties   237
14.3 Spillover Effect of 1992 Perot Activism on Activity in 1994
      Republican House Campaigns by Contact from Republican
      Campaign   240
14.4 Mean Position on Perot Issues for Core Republicans,
      Democrats, Reformers, and Reformers Mobilized by the
      Republican Party, 1996–2004   241
14.5 Relative Major Party Campaign Activity for Reform
      Contributor Sample, 2000–2004   244
15.1 Democracy Corps Poll Feeling Thermometers Regarding
      Ralph Nader, August 2000–November 2004   254
16.1 By-products of Partisan Polarization, 1952–2004   271
17.1 The Effect of Religiosity and Class on Partisanship   284
18.1 Path Analysis of Ideology and Party Identification for White
      Respondents in 1992–1996 NES Panel Survey   309
19.1 Trends in Conservative Positions, 1970–2004   318
19.2 Percentage with Conservative Position Identifying with
      Republican Party, 1970–2004   321
19.3 Percentage of Those with Conservative Views Voting for
      Republican Presidential and House Candidates, 1976–2004   322
19.4 Percentage of Those with Conservative Views Identifying
      with the Republican Party and Percentage of Party from
      Conservatives, 1976–2004   322
19.5 Distribution of House Republican Members' Voting Records,
      1900–2000   323
19.6 Percentage of House Conservatives within the Republican
      Party, 1900–2000   324
19.7 Correlation of House and Presidential Vote Results,
      1900–2004   326
21.1 Party Strength, Majority Size, and Polarization, 1965–2004 345
22.1 Republican Percentage in the U.S. House and Senate   361
22.2 Number of Governorships and State Legislatures Controlled
      by Republicans   362
22.3 Republican Percentage in the U.S. House and Senate, by
      Region   363

Acknowledgments

The research effort that produced this book is the product of more than a decade of scholarship. The first edition originated from research coordinated in 1993 at the Ray C. Bliss Institute of Applied Politics on the changing role of political parties in American politics. The second edition reflected the impact of the 1994 elections on political parties, while the third and fourth editions reported further changes after the 1996 and 2000 elections, respectively. The present, fifth edition considers the impact of the 2004 election and subsequent events.

From the beginning of this effort, our goal has been to bring together party scholars from around the nation to discuss the state of U.S. party politics and new avenues of research. On each occasion, we have been privileged to field a "dream team" of contributors, and although the roster has differed a little each time, the team for this edition is just as strong, including a mix of veteran and emerging scholars. Taken together, the essays in this volume offer insight into the "state of the parties" now that the twenty-first century is under way.

The development of this volume was greatly aided by the staff of the Bliss Institute. Janet Bolois was not only instrumental in compiling the chapters and managing the layout but has also honed the unique skill of putting up with the editors—no simple task, to be sure. Kimberly Haverkamp deserves special mention for her invaluable assistance with logistics, and Patricia Hallam provided a careful reading of the manuscript and a critical eye. As before, we owe a debt of thanks to Jennifer Knerr and her successor at Rowman & Littlefield, Niels Aaboe, and their associates. Finally, we would surely be remiss if we did not acknowledge our families, principally Lynn Green and Mary Coffey. Without their unwavering support and encouragement, *The State of the Parties* would not have been possible.

1

The State of the Parties in a Polarized Nation

Daniel J. Coffey and John C. Green

The 2004 campaign was among the most hotly contested in American history. Following the bitter 2000 election, both of the major political parties expected another close battle. In some respects, each party returned to older forms of campaigning, focusing on grassroots mobilization, but with new methods. The Democrats, stung by the events that took place in Florida in 2000, conducted nationwide get-out-the-vote drives with special help from interest group allies. Meanwhile the Republicans organized a voter canvass that reached down to the precincts using modern targeting and communication techniques. On election night, 60 percent of Americans turned out to vote, the highest percentage since 1968. This surge in participation produced a closely divided result, with a very narrow majority for the Republicans.

The critical role of political parties in generating these results suggests that the era of party decline has long since passed. Party scholars argue that it is no coincidence that a more active and vibrant party system has led to greater levels of citizen participation. Of course, the resurgence of parties leads to a new set of questions. Has there been a fundamental change in the party system? Have changes in campaign finance law changed the role of parties and their interest groups allies in campaigns? Will the parties put as much effort into grassroots mobilization in future elections? Has the public become too polarized? Can government institutions function well under these circumstances?

This collection of essays is the fifth in the series that assesses the state of the parties after a presidential election (the earlier editions were Shea and Green 1994; Green and Shea 1996, 1999; and Green and Farmer 2003). In this volume, a group of prominent and emerging scholars examines the state of the parties from a variety of perspectives. Overall, research on political parties often is subsumed by other issues, such as legislative studies, public opinion research, and studies of campaign finance and elections. As the following chapters show, however, political parties are vibrant institutions, central to all these aspects of politics in a functioning democracy. As such, political parties are worthy of study in their own right.

Here we break down the study of parties into six sections: the party system, party resources, party activities, minor parties, partisanship in the public, and the party in government. Before we do, so, however, it is useful to review the 2004 election.

The Election of 2004

Once again, the 2004 presidential election came down to a few battleground states, with twelve states decided by less than 5 percent of the vote. To the surprise of many, Florida, the center of the controversy in the 2000, election, backed George W. Bush with 52 percent of the vote. Instead, Ohio was the deciding state. The vote count was not as close as Florida in 2000 and the balloting controversies were settled fairly quickly. With victories in Ohio, Iowa, and New Mexico, Bush won with 286 electoral votes and was reelected to a second term.

In the end, 2004 was a banner year for the GOP, reinforcing its victory in the 2002 midterm elections. Bush became the first president since his father in 1988 to win more than 50 percent of the popular vote. In all, the GOP picked up four Senate seats, to bring their margin to 55–45, and three House seats, increasing their margin of control to 232–202. The Republicans then had more seats in Congress than at any time since 1948. Bush entered his second term in office with his party controlling the Congress, something that had eluded Richard Nixon and Ronald Reagan when they were reelected.

A Durable Republican Majority?

These results lead to the larger historical questions: Has the Republican Party become the majority party in the United States? Has a partisan realignment occurred? Many observers answer with a qualified yes. Since 1994, Republicans have consistently won elections at all levels of government. They have constructed strong and effective party organizations. The minor party agitation of the 1990s has declined, largely to their benefit. Despite some scholars' predictions of an "emerging Democratic majority" (Judis and Teixeira 2002), the Republicans also have gained parity with the Democrats in the allegiance of the voters, doing surprisingly well among many Democratic groups in the electorate, including Hispanics, women, and Roman Catholics. And they have governed in a consistently conservative fashion, despite great controversy and fierce opposition.

However, other observers are still skeptical of a Republican realignment. Despite the party's successes, the Unites States is still a "fifty-fifty nation," with Bush winning just over 50 percent of the popular vote. The Republican party organizations have no monopoly on new resources and techniques, and some of the most innovative features of the 2004 campaign came from the Democrats and their allies. A polarized public shows no inclination to strongly embrace the Republicans, and it contains huge pockets of discontent. Although polls have shown time and again that the public believes the Republicans can do a better job dealing with terrorism, the September 11, 2001, terrorist attacks and the subsequent War on Terror have not appeared to have caused a mass realignment as the Great Depression did. This is in part due to the Bush administration's aggressive antiterrorism policies. As evidence of this, nearly 40 percent of citizens in a January 2006 Gallup poll felt that the Bush administration had gone too far in restricting individual liberties to fight terrorism. President Bush has, not surprisingly, remained a highly polarizing figure.

Moreover, the Republican margins in government are also razor thin. For example, the GOP's historic majority of 232 seats in the House of Representatives would have been the *smallest* Democratic majority in their long period of control from 1954 to 1994. And after the 2004 election, each of the major parties held exactly 3,657 state legislative seats (National Conference of State Legislatures 2005). And as the Republicans discovered in 2005 and 2006, unified party control is a double-edged sword. When one party holds the reins of government, it is more likely to be held accountable for the problems that occur under its watch.

Along these lines, a number of scandals in 2005 appear to place the Democrats in an advantageous position going into 2006. Fundraising scandals, ties to corrupt lobbyists, the administration's slow response to the catastrophic Hurricane Katrina (contrasting so sharply with the administration's quick response to 9/11), and revelations of domestic spying by the National Security Agency all threaten the GOP's majority party status.

Democrats will nevertheless face an uphill battle to regain control of Congress in 2006. This is especially true given Republican control of the redistricting process in several states. As Jacobson (2005a, 165) points out, after the 2000 census, the GOP managed to gain fifteen congressional seats in states where Republicans directed the redistricting process through partisan gerrymandering. Democrats are still plagued by fighting between centrists and progressives over the direction of the party, especially in how it responds to President Bush's policies. Moreover, although scholars continue to debate the significance of the Republicans' success in the 1994 midterm elections, a Democratic sweep in 2006 or 2008 may not necessarily presage the end of Republican dominance. In fact, mid-realignment breaks, when the out-party gets a few years in power, appear to occur with some regularity.[1]

Clearly, however, the 2006 midterm elections and the 2008 presidential contests will be important tests of a durable Republican majority. Significantly, as the first presidential election since 1928 without a sitting president or vice president on the ballot, the 2008 nomination could lead to one of the most divisive primary seasons in years for both parties.

New Finance Rules

The 2004 elections were the first campaign to operate under the Bipartisan Campaign Finance Reform Act of 2002 (BCRA) and its new finance rules. BCRA banned "soft money," otherwise illegal contributions raised by the political parties, and it set limits on "issue advocacy" broadcast spending paid for by corporate or union treasury funds within sixty days of a general election. While the hope of most reformers was to reduce the amount of money in politics, BCRA appeared to have little influence on the overall amount raised and spent, as the major parties took advantage of higher contribution limits and Internet fundraising to raise additional "hard money" donations. In fact, the Democratic and Republican National Committees raised more hard money in 2004 than hard and soft money combined in 2000.

BCRA did, however, have a major impact on *how* money was raised and spent. Even without soft money, parties were able to spend unlimited funds on uncoordinated expenditures. Meanwhile, interest groups turned to "527 committees"—advocacy organizations falling under Section 527 of the Internal Revenue Code—to raise and spend unregulated funds. Here, the new restrictions on issue advocacy meant that such spending occurred prior to the sixty-day blackout before the election or went into nonbroadcast expenditures such as direct mail and grassroots activities. All told, the 527 committees raised and spent nearly $600 million in the 2004 election (Curriander 2005, 123).

Democrats appeared to benefit the most from the 527 committees, reflecting their historic disadvantage in raising hard money. The highly polarized context of the election led to the formation of new groups supporting and opposing President Bush. On the Democratic side, America Coming Together, the Media Fund, and MoveOn.org were three of the most prominent (Curriander 2005, 123). These and other progressive groups were part of a broader coalition, America Votes, designed to coordinate such campaigning. On the Republican side, prominent 527 committees included Progress for America and Swift Boat Veterans for Truth. The latter made charges against John Kerry's Vietnam service that had an impact on the outcome.

These innovations were part of the extraordinary voter mobilization on both sides. But 2004 was a major disappointment for the Democrats. Contrary to conventional wisdom, the dramatic increase in turnout did little to help the party. Moreover, Kerry's campaign, which raised more money than any other Democratic campaign in history, lost its edge to the Bush campaign where the Democrats have traditionally been strongest: at the grass roots.

These organizational innovations are in a state of flux and thus are important factors to watch in the upcoming campaigns.

A Polarized Electorate

In 2004, the electorate was polarized, a fact captured somewhat crudely in the distinction between "red" (Republican) and "blue" (Democratic) states. However, the switch of Iowa and New Mexico to the Republican column and New Hampshire to the Democratic means that the Electoral College map is now almost as neatly segmented as it was in the election of 1896. Thus, region has reappeared as a feature of national politics. Democratic strongholds are now relegated to the Northeast, Upper Midwest, and Pacific Coast, while the Republican bastions include the South, Plains and Mountain states, and Lower Midwest. The South is critical to this new regionalism, having completed its long movement from a Democratic- to a Republican-dominated region. As Nelson (2005, 5) points out, President Bush became the first president since Franklin Roosevelt to win more than 1,000 Southern counties in consecutive elections.

These regional differences mirror a sharp division in voter preferences. After the 2004 election, a popular political cartoon joked that the blue states should secede from the nation and join the "United States of Canada," while the red states were dubbed "Jesus Land." This joke reflects important differences in the values of many Americans. To the surprise of many observers, the 2004 exit polls found "moral values" to be the central concern of a plurality of voters (22 percent). This concern should not be overstated, however, because "moral values" was only marginally more important than the war in Iraq (15 percent), terrorism (19 percent), and the economy and jobs (20 percent).[2] But it does suggest that cultural disputes have become an important part of the political agenda. A good example is the role of same-sex marriage in the 2004 campaign, during which anti-same-sex marriage amendments passed in eleven states, including the battleground states of Ohio, Michigan, and Oregon (Donovan et al. 2005).

The "moral values" voters reflected a growing difference between secular and religious Americans. According to exit polls, 78 percent of white born-again Protestants—making up 23 percent of the electorate—voted for Bush in 2004. Just as important, the religious versus secular divide appeared to grow in 2004. Church attendance was significantly related to Bush support; 61 percent of those attending church weekly voted for Bush, compared to only 36 percent of those who never attend and 47 percent who report they attend services only occasionally. One of the biggest differences was a "marriage gap." Married people voted at a rate of 57 percent for Bush (up from compared 53 percent in 2000), while only 40 percent of singles did so.

These regional, issue, and demographic differences produced an extraordinary partisan division in 2004: 93 percent of self-identified Republicans voted for Bush and 89 percent of self-identified Democrats backed Kerry. The independents broke almost evenly (48 percent for Bush to 49 percent for Kerry).[3]

The Party System

Part 1 of this book considers the state of the broader party system in this highly polarized electorate. In chapter 2, James Reichley argues that American party alignments operate on sixty- to seventy-year cycles, as opposed to the more typical thirty-year realigning cycles. From this perspective, the 1990s were a realigning period in which the Republicans tentatively replaced the Democrats as the nation's majority party. Reichley sorts through the complexities of the 2004 campaign and concludes that the Republicans may well become the normal majority party. Thus, 2004 reveals the operations of a new party system.

According to Howard Reiter in chapter 3, the sharp partisan divisions of the present era have dampened intraparty factionalism. Reiter points out, however, that this does not mean the end of party factions. Like "old war wounds," these divisions remain latent within the major party coalitions. So, for example, Howard Dean's candidacy revived the division between centrist and liberal Democrats, and the war in Iraq may presage a cleavage between conservative and moderate Republicans. Regional differences are a critical factor in such factions, which may play a crucial role in the 2008 presidential nomination contests.

Chapter 4 turns to the "state of party elites," where John Jackson, Nate Bigelow, and John Green analyze the attitudes of national party convention delegates between 1992 and 2004. They find strong and systematic differences between Democratic and Republican delegates over the period. These cleavages were especially deep on the social welfare questions, reinforced by cultural and foreign policy disagreements. At the same time, however, there was a consolidation of factions with the parties, so that in 2004 a centrist faction played a dominant role in each party—the "New Democrats" and the "Moderate Republicans," respectively. These factions have a clear regional character as well.

This polarization of party activists also extends to state political parties. In chapter 5, Daniel J. Coffey analyzes the ideological content of state party platforms and finds sharp differences between the Democrats and Republicans. Importantly, this study finds almost no link between the ideology of state party platforms and median public opinion. Instead, the issue polarization is strongly related to the views of party activists and political competition. While this ideological coherence strengthens state party coalitions in important respects, Coffey's analysis shows that parties may be in danger of losing popular support if ideologically motivated activists take the parties too far from the political center.

Party Resources

Part 2 turns to party resources, where there were major innovations in 2004. In chapter 6, Diana Dwyre, Eric Heberlig, Robin Kolodny, and Bruce Larson demonstrate that the new campaign finance laws did not reduce national party committee finances because the parties found new ways to raise and spend money. They were able raise record amounts of "hard dollar" contributions and incumbent members of Congress became a significant source of party funds. They also found new ways to spend a record amount of money in campaigns, including the expansion of independent expenditures on behalf of candidates. However, these trends did not increase competition in congressional elections and they raise troubling questions about the role of money in politics.

In chapter 7, Ray La Raja, Susan Orr, and Daniel Smith find that the new campaign finance laws had a similar effect on state party finances. State parties actually raised more "hard money" in 2004 than in 2000, and in battleground states, the parties increased candidate support for mobilizing voters. However, in nonbattleground states, the state parties were less able to carry out voter mobilization efforts. Indeed, the national laws appear to have had less of an impact on state parties than the electoral and legal context of the state. The import of local circumstances makes the long-term impact of the federal campaign finance laws far from clear.

The 2004 campaign also saw innovations in the campaign spending of interest groups. David Magleby, Quin Monson, and Kelly Patterson explore these developments in chapter 8 with their analysis of America Votes (AV), a coalition of thirty-two progressive interest groups that sought to coordinate their campaign efforts. Some of the AV members were 527 committees newly minted to take advantage of the latest campaign finance laws; the best known of these committees was America Coming Together. This analysis finds that AV behaved much like coalitions of lobbying groups, allowing its members to specialize in particular activities. Whether this innovation will persist in 2008 is unclear.

One of the most interesting aspects of the 2004 election was Howard Dean's presidential nomination campaign. Dubbed the first "Internet campaign," it has implications beyond the 2004 election—especially because Dean became the chairman of the Democratic National Committee in 2005.

In chapter 9, Scott Keeter, Cary Funk, and Courtney Kennedy report on an innovative survey of Dean's campaign volunteers. The "Deaniacs" were to the left of the general population and rank-and-file Democrats on many issues but were quite similar to other liberals. The impact of technology in mobilizing new resources from distinctive party factions could dramatically alter party politics in the future.

Party Activities

Part 3 reports on the operation of political parties circa the 2004 election. In chapter 10, Peter Ubertaccio explores Republican efforts to strengthen their grassroots party organization. Ubertaccio shows that the Republicans successfully applied the techniques of "multilevel marketing" (MLM) companies, such as Amway, to improve their ability to register and turn out voters. The best example was the "72-Hour Task Force" that allowed Republicans to match the traditional Democratic get-out-the-vote advantage in 2002 and 2004. Ubertaccio argues that MLM techniques represent a new model of local parties that relies on neither patronage-based nor consultant-driven organizations. The Bush campaign employed this approach successfully in 2004 and the Democrats may pursue it in the future.

The Democrats and their allies opted for another approach in the 2004, mixing new and old grassroots techniques. In chapter 11, Melanie Blumberg, William Binning, and John Green offer a case study of this campaign in Mahoning County, Ohio, a crucial Democratic stronghold. Here they detail the impressive grassroots efforts of America Coming Together, organized labor, the Kerry campaign, and Democratic Party organizations. The study concludes that the inability of the Democratic campaign to coordinate the diverse elements of the campaign proved costly on Election Day, and furthermore, the new campaign finance laws contributed to the "uncoordinated" campaign.

In chapter 12, David Dulio and R. Sam Garrett report on the continued professionalization of party organizations by reviewing the relationship between campaign consultants and state party operatives. Using a new measure of state party organizational strength, they find that consultants are *allies* of state parties rather than *adversaries*. The latter view is advanced by not only some scholars but also some party activists, as demonstrated by Howard Dean's critique of professionalized politics as chair of the Democratic National Committee. Dulio and Garrett demonstrate that, in fact, consultants and parties perform complementary roles in the campaign process, and both weak and strong parties benefit from their specialized services.

Dan Shea and John Green turn to a study of local party activities and the mobilization of young voters in chapter 12. Although local party organizations have experienced gains in organizational strength in recent times, it is far from clear that they are effectively connecting with young voters—who are, after all, critical to the parties' future success. This failure is due primarily to the perception that youth mobilization is too difficult and to a lack of innovative outreach. The authors argue that local parties can contribute to rejuvenating political participation in the United States by successfully reaching out to the youth vote.

Minor Parties

As discussed in part 4, minor party candidates had a negligible direct effect on the presidential election in 2004, unlike 1992 and 1996, when Ross Perot was on the ballot, or 2000, when Ralph Nader made a difference. However, in chapter 14, Ronald Rapoport and Walter Stone demonstrate that the Perot phenomenon continued to matter to the major party coalitions. Reporting on an innovative twelve-year panel study of Perot activists, they find that the Republican success between 1994 and 2004 was due in part to the support of these individuals. This pattern aptly illustrates the "dynamic of third parties," whereby the major parties bid for the support of a successful minor party's constituency in subsequent elections. Interestingly, they find that these Perotistas have become disenchanted with the Republicans under President Bush and may be available to the Democrats in 2008.

In chapter 15, Christian Collet and Jerrold Hansen report on the desultory Nader campaign of 2004. Nader's shunning of the Green Party in 2004 damaged its prospects of becoming a viable minor party, while Nader's increasing shrill populism harmed his own reputation. Due to the memories of the bitterly contested 2000 election, Nader's core supporters in 2000—liberals in the Mountain West and New England—deserted him in favor of Kerry. The Nader 2004 supporters amounted to a disparate set of alienated voters of various sorts rather than the progressive constituency of 1992 and 1996. The authors are pessimistic about the prospects for an effective third-party candidate in the present period of party polarization.

Partisanship and the Public

Part 5 reviews the "party-in-the-electorate" or "party-in-elections" (Aldrich 1995). In chapter 16, David Kimball and Cassie Gross examine the much-debated polarization of the mass electorate. They note an important psychological aspect of polarization, an "us versus them" mentality, missed by other analyses of the electorate. President Bush was a highly polarizing political figure, aided and abetted by the mobilizing activities of party elites and their interest group allies. Party polarization was concentrated among the most partisan and attentive citizens. It will be interesting to see if this level of polarization persists in the 2008 election.

In chapter 17, John R. Petrocik helps explain this polarized electorate by looking at the components of the major party coalitions. He argues that the core values of a party are largely determined by the social characteristics of the groups that make up each party's coalition, and he shows how the Democratic and Republican coalitions have changed since the New Deal era. A key difference is the increased importance of religious commitment in 2004. As a consequence, cultural issues were important enough in the minds of many voters to trump economic and foreign policy issues. Thus, contemporary parties represent a significantly different alignment of social groups than those of a generation ago.

Kyle Saunders and Alan Abramowitz offer another insight into voter polarization in chapter 18: the electorate has become more ideological. They argue that voters' self-identified ideology is a far more powerful force in determining partisan identification and that it has become more so over time. In their view, this ideological cleavage in the vote is a product of citizens' rational assessment of each party's policies, which have grown increasingly distinctive. This high level of consistency between citizens' policy assessments and partisan leanings suggests that the current era of polarized politics will continue in the future.

In chapter 19, Jeffrey Stonecash explores the conventional wisdom that the public has become more conservative in this era of partisan polarization. He shows that there is only modest evidence that the citizenry has adopted more conservative views. Instead, he finds that conservatives have become more concentrated in the Republican Party, reducing its internal divisions and producing a more unified conservative posture. While Stonecash analyzes only the GOP, the same may be true of the Democrats, where liberals have become highly concentrated as well.

Party in Government

Part 6 considers party in government. In chapter 20, Richard Skinner argues that scholars need to reevaluate the role of partisanship in the White House. He argues for a "partisan presidency" that stands in sharp contrast to the "modern presidency" of the mid-twentieth century. Indeed, since the New Deal, the presidency has largely been independent of the parties, as each president seeks to enact a personal agenda. For Skinner, the partisan presidents include Ronald Reagan and Bill Clinton, but especially George W. Bush. Bush's aggressive campaigns for congressional Republicans, strongly partisan legislative agenda, and overtly partisan administrative practices have produced something like unified party government in Washington, D.C. Whether this kind of party unity will persist in the future remains to be seen.

There is no greater exemplar of party polarization than the House of Representatives. In chapter 21, Lawrence Butler argues that scholars need a better understanding of the role of the leadership within the House in enforcing party unity. Scholars, he argues, need to distinguish between party unity and party effectiveness in passing legislation. After the Republican "revolution" of 1994, a more centralized leadership was implemented. This new order may well have allowed the GOP to pass legislation despite the very narrow Republican margin of control of the body. This leadership will be tested during President Bush's second term.

In chapter 22, Shannon Jenkins, Doug Roscoe, John Frendreis, and Alan Gitelson offer an evaluation of the key 1994 election—which put the GOP in charge of the U.S. Congress and many state governments—from the perspective of a decade later. Contrary to some early assessments, these authors show that the election was indeed significant, with sudden Republican gains that largely persisted ten years afterward. However, this dramatic change had two parts. In the South, the 1994 election was the result of steady Republican gains, but in the North it was a sudden surge. The authors conclude that the Republican gains created a new partisan equilibrium in national politics.

In chapter 23, David Ryden analyzes the role of the U.S. Supreme Court in determining the state of the parties. The Court has shown an increasing willingness to rule on nearly every aspect of the electoral process, including redistricting and campaign finance reform, two areas Ryden reviews in detail. In this regard, the Courts for political parties operate in and outside of government. Ryden argues, however, that the Court has yet to develop a clear doctrine of regarding political parties to guide its deliberations. Thus, its decisions are frequently problematic for the functioning of a democratic politics. In this final chapter, the book comes full circle: the laws the Courts develop are a key feature of the broader party system.

Unanswered Questions

These essays leave a number of questions on the table about the state of the parties in the near future. Among the most important are:

- Will the GOP cement its role as the majority party? Or will the Democrats stage a comeback? Will the party system return to an even match in partisan terms?
- Will the parties maintain strong and vital organizations? How will state parties perform in the long run without soft money? Will interest

group coalitions such as America Votes and 527 committees such as America Coming Together continue to matter?

- Will the parties continue to make concerted efforts to mobilize citizens at the grass roots? If party competition dies down, will voter turnout decline as well? Will local parties seek to find new supporters, especially among the young?
- Have we seen the end of important third-party movements, or will third-party support reemerge if public disapproval for the parties rises?
- With 2008 approaching, will the departure of President Bush from the White House reduce the polarization of the voters? Will regional divisions persist and will cultural differences remain a part of the political agenda?
- How well will government institutions perform in a polarized politics? Will the partisan presidency endure or pass away? How will the Courts regulate the political process?

Notes

1. In previous realignment cycles, the minority party has managed to win brief but unified control of the federal government: the Whigs in 1841–1843, the Democrats in 1893–1894 and again in 1913–1917, and the Republicans in 1953–1954. On two other occasions, the minority party has managed to win control of both houses of Congress: the Democrats in 1879–1880 and the Republicans in 1948–1949.

2. Exit poll data from CNN, http://www.cnn.com/ELECTION/2004/pages/results/states/US/P/00/epolls.0.html.

3. Ibid.

Part I

The Party System

The Future of the American Two-Party System in the Twenty-First Century

A. James Reichley

American political parties are back. After several decades in which they were variously pronounced "weakened by years of neglect" (Broder 1971), "mere jousting grounds for embattled politicians" (Burns 1973), afflicted by "a massive loss of public confidence" (Burnham 1982), "in disarray— more so than at any time in the last century" (Keefe 1988), replaced by "the news and publicity media as primary organizers of citizen action and legitimizers of public decisions" (Polsby and Wildavsky 1988), and "in a late stage of a century-long decline" (Shafer 2003), parties are once more at the very heart of American politics, thriving, unified, well financed, and shaping voter decisions.

During the 1990s there were growing signs of party revival. Party unity on roll-call voting in Congress rose steadily throughout the decade (Pomper 2003). National party organizations raised and spent unprecedented campaign war chests (Corrado, Barclay, and Gouvea 2003). Party loyalty in elections increased, and ticket splitting sharply declined (Ceaser and Busch 2001; Hetherington 2001). By the end of the decade L. Sandy Maisel (1999) found parties once more "the vital linking institution" in American government.

As the new century began, some thoughtful political analysts, while welcoming the resurgence of party activity, continued to question the staying power of parties as effective forces in national politics. "The role of parties in elections," Maisel warned, "remains in doubt." John Kenneth White and Daniel Shea observed that parties still had failed "to reestablish their connection with the voters" (2000).

During the first term of President George W. Bush, however, both major national parties achieved increased organizational strength and appeared to tighten their grips on voter loyalties. In Congress, both parties—particularly the dominant Republicans—were "cohesive and elaborately organized" (Sinclair 2002). In the House of Representatives, committee leaders were "more accountable to their party colleagues," and the Republican majority leadership exerted tighter procedural control than at any time since Speaker Joseph Cannon was stripped of some of his powers in 1910. In the Senate, power remained more diffuse, and the filibuster weapon restricted the majority's freedom to act, but party unity on roll-call votes continued to be high.

In the 2004 presidential election, 93 percent of Republicans and 89 percent of Democrats voted for the candidates of their respective parties—both figures unprecedented highs since modern polling began measuring the electorate. In voting for the House of Representatives, 91 percent of Republicans and 88 percent of Democrats cast ballots for their party's candidate—both also record highs in modern polling (White 2004). Only 14 percent of congressional districts elected House members from a different party than had carried them for president. About 25 percent of voters told pollsters on Election Day they regarded themselves as independents, but many of these in recent elections have consistently supported one party or the other. The 2004 National Election Study found that only 5 percent of those who actually voted were "pure independents," down from 7 percent in 2000. National turnout rose to 61 percent—the highest level since 1968.

Contrary to predictions by many analysts (including me), enactment of the 2002 McCain-Feingold campaign finance reform act did little to undermine the fundraising capacities of national parties. While prohibited from receiving unlimited corporate, union, or individual contributions—so-called soft money—both national parties in 2004 broke previous records in fundraising. The Democratic National Committee for the first time in recent history actually raised slightly more than the Republican National Committee, although overall the campaign of Bush and his Republican supporters slightly outspent Senator John Kerry and the Democrats—$1.14 billion to $1.08 billion (Federal Election Commission 2005b; Malbin 2006).

Modern national parties are, of course, far different from the parties of fifty years ago—more centralized, less based on patronage and more on ideology, more linked to high-priced political consultants and professional fundraisers. Halfway through the first decade of the new century, the cry of most reformers, media critics, and much of the public is not that parties are *too weak* but that they have become *too strong*, splitting the nation into bitterly polarized ideological camps, blocking compromise and cooperation in Congress, and favoring ideological extremes at the expense of the neglected middle.

Nevertheless, contemporary American political parties appear to come close, at least structurally, to the model proposed by the famous 1950 American Political Science Association report urging a "more responsible two-party system" (see Green and Herrnson 2002). As called for by the report, parties in the early years of the new century offer voters a genuine choice, more focused on policy alternatives than on ancient prejudices, and the majority party through congressional enactment or executive order is able to implement a large part of its program. If the political outcome so far is not exactly what many of the reformers had in mind, the party system may simply be giving expression to underlying currents in American democracy.

An Enduring Two-Party System

Strengthened parties have continued to function within the traditional two-party system that goes back at least to the years immediately after the Civil War and is rooted in party differences that emerged during George Washington's first term. The uprising of third parties in the 1990s that brought Ross Perot 19 percent of the popular vote in the 1992 presidential election (though no electoral votes) has for now largely subsided. Third-party candidates for president, including Ralph Nader, received less than 1 percent of the popular vote in 2004. The Congress elected in 2004 included only one member in the House not of a major party (Socialist Bernard Sanders of Vermont) and one in the Senate (Independent James Jeffords, also of Vermont), both of whom received committee assignments from their body's Democratic caucus.

Why has the two-party system, which in its rigor is almost unique in modern developed democracies, persisted so long in the United States? Maurice Duverger pointed out many years ago (in his formulation known as Duverger's Law) that polities maintaining single-member, first-past-the-post systems of election—principally the United States and Great Britain and some of its dominions—tend to promote the development of two major parties whose candidates have a real chance of winning elections (Duverger 1954).

Even polities such as Britain, Canada, and Australia, however, which like the United States use the first-past-the-post system, have generally had at least one significant minor party represented in parliament alongside the two major ones. Why have enduring minor parties with substantial impacts been so rare in the United States?

The first-past-the-post election system pushes us toward a two-party political system. But the constitutional factor that really has kept the system locked in place has been the institution of the Electoral College for choosing presidents.

Quite contrary to the intentions of the founders, almost all of whom hated parties, the Electoral College, as long as most states retain the at-large system for choosing electors, heavily favors the presidential nominees of the two major parties that can pile up large blocs of electoral votes in heavily populated states. The system even makes it improbable that a minor party could hold the balance of power between the two major parties, as has sometimes occurred in Britain and Canada.

Constitutional change to eliminate the Electoral College would entail a political effort that is not likely to be forthcoming. The less populated states benefit from being constitutionally overrepresented in the College (each state receives the combined total of its members in the Senate and the House), while the more populous states gain political clout from the at-large system of choosing electors. Together these interests maintain a formidable barrier against change.

The high visibility of the presidential election shapes the structure of our entire political system. As long as the Electoral College confines the real presidential competition to the candidates of the two major parties, the United States will probably continue to have a two-party system in most congressional and state elections.

Reinforcing the effects of the Electoral College and first-past-the-post elections, representatives of the two major parties have taken pains to enact state election laws that strongly advantage major-party candidates. In Pennsylvania, for example, major-party candidates for the state senate need only 2,000 signatures on petitions to get their names on the ballot, whereas independent or minor party candidates require 29,000 (reduced from 56,000 by court order).

A major national calamity or conflict might lead to the creation of a new major party, as the struggle over slavery gave birth to the Republicans in the 1850s. Barring such a catastrophe, though, it is probable not only that we will continue to have a two-party system but also that the Republicans and the Democrats will be the main contestants. After all, even the Great Depression of the 1930s failed to make enduring cracks in the two traditional major parties' shared monopoly of political power.

Why have the Democrats and the Republicans endured for so long as main beneficiaries of constitutional and statutory factors favoring a two-party system? There may be something to W. S. Gilbert's observation in *Iolanthe*:

> *That every boy and every gal*
> *That's born into this world alive,*
> *Is either a little liberal,*
> *Or else a little conserva-tive.*

Democrats and Republicans, if this formulation is correct, may represent an inherent division of humankind between natural liberals and natural conservatives.

More specifically to American experience, I have elsewhere argued that Republicans and Democrats embody traditions of values and interests that have competed for national political power since the very beginning of American history (Reichley 2000). One—which I call the *republican tradition*, coming down along a line from the Federalists and the Whigs to the modern Republicans—has emphasized social order, economic growth through market capitalism, and religion-based morality. The other—the *liberal tradition*, proceeding from the Jeffersonian Republicans to the modern Democrats—has emphasized social equality, economic sharing, and strict separation between church and state. Both traditions—distinguishing them from feudal and socialist traditions in Europe—have championed personal freedom: the republican tradition accentuating economic freedom and the liberal tradition stressing freedom of expression. In foreign policy, both traditions have had nationalist and internationalist wings.

Throwing the Rascals Out

In earlier editions of this volume, I have theorized that alternations in national control by parties representing the rival ideological traditions have roughly followed two patterns of political cycles. I will here briefly summarize how these cycles have operated before discussing what clues they may give on possible developments in national politics as the twenty-first century unfolds.

The first pattern is a series of short cycles that is relatively simple and rises pretty clearly from the empirical data. These are what may be called "throw the rascals out" cycles. After a party has held the presidency at the national level or the governorship at the state level (increasingly even in what used to be thought of as one-party states) for two or three terms (eight to twelve years), voters tend to grow dissatisfied or bored with the party in power and are receptive to pleas by the opposition that it is "time for a change." All other things being equal, this tendency produces pressures that lead to the incumbent party being voted out of office, often by a large majority, and the former opposition being installed.

Since the early 1950s the Republicans and the Democrats have fairly regularly alternated in control of the White House, with four two-term periods (not counting the current Republican run of at least two terms), one of three terms (the Reagan–Bush I years), and one that was confined to a single term (Carter). Going further back in history, since the Republicans and the Democrats became the major parties competing for national power in the 1860s, the average duration of party control of the White House has been eleven years. The only markedly longer periods of party dominance were the twenty-four-year tenure of the Republicans during and after the Civil War and the twenty-year period of Democratic supremacy during and after the Depression. Both of these exceptions may reflect the effects of the system of long-term cycles that I will discuss below.

Similar short-term cycles have operated for governorships in states with competitive two-party systems. In the seven most populous states with historically competitive systems, the average period of party control of the governorship from 1950 to 2004 was a little more than eight years. In Pennsylvania and New Jersey, the two parties exchanged control of the governor's office every eight years with almost rhythmic regularity. In New York, Ohio, and Michigan, parties tended to hold gubernatorial dominance for slightly longer periods, but alternation nevertheless occurred. In Illinois there was regular alternation until 1976 when the Republicans began a twenty-six-year tenure, finally giving way under clouds of scandal to Democratic governor Rod Blagojevich in 2002. In California the two parties exchanged control of the governorship every eight years until the Republicans won four straight terms in the 1980s and 1990s, followed by two Democratic victories, the last cut short by Governor Gray Davis's replacement through recall by Republican governor Arnold Schwarzenegger in 2003. Cyclical party turnover now seems to be developing in some of the Southern states where Democrats used to enjoy one-party dominance, such as Texas, Virginia, and Florida.

From 1954 to 1994, regular shifts in party control did not occur in Congress. Between the Civil War and the Eisenhower administration, changes in control of Congress usually accompanied, or slightly proceeded, the presidential cycle (Norpoth and Rusk 2005). In only four two-year periods did the president's party not control at least one house of Congress (under Hayes, 1879–1880; Cleveland, 1895–1896: Wilson, 1919–1920; and Truman, 1947–1948). From 1954 to 1994, however, the Democrats controlled the House of Representatives without interruption and the Senate for all but six years. As a result, Republican presidents during this forty-year span regularly confronted Congresses dominated by their political opposition. After the 1994 election, the shoe was on the other foot, with a Democratic president for six years facing a Republican Congress. Whether the 1994 turnover will lead to more normal short-cycle alternations in party control of Congress or will turn out to have been the harbinger of a new long cycle giving the Republicans extended dominance in Congress, as the Democrats enjoyed after 1932, remains to be seen.

The Long Cycle

Probably the best known of the theories that a long-term cycle has operated in American national politics is that of historian Arthur Schlesinger Jr. (1986), carrying on work begun by his father. Schlesinger's theory is more closely related to political ideology than to parties, but it also has party manifestations. According to Schlesinger, there have been throughout U.S. history regular alternations between spans of political liberalism and conservatism, each lasting about sixteen years, or four presidential terms. The most recent spans were the liberal one launched by John Kennedy in 1960 and its conservative successor, which began in the late 1970s. Right on time, Schlesinger claimed after the 1992 election, Bill Clinton had initiated a new liberal era.

Like most cyclical theories, Schlesinger's theory seems to work better in retrospect than as a predictive tool—though even in retrospect it requires some rather odd combinations, such as bunching Richard Nixon and Gerald Ford into a common liberal phase that began in 1960. The Republican landslide in the 1994 midterm elections, followed by George W. Bush's arrival in the White House in 2001, seemed to bring a premature end to the new liberal era introduced by Clinton.

Among political scientists, who generally have been more open to cyclical theories than historians, most theories of long cycles are linked to the concept of "critical" or "realigning" elections introduced by V. O. Key (1955). Critical elections, Key claimed, have periodically purged American politics and government of accumulated debris and opened the way for new departures. Key's work has been carried on by, among others, Walter Dean Burnham (1970), Gerald Pomper (1970), and James Sundquist (1983). In most versions of this theory, realigning elections, ending the dominance of one political party and establishing normal political control by its major rival, have occurred every twenty-eight to thirty-six years.

There is some dispute over which were the actual realigning elections, but general agreement places realignments at or just before the elections of Thomas Jefferson in 1800, Andrew Jackson in 1828, Abraham Lincoln in 1860, William McKinley in 1896, and Franklin Roosevelt in 1932. (Some scholars drop the elections of Jefferson and Jackson on the ground that the two-party system did not achieve full development until the 1830s.)

A puzzle for believers in the traditional theory of realigning elections is the apparent failure of one to occur on schedule in the 1960s. Burnham argues that a realignment *did* occur with the election of Nixon as president in 1968 and the creation of a new Republican majority in presidential politics. Certainly the shift of the South away from the Democrats at the presidential level after 1968 was a major change in national politics. But if this was a realignment, why did it not produce a change in control of Congress or most of the major states, as had occurred with previous realignments?

The theory of realignments that I have proposed deals with this problem—and some of those that rise from Schlesinger's rival formulation—by proposing that long cycles in their fullness have actually covered not sixteen years (Schlesinger) nor twenty-eight to thirty-six years (Key and his successors) but *sixty to seventy years* (Reichley 2000). Truly realigning elections in my view have occurred—at least prior to the major realignment that may now be under way—only three times in American history: 1800 (Jefferson), 1860 (Lincoln), and 1930 (FDR). The elections of Jackson in 1828 and McKinley in 1896 were important political events, but they were in fact restorations and climaxes of eras that had begun about thirty years before, rather than true realignments or, in the broader sense, enduring changes in national political direction.

Jackson won in 1828 after a period of about ten years in which national politics had been in flux and the old hegemony of Jefferson's party appeared shaken. But Jackson was clearly in the line of Jefferson, as was generally recognized at the time—including, before his death in 1826, by Jefferson himself (Meyers 1957). Martin Van Buren, one of Jackson's principal lieutenants and his successor as president, wrote, "The two great parties of this country, with occasional changes in name only, have, for the principal part of a century, occupied antagonistic positions upon all the important political questions. They have maintained an unbroken succession" (Van Buren 1967). Jackson carried every state Jefferson carried in 1800 and lost every state Jefferson lost. Jefferson's narrow victory over John Adams in 1800 was converted into Jackson's landslide triumph over John Quincy Adams in 1828 by the addition of seven new Western states in which the Democrats were strong. So the 1828 election and Jackson's subsequent triumph over forces in Congress led by Henry Clay *restored* the dominance of the (renamed) Democrats instead of bringing in a new majority party.

Similarly, McKinley's victory in 1896 followed a period of about twenty years during which there had been no clear majority party. The 1896 election represented a rallying of the forces, temporarily in eclipse, that had made the Republicans the majority party from 1860 to 1876. McKinley won through renewal of the coalition of Northeastern and Midwestern states on which the Republican Party had been founded. William Jennings Bryan, his Democratic opponent, swept the South, the Democrats' principal stronghold since the end of Reconstruction. Bryan also tapped the farmers' revolt and the silver issue in the West to win some of the Western states, normally Republican, that had been admitted to the Union since the Civil War. But within a few years most of these were back in the Republican column, where they normally remained until the Great Depression of the 1930s. The 1896 election, therefore, did not displace the former majority party but renewed and strengthened the party that had become dominant after the last major realignment.

The mystery of why no true overall realignment occurred in the 1960s is thus explained: it was not due. What actually happened in the 1960s was the renewal and climax of the cycle dominated by liberalism and the Democratic Party that began in the 1930s. In 1964 Lyndon Johnson decisively defeated Barry Goldwater, representing a radical version of the laissez-faire economic ideology that had prevailed during the preceding cycle. The movement of the South away from the Democrats at the end of the 1960s was an early sign of the breakup of the New Deal cycle—similar to the move of the

Northeast away from the Democrats in the 1840s and the swing of major Northern cities away from the Republicans after 1912.

Briefly stated, each of the sixty- to seventy-year cycles moved through roughly similar phases: (1) a breakthrough election in which the innovating party gained power under an inspiring leader (Jefferson, Lincoln, FDR), followed by an extended period during which the new majority changed the direction of national life and enacted much of its program; (2) a period of pause during which the dominant party lost some of its dynamism and forces reflecting the ethos of the preceding cycle staged a minor comeback (John Quincy Adams, Cleveland, Eisenhower); (3) a climactic victory by the majority party over a more radical expression of the ideology of the preceding cycle (Jackson over Clay, McKinley over Bryan, Johnson over Goldwater), followed by enactment of remaining items in the majority party's program; and finally (4) the gradual decline and ultimate collapse of the old order, opening the way for a new realignment and a new majority.

The phases of the sixty- to seventy-year cycles correspond roughly to some of Schlesinger's sixteen-year spans. The long-cycle theory, however, explains why the Jeffersonians after 1800, the Republicans after 1860, and the Democrats after 1932 held onto power for longer than Schlesinger's theory would predict. These were all periods covered by the initial phase of the long cycle, during which the majority is fresh and holds the support of the public through an extended period of elections. The separate cycles posited in the twenty-eight- to thirty-six-year theory correspond neatly to the rise and decline segments of the long cycle.

Political cycles are probably rooted, at least partly, in generational change. Schlesinger argues that his sixteen-year spans reflect the succession of political generations. Members of the political generation of John Kennedy, for example, were putting into effect values and attitudes acquired during their youths in the liberal environment of the 1930s. The Reaganites of the 1980s were applying values they had developed during the relatively conservative 1950s (though many Reaganites regarded themselves as revolting *against* Eisenhower's moderate Republicanism). Members of the generation of the 1990s, in this theory, should have been eager to reintroduce the liberal values with which Kennedy inspired them during their college years in the 1960s.

Schlesinger's analysis, like his larger cyclical theory, captures part of the truth. Genuinely major changes in political direction, however, seem to occur only after persons holding political values and party loyalties formed by the last major realignment have largely passed from the political scene. So long as generations whose party allegiances were shaped by the Civil War and its aftermath remained politically active, the normal Republican majority in national elections was hard to shake. Similarly, party loyalties formed by the Depression and the New Deal have been remarkably durable.

But the generations most deeply marked by the New Deal era, roughly those born from 1905 to 1930, now make up a sharply declining share of the potential voter population—less than 8 percent, according to the 2000 census.

The last two major realignments, in the 1860s and the 1930s, came at times of massive traumas within the larger social system—the Civil War and the Great Depression. The first realignment, in the 1800s, coincided with huge territorial growth and population migration. Probably a major realignment requires *both* an electorate in which loyalties formed by the last great political divide have grown weak *and* powerful sources of new division.

The first condition now clearly exists for much of the voting public. Do social and political forces currently at work in national life provide the second?

Republican Realignment

After both of Ronald Reagan's presidential election landslide victories in the 1980s, many Republican political activists, some conservative journalists, and a few political scientists argued that realignment favoring the Republicans was in fact under way (Chubb and Peterson 1985). When Reagan left the political scene in 1989, however, the Republicans remained the minority party in public opinion polls, Democratic majorities in the House of Representatives appeared secure, and talk of Republican realignment had subsided (Shafer 2003).

In 1992 Bill Clinton restored the Democrats to control of the White House, though with less than a majority of the total vote. The amazing 19 percent of the popular vote won by Ross Perot's independent candidacy gave clear evidence that ties to the existing major parties, formed by the last great realignment, had grown weak.

The huge Republican victory in the midterm congressional elections of 1994, producing Republican majorities in both houses of Congress for the first time in forty years, coupled with big Republican wins in gubernatorial elections in most of the major states, once more aroused hope or dread, depending on subjective preference, that Republican realignment at last was in motion. Two years later, voters maintained Republicans in control of Congress by reduced majorities but kept Clinton in the White House with a plurality of the popular vote.

In 2000 the presidential election seemed to show an almost exactly evenly divided electorate. George W. Bush eked out the narrowest of Electoral College victories, awarded by a one-vote majority on the Supreme Court five weeks after the election, but in the popular vote ran more than 300,000 behind Vice President Al Gore.

Some early interpretations of the 2004 election suggested that not much had changed since 2000. While Bush this time indisputably won in both the electoral and popular vote, commentators were quick to point out that his electoral vote margin was the smallest for an incumbent president winning reelection since Woodrow Wilson in 1916. Exit polls conducted for a consortium of major news media reported that Bush had been supported by only 45 percent of young voters (18 to 29 years of age) and 45 percent of self-identified moderates—hardly evidence, it was said, of ongoing realignment (White 2004).

Examination of swings among other crucial voter groups, however, presents a somewhat different picture. Bush's popular vote majority, while relatively small, was solid—the first actual popular vote majority won by a presidential victor since his father in 1988. He made significant gains among groups vital to recent Democratic coalitions: up twelve percentage points among Hispanics (some analysts challenged the size of Bush's gain among Hispanics but conceded he probably won about 40 percent—the Republicans' preelection target; Leal et al. 2005); up five points among women, shrinking the Democrats' lead among women to only three percentage points compared to eleven in 2000; up seven points among voters over age 60; up five points among Catholics to a majority of 52 percent; and up six points among Jews.

The 2004 National Election Study found that among actual voters, those identifying themselves as Republicans actually outnumbered Democrats by 36 percent to 32 percent, compared to an eight-point Democratic lead in 2000. If leaners—those identifying themselves as independents but expressing a preference for one party or the other—are thrown into the mix, Democrats held a minuscule lead of 47.6 percent to 47.1 percent (Weisberg and Christenson 2005).

Republican realignment among working-class and lower-middle-class whites, once predominantly Democratic constituencies, grew stronger in 2004. White voters from families with incomes between $30,000 and $50,000 supported Bush over Kerry by 58 to 41 percent. Even white voters with incomes between $15,000 and $30,000 went for Bush by 51 to 48 percent (Pew Research Center 2005a). Republican strength among white lower-middle-class and working-class voters produced large gains for Bush in old steel-producing and coal-mining counties in southwestern Pennsylvania around Pittsburgh and blue-collar suburban areas in southeastern Michigan around Detroit (offset in both states by swings to Kerry in upscale suburban counties, which I will discuss below). When the Democratic candidate for president loses coal-mining West Virginia by 13 percentage points, it can fairly be said that the Democratic Party is in trouble.

A postelection analysis by a centrist Democratic study group called Third Way found that the "economic tipping point—the income level above which white voters were more likely to vote Republican than Democrat—

was $23,700." The survey found that middle-class blacks continued to vote heavily for the Democrats, but Hispanics rising into the middle class trended toward the Republicans. Among the white middle class, the study concluded, "Democrats were not competitive at all."[1]

Besides holding the presidency, Republicans also made gains in the Senate and the House of Representatives. Among voters for Bush, 91 percent cast ballots for Republican candidates for the House of Representatives, up from 86 percent in 2000. Shifts to Bush and the Republicans among critical voter groups appear to have been largely due to two main factors: the influence of the war against terrorism and consolidation of major traditional religious groups in support of the Republican Party (Stanley and Niemi 2005; Weisberg and Christenson 2005; Shanks et al. 2005; Verba and Schlozman 2005).

Preference for Bush as a wartime leader, coupled with the Republicans' long-standing advantage on defense-related issues, had significant impact in the voting booth. Exit polls reported that 58 percent of voters said they trusted Bush "to handle terrorism," while only 40 percent trusted Kerry. Among the 54 percent who answered that the United States was safer from terrorism than it had been in 2000, 79 percent voted for Bush (Abramowitz 2004). Based on the findings of the 2004 National Election Study, Herbert Weisberg and Dino Christenson (2005) concluded, "September 11, 2001, gave George Bush the opportunity that November 7, 2000, had not given him, and his campaign did not let that opportunity slip through their hands."

The other crucial factor building the Republican majority was mobilization of highly observant members of major religious groups. Exit polls found that among the 41 percent of voters who reported attending church at least once a week, 61 percent voted for Bush and only 39 percent for Kerry—a disparity more than three times the size of the gender gap. A more detailed postelection survey by the Survey Research Center at the University of Akron found that 88 percent of "traditionalist" evangelical Protestants (regular church attenders, holders of traditional Christian beliefs), 68 percent of traditionalist mainline Protestants, and 72 percent of traditionalist non-Latino Catholics voted for Bush (Green et al. 2005). (On the other hand, the Akron survey reported that only half of at least nominal mainline Protestants overall voted Republican for president, which I will discuss below.)

For the first time in U.S. history, the more highly observant members of all numerically major religious groups except African-American Protestants have come together in support of the same political party. How durable this faith-based political coalition will be remains to be seen, but its effects on current politics have been substantial. A recent Pew Research Center survey (2005b) found that church attendance now ranks behind only race as a predictor of party affiliation—ahead of gender, income level, union membership, and level of education.

Referenda on the same day as the 2004 election in eleven states on constitutional amendments prohibiting same-sex marriage, all of which passed overwhelmingly, had particularly strong effects in mobilizing voters motivated by moral values derived from religion. "Two-fifths of survey respondents," according to one study, "said that same-sex marriage was an important issue in the presidential race." Ohio's referendum on the issue may well have helped bring out and unite religiously conservative voters who gave Bush the state and the election (Lewis 2005).

Many political analysts identify issues like public prayer and same-sex marriage as "wedge" issues, suggesting that only economic issues and those embraced by liberal ideology should be "real" issues. But for millions of Americans, concerns such as the future of the traditional two-parent family, the place of religion in public life, and protection of the unborn hold preemptive political importance.

The 2004 election occurred under relatively unfavorable conditions for an incumbent president or party. The Iraq war had turned out to be unexpectedly long and bloody, with no end in sight. Many voters felt the administration had been deceptive in justifying the war and were disturbed by revelations of abuses of captured prisoners. The economy was recovering only gradually from the 2001 recession, with slow job growth, and the stock market slumped during most of the campaign. The large federal government surplus that greeted Bush when he took office had been transformed into a skyrocketing deficit. After a strong performance at the Republican convention, Bush lost badly in the first debate with Kerry and only partly recovered in two later encounters. Yet the slim majority supporting Bush and the Republicans seemed hardly to waver, giving evidence of a commitment that had become firm and might be enduring.

During the first year of Bush's second term, troubles continued. The Iraq war showed no sign of a resolution and both American and Iraqi casualties mounted. Opposition to the war increased and became more vocal. Economic growth picked up, but many people reported finding no improvement in their own pocketbooks. Gas prices exploded, causing outrage among motorists and threatening the general economy. Bush's efforts to build support among Democrats in Congress and in the public for reforms of Social Security had negative effects. The president's approval ratings sank, and polls showed dissatisfaction with Republicans in Congress (Gallup 2005a).

Yet discontent with the Republicans did not seem to translate into support for the Democrats. A Pew survey in the summer of 2005 found Republicans leading Democrats in party identification by four percentage points among whites in the second lowest economic quintile, including families with incomes between approximately $19,000 and $30,000, and by increasingly larger margins in all higher quintiles (Pew Research Center 2005a). Polls showed almost identical majorities disapproving of both Democrats and Republicans in Congress. A Gallup poll in August 2005 found Rudy Giuliani and John McCain, who ranked first and second in trial heats among Republicans for their party's 2008 presidential nomination, running five points ahead of Hillary Clinton, who topped the Democratic poll, and 13 points ahead of John Kerry (Gallup 2005b). Focus groups conducted by Democratic researchers in swing and rural states in the summer of 2005 found Democrats favored on economic and most domestic policy issues but that "powerful as concern over these issues is, the introduction of cultural themes—specifically gay marriage, abortion, the importance of the traditional family unit, and the role of religion in public life—quickly renders them almost irrelevant in terms of electoral politics at the national level" (Democracy Corps 2005).

All of these findings came before the devastation wrought on the Gulf Coast by Hurricane Katrina in the first days of September 2005. In the early fall of 2005, some Democrats clearly expected, and some Republicans feared, that effects of this disaster would send a transforming shock through the entire national political system. Long-term political consequences will depend on the results of inquiries into causes for the bungled responses by government at all levels to the chaos in New Orleans, the perceived effectiveness of Bush's leadership in relief and recovery, and the impact of storm losses on the larger economy.

The national security and moral values issues that played major roles in producing the Republican majority in 2004 seem likely to be important factors in American politics for many years to come. The war against Islamic terrorists, even after most U.S. fighting units are finally withdrawn from Iraq, will probably stretch long into the future—perhaps at least as long as the forty-year Cold War with the Soviet Union. This struggle will have its ups and downs, helping or damaging the parties of particular administrations in office. But the long-standing preference of a majority of the public for the Republicans on security issues may well, on balance, advantage the Republicans, as it did during most of the Cold War. It should be remembered that the Cold War deeply divided the Democratic Party but helped keep the Republicans united and in control of the White House from 1968 to 1992, except for Jimmy Carter's narrow victory in 1976 after Watergate. The public's trust in the current struggle will no doubt ultimately depend on whose leadership is deemed most effective.

The likely political effects of moral values concerns may be more mixed. As I will discuss in the next section, identification of the Republicans with traditional morality and a religious presence in public life has already produced gains for the Democrats among some constituencies. In a nation that remains predominantly religious, however, the issue provides a powerful base of support for the Republicans. A Pew survey in August 2005 found only 29 percent viewing the Democratic Party as "generally friendly" to religion, down from 42 percent in 2003, while 55 percent regarded the Republican Party as friendly to religion (Pew Research Center 2005b).

African Americans so far have overwhelmingly resisted being drawn into a Republican realignment. In 2004 Bush won only 11 percent of the African-American vote, up only three percentage points from 2000. Part of the reason for the loyalty of most blacks at all social and economic levels to the Democrats may be that realignment among African Americans—who from the 1860s to the 1930s were massively Republican—was not completed, particularly in the South, until 1964. As late as 1960, Richard Nixon won 32 percent of the black vote against John Kennedy. But in 1964 Barry Goldwater, the Republican candidate for president, opposed passage of the Civil Rights Act, and African Americans that year gave more than 90 percent of their vote to the Democrats. Black support for the Democrats has largely remained at that level ever since.

The social and moral conservatism of many African Americans, who have been more politically organized through their churches than any other group, has from time to time attracted the attention of Republican strategists. During Bush's first term, the administration's "faith-based initiative," which would direct federal funds into religiously sponsored welfare programs, was warmly supported by many black churches. More recently, the same-sex marriage issue has caused some socially conservative black clergy to question the viability of continued alliance with Democratic liberalism. If African-American support for Republicans rose to as little as 20 percent, the Republican Party would gain a critical edge in crucial swing states such as Pennsylvania, Michigan, Ohio, and Florida.

In light of the 2004 election, the Republicans seem to have more room to grow than the Democrats. States carried by Bush were predominantly in the South and the mountain West, where population continues to rise. A survey by the *Los Angeles Times* found that Bush carried ninety-seven of the nation's one hundred fastest-growing counties. Some of these counties are relatively small, but many are located in exurban regions where population increase is now greatest. Kerry won with less than 55 percent of the vote in fourteen states that total 189 electoral votes, while Bush won by less than 55 percent in only ten states, with 113 electoral votes.

A significant factor in growing Republican strength in recent elections may be that Republican operatives have simply been better at running political campaigns. While the Republicans have actually lost some of their long-standing dominance in fundraising, by common consent among political professionals, journalists, and political scientists they have been more effective at conducting campaign "ground wars"—canvassing door-to-door, registering voters, putting out yard signs, writing letters to the editor, operating phone banks, and getting out the vote on Election Day. In 2004 Democrats relied largely on auxiliary organizations, the so-called 527 groups, to manage grassroots efforts by often imported workers, while the Republican campaign built up a vast army of local volunteers. Republican volunteers were specifically assigned to contact persons within their communities who shared their religious, social, or recreational interests. A study by Sidney Milkis and Jesse Rhodes (2005) found that for the first time in history the Republicans created "a national party machine, composed of more than a million campaign volunteers across the country," with potential effects on future elections.

In the years immediately ahead, the short-term "throw the rascals out" cycle and a long-term Republican major realignment cycle that may be emerging will be pulling in opposite directions. In 2006 the Republican congressional majority produced by the 1994 election will be twelve years old. In 2008 the Republicans will have held the White House for two consecutive terms. Democratic congressional gains in the 2006 midterm elections, particularly in the House, appear likely. The Republican candidate for president in 2008 will have to deal with eight years of accumulated voter frustration and discontent of a kind that, with only one exception since 1952, has helped limit the incumbent party to no more than two terms in control of the White House. If Republican losses in Congress are relatively small and if a Republican once more wins the presidency in 2008, we will have pretty clear evidence that the nation has entered a major new cycle in political history.

Democratic Counter-Realignment

Realignments do not work all in one direction. While some groups come together in a new majority party, others may coalesce to give enduring support to a vigorous alternative majority. The Civil War and its aftermath, which helped establish the Republicans as the normal national majority party for most of the next seventy years, also firmly anchored the South to the Democrats for almost a century. As James Sundquist (1983) has pointed out, major realignments usually come when the two major parties are clearly distinguishable on highly contentious issues.

In 2002 John Judis and Ruy Teixeira published a best-selling book called *The Emerging Democratic Majority* in which they argued that existing trends pointed to development of an enduring Democratic majority in national politics. Among the factors they cited were continued strong support for the Democrats among women, blacks, Hispanics, and Jews; growing Democratic strength in once heavily Republican middle-class suburbs; and weakening of traditional religion. The Republicans proceeded to win the next two elections, but some of the trends that Judis and Teixeira identified have continued to operate.

Among the bright spots for John Kerry and the Democrats on Election

Night 2004 were victories in former Republican suburban strongholds outside New York City, Philadelphia, Detroit, and Chicago, which were crucial to Democratic majorities in New York, New Jersey, Connecticut, Pennsylvania, Michigan, and Illinois. Some of these suburbs remain normally Republican in local and state elections, but the gradual swing to the Democrats even at these levels is evident, something like the earlier move in the South from the Democrats to the Republicans.

Growing Democratic strength in upscale suburbs reflects a Democratic trend among parts of the upper middle class. In 2004, voters with postgraduate education supported Kerry 55 to 44 percent, in contrast to a narrow Republican lead in 1988 among holders of postgraduate degrees. Among college graduates, Bush led by only 52 to 46 percent, down sharply from a Republican advantage of 62 to 37 percent in 1988. Disaffection from the Republicans among professionals and some corporate managers and their spouses springs in part from cultural discomfort with the religious Right. But causes probably go deeper and may be long-lasting.

One source of the swing may be the long-term effects of advanced education. A study of attitudes among college faculties released in the spring of 2005 found 72 percent of faculty members identifying themselves as liberals and only 15 percent as conservatives. Democrats outnumbered Republicans 50 percent to 11 percent. The more elite the school, the greater the preponderance of liberals and Democrats. Liberal dominance was greatest in the English literature, philosophy, political science, and religious studies departments, where at least 80 percent identified themselves as liberals and no more than 5 percent were conservatives.[2]

For many years, U.S. college faculties have been predominantly liberal, with little apparent lasting effect on partisan preferences among most college graduates. But political and cultural attitudes acquired in colleges and graduate schools may now increasingly be finding their way into voting booths. In addition, overwhelming support on university faculties provides the Democrats with valuable resources of economic, administrative, and foreign and domestic policy expertise.

A downside for the Democrats from their close identification with dominant intellectual elites, and with allied opinion molders in the media and the entertainment industries, is that the Democratic Party risks becoming the target for populist resentment of a kind that historically has been focused on big business and inherited wealth. In 2004 John Kerry proved particularly vulnerable as a symbol of this identification.

Changes in attitudes toward religion among a fairly large part of the public, particularly in the middle class, have also worked in the Democrats' favor within some constituencies. The University of Akron survey of religious alignments cited earlier found that among "modernist" mainline Protestants (those low in church participation and holding nontraditional religious beliefs), Kerry won by a majority of 78 to 22 percent. Among modernist white Catholics, Kerry won by 69 to 31 percent. Even among "centrists" (the large group placed between traditionalists and modernists by John Green and his colleagues analyzing the Akron data), Kerry was supported by 42 percent of mainline Protestants and 45 percent of white Catholics. Kerry's overwhelming lead among modernist mainline Protestants enabled him to break almost exactly even among mainline Protestants overall, a reliable Republican constituency since the Civil War. Among white Catholics overall, an equally reliable Democratic constituency during most of American history, Bush won narrowly by 53 percent (Green et al. 2005).

The "modernist" category employed by Green and his colleagues mixes together two tendencies in contemporary American religion that, while related, are distinct: religious liberalization and secularization. Religious liberalism, in the sense of major reinterpretation of many traditional Christian beliefs and doctrines in response to the findings of modern science and scholarship, coupled with advocacy of liberal political and social action, has been a significant force among mainline Protestants, and to a lesser extent Roman Catholics, for more than fifty years. Many modernists in this sense are highly active in their churches and motivated by religious convictions in their political action.

During the pontificate of Pope John Paul II, the U.S. Catholic hierarchy became increasingly conservative on personal moral and cultural issues, though not on economic or peace issues. The Vatican and many American bishops have sought actively to restrain social liberalism among priests and laity. Since the 1960s, however, religious liberals have been dominant in the national leaderships of most mainline Protestant denominations. Until very recently, the liberalism of mainline leaders seemed to have little effect on the behavior of their laities, who remained predominantly conservative-to-moderate in their social attitudes and Republican in their politics. The Democratic trend among some mainline Protestants in 2004 may indicate that the liberal attitudes of denominational leaders, whose views now are shared by many local clergy, are influencing a growing share of laity.

Accompanying religious liberalization, and sometimes rising from it, has been the even stronger force of secularization—disassociation from any kind of organized religion. By 2004 the percentage of Americans telling pollsters they identified with no religious faith had risen to just over 15 percent—up from 5 percent in 1984. In 2004, 72 percent of declared seculars voted for Kerry. To these may be added the sizable number whom sociologists categorize as "behavioral seculars"—those who identify themselves to pollsters as Methodists or Catholics or Jews or some other denomination but who almost never attend religious services and do not regard traditional religion as an important factor in their lives. It seems reasonable to conclude that most of the 35 percent of modernist mainline Protestants and 30 percent of modernist Catholics who responded to the Akron survey that they "rarely" attend religious services (defined as "seldom or never") are in fact behavioral seculars, with no meaningful attachment to any religious faith.

If avowed seculars, behavioral seculars, and liberal white Protestants and Catholics are added (with some overlap) to the still heavily Democratic bodies of African Americans, Hispanics, Jews, union members, people living in poverty, and single women, the Democrats still have close to a majority within the national electorate—as reflected by the 2000 and 2004 elections. If the trend toward secularism continues—if the United States is destined to become increasingly like Western Europe, where organized religion now plays little part in the lives of most people—the Democrats can fairly expect, given normal public reaction against incumbent Republicans, to regain control of national government soon. If that happens, it may then be the Democrats who emerge, as Judis and Teixeira predicted, as the normal majority party in a new realignment, giving shape and direction to public life well into the twenty-first century.

A problem for the Democrats is that many of the liberal interest groups at the core of their current coalition seem unwilling to allow them to deviate from a strict ideological line on contentious social and moral issues such as abortion, same-sex marriage, affirmative action, and federal judicial appointments. This development has already lost them majority support among white Catholics and may foster further erosion among social conservatives in some of their traditional constituencies such as African Americans, Hispanics, Asians, and working-class whites.

An End to Long-term Realignment?

Some political scientists and historians have always doubted the existence of long-term political cycles (Shafer 1991; Ladd 1991). A recent influential book by David Mayhew (2002) challenges the thirty-year cycle theory proposed by Burnham and others. Mayhew particularly, but not exclusively, argues that the 1896 election, which is essential for the thirty-year theory, does not meet criteria for a realigning event—a conclusion that I share. My own view, as stated earlier, is that major realignments, introducing a new cycle in national political life, have in the past come not at approximately thirty-year intervals but every sixty to seventy years, when generational change has weakened traditional party loyalties and in response to profound national traumas or transformations.

It may be, however, that conditions early in the twenty-first century simply do not permit development of the kind of bonding political commitments that came out of earlier realignments. The clamor of competing media, the distractions of the consumer society, the nihilistic pressures of modern culture may atomize contemporary life to a degree that enduring political cohesion is unlikely to take root. Or it may be that current national and international problems—the collision between promised government benefits and acceptable levels of taxation or borrowing, the economic and cultural perils of globalization, the threat of nuclear proliferation, and the continuing struggle against terrorism, among others—are so complex and intractable that solutions offered by any one party or group of political leaders will not be supported for long by the voting public. Recent political experience in Europe suggests this may be the case.

Yet the generations that went through the Civil War and the Great Depression faced enormous and what seemed at the time almost insurmountable challenges. In both of those earlier periods, a new majority party emerged, implementing proposed solutions—never wholly successful or universally popular, but able to move the nation forward and commanding widespread political support for an extended period. My bet is that it will happen again, with the Republicans still advantaged to play the role of normal majority party.

Notes

1. Dan Balz, "For Democrats, A Troubling Culture Gap," *Washington Post*, August 10, 2005.

2. Howard Kurtz, "College Faculties a Most Liberal Lot," *Washington Post*, March 29, 2005.

3

Party Factions in 2004

Howard L. Reiter

About ten weeks into George W. Bush's second term, a reporter for the *New York Times* compiled an inventory of the blocs within Bush's Republican Party. He listed four "broad coalitions": the Cultural Coalition, the Leave-Us-Alone Coalition, the Security Coalition, and the Old Guard Coalition. Within these groupings, there were no fewer than ten blocs, including Biblical, America First, Tax-Cutting, and so forth.[1] On the same page of the newspaper, another reporter wrote of tensions within the Democratic Party between liberals and centrists.[2]

Factionalism within major American parties is a subject that never goes away. It is difficult to describe the Republicans and Democrats without getting into a discussion of moderate, business, and religious-Right Republicans, or Southern, liberal, and feminist Democrats. However, while journalists, politicians, and political junkies use such terms all the time, political scientists have done little to clarify the fault lines that run within each party, the only major exception being those who study legislative roll-call voting. Indeed, some of the classic definitions of a political party, such as Edmund Burke's "a body of men united, for promoting by their joint endeavors the national interest, upon some particular principle in which they are all agreed" (1971, 1:151) and Anthony Downs's "a team of men seeking to control the governing apparatus by gaining office in a duly constituted election" (1957, 25), treat parties as monolithic. But even the most casual observer knows that each American major party is a grab bag of disparate groups with different agendas.

Several features of major U.S. political parties guarantee that they will have internal divisions. First, the United States is a large and heterogeneous country, with many groups divided along class, ethnic, gender, racial, religious, geographic, ideological, and other lines. Second, there are only two major parties in the United States; combined with the first feature, this means that each party is necessarily made up of numerous disparate groups.

Third, the federal structure of American government enables each party to take a somewhat different profile in different states; parties in Utah and Mississippi are likely to be more conservative than their counterparts in Massachusetts and California. Finally, American political parties have traditionally been less united around a political program than many parties in other nations; therefore there has been more toleration of a wide variety of perspectives within each party. As we shall see, however, this factor has changed in recent years.

What is a faction, and why are factions important to study? Two scholars once defined a faction as "any relatively organized group that exists within the context of some other group and which (as a political faction) competes with rivals for power advantages within the larger group of which it is a part" (Beller and Belloni 1978, 419). As a definition, this seems reasonable, as it is neither overly vague nor too precise in its requirements for what a faction is. These authors went on to note that "factions structure the processes of intraparty politics and decision-making; . . . define the struggle for control of the party, its policies, its leadership and offices, its doctrines, its treasury, etc.; . . . are devices for the distribution of party patronage—and, for governing parties, of government patronage; and they are instruments for generating and supporting rival candidacies for public office" (437).

Most important of all, divisions within parties affect their ability to perform the functions that parties are supposed to carry out as a vital part of the democratic process. Among these are structuring the vote for the electorate, recruiting candidates for public office, organizing government, and in general providing linkages between the electorate and public officials. All of these functions, and how well they are performed, are conditioned by the nature of the divisions within parties and the intensity of those cleavages. For example, parties help simplify the voting process for voters by symbolizing particular ideologies or issue positions. However, if a party is deeply divided, the voter may not know which faction is represented on the ballot, and so the party label means less. Another example is that parties normally organize legislatures, and a factionalized majority party may be unable to form majority voting blocs and get legislation passed.

Is factionalism beneficial or harmful to political parties? There is no question that factions have a bad reputation. "Simply stated," Terence Ball has written, "a party is a faction of which one approves, and a faction a party of which one disapproves" (1989, 156). A party riven by factionalism may have difficulty functioning effectively, but factionalism may also give partisans opportunities to work within the party rather than face the unpalatable choice of knuckling under to the party majority or defecting. Factions can also be a way for party members to communicate with party elites (Bowler,

Farrell, and Katz 1999, 14–16). Factionalism may, in other words, provide a relatively harmless way of letting off steam—or it can divide the party into warring contenders who have lost sight of collective goals. Different kinds of factions might have different effects on the parties of which they are part (Beller and Belloni 1978, 439–42). To a great extent, a party is defined by its factional composition. If the party is divided, it matters greatly whether those blocs are based on ideology, patronage, personal ties, ethnicity, geography, or something else. Some cleavages, such as those based on ideology, pose more of an enduring threat to party unity than others, such as those based on personalities that come and go.

These considerations should make us cautious about predictions of party splits. Every major American party contains disparate and even contradictory elements, and yet the parties usually manage to hold these groups together. Those who predict that social and economic conservatives cannot long coexist in the Republican Party (e.g., Lowi 1995) must confront the fact that they have done so for at least a quarter of a century now and have been fairly successful at submerging their differences in order to win office and govern. Older examples pervade U.S. history, such as the inclusion of Northerners and Southerners in the Democratic New Deal Coalition and the Republican combination of progressives and conservatives in the early twentieth century.

As noted earlier, political scientists who study legislative roll-call voting have paid attention to factions within parties (Kolodny 1999; Hammond 1997; Rohde 1991), but legislatures are only one arena in which partisans act. Moreover, they may not be the best place in which to observe the factions of a party. Unlike national conventions, national committees, and other party institutions, legislatures were not created by the parties; the legislative agenda is not one that is drawn up primarily to accommodate different party factions. Voting behavior in a legislature is influenced by the presence of the other party, which may produce an artificial unity within a party by encouraging its members to band together in the face of a common threat. Moreover, unlike national conventions, legislatures do not necessarily include numerous members of each party from each state. Until the Republican Party began to grow in the South in recent decades, for example, it would have been difficult to study Southern Republicans by observing Congress. Instead of looking only at Congress, we should also look at party institutions— national conventions and voters in primaries and caucuses—whenever there is a contest, because analysis of such institutions gets us closer to the real battle within a party and provides us with evidence from most if not all the states.

If factionalism is important to understand, then we are justified in asking what the factional makeup of the Democratic and Republican parties looks like, particularly in the context of the 2004 presidential campaign. After all, any faction worth its salt should regard the presidential nomination as the highest prize a party can offer. But before we can understand factionalism in 2004, we need a brief overview of how party factionalism evolved over the years.

Party Factions through History

Modern American political parties arose in the 1830s, during the age of Andrew Jackson. In that period, parties developed many of the features we now know: national conventions, platforms, congressional coordination, and national committees. During the period from the 1830s through the 1850s, Democrats and Whigs divided along sectional lines at their national conventions. Northern and Southern Whigs squared off, and Democrats experienced both North-versus-South and East-versus-West divisions around such issues as the extension of slavery to the territories, trade, and the proposed transcontinental railroad. In Congress, too, sectional differences emerged within each party. When sectional strife began to reach the boiling point in the 1850s, the Whigs disintegrated, and the Democrats suffered a split in 1860 that produced two sectional presidential candidates (Reiter 1996). Later that year, the young Republican Party won its first presidential election, but the South then seceded and the Civil War broke out.

After the Civil War, both parties endured many decades of unstable factionalism. The blocs of states that banded together at one national convention often had no similarity to the blocs that emerged four years later. Neither socioeconomic ties nor candidates' personalities nor the coalitions around the Populist or Progressive movements produced lasting alliances among states (Reiter 1998). Instead of blocs based on sectional differences, like those before the Civil War, states would form alliances of convenience, based on specific favors such as promises of control over government patronage jobs or cabinet positions. State and local party leaders used their convention delegates as bargaining chips in complex negotiations. Consequently, the states one voted with at the last convention might bear little resemblance to one's current allies.

All that changed during Franklin D. Roosevelt's New Deal in the 1930s. By vastly expanding the role of the federal government in American society through new regulatory powers and social welfare programs, the New Deal helped produce a more national political system. Just as state and local government came to enjoy less autonomy than before, the state and local parties began to lose their peculiarities as voters looked more and more to national political issues as they decided how to vote. One consequence was that many voters in what had been strongly Republican or Democratic regions began to build the minority party and create more political competition. Over the years, Southern conservatives began to move away from the Democratic Party, which became a party that championed civil rights, and Northern liberals began to move away from the Republican Party, which increasingly stood against the progressive programs that many Republicans had favored. The Solid South began electing Republicans, and states like Vermont and New Hampshire began electing Democrats.

Early in this process, each party began to develop stable factions. For the Democrats, the South began to rebel against its Northern counterparts as early as the late 1930s over such issues as Roosevelt's attempt to enlarge the size of the Supreme Court and his administration's attempt to ensure that federal contractors did not discriminate on the basis of race (Patterson 1967; Garson 1974). Over the next couple of decades, there was a clear North-South division at national conventions, in the Democratic National Committee, and in Congress, with the South clearly the more conservative region (Reiter 2001a). At national conventions, there was also a division between, on the one hand, states whose politics were dominated by old-fashioned political machines and the patronage culture that went with them and, on the other, states where progressive political reform was more influential. A series of candidates presented themselves as critics of politics-as-usual and became targets of machine politicians. They tended to run best in the Upper Midwest and the Far West, where the Progressive movement of the early twentieth century was most influential, and in New York and New England as well.

On the Republican side, the first issues that led to lasting factions involved foreign policy. In the late 1930s, the question facing Americans was whether to aid Great Britain, France, and other European nations that faced Nazi aggression. Republicans in the Northeast, who had business ties across the Atlantic, were most eager to help those nations after Germany invaded Poland in 1939, while Midwestern Republicans preferred to stay out. Northeastern Republicans were also more prone to advocate domestic policies that were more moderate versions of the New Deal, while Republicans elsewhere preferred to fight Roosevelt's programs head-on. Over the years, Northeastern Republicans increasingly became a relatively liberal minority within their own party.

These factional patterns persisted long past the 1930s and 1940s, and in fact these fissures—the Democrats' between North and South and between reformers and machine politicians, the Republicans' between the Northeast and the rest of the country—have continued in some form to the present day. However, they have been somewhat attenuated by an extremely important trend in American politics: the growing ideological homogeneity within each party (Hetherington 2001). Arizona senator Barry Goldwater's Republican nomination in 1964 jump-started the process by which numerous conservative Democrats, especially in the South, began their migration into the Republican Party, while many liberal Republicans, especially in the Northeast, moved toward the Democrats. Today, each party is more united and less factionalized than it has been since at least the early twentieth century. As we shall see, this fact has many implications for the state of party factionalism in the early twenty-first century.

Democratic Party Factionalism Today

When Bill Clinton ran for president in 1992, his base of support reflected the older factional lines. Running against Paul Tsongas and Jerry Brown, who were critics of Democratic orthodoxy, Clinton ran well not only in the South but in traditional machine states as well. In 1996 and 2000, there were no divided votes at the Democratic National Conventions. The first year saw Clinton's unopposed renomination, and in the latter year, former New Jersey senator Bill Bradley's challenge to Vice President Al Gore died when Bradley lost all of the early primaries and caucuses. With the Democratic Party fairly united, there is little evidence that the Gore-Bradley contest reflected any of the patterns I have been discussing. Exit polls indicate that Gore won key constituencies, such as labor, African Americans, and gays, that might have been expected to be open to an insurgent candidate due to dissatisfaction with some of the Clinton-Gore policies; however, Bradley was too close to Gore ideologically to make a compelling case for change, and most Democratic constituencies had long been rallying behind Clinton in response to Republican attacks (Mayer 2001, 33).

In 2004, were there echoes of the liberal-conservative disputes that had wracked the Democratic Party in earlier years? We can answer this question with regard to both elites and the Democratic masses.

Party Elites

In Congress, what sorts of Democrats voted with the rest of their party most often? Every year, the respected journal *Congressional Quarterly* examines all the votes in Congress on which a majority of Democrats voted against a majority of Republicans, giving each member a score representing the percentage of votes on which that member voted with his or her party. Figure 3.1 shows the results for the Democrats in 2004, by region (*CQ Weekly* 2004a). The data indicate above all the very high level of support that the average Democrat gave to the party.

What were the factors associated with high or low party loyalty? The most obvious is ideology, which I measure with a combination of the scores

Figure 3.1 Party Loyalty of Democratic Members of Congress, by Region, 2004

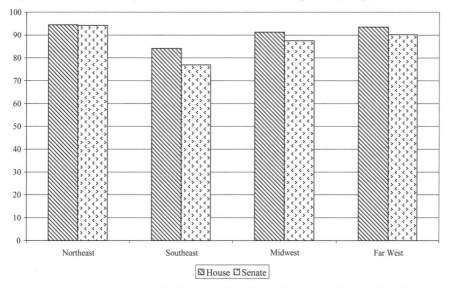

Source Congressional Quarterly (CQ Weekly. 2004a. "Party Unity." December 11: 2952–56).

awarded in 2002 by two ideological organizations, the liberal Americans for Democratic Action and the American Conservative Union (Barone 2003). Using data from 2002 instead of 2004 avoids the problem of using some of the same votes to measure ideology and party loyalty; the ideology of a major politician does not change very much in two years. The more liberal a Democrat was, the more he or she voted with other Democrats; the correlation between ideology and partisanship was + .771 in the Senate and + .817 in the House of Representatives. There were sectional differences, too, with Southerners the least supportive and Northeasterners slightly more loyal than others outside the South. This is largely because Southern Democrats continue to be somewhat more conservative than Democrats elsewhere; the least loyal Democrat in each house, Senator Zell Miller of Georgia (who backed his party only 2 percent of the time) and Representative Charles Stenholm of Texas (59 percent), was a Southerner. Northeastern Democrats were more liberal than Democrats elsewhere, especially in the Senate.

Party Masses

While Massachusetts senator John Kerry swept nearly every primary and caucus, there was little variation in his vote from state to state (Burden 2005, 22–34; Ceaser and Busch 2005, 69–105, 109–11, 114–18; Day, Hadley, and Stanley 2005, 74–86; White 2005, 3–20; Institute of Politics 2006). Exit polls reveal that Kerry appealed to different kinds of Democrats in different primaries and caucuses. In seven states, he ran at least 10 percent better among conservatives than among the very liberal; in two states, the reverse was true; and in thirteen states, less than 10 percent separated the two groups. Similarly, it did not make a lot of difference whether a Democrat thought that the war, the economy, health care, education, or taxes was the main issue; all of these groups supported Kerry in roughly the same proportion. Instead, what defined the Kerry voter was a desire to win; on average, voters who said they chose a candidate on the basis of his potential to beat President Bush were 24 percent more likely to vote for Kerry than were voters who chose a candidate based on the issues. The Massachusetts senator was the candidate of voters who made a cool calculation that he could win in November rather than going with their ideological heart.

There was a further pattern to Kerry's support, however; his appeal to relatively conservative Democrats was strong in the earliest events—the Iowa caucuses, the New Hampshire primary, and especially the Vermont primary. These events all had in common the fact that former Vermont governor Howard Dean ran a relatively strong race. That Dean—with his slashing attacks on the war, his criticism of the Democratic establishment, and his claim to represent the "Democratic wing of the Democratic Party"— appealed to liberals is not surprising (on the Dean campaign and his appeal to liberals, see chapter 9 in this volume). In the five states where Dean received more than 10 percent of the vote, Kerry's appeal to conservative Democrats was highest; in the other states, Kerry's supporters were all over the ideological map. The conclusion to be drawn is that only the Dean candidacy revived old internal battles among Democrats. Where he was strong, he appealed mainly to the most liberal Democrats, leaving Kerry to win moderates and conservatives. Dean also had an antiestablishment appeal, but no candidate since Jimmy Carter has won a presidential nomination from either party without the support of the party establishment (Cohen et al. 2001). Unfortunately for Dean, his bubble burst on the night of the Iowa caucuses, and in most of the primaries, Kerry was free to win Democrats of all stripes.

As the November election approached, a cross-section of Americans was surveyed about the campaign by the National Election Study. Who among the Democrats had reservations about Kerry?

In answering this question, I included all people who considered themselves Democrats, registered or not. It has been shown that people who call themselves independents but say that they lean toward a party behave in similar fashion to those who identify themselves with that party, albeit less strongly (Keith et al. 1992). Therefore, in order to maximize the size of the sample, I combined self-identified Democrats with those independents who felt closer to Democrats than to Republicans.

At first glance, this group was highly supportive of Senator Kerry; about nine out of ten voters in the sample voted for him. But how many had reservations about Kerry? All respondents were asked, "Is there anything in particular about John Kerry that might make you want to vote AGAINST him?" Fully 28 percent of Democrats and Democrat-leaning independents replied in the affirmative. The most frequent comments were that Kerry was indecisive, was dishonest, and had a bad war record; this suggests that Republican accusations that Kerry "flip-flopped" and had lied about his war record had had some effect, even among Democrats. As figures 3.2 and 3.3 show, there was not a consistent relationship between ideology and people's inclination to say negative things about Kerry; this fits his record in the primaries. There were sectional differences, however, with Southerners least negative about him and Westerners most negative. About half the Southern Democrats in the sample were African Americans, who are among the most loyal of Democrats.

Republican Party Factionalism Today

While there have been no divided roll-call votes at Republican National Conventions since 1976, surveys of delegates have shown that the earlier Northeastern exceptionalism has persisted. In 1988, while Vice President

Figure 3.2   Percentage of Democrats Who Said There Was Something about Kerry They Disliked, by Ideology, 2004

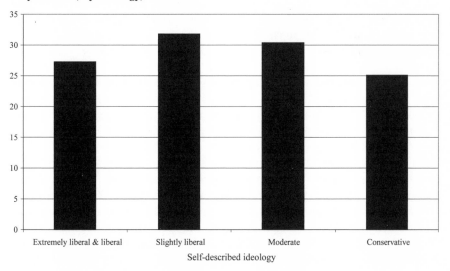

Source: American National Election Studies, www.umich.edu/~nes

Figure 3.3   Percentage of Democrats Who Said There Was Something about Kerry They Disliked, by Region, 2004

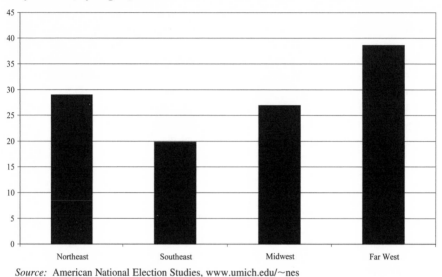

Source: American National Election Studies, www.umich.edu/~nes

George H. W. Bush's delegates were ideologically similar to those of his chief rival, Kansas senator Bob Dole, Bush's Northeastern delegates were markedly less conservative than his delegates from the rest of the country. In 1996, when abortion was the main issue among delegates, nominee Dole's Northeastern delegates took substantially more pro-choice positions than his delegates outside the Northeast did. In 2000, exit polls of Republican voters through Super Tuesday showed that the insurgent Senator John McCain received at least 33 percent of the vote in every state in the Northeast but did not reach this percentage in any state outside the Northeast except his home state of Arizona. McCain ran 25 percentage points better among self-described Republican moderates than among conservatives (Reiter 2001b).

In 2004, Republican factionalism was nonexistent. Like other recent presidents—Ronald Reagan in 1984 and Bill Clinton in 1996—George W. Bush faced not a whisper of opposition from any other prominent member of his own party in his bid for renomination (Burden 2005, 34–35; Ceaser and Busch 2005, 111–15, 120–22; Institute of Politics 2006). In order to assess the state of Republican factionalism in 2004, therefore, we need to go outside the primaries and caucuses that we examined for the Democrats. What kinds of Republicans gave President Bush their strongest support, and who were his chief critics? I will answer those questions by examining both party elites and party masses. Those answers can help us speculate as to what a challenge to the president's renomination might have looked like— and what may happen in the future.

Party Elites

In 2004, according to *Congressional Quarterly*, the average Republican senator or representative voted President Bush's way about 83 percent of the time (*CQ Weekly* 2004b). Figure 3.4 shows some of the patterns, broken down by region. In the Senate, only seven members out of fifty-one voted Bush's way less than 90 percent of the time, and four of those were Northeastern moderates: Lincoln Chafee (Rhode Island), Susan Collins and Olympia Snowe (Maine), and Arlen Specter (Pennsylvania).

In general, what were the factors associated with high or low support of Bush? The most obvious is ideology; the relationship between ideology and support for Bush among Republican senators in 2004 was quite strong, with a correlation coefficient of $+.733$. The fact that Northeastern Republican senators were among the least supportive of Bush was mainly due to the fact that so many of them were moderates. In the House of Representatives, Northeasterners were also especially likely to be among President Bush's weakest supporters within his own party. Although Northeasterners comprised only one-sixth of House Republicans, they made up half of the thirty representatives who supported Bush no more than 75 percent of the time.

Figure 3.4   Support for Bush by Republican Members of Congress, by Region, 2004

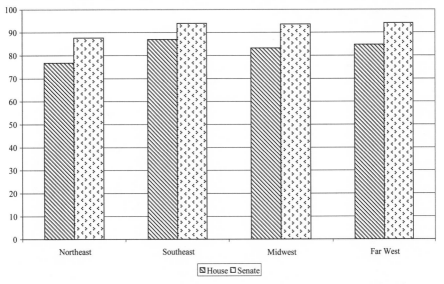

Source: Congressional Quarterly (QC Weekly. 2004a. "Party Unity." December 11: 2952–56).

Unlike in the Senate, Midwestern Republican representatives were a bit less likely to back Bush than were those from the Southeast and Far West. In the House, the correlation between conservatism and support for Bush was +.628. The fact that so many moderates were from the Northeast explains why Bush's support was lowest there. In short, whether a Republican member of Congress supported Bush was primarily a function of how conservative that person was. In light of Bush's mostly conservative policies, this is not surprising.

Party Masses

What about the mass of ordinary people who consider themselves Republican? In the National Election Study survey from the fall of 2004, Republicans were highly supportive of President Bush; more than nine out of ten voters in the sample voted for him. What kinds of Republicans had reservations about Bush? As with the Democrats, all Republican respondents were asked whether there was anything in particular about their party's candidate that might make them want to vote against him. Fully 37 percent of Republicans replied in the affirmative. As figure 3.5 shows, liberal and centrist Republicans were more likely than conservatives to express reservations about Bush; this is in keeping with the findings about congressional support for Bush.

Figure 3.5   Percentage of Republicans Who Said There Was Something about Bush They Disliked, by Ideology, 2004

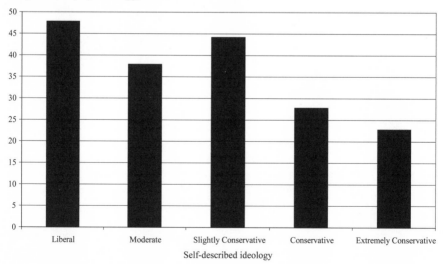

Source: American National Election Studies, www.umich.edu/~nes

The geographic patterns shown in figure 3.6, however, are somewhat surprising. While Northeastern Republicans were, as usual, Bush's greatest critics, those from the Far West were nearly equally so. This may be the result of the survey sample, which overrepresented the blue states of California, Oregon, and Washington; the only other Western states in the sample were Colorado and Utah. The survey thus may have contained an oversample of moderate Western Republicans. The three blue states, whose citizens represented 61 percent of Bush's Far Western voters, were 79 percent of the National Election Study's Far Western Republican sample.

What specifically did Republicans cite as reasons not to want to vote for Bush? The most frequent reason was dissatisfaction with the war in Iraq, which was cited by more than one-third of the Republicans who cited any reason at all. Among those expressing reasons not to vote for Bush, those describing themselves as extremely conservative were far less likely to mention the war than other ideological groups, but that was the only predictable link between ideology and views on the war. Furthermore, Midwesterners were more likely than Republicans in other parts of the country to mention the war. Other relatively common responses referred to Bush's family, his level of intelligence, bad economic times, the national debt, and dishonesty.

The many references to the Iraq war tantalizingly suggest that an antiwar Republican insurgency might have secured a sizable minority of votes in

Figure 3.6   Percentage of Republicans Who Said There Was Something about Bush They Disliked, by Region, 2004

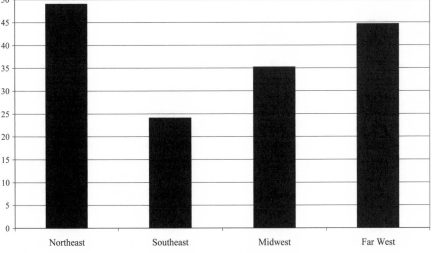

Source: American National Election Studies, www.umich.edu/~nes

some of the primaries and caucuses in 2004. There is other evidence that many Republicans lacked confidence in Bush's conduct of the war. In a Gallup/CNN/*USA Today* survey conducted in late January and early February, just as the primaries were starting, one-third of Republicans gave an antiwar or anti-Bush response to at least one of the following questions: whether they approved of Bush's conduct of the war, whether the war was worth getting involved in, whether the Bush administration had deliberately misled the public about Iraqi weapons of mass destruction (WMD), and whether the war could be justified only if WMD were found or would not be justified even then. Since on all of these questions independents were far more critical than Republicans of Bush, an antiwar candidate might have made an especially strong showing in open-primary states.

Conclusion

Many decades after the New Deal produced lasting factional divides within each of the major parties, those cleavages continue to be relevant. In 2004, members of both parties in Congress voted in predictable ways, with liberal Democrats and conservative Republicans being most loyal to the party or to Bush, respectively. Ordinary Republicans, too, reacted to Bush as we might expect, with conservatives happiest with him. Where Howard Dean ran well in the primaries and caucuses, he attracted more liberal Democrats than John Kerry did; Dean represented both ideological and antiestablishment appeals and so was able to activate old cleavages among Democrats.

However, 2004 also saw novel forms of intraparty disputes. Where Dean did not run well, Kerry's support was across the board and not ideologically distinctive. This pattern is a reflection of the great cohesiveness of the party, where differences between candidates revolve around degrees of liberalism and where an emphasis on Kerry's electability cut across many groups. On the Republican side, dissatisfaction with Bush's leadership of the war in Iraq similarly cut across ideological lines and provides us with a good example of how a particular issue can transcend older intraparty lines. Both the Kerry candidacy and the war, however, were temporary phenomena, and there is no reason to think that either of them will cause a lasting shake-up in party factions. These patterns do, however, suggest that the alignments that developed a half-century ago are like old war wounds. Under the right circumstances, such as the Dean candidacy, the old fault lines can be reactivated. At other times, the divisions within the parties are more obscure or are based on circumstances of the moment such as the war in Iraq.

Perhaps we can best understand this mixed portrait as a result of the increased ideological homogeneity of both major parties over the past half-century, which was caused by a gradual realignment of voters into the party that best represents their ideology. The net effect has been to unify both parties and render them more ideologically monolithic (Jacobson 2000, 17). This process has been well documented by congressional scholars. Fleisher and Bond (2000, 3–4) have graphically shown the rise in party voting and party unity scores in Congress since the late 1960s, and Sinclair (1996, 93) has documented the shrinking gap between the voting records of Northern and Southern Democrats in both houses. Hetherington (2001) has provided an especially useful analysis of these trends. (On the ideological differences between Democratic and Republican national convention delegates, see the next chapter in this volume.)

As the parties become more unified programmatically, and as the pressures for hanging together intensify due to the closeness of recent presidential and congressional races, we should expect that factions within the party will become less polarized over policies and shaped more by evanescent factors such as the personalities of presidential candidates and short-term policy controversies. In addition, presidential candidates of the same party are likely to differ less on ideology than on the emphasis placed on different parts of the agenda. Dean stressed the war in Iraq, while North Carolina senator John Edwards emphasized economic conditions. To some extent, these controversies may reflect different strategies for winning elections (Reiter 1981).

The consequences for the parties are in many ways quite positive. When factions were lasting and based on ideological differences, as they were for years after the New Deal, it was often difficult for the parties to unite in campaigns or to govern. Today, by contrast, each party enjoys more unity than it has experienced for decades, perhaps more than ever. That unity enables it to carry out many of its functions better than it could if it were still as divided as it was during the post–New Deal period, when many voters seemed to lose interest in partisanship (Wattenberg 1984). Today, election campaigns present a more unified image, with fewer prominent defectors, and the majority party in Congress is able to govern more effectively than before. There may still be echoes of earlier struggles when a party chooses a presidential candidate or when the right issue arises, but bitter intraparty rivalries that make governance difficult do not characterize the present era.

What about party factions in the immediate future? There is good reason to believe that these patterns will persist in 2008. With President Bush unable to run again and Vice President Dick Cheney unwilling to run for president, both parties will have an opportunity for wide-open nominating races in 2008. Once again, the Democrats will choose from an array of candidates who range from the very liberal to the moderately liberal. Potential candidates with a liberal reputation, such as New York senator Hillary Rodham Clinton, have already been moving toward the center, with an eye toward the general electorate, while lesser-known figures like Virginia governor Mark Warner will surely be displaying their liberal good faith in order to woo Democrats in the primaries and caucuses. On the more ideologically homogeneous Republican side, the hero of the moderates, Arizona senator John McCain, has been mending fences with the Bush administration and other conservatives, while more centrist figures like New York governor George Pataki and Massachusetts governor Mitt Romney have begun to move rightward. At this early stage, there is every reason to believe that the ideological range of candidates within each party will be limited and that each party will be able to unite behind its nominee as soon as he or she clinches the nomination.

Notes

The author wishes to thank John Gerring and J. David Gillespie for advice on an earlier draft of this chapter and Marc Maynard, Marilyn Milliken, and Lois Timms-Ferrara of the Roper Center for Public Opinion Research for assistance in obtaining data used in this study. The Gallup/CNN/*USA Today* Poll #2004–07, conducted from January 29 through February 1, 2004, was accessed from the Roper Center.

1. Bill Marsh, "A Guide to the Republican Herd," *New York Times*, April 3, 2005.

2. Nicholas Confessore, "Here's Why the Centrist Democrat Is Feeling Unloved," *New York Times*, April 3, 2005.

4

The State of the Party Elites

National Convention Delegates, 1992–2004

John S. Jackson III, Nathan S. Bigelow, and John C. Green

The state of the party elites after the 2004 election can be succinctly summarized in one word: polarized. The major party activists were sharply different from each other on self-identified ideology and the major issues of the day, advocating two quite different views of American government in a systematic way. Although there is some variation by issue and within each party, there can be no mistaking the sharp divisions between the leadership echelons of the two major parties. Of course, this polarization is not entirely new. Past studies, including our own, indicate that such divisions have existed for more than a decade, standing in stark contrast to the predominantly pragmatic, nonideological parties of previous eras (see Jackson, Bigelow, and Green 2003).

This essay is built on an empirical base of eight surveys of national convention delegates in the four presidential elections from 1992 to 2004. This twelve-year period took the nation from President George H. W. Bush's failed reelection bid to the reelection of his son, George W. Bush. On the Democratic side, the period spans the 1992 election of Bill Clinton, a relatively unknown governor of Arkansas, through the unsuccessful 2004 quest for the presidency by Senator John Kerry of Massachusetts. Much has changed in this twelve-year period, especially on the defense and foreign policy fronts. But much has also remained relatively stable, particularly with regard to domestic issues. However, neither party is fully united on issues, despite an increase in the prominence of moderate factions since 1992.

The Importance of Party Elites

The value of using national convention delegates to study the party elites has been amply discussed and debated in the literature (Miller and Jennings

1986; Kirkpatrick 1976; Maggiotto and Wekkin 2000; Abramowitz, Mc-Glennon, and Rapoport 1986). While there are admittedly some drawbacks and limitations to such an approach, there are also some significant advantages. Although the national conventions no longer determine presidential nominations, the delegates constitute what Jeane Kirkpatrick called "the presidential elite" within the two national parties (Kirkpatrick 1976). Once every four years they *are* the embodiment of the national party organizations. For one week, meeting at the designated time and place, they are the party's highest plenary body, exercising the power and authority of the entire national party. In addition to formally nominating the candidates for president and vice president of the United States, they perform significant additional functions, such as adopting the party's platform and the rules under which the next presidential nominations will be conducted and holding a giant "pep rally" for the party's candidates (David, Goldman, and Bain 1960). The success or failure of the national conventions goes far in signaling the extent to which the party is united and ready for the general election in the fall.

Convention delegates are often representatives of state and local party organizations, displaying distinctive regional political cultures. They are also often envoys from the party's interest group allies. And once the convention is over, they become emissaries back to local party and interest group organizations, where they can play a critical role in rallying them for the presidential campaign. Thus delegates are a slice of life at the party's grass roots and the broader activist pool, at least in the year of the presidential election. In short, convention delegates can teach us much about the state of the presidential echelon of party activists in their election year.

One thing delegates can reveal is the distribution of issue positions between and within the major parties. In this regard, each party's delegates embody the key policy differences with their rival party and also important factional differences within each party's coalition—and they tend to hold these views in a more consistent and sophisticated way than the mass public (Jackson, Brown, and Bositis 1982). Scholars have found that these differences have become increasingly large and significant over the last several decades (Jackson, Bigelow, and Green 2003; Green, Jackson, and Clayton 1999; Jackson and Clayton 1996). Indeed, one of the central pieces of evidence for party polarization in recent times has been the increasingly sharp issue differences of these party elites (Pomper 2003). Social welfare issues have long been fundamental to this polarization, but foreign policy and cultural issues have been added to the mix in recent times (Herrera 1995).

Indeed, the high level of party polarization could be a manifestation of a new "values divide" and the advent of "culture wars" in American politics, especially divisions over sexual and family issues. The values divide was hotly debated after the 2004 election, but culture wars were widely discussed during the 1990s—especially after Pat Buchanan publicly proclaimed a culture war at the 1992 Republican National Convention. Although foreign policy questions were not a focus of this debate in the 1990s, they have often been related to values disputes—and may be once again due to the Iraq war and other contemporary controversies (Guth et al. 2005).

As with many concepts, there are two schools of thought. One argues that the culture wars are real, rooted in deep value divisions in American society. The public is polarized, with little middle ground or room for compromise. As a consequence, politics has degenerated into warring camps, where political leaders reflect the disputes in the public (White 2003; Greenberg 2004). The contrarian school claims that the culture wars are much exaggerated. A degree of conflict over values has always existed in society, and it is no worse than in the past. Moreover, the public is not especially polarized on such matters, and most Americans hold moderate issue positions that make compromise possible. What passes for culture wars is the product of small but intense minorities—and the decisions by political leaders to pursue such divisions (Williams 1997; Fiorina 2005).

One of the few things these two schools agree upon is that political leaders, including party elites, are most likely to exhibit the values divide and participate in the culture wars, whatever their character or source. Our data can help determine the extent to which these new divisions contribute to party polarization alone or in combination with other older divisions. After briefly describing the source of our data, we will first review differences between the parties over the last four elections and then turn to divisions within the parties.

The Surveys

The data in this study are part of the ongoing Party Elite Study and are drawn from national surveys of the delegates to the Republican and Democratic national conventions for the years 1992–2004. In each year, the methodology remained essentially the same. We obtained the official roster of the delegates, listed by state, from the Democratic and Republican national committees. A systematic random sample was then drawn from each list using a skip interval designed to produce approximately one thousand original names and addresses from each party list. The questionnaires were mailed initially the week after the national conventions were held. Each questionnaire contained a cover letter from the study directors explaining the study's purpose. Approximately one month after the first wave of questionnaires was mailed, a follow-up questionnaire was sent to nonrespondents. The returned questionnaires were gathered up through the day of the national elections.

Overall, we obtained a very respectable response rate in the range of

40–50 percent. In almost all cases, those who responded were not systematically different from nonrespondents. In the small number of instances where
systematic differences were discovered, we weighed the data to overcome
some demographic deficits among the respondents. Thus, we are confident
that the respondents are representative of all delegates to the national conventions in the year studied. The surveys contained a series of questions that
have been repeated, with their wording largely unchanged, across the entire
twelve years. In most cases, the questions were adopted from the National
Elections Study questions used on voters generally. Thus, the results should
be comparable across time and across both parties.

Party Divisions by Issues, 1992–2004

We begin with the self-identified ideology of the national convention
delegates. The question employed offered responses ranging from "very liberal" to "very conservative," with a "moderate" option offered between the
two ideological alternatives. Figure 4.1 provides the overall results for all the
national convention delegates from 1992 through 2004.

The ideological gap between the two parties is notable. The dominance
of self-identified conservatives among the Republicans is especially marked,
attracting between 71 and 81 percent of the Republican delegates during
these four elections. Most of the remainder, from one-fifth to one-fourth of
the total, called themselves moderates; there were almost no liberals. It is
also interesting to note that 1996, Bob Dole's convention, marked the apex
of the conservative dominance, a pattern that declined slightly in George W.
Bush's conventions of 2000 and 2004.

Figure 4.1   Ideology

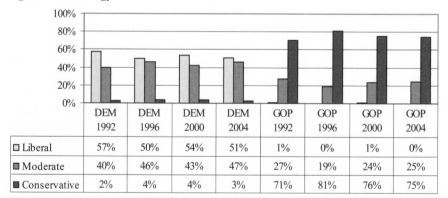

	DEM 1992	DEM 1996	DEM 2000	DEM 2004	GOP 1992	GOP 1996	GOP 2000	GOP 2004
☐ Liberal	57%	50%	54%	51%	1%	0%	1%	0%
▦ Moderate	40%	46%	43%	47%	27%	19%	24%	25%
■ Conservative	2%	4%	4%	3%	71%	81%	76%	75%

Note: Figures do not add up to 100 percent due to rounding.

On the Democratic Party's side, the picture is more mixed. Figure 4.1 shows that a majority called themselves liberals, but it is a narrow majority. Of course, the term *liberal* was stigmatized in the 1990s, so that Democratic activists may have preferred a "moderate" (or "progressive") label even if they held liberal issue positions. In any event, there were almost as many self-identified moderates as liberals among the Democratic delegates in the last four presidential campaigns. In addition, the gap between the two categories was the narrowest during John Kerry's 2004 convention. Indeed, this nearly even division probably reflects some of the larger battles between the liberal wing of the party rallied by liberal groups and the more moderate wing represented by the Democratic Leadership Council. This division goes back at least to the Carter-Kennedy nomination battle of 1980 and perhaps back even further to the McGovern insurgency in 1972 and the social movements of the 1960s. Clearly, "conservative" is not a popular label among Democrats, and very few delegates chose the term over this period. Thus the facile stereotype that Democrats are pure liberals is not borne out by these data. In fact, the Republican elites are more ideologically consistent.

Social Welfare Issues

We turn next to specific issues that divide the two parties, beginning with economic issues. The first of these is about the scope of governmental services, a defining difference between the two parties for many decades. Since the New Deal, the Democrats have been known as the party that favors having the government provide a higher level of public services, particularly to the poor and needy, while the Republicans have been opponents of "big government," at least with regard to economic matters. Figure 4.2 provides the results of a question about this issue.

Clearly, the question of providing more or fewer governmental services does divide the two parties markedly. For the past three national elections, 80 percent or more of the Democratic delegates favored the "continue" or "provide more" government services position, with only a smaller and smaller percentage choosing the "provide fewer services" option.

On the Republican side, well over half favored the "fewer services" position, and this was the choice of more than 80 percent of the 1992 and 1996 delegates. It is interesting to note, however, that the 2000 and the 2004 convention delegations were somewhat more moderate on government services, with only 61 and 62 percent, respectively, preferring a cut in government services. Perhaps President Bush's "compassionate conservatism" appeal had some resonance with these delegations. In addition, it may make a difference *which* government services are considered. The potential for cutting farm subsidies and government support for American businesses have both engendered deep divisions within the Republican majority in Congress dur-

Figure 4.2   Government Services

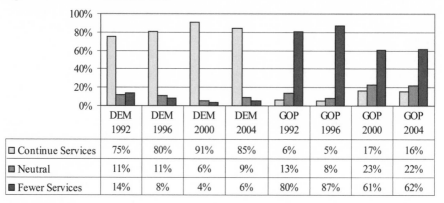

	DEM 1992	DEM 1996	DEM 2000	DEM 2004	GOP 1992	GOP 1996	GOP 2000	GOP 2004
▢ Continue Services	75%	80%	91%	85%	6%	5%	17%	16%
▨ Neutral	11%	11%	6%	9%	13%	8%	23%	22%
■ Fewer Services	14%	8%	4%	6%	80%	87%	61%	62%

ing the Bush administration. It may also be that cutting services is more easily advocated by the "out party" than by the party in power, which is faced with the burden of actually governing, making policy, and formulating budgets. Or perhaps the Republicans have become more diverse as they have experienced electoral success and grown in numbers. Whatever the dynamics, it is notable that the 2000 and 2004 presidential elections, both of which the Republicans won, have produced somewhat more internal party division on this issue.

Another deeply contentious issue between the two major parties has been the question of providing health insurance. Harry Truman first proposed health care insurance for the elderly, but it was not until Lyndon Johnson led a large majority of Democrats in the Congress twenty years later that Medicare and Medicaid were adopted. Bill and Hillary Clinton attempted to extend this idea to all of the uninsured in 1993 and 1994, but their plan for a complicated form of national health care failed in the face of determined opposition from the insurance industry, many in the medical community, and a united Republican Party. Since then, there has been a constant chorus of complaints against the current system, particularly the problems of forty-five million Americans who have no health insurance. Figure 4.3 provides the views of the delegates on this topic.

It is very evident that the elites of the two parties are very polarized on this issue. In 2004, 84 percent of the Republicans preferred private health insurance plans, compared to 81 percent of the Democratic elites who preferred some form of government insurance. Only 9 percent of the Republican delegates and 6 percent of the Democratic delegates took the other party's characteristic position on this item. In addition, the Democrats' majority support for the government insurance position has increased steadily since

Figure 4.3 Health Insurance

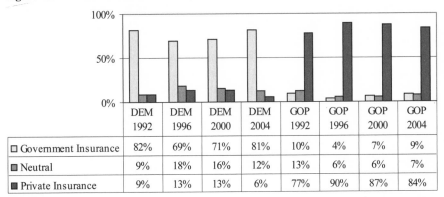

	DEM 1992	DEM 1996	DEM 2000	DEM 2004	GOP 1992	GOP 1996	GOP 2000	GOP 2004
☐ Government Insurance	82%	69%	71%	81%	10%	4%	7%	9%
▨ Neutral	9%	18%	16%	12%	13%	6%	6%	7%
■ Private Insurance	9%	13%	13%	6%	77%	90%	87%	84%

its low point of 1996. That was immediately after the collapse of the Clinton health plan in 1994 and their significant midterm congressional election losses of 1994. Even in face of that massive repudiation, fully 69 percent of the Democratic delegates supported a governmental insurance plan, while 90 percent of the GOP delegates opposed it. On this matter, the two parties' elites could hardly be more polarized. It is uncertain whether there could be any middle ground found in such circumstances.

A new issue on the agenda in 2004 was the major tax cuts advocated by President Bush and enacted by the Republican-controlled Congress. Although not strictly a social welfare issue, the major parties saw powerful links to social welfare programs. The Democrats felt that the tax cuts benefited the rich and would reduce the capacity of the federal government to help the poor, while the Republicans felt such cuts would restrain the size of government and generate economic growth and reduce poverty. These party elites were deeply polarized on Bush's tax cuts: 98 percent of Democrats opposed them and 95 percent of Republicans supported them (data not shown).

Another closely related domestic issue is whether government should provide aid or special assistance to minority groups. Race has long been a divisive issue in American politics, and conflict over race has been difficult for the political system to process. The Civil War and the civil rights revolution of the 1950s and 1960s were among the most disruptive and conflict-ridden periods in American history, and we are still facing their legacy. More recently, conflict over affirmative action programs divided the Republicans, who are generally opposed to them, from the Democrats, who are generally in favor. African Americans have become one of the bedrock components of the Democratic Party, providing one of the most dependable bloc votes for the Democrats. Meanwhile, white Southerners have become almost equally dedicated to the Republican Party. Thus, any question overtly dealing with race is likely to show very distinct differences. Figure 4.4 provides these results.

Figure 4.4 indicates very distinct partisan differences on this difficult issue. However, the two parties are somewhat less polarized on this issue than they were on health insurance. This more modest level of polarization is due largely to the decline of the Republicans' opposition to affirmative action from 75 percent in 1996 to 60 and 62 percent in 2000 and 2004, respectively. By comparison, the Democrats were more consistently in favor of the liberal option, with a steady support in the range of almost three-fourths of the delegates in each year. Again, it is the two George W. Bush nominating conventions that provided some modicum of diversity on this matter. The Bush administration has made a point of reaching out to minorities, especially Hispanics and to a lesser degree African Americans. If the GOP begins to make inroads in these communities, its internal heterogeneity is likely to increase.

Defense Spending

Defense spending has been a particularly contentious issue that divides the parties internally as well as polarizing them. But it is also an issue that seems to be particularly susceptible to changes over time, depending on who is in the White House and what is happening abroad. Figure 4.5 reflects these long-term patterns.

In 1992, at the end of the George H. W. Bush administration, Democrats were heavily in favor of decreasing defense expenditures, by a margin of 83

Figure 4.4   Minority Group Help

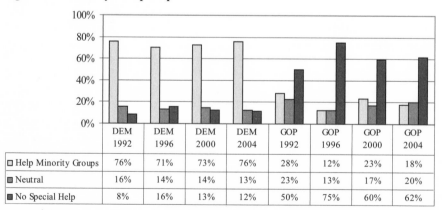

	DEM 1992	DEM 1996	DEM 2000	DEM 2004	GOP 1992	GOP 1996	GOP 2000	GOP 2004
☐ Help Minority Groups	76%	71%	73%	76%	28%	12%	23%	18%
▨ Neutral	16%	14%	14%	13%	23%	13%	17%	20%
▪ No Special Help	8%	16%	13%	12%	50%	75%	60%	62%

Figure 4.5   Defense Spending

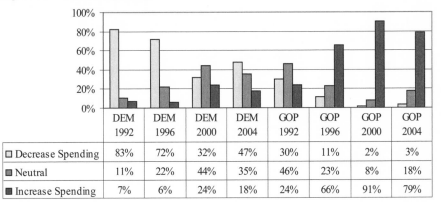

	DEM 1992	DEM 1996	DEM 2000	DEM 2004	GOP 1992	GOP 1996	GOP 2000	GOP 2004
☐ Decrease Spending	83%	72%	32%	47%	30%	11%	2%	3%
▨ Neutral	11%	22%	44%	35%	46%	23%	8%	18%
■ Increase Spending	7%	6%	24%	18%	24%	66%	91%	79%

percent to 7 percent. At the same time, the Republicans were deeply divided over the Bush administration's policy of decreasing the defense budget in response to the end of the Cold War and the fall of the Soviet Union: 30 percent of the Republican delegates wanted to decrease expenditures while 24 percent wanted to increase expenditures; 46 percent were in the neutral category. This ambivalence may have resulted partially from a desire to support their own party's president. Four years later, at the end of the first Clinton administration, this pattern had changed dramatically, with fully two-thirds of the Republicans wanting defense expenditures increased and only 11 percent wanting them decreased. Meanwhile, Democratic delegate demands for decreased defense spending fell a bit to 72 percent.

By 2000, the Republican delegates' support for increased spending had increased to fully 91 percent, a pattern that undoubtedly reflected a near-consensus among the GOP that Clinton had weakened the U.S. military—a charge George W. Bush raised repeatedly against Al Gore in the 2000 campaign. Thus, defense expenditures would probably have increased under the second Bush administration even in the absence of 9/11 and the war in Iraq. As it was, those two influences combined to dramatically expand the defense budget by 2004. By that year, it was the Democrats who were divided, with 47 percent of the delegates advocating a decrease, 35 percent taking a neutral position, and 18 percent advocating further increases. John Kerry's tentative and contradictory handling of the issue vis-à-vis his contradictory armaments funding votes in the U.S. Senate in the 2004 campaign only reflected the divisions among his own partisans.

In 2004, there were new foreign policy issues on the agenda, such as the war in Iraq, and they divided the parties sharply. For example, 70 percent of Democratic delegates believed the Iraq war was "completely unjustified,"

while 76 percent of Republican delegates thought it was "completely justified" (data not shown).

Cultural Issues

In the parlance of the "values divide" and "cultural wars" language, few
issues have been as divisive as the battle over abortion. In fact, one could
make the case that the Supreme Court's landmark case of *Roe v. Wade*
(1973) helped ignite the culture war and was the major stimulus for millions
of evangelical Christians to enter the political process *qua* religious advocates for the first time. Given the respective party platform statements on this
issue, one might expect extensive polarization of the party elites. After all,
the Republican platform was unequivocal in its pro-life position and the
Democratic platform just as unequivocal in its pro-choice advocacy during
the period under study. Certainly the popular stereotypes of the two parties
place them at loggerheads on this highly salient issue. Figure 4.6 provides
the results.

The problem with the popular stereotype is that it contains some distor-
tion. The Democrats generally live up to their pro-choice image. Over the
first three national conventions in this era, the pro-choice position support
ranged from 82 to 90 percent. Interestingly enough, only in 2004 was there
some decline, down to 76 percent pro-choice and 23 percent taking the more
ambivalent position among the Democrats. Among Republican delegates,
ambivalence and moderation were the popular positions: in all four conventions, well over half of the Republicans wanted to approve abortions in some
cases and less than 20 percent took the pure pro-life position of the party's
national platform. This issue is an example of how an intense minority can

Figure 4.6   Abortion

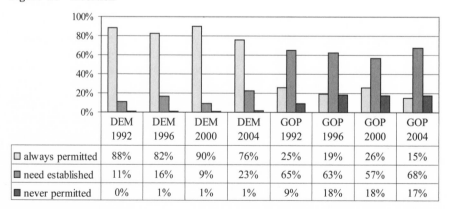

	DEM 1992	DEM 1996	DEM 2000	DEM 2004	GOP 1992	GOP 1996	GOP 2000	GOP 2004
□ always permitted	88%	82%	90%	76%	25%	19%	26%	15%
■ need established	11%	16%	9%	23%	65%	63%	57%	68%
■ never permitted	0%	1%	1%	1%	9%	18%	18%	17%

dominate a party's public policy position. The pro-life components of the Republican Party's base are very vocal and very mobilized, and they are able to dominate the political discourse in speaking for the Republican Party. However, the data in figure 4.6 indicate that they do not speak for the majority of GOP party elites.

At least on the Republican side of the equation, this is one "value" issue where the moderates predominate. The problem is that the Democrats do not offer much moderate cover here. In addition, the Democrats are also not the governing party at this time; they only have the challenge of maintaining the status quo, which is much easier to do than advocating fundamental change—and can be done with a minority of votes in the U.S. Senate. The parties are certainly divided on abortion but not fully polarized: a strongly pro-choice Democratic majority faces a moderate to pro-life range on the Republican side. In fact, it may be the Republicans who better reflect the ambivalence about abortion evident in most public opinion polls. This fight was focused in the second term when President Bush nominated two new Supreme Court members and will undoubtedly continue.

A new but closely related issue appeared on the political agenda in 2004: the legalization of same-sex marriage. After the state supreme court legalized the practice in Massachusetts, the issue became a critical feature in the campaign, with President Bush endorsing an amendment to the U.S. Constitution to prevent same-sex marriage and Christian Right groups putting eleven initiatives on state ballots with the same goal (data not shown). On this issue, the delegate opinion was in some ways a mirror image of opinion on the abortion issue. Among Democrats, 48 percent favored same-sex marriage, with the remainder opposing it (but with 40 percent in favor of civil unions). For the Republicans, just 4 percent supported same-sex marriage and 72 percent favored traditional marriage only (and another 24 percent open to civil unions).

Over the recent decade, the question of school choice has come to be deeply divisive in the United States. It is an issue carrying the weighty concerns over education for schoolchildren overlaid with issues of race and religion. Should public tax money, in the form of vouchers, be provided to parents to transfer their children out of often troubled public schools, especially in the central cities, and into more successful schools—public or private, and potentially religious based—often in the suburbs? Democrats, who have a heavy contingent of teachers and their unions in their base, say no. Republicans, with a heavy contingent of evangelical Christians in their camp, say yes to school choice and to vouchers. Figure 4.7 provides the results for four elections.

The data paint a picture of dramatically polarized party elites. Well over 80 percent of the Democrats were opposed to school choice in the past three elections, while almost as many Republicans favored it. Only the Democrats in 1992 showed much variation in this monolithic party polarization. This

Figure 4.7   School Choice

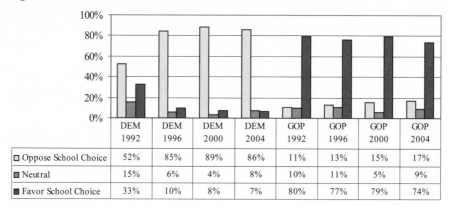

	DEM 1992	DEM 1996	DEM 2000	DEM 2004	GOP 1992	GOP 1996	GOP 2000	GOP 2004
□ Oppose School Choice	52%	85%	89%	86%	11%	13%	15%	17%
▨ Neutral	15%	6%	4%	8%	10%	11%	5%	9%
■ Favor School Choice	33%	10%	8%	7%	80%	77%	79%	74%

issue will remain on the agenda because the Republican majority in Congress is in favor of some form of school choice and President Bush has persistently advocated it. The Democrats are reduced to a position of attempting to block change here, and it is unclear how long their veto of some form of vouchers or school choice plans can be maintained. A number of school systems have already adopted some variation on this theme, and many others are considering this change with the active support of the U.S. Department of Education behind them.

The next item shows how a party's position can wax and wane depending on the circumstances. In the early to mid-1990s, term limits were very popular, especially among some conservatives and Republicans. Newt Gingrich's 1994 "Contract with America" promised term limits for Congress. Meanwhile, some twenty states adopted term limits for their legislative and executive branches, and most of those would probably have extended those same limits to the U.S. Congress if the Supreme Court had not declared such limits enacted by the states to be unconstitutional. Then the Republicans took over the majority in the Congress in 1994, maintaining that majority ever since except for a brief interlude in the Senate from January 2001 to December 2002. Some states have even contemplated abandoning their term limits now that they have more experience, although the "rollback" position does not enjoy widespread popularity. Figure 4.8 reflects those changes.

Almost three-fourths of the GOP delegates in 1992 favored term limits, but by 2000 this position had declined to well below a majority. Clearly the Republicans are now deeply divided internally on this issue. A Democratic majority was always opposed to term limits, and they have not changed much on this position. Democratic support for term limits started at 25 percent in

Figure 4.8   Term Limits

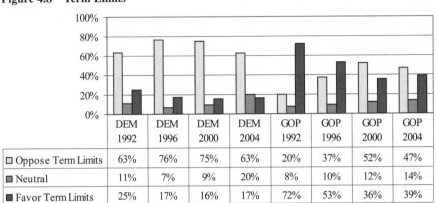

	DEM 1992	DEM 1996	DEM 2000	DEM 2004	GOP 1992	GOP 1996	GOP 2000	GOP 2004
☐ Oppose Term Limits	63%	76%	75%	63%	20%	37%	52%	47%
▣ Neutral	11%	7%	9%	20%	8%	10%	12%	14%
■ Favor Term Limits	25%	17%	16%	17%	72%	53%	36%	39%

1992 and has stood at 16 or 17 percent ever since. This issue seems to be an instance where the more the political elites learned about a policy and its application in the real world of practical politics, the less they liked it.

Issues Dimensions, 1992–2004

How did these attitudes fit together among Republican and Democratic delegates between 1992 and 2004, and how did the structure of opinion vary over time? To answer these questions, we performed a factor analysis on self-identified ideology and the seven issue questions found in all four surveys, for each year and then for all four years combined.[1]

Table 4.1 presents the results of this analysis for both sets of party elites. The first column shows the results from 1992 to 2004, and the next four columns replicate the analysis for each year individually. The results confirm our previous finding that the rival party elites are quite polarized. The gulf between the parties is greatest on self-identified ideology, followed by social welfare issues such as government services, national health insurance, and help for minorities. The social issues were modestly less polarizing overall, but abortion and school choice became more so after 1992. Defense spending and term limits were less important overall (1992–2004) largely because of the dramatic changes in the pattern of opinion already noted: defense spending had become more divisive by 2004 and term limits less so. But regardless of specific issue patterns, it is clear that major party elites were sharply divided along liberal-conservative lines.

Table 4.1   Structure of Opinion, National Convention Delegates, 1992–2004

Factor Loadings	1992–2004	1992	1996	2000	2004
Liberal Ideology	.87	.87	.88	.87	.87
Maintain government services	.84	.83	.87	.86	.83
Support national health insurance	.83	.82	.83	.83	.85
Support minority assistance	.75	.74	.77	.73	.75
Oppose school choice	.76	.66	.82	.81	.80
Support abortion rights	.73	.69	.73	.76	.73
Decrease defense spending	.69	.67	.78	.76	.75
Oppose term limits	.44	.60	.54	.37	.25
Eigenvalue	4.5	4.4	4.9	4.7	4.5
% variance explained	56%	55%	61%	58%	57%
Weighted N	4,000	1,000	1,000	1,000	1,000

The Internal Structure of Democratic Opinion

Within this overall pattern of interparty division, there is considerable variation within each party. Two dimensions of opinion emerge from this analysis when the Democrats were analyzed alone (Jackson, Bigelow, and Green 2003). The first dimension might be called "welfare liberalism"; it is composed of self-identified ideology and attitudes on defense spending, national health insurance, and help for minorities. Delegates on one end of this dimension of opinion strongly identified as liberals and supported the central priorities of the welfare state (with reduced defense spending to free up resources for domestic priorities). Delegates on the other end of this dimension were more likely to identify as moderates, less eager to cut defense spending and skeptical of new welfare initiatives.

The second dimension can be cautiously labeled as "antigovernment populism"; at its core were attitudes on school choice, term limits, and the scope of government services. We use the term *antigovernment* to distinguish the targets of this populism—public officials, as opposed to business and corporate officials, which represented another form of populism advocated by the Left.[2] This measure reveals that hostility to government elites was a significant part of the structure of opinion among some Democratic delegates. Delegates on one end of this dimension favored school vouchers, term limits, and modest reductions in the level of government services; delegates on the other end, who were much more numerous, had an unfavorable view of such limitations, implying a more positive view of government officials. It is worth noting that abortion loads on both factors, revealing the nearly uniform pro-choice positions of these delegates. Of course, abortion rights can be thought of both as an element of welfare liberalism and as opposition to the power of government officials. These two dimensions of Democratic opinion were quite stable in the four years under study, with a slight weakening of the populist dimension by 2004.

The Internal Structure of Republican Opinion

The Republican delegates have a more complex structure of opinion. Readers accustomed to thinking of the Democrats as more diverse than the Republicans may find this result surprising, but other studies of Democratic and Republican elites in the 1980s found similar patterns (see Green and Guth 1991). Three dimensions emerge from this analysis (Jackson, Bigelow, and Green 2003). The first dimension, which we label "anti–welfare state conservatism," contains attitudes on minority assistance, government services, and national health insurance. In many respects, this dimension is the opposite of the "welfare liberalism" dimension among the Democratic delegates. Republicans on one end of this dimension strongly opposed these public programs, while those on the other end expressed considerable support. Presumably, this conservatism is associated with support for free market ideology.

The second dimension might be called "cultural conservatism" and includes views on abortion, self-identified ideology, and to a lesser extent school choice. On one end of this continuum are the cultural conservatives who became prominent in the GOP during the 1990s; on the other end are the cultural moderates once dominant in the party.

Finally, the third Republican dimension is a counterpart to the "antigovernment populism" found among the Democrats. For Republicans, this dimension is defined by support for term limits, and to a lesser extent, school choice and increased defense spending. So, these Republican populists supported some limits on public officials but were also strongly nationalistic; nonpopulists were deeply skeptical of such limits on public officials and less supportive of a larger defense budget.

Unlike the Democratic dimensions, these Republican dimensions were much less stable over time, varying considerably from year to year. The three basic dimensions appeared in 1992, 1996, and 2004, but with slightly different loading in each year. The most consistent dimension was antigovernment populism, and the major exception was in 2000, when the welfare and cultural issues merged into a single dimension (thus paralleling the two-dimension structure of the Democrats). This bridging of economic and social conservatism may well have arisen from the strong desire to win back the White House in 2000. However, in 2004 the GOP delegates were again divided along economic and social lines, much as in 1992 and 1996.

Factions among Party Elites, 1992–2004

To better visualize this structure of opinion among the delegates, we created a crude measure of factions among the party elites.[3] Here we dichotomized the issue dimensions at the mean and then cross-tabulated them to group the delegates with various combinations of "high" and "low" scores. For the Democrats, the two issue dimensions produced four such "factions." For the Republicans, this strategy produced eight groups, but upon inspection we combined three very similar categories for a total of six factions.[4]

Democratic Factions

The four Democratic factions represent various combinations of welfare liberalism and antigovernment populism. The most recognizable of these groups we labeled the "Traditional Liberals" because they scored high (above the mean for all Democrats) on welfare liberalism and low on populism. Another group was essentially the opposite, scoring low (below the mean for all Democrats) on welfare liberalism and high on antigovernment populism; we called this group the "Traditional Centrists."

The other two factions represent additions largely peculiar to the 1990s. We call one the "Populist Liberals" because they score high on welfare liberalism but also high on antigovernment populism. With some apprehension, we label the remaining faction the "New Democrats"; they scored low on welfare liberalism (consistent with the fiscal restraint of the Democratic Leadership Council) as well as low on the populist dimension (fitting with the Council's pro-government vision). These groupings—and their labels—should be viewed with caution, since they reflect differences within parties that are often much smaller than interparty differences on the issues. However, they allow us to observe the changes in the makeup of the Democratic convention delegates from 1992 to 2004 (see figure 4.9). Some of these changes reflect shifts in opinion over time among party elites, but others arise from the presence of new elites with different opinions. It is beyond the scope of this essay to delineate the relative impact of these two sources of change. What we can observe is the "state of party elites" on the eve of each presidential campaign.

The 1992 Democratic National Convention was a low point for the Traditional Liberals in the 1990s: they made up only about one-fifth of delegates that year. This situation may reflect some discouragement with liberal activism leftover from three straight presidential defeats at the hands of Ronald Reagan and George H. W. Bush. However, the Traditional Liberals rebounded in 1996, rising to more than one-third of all delegates, and then declined to a bit under one-third in 2000 and remained at about that level in

Figure 4.9   Democratic Faction Groups

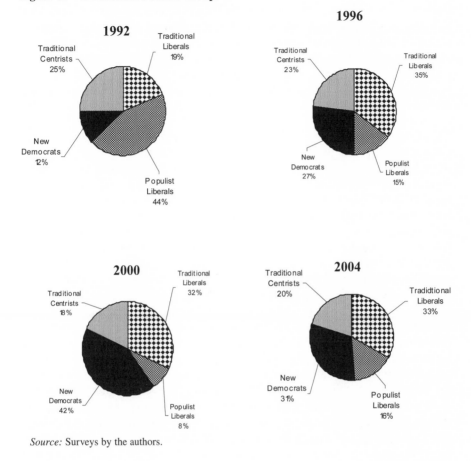

Source: Surveys by the authors.

2004. This change reflects the polarization of the Democratic elites on social welfare issues we observed above.

The trajectory of the Traditional Liberals was influenced by the rise and fall of the Populist Liberals. In 1992, they were the single largest faction, making up more than two-fifths of the total. No doubt these delegates were influenced by the populism sweeping across the nation at the time and the critique it offered of welfare liberalism. This faction declined sharply after 1992, making up between one-sixth and one-tenth of the delegates in subsequent years. The decline was propelled by a shift away from support for school choice, and to a lesser extent, term limits among the delegates who served in these conventions.

The Traditional Centrists made up about a quarter of the delegates in

1992, outnumbering the Traditional Liberals. They remained essentially unchanged in size in 1996, declined slightly in 2000, and rebounded somewhat in 2004—ending the period with a little more than one-fifth of the delegates, almost half the size of the Traditional Liberals in 2000 and 2004. The decline of support for school choice hurt this faction, but it was buoyed by the shift in defense priorities among Democratic delegates.

The Traditional Centrists had to compete with a new "centrist" faction during this period, the New Democrats. This faction was quite small in the 1992 convention, accounting for about an eighth of the delegates. This suggests that Bill Clinton and Al Gore were first nominated by a variety of other Democratic factions but then increased their following by one means or another: the New Democratic delegates more than doubled by 1996, making up more than one-quarter of the total, and then expanded to more than two-fifths in 2000, becoming the single largest faction among the Democrats. In 2004, the New Democrats experienced a slight decline (to 31 percent) but remained the second largest faction within the party. Thus, the fortunes of the New Democrats are inversely related to the popularity of antigovernment populism.

Overall, it appears that Clinton fundamentally changed the Democratic Party elites. In 1992, Populist and Traditional Liberals, along with Traditional Centrists, dominated the party elites. Since then, the New Democrats have supplanted the antigovernment populists and challenged the more liberal wing of the party. But this latter argument is far from settled and is likely to be on display again in the 2008 election. Some, like former presidential candidate and Democratic National Committee chair Howard Dean, argue that only by stressing core liberalism will the Democrats regain majorities in Congress and retake the White House. Others, perhaps including Hillary Clinton, argue that the New Democrat approach is the best way to regain power in a country that may have shifted rightward on at least some matters.

Republican Factions

The six Republican factions are displayed in figure 4.10. The GOP was rife with factions in the early 1990s, representing both the successes and failures of the Reagan-Bush era. By 2000 and 2004, the Republicans had solidified around two dominant factions, even though the others did not disappear altogether.

"Traditional Conservatives" are those delegates who score low on both social welfare and cultural conservatism but less so on antigovernment populism issues. In partial contrast, the "Populist Conservatives" score high on all three dimensions, adding strong support for school choice and especially term limits to conservative positions on economic and social issues. The core of the Christian Right can be found among the Populist Conservatives, in addition to other elements of the "hard Right," such as gun owners and anti-

Figure 4.10   Republican Faction Groups

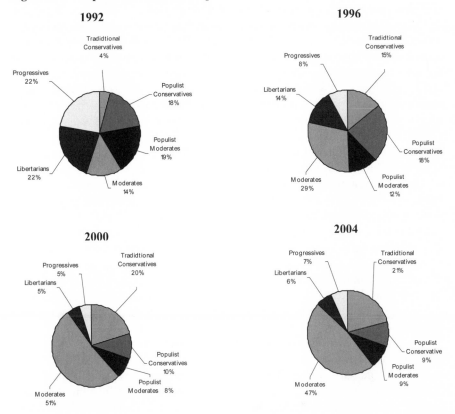

tax advocates. However, some of these constituencies are found among the Traditional Conservatives as well.

A similar division occurs among the historic rivals of the hard Right in Republican circles. These factions include the "Moderates" and the "Populist Moderates." Both score relatively low on welfare and cultural conservatism, but the former are also low on antigovernment populism, while the latter have high scores on populism. These two factions contain much of the traditional business and professional constituency of the Republican Party. (Of course, these "Moderates" were still far more conservative than the Democratic delegates.)

"Libertarians" score high on economic conservatism and low on social conservatism, as well as high on the issues related to populism, largely on the grounds of personal liberty. Finally, the "Progressives" are the remnant of the once-potent "Liberal Republicans," who score the most liberal on welfare and cultural issues and low on populism. The Progressives have shrunk to less than 10 percent of the total since 1992.

Much as it did among the Democrats, the populism of the 1990s re-arranged the factions within the GOP. The Traditional Conservatives made up only under one-twentieth of the delegates in 1992, largely because of the Populist Conservatives, who made up almost one-fifth of the total. However, the Traditional Conservatives made a rebound in 1996, growing to about one-fifth of the delegates in 2000 and 2004. Fueled in part by the decline in support for term limits, this expansion was especially evident after the GOP victories in the 1994 elections. However, the Populist Conservatives main-tained nearly one-fifth of the delegates in 1996 before declining to one-tenth in 2000 and less than one-tenth in 2004.

The Moderates experienced a similar trajectory. In 1992, they made up about one-sixth of the delegates, eclipsed by the Populist Moderates at al-most one-fifth. However, the Moderates made a big comeback in 1996, dou-bling in size to almost one-third. Much of this gain appears to have been at the expense of the Populist Moderates, whose numbers declined, falling to about one-tenth of the GOP delegate pool. This trend continued in 2000, where the Moderate faction expanded to an outright majority of the GOP delegates, and the Populist Moderates declined to less than one-tenth. In 2004, the Moderates slipped just below their outright majority but remained the dominant faction.

So, the long-standing debate over how conservative the GOP should be was submerged briefly by a surge of populism in 1992 but then resurfaced once the surge subsided. Both the Libertarians and Progressives suffered dramatic declines over the period. Each made up over a fifth of the delegates in 1992 but fell steadily to less than a twentieth by 2000 and remained just above that level in 2004. The merging of the economic and social conserva-tism in 2000 sharply reduced the distinctiveness of these small factions, but they did not entirely disappear.

The Character of the 2004 Party Factions

What types of delegates made up these different factions in each party in 2004? Although a full description is beyond the scope of this essay, a few salient features are worth discussing. Convention delegates are chosen at the state level, so it should come as no surprise that the factions had a distinctive regional distribution. The centrist Democratic factions were overrepresented by Midwestern and Southern delegates, while delegates from the liberal fac-tions were mostly from the North and West. In part, this regional distribution represents the effects of political competition: Democratic delegates from safe Republican states were the most likely to come from the centrist factions of the party, while the more liberal factions dominated safe Democratic states. Interestingly, delegates from battleground states represented an almost even distribution of the Democratic factions.

In part, the regional distribution reflects different political cultures. Although there were no significant gender or racial differences among these factions, there were important religious divisions. The more liberal factions contained the largest number of secular delegates and delegates from non-Christian faiths. Black Protestants were common in all the factions but especially among the Populist Liberals and New Democrats. Catholics were most common among the centrist factions, and so were both mainline and evangelical Protestants.

These religious differences are reflected in the issue of same-sex marriage. The two centrist factions opposed same-sex marriage, but with a majority in favor of civil unions. In contrast, some two-thirds or more of the liberal factions backed same-sex marriage and less than one-tenth supported traditional marriage only. But the Democratic delegates were nearly unanimous in their opposition to the Iraq war, with only very modest variation across factions.

By the time they convened in Boston at the end of July 2004, most Democratic delegates expressed strong support for John Kerry—their presumed nominee. However, when asked which candidate they originally supported, the four Democratic factions expressed some notable differences. The two moderate factions (Traditional Centrists and New Democrats) were most likely to favor John Kerry or John Edwards. The Traditional and Populist Liberals were the most likely to support Howard Dean or Dennis Kucinich.

There were also strong regional patterns for the Republican factions in 2004. Southerners made up two-fifths of the two most conservative factions but made up roughly one-third of the other factions as well. Westerners were also most common among the two most conservative factions at more than one-quarter and then declined elsewhere. Northerners were most common among the more moderate factions, especially the Progressives and Populist Moderates. It is worth noting that the dominant Moderate faction had the most even regional distribution. Like their Democratic counterparts, Republican delegates from safe Republican states were most likely to represent a conservative faction within their party. The moderate factions were also likely to come from safe Republican states, while the small group of Libertarians was overrepresented in battleground states and the tiny Progressive faction in Democratic states.

In terms of religion, evangelical Protestants dominated all the Conservative and Populist factions. Indeed for the two most conservative factions, evangelicals outnumbered the next largest group, mainline Protestants, by more than two to one. Evangelicals were less common among the more moderate factions, and their place was taken by mainline Protestants, the single largest group, but also by Catholics, who were a close second. The few Republican delegates who identified themselves as secular were most likely members of the Libertarian faction. Other religious minorities were rare in all the factions.

These patterns of religious affiliation help explain the factions' views on marriage. A majority of all but one of the factions favored traditional marriage only, usually by very large margins. The exception was the Progressives, where a large majority favored civil unions. Indeed, support for civil unions increased steadily from the most conservative to most liberal factions. There was little support for same-sex marriage, with the exception of the Libertarians, among whom about one-sixth backed the option. In 2004, the more conservative factions of the Republican Party united behind President Bush, including support for the Iraq war. Note, however, that there was some modest skepticism about the war on the part of the more liberal factions.

Conclusion

In 2004, the major party elites were strongly polarized on a wide variety of issues. This pattern of polarization was common in the 1990s, and in some modest respects, the patterns in 2000 and 2004 reflect a bit more moderation compared to 1992 and 1996 (see Jackson, Bigelow, and Green 2003). But such modest changes were overwhelmed by the strong and persistent divisions between the major parties on key social welfare issues, such as the scope of government services and health insurance. And new issues that arose in 2004, such as the Iraq war, the Bush tax cut, and same-sex marriage, tended to strongly reinforce the existing party differences.

Clearly, cleavages over social welfare were the most important divisions between the major party elites. Foreign policy was often a strong source of division, but it was more variable over time, reflecting the international situation as well as the party that held the White House. Similarly, the values divide and culture wars disputes reinforced the ideological differences between the parties, though in a less consistent way. It is interesting that the hot-button cultural issues created asymmetrical patterns within the parties. For example, the Democratic delegates were strongly pro-choice on abortion, but the Republicans were not comparably pro-life, with a plurality holding moderate positions. A comparable asymmetry occurred on marriage: the GOP delegates were very strong supporters of traditional marriage only, while the Democratic delegates had more diverse opinion, with the largest numbers favoring civil unions rather than same-sex marriage.

However, within this pattern of interparty polarization, neither party is fully united. Over the period of study, the Democrats were characterized by four factions, ranging from consistently liberal to centrist, while the Republican had six factions, reaching from consistently conservative to moderate. These patterns suggest that the Democrats are more divided by demography and the Republicans by ideology. It is worth noting that these findings on intraparty differences are greater than has been observed in studies of elected officials, such as members of Congress (see chapter 3 and also Pomper 2003). This may result from the fact that the nation's regions are more fully represented among delegates than other kinds of political elites. After all, conventional delegates always include Southern Democrats and New England Republicans, whereas these groups are markedly less likely to be elected to Congress.

The relative size of these factions was not especially stable over the period in question. In fact, there was considerable change in the relative size of the factions, with two factions, the New Democrats and Moderate Republicans, becoming dominant over the period. In part, these changes reflect shifts in elite opinion, such as a decline in support for term limits, but also the appearance of new delegates, many of them elected in support of Bill Clinton and George W. Bush. The increased influence of these moderate factions reflects to some extent an increase in party unity. So by 2004, the major parties had become more distinctive and united on many issues.

This state of party elites has important implications for the party system. For one thing, it means that party organizations are less likely to be riven by bitter ideological disputes and that the disputes that do occur are more likely to have positive consequences for the party as a whole. It also means that factionalism is less likely to stand in the way of competing for votes against the rival party that is characterized by quite different issue positions. Finally, it means that voters are more likely to hear consistent political messages that reflect the underlying values of the party. All this can contribute to clearer choices at the polls and more consistent government after the election. Of course, this situation also means that national politics is likely to be characterized by fierce partisanship between disciplined armies with opposite visions for government and an inability to compromise on policy. If the state of party elites is any guide, there is no reason to believe that such a high level of partisanship will decline anytime soon.

Notes

1. For purposes of this analysis, we used the full range of the survey items. To assure the number of cases in each of the studies did not bias the results, we weighted each set of party delegates and each year equally. We performed a principal components analysis with a varimax rotation; see Jackson, Bigelow, and Green 2003 for a full discussion.

2. Items for the individual surveys suggest that opposition to corporate elites is likely to be strongly associated with welfare liberalism.

3. Here, we define factions by issue positions rather than membership in or affect toward factional organizations. Of course, issue positions and affiliation with such organizations are highly correlated (Green, Jackson, and Clayton 1999).

4. For these purposes, we used factor scores generated by pooling all four surveys. For the Democrats, the results are straightforward because the same two-factor solution emerged in the pooled data. The Republicans were more complicated: the pooled data generated a three-factor solution, with economic conservatism (government services, national health insurance, and help for minorities), social issue conservatism (ideology, abortion, school choice), and populism (term limits, school choice, and defense spending) factors. We used factor scores from this analysis to define the GOP factions.

5

State Party Activists and State Party Polarization

Daniel J. Coffey

In recent years American political parties have become increasingly polarized. Numerous studies of party activists and elected officials have shown that the degree of ideological homogeneity within each party across issues has increased significantly since the mid-1970s (Aldrich 1995; Carsey and Layman 2002). Some have gone so far as to argue that American parties have become as ideologically coherent and programmatic as their European counterparts (Pomper 2003). Moreover, the rise in the ideological differences between the parties coincides with substantial increases in the organizational strength of the parties. American party organizations have more money, staff, and technology and have been making efforts to coordinate their activities down the to county and precinct level (Aldrich 2000; Morehouse and Jewell 2003b; Clark and Prysby 2004).

Changes in mass public opinion, however, do not appear to be the guiding force behind the polarization of the parties. Fiorina (2005), for example, finds that on most issues, differences between the views of Democrats and Republicans in the electorate are modest at best and do not appear to be increasing over time. However, there is some disagreement on this point. For example, Abramowitz and Saunders (1998), Bartels (2000), and Hetherington (2001) all have found evidence that increases in elite polarization have increased the public's awareness of partisan differences, which has in turn increased the salience of party identification for the mass public, leading to less split-ticket voting and increases in party attachment. At the same time, however, the high degree of polarization among elites cannot be fully explained by what have been modest increases in partisanship in the general public. For example, several studies have shown that party unity scores and the ideological differences between party members in Congress are at their highest levels in nearly a century (Poole and Rosenthal 1997; Pomper 2003). In contrast, in 2004, while 76 percent of citizens believe that there are important differences between the parties—the highest proportion in nearly fifty years of National Election Studies—the percentage of citizens who strongly identify with either party is modestly higher (31 percent) than it was in 1988, when only 60 percent saw important differences between the parties, and is considerably lower than the 38 percent of citizens who were strong partisans in 1964, when just 55 percent of respondents perceived that there were important differences between the two parties (American National Election Studies).

One reason for the lack of polarization is the structure of modern political parties. Shea (2003) argues that the resurgence of party organizations in recent years has actually led to lower levels of turnout, citizen trust in government, and participation in civic organizations. This is partly because parties tend to focus on providing numerous technical services for candidates, such as raising money, providing seminars in effective campaign tactics, and distributing poll results. As a result, the public remains largely disengaged from the parties. Moreover, the revival of political parties in recent years has been the result of the mobilization of ideological activists. As Bibby (1999) points out, modern parties are in many ways networks of allied interest groups and issue advocates. The dependence on such groups for financial and electoral support has produced more ideologically polarized candidates and parties, who have little incentive to reach out to citizens not affiliated with these groups, as mobilizing voters is costly and uncertain (Shea 2003). As a result, as White and Shea (2004, 65–67) note, in some polls only about one-quarter of respondents feel that the two-party system is appropriate for solving the nation's problems.

One consequence of these developments is a substantial disconnect between the views of political party activists and the larger citizenry. As the primary representative institutions in American politics, the ability of parties to represent the broader public is of fundamental importance (Schattschneider 1942; Key 1949; Epstein 1986). It is true that party activists have always been more ideological than the electorate and than the rank and file in their own party (Abramowitz, McGlennon, and Rapoport 1986). What is less appreciated is that to a large extent, parties may not be capable of representing the larger citizenry because the views of party activists are considerably different from the larger public's views (Fiorina 2005).

This problem is especially true at the state level, where open party structures allow ideological activists to control state party organizations (Usher 2000). Several studies, for example, have shown that activists associated with the Christian Right are very strong within numerous state Republican parties (Green, Rozell, and Wilcox 2000; Layman 2001). For instance, as Hacker and Pierson's (2005) study of the 2001 tax cuts indicates, the cultivation of activist support by elected officials can result in public policies that diverge significantly from the preferences of the median voter. They argue that modern politics produces powerful incentives for elected officials to craft legislation and make campaign appeals to avoid punishment by well-organized interest groups and an ideologically extreme base of supporters who control important financial resources. While their study focuses on the skewed policies that have resulted from the Republican Party's mobilization of conservative activists, the same can be said of the Democratic Party and its dependence on liberal interest groups (Berry 1999). As a result, both parties have significant financial and electoral incentives to pursue agendas or take policy positions that are significantly to the right or left of the state political center. In such an environment, party agendas should be more likely to be driven to satisfy a reliable core of supporters instead of the general public, and this should help to account for the lack of voter attachment to increasingly well-organized, well-funded, and competitive state parties.

How does party ideology vary across state parties? There is substantial research that parties and elected officials are highly responsive to public opinion (Downs 1957; Page and Shapiro 1992). Research on state politics has found that public opinion has a substantial effect on state public policy. Specifically, Erikson, Wright, and McIver's (1993) comprehensive analysis of state public opinion provides strong evidence that differences in the ideology of elected officials and public policy from state to state are caused by differences in median public opinion. Their research is supported by several studies showing a strong link between public opinion, elite ideology, and state public policy (Hill and Leighley 1993; Berry et al. 1998).

The analysis that follows will compare the relative influence of median pubic opinion and party activist opinion on state party agendas. Using data from state party platforms, I find that activist opinion is more strongly correlated with the ideology of state party platforms and especially the polarization between platforms within the same state. In addition, state political culture significantly influences party platform ideology, with moralist states having more ideological platforms than individualist states. Finally, counterintuitively, more competitive state party systems are more ideologically polarized than states in which there is relatively little competition between the parties. In every specification of models of party platform ideology below, I find that median statewide public opinion has no influence on platform ideology.

Why Party Platforms?

This chapter analyzes party representation using an unconventional method. Instead of looking at state legislative roll-call voting (as was done in Aldrich and Battista 2002) or public opinion surveys (like Erikson, Wright, and McIver 1993 and Berry et al. 1998), I use state party platforms to measure party ideology. Previous studies that analyzed state party platforms have found that they are reliable indicators of state party positions

(Elling 1979; Paddock 1998). Paddock (1992), for example, measured party ideology using state party platforms and found party ideological differences became increasingly polarized between 1956 and 1980, while Elling found that once in office, legislative parties make serious efforts to fulfill the commitments of the state party platform.

The analysis of state platforms has several advantages. Across states, there is variance in political culture, levels of turnout, party organizational strength, and intraparty competition (Morehouse and Jewell 2003b). As a result, a variety of hypotheses about the relative influence of public opinion and activist opinion on party positions can be tested.

As such, an examination of state party agendas is ideal for analyzing how state parties represent citizens, as they provide an excellent comparative measure of party ideology. At first glance, state party platforms may seem of little importance. None of the provisions are binding on politicians within the party, and most interest groups place their efforts on direct lobbying or mobilizing grassroots support in elections to influence party positions on issues. Yet there are several reasons why an analysis of party platforms is an appropriate tool for analyzing intra- and interparty differences across state parties. State party platforms provide a standard unit of analysis for measuring party ideology across the states. Given the difficulties of measuring party elite and activist ideology at the state level, platforms are indicators of party positions that can be obtained by researchers with little effort.

In essence, this approach allows parties, through activists and elites, to put into their own words what matters most in politics. As Gerring argues, "Any study of party ideologies is . . . a study of what politics is all about. Since political parties are one of the chief disseminators of political culture, partisan rhetoric provides a window into the values and attitudes that have guided American politics" (1998, 21). Parties provide citizens with their positions on specific policies over a range of issues. It should be noted that most state platforms were obtained directly from party websites, often under links titled "Who We Are," "What We Stand For," or "About Our Party." In other words, when the Internet is a major source of information for most citizens, the state parties are doing their best to advertise the platforms as the definitive statement of the organization's core beliefs.

Content Analysis Description and Procedures

The primary concern for this chapter is how state party platforms vary in terms of ideology. Why are some platforms moderate and others very liberal or very conservative? A first step, therefore, is to measure party ideology.

Party ideology was characterized for this purpose by calculating by the proportion of liberal and conservative sentences in each State of the State speech. Specifically, the calculation used was the number of liberal sentences minus the number of conservative sentences, divided by the total number of sentences in the platform.

To measure ideology in this manner, an ideological judgment was made about each sentence: liberal, conservative, or neither. The denominator is the total number of sentences in the platform, thereby factoring moderate sentences into the ideological calculation and moving the score closer to a neutral score of 0. For example, the Wisconsin Democratic platform is 164 sentences long, of which 147 are liberal, while only 3 are conservative. The corresponding score, then, is .88. In contrast, the moderate Hawaii Republican platform is 206 sentences long, of which 57 are liberal and 125 are conservative, yielding a score of − .33. I have previously used this scheme to code gubernatorial State of the State speeches, and the method produces reliable and valid indicators of ideology (Coffey 2005). In many ways, this scheme is similar to that used by other researchers who have coded party ideology (Laver and Garry 2000).

What makes a sentence liberal or conservative? Ideology is difficult to define, and many scholars argue that American parties (and politics in general) are distinct for being nonideological—their fragmented organizational structures cause them to be more focused on winning elections and maintaining social cohesion than pushing dogmatic agendas (Epstein 1986). Recent studies have challenged this conventional wisdom. Klingemann, Hofferbert, and Budge (1994) find that American national party platforms are nearly as distinct from each other as many manifestos in European party systems. Gerring's (1998) extensive study of campaign speeches and national party platforms from 1828 to 1996 finds that American parties have distinct philosophies that are clearly articulated in national party platforms across decades.

My coding of sentences as liberal and conservative is generally similar to Gerring's scheme. Gerring defines party ideology as messages or positions that are "internally coherent, externally differentiated (from one another) and stable through time" (1998, 3). Using this framework, I coded sentences as liberal if they call for one of the following:

- intervention in the free market to protect working-class and lower-income citizens
- greater spending on social welfare programs
- support for the protection and expansion of the rights of marginalized groups

Conservative sentences generally have one or more of the following characteristics:

- oppose government regulation of the economy
- call for the protection of individual opportunity (especially lower taxes and private property right) in the marketplace
- advocate a strict regulation of individual behavior
- promote a greater role for religion (often Christianity) in the public sector

The sentences were usually fairly easy to interpret. I erred on the side of caution, however, as the primary claim of this study was that state political parties are ideologically polarized. Ideological sentences had to encompass some specific policy proposal (or criticism) that embodies a vision of what is "good" (or "bad") for a state's government and society. If a sentence was ambiguous in its ideological position, I coded it as moderate. I used two basic guidelines:

1. Would such a sentence appear in the opposition party's platform?
2. How would a reasonable person interpret such a sentence?

These guidelines often caused me to reject a sentence as not having ideological content.[1]

Party Platform Ideology

I coded sixty-seven state party platforms written between 2000 and 2002; in a few cases (Arkansas and Virginia Democrats; Louisiana and Illinois Republicans), I decided to use the 2004 platform. Where more than one platform was written between 2000 and 2002 for a state party, I used only the most recent platform.

The platforms clearly distinguish the parties across the states. The Democratic average score is a fairly liberal .66, while the average GOP platform is −.64 (see table 5.1 for each state party's score). There is no overlap between the parties; the most liberal GOP platform, from Indiana, has a score of −.25. In comparison, the most conservative Democratic platform, Alabama's, has a score of .42.[2] Despite the substantial ideological differences between the party platforms, there is a fair amount of variance within each party. The absolute range of the platform ideology is .45 for the Democratic Party and .61 for the Republicans.[3]

The polarization of parties at the state level is consistent with partisan polarization at other levels of government. Numerous studies have documented the increasing polarization of the parties in Congress, as party unity scores have reached their highest levels in decades (Poole and Rosenthal 1997; Bond and Fleisher 2000; Sinclair 2002; Stonecash, Brewer, and Mariani 2003). Pomper (2003) has found that national party platforms have

Table 5.1   State Party Ideological Scores

State	Republicans	Democrats
AK	− .79	.65
AL		.42
AZ		.78
AR		.63
CA	− .80	.80
CO		.73
CT		.71
DE		.43
HI	− .32	.63
ID	− .60	.62
IL	− .70	.66
IN	− .25	.52
IA	− .63	.80
KS		.43
LA	− .75	
ME	− .72	.75
MA	− .51	.74
MI		.80
MN	− .86	.76
MS	− .70	
MO	− .68	
MT	− .50	.70
NE	− .59	.70
NH	− .47	.49
NM	− .52	.66
NC	− .69	.51
ND		.70
OH	− .44	
OK	− .78	.80
OR	− .71	.84
RI		.55
SC	− .73	
SD	− .47	.71
TX	− .81	.62
UT	− .59	.51
VA		.68
VT	− .62	.69
WA	− .83	.85
WV	− .67	.48
WI	− .83	.87
WY	− .68	.59
Average Platform Score	− .64 (.15)	.66 (.12)

Note: Cell entries are party platform scores as a ratio of liberal to conservative sentences; for the average platform score, the standard deviation is in parentheses.

grown increasingly programmatic over the last three decades. As noted in the previous chapter, activists attending the national party conventions are especially polarized along ideological lines. Moreover, as studies of public opinion have demonstrated, ideological polarization has extended to the mass public, although it appears to be concentrated among the most partisan and attentive citizens (see chapter 16).

Causes of State Party Platform Ideology

Have party activists distorted party positions? What factors explain the variance in state party ideology? Public opinion, as Erikson, Wright, and McIver (1993) have shown, has a substantial impact on state elected officials. The assumption is fairly simple: liberal states should have liberal party platforms, and relatively conservative states should have conservative platforms. If activists are responsible for the ideological polarization of the parties, however, the relationship between party ideology and median public opinion may be distorted.

As Erikson and his colleagues also found in their study, political activists have a significant influence on the positions of parties. Party activists prevent elected officials from converging on the mean of state public opinion; conservative activists pull elected Republican officials to the right, while liberal activists pull elected Democrats to the left of the ideological spectrum. From state to state, however, the correlation between activist opinions is highly correlated with median public opinion. This pattern results from the fact that activists are drawn from the larger state population and in general share the same beliefs and attitudes about public policies and the proper role of government in society. Based on their surveys of party activists in the late 1970s and early 1980s, Erikson, Wright, and McIver found that activists are more polarized but that relative differences from state to state correlate with the variance in median public opinion from state to state.

This may no longer be the case, however. Activists associated with each party are pushing their candidates to take more polarized positions. As Berry and Schildkraut have noted about the national party platforms since 1980, "Regardless of motive, citizen groups work to accentuate the differences between the parties, to drive a wedge in further so that the parties do not gravitate toward a more moderate position" (1998, 148). Activists are most involved in the writing of the party platform (Jewell 1984). Party activist opinion, therefore, should have a stronger influence on platform ideology than general state opinion.

Figure 5.1 shows the relationship between median public opinion and Democratic platform ideology. To measure public opinion, I have used the updated Erikson, Wright, and McIver data set, which includes surveys of

Figure 5.1   Democratic Party Platform Ideology and State Public Opinion

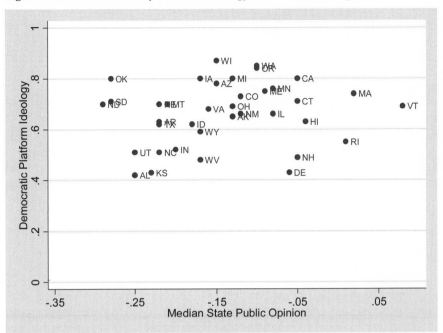

Source: Author's analysis: Erikson, Wright and McIver (1993).

Note: Democratic platform ideology (y-axis) ranges from 0 (moderate) to 1 (very liberal); public opinion (x-axis) ranges from conservative (− .35) to liberal (.10).

state public opinion from 1995 to 1999.[4] One benefit of using these data is that they precede the writing of the party platforms. The initial evidence suggests that there is little in the way of a relationship between state public opinion and party platform ideology.

Figure 5.1 shows that while there appears to be a slight positive relationship (r = .16) between median public opinion and Democratic Party liberalism, the relationship is weak at best. In some states, public opinion is related to platform ideology; Massachusetts, for example, has liberal citizens and a liberal platform. In contrast, however, Oklahoma and South Dakota have fairly conservative populations and Wisconsin is a relatively moderate state, but those states' platforms are extremely liberal. There is a similar pattern for Republican platforms (r = .10); Minnesota, California, and Washington all have much more conservative platforms than would be expected based on median public opinion in those states (data not shown).

What then are the systematic factors driving party ideology? I have estimated two models for each party to compare the relative influence of citizen and activist ideology on state party platforms. Since party ideology is measured on a ratio scale ranging from 1 to -1, it is appropriate to use OLS regression to analyze what variables systematically affect party ideology. In this analysis, there are two dependent variables: Democratic Party ideology and Republican Party ideology. For each party, the ideological model must be estimated separately, since the independent variables for each party are the same for each state.[5]

One concern with the analysis is the low number of observations. The regression results, therefore, must be interpreted with some caution. As a result, I have estimated the models with few variables to avoid overspecification. Since the primary claim is that activists are driving state party agendas, each model includes the measure for median public opinion used above. In addition, the Erikson, Wright, and McIver data provide information about the percentage of conservatives, liberals, and moderates in each state, which is also used in some of the models below. For activist opinion, I have used the Party Elite Studies of each party's national convention delegates from 1992 to 2004.[6] Activist opinion is measured by the pooled average ideology of each state's party delegation for the four national party conventions from 1992 to 2004.

The model includes three control variables: state political culture, state party competition, and electoral turnout. In theory, party ideology should moderate with increases in party competition, because parties tend to moderate in order to avoid losing votes (Downs 1957). Party competition is measured by the Ranney competition index (Bibby and Holbrook 2004). This measure ranges from .50 (no competition) to 1 (the parties are perfectly competitive). The measure takes into account the percentage of seats won by the parties in the state legislature, each party's percentage of the vote in gubernatorial elections, the frequency of divided government, and the length of time the parties have controlled the governorship and the legislative houses (Bibby and Holbrook 2004, 87). Each model also includes a variable for turnout in state elections, measured by the average turnout in senatorial, gubernatorial, and presidential elections between 1997 and 2002, which is prior to the writing of most of the state party platforms analyzed (Bibby and Holbrook 2004).

Finally, I have included dummy variables for state political culture based on Elazar's (1972) typology. Elazar classifies state political culture in three subcultures: moralist, traditionalist, and individualist states. He points out that history, the demographic makeup of the state, and a range of other factors significantly affect citizens' understanding of the proper role of government in society. In moralist states, there are high levels of citizen participation in politics and a general view that government can be used to improve society. These states are more likely to have platforms, regardless of party. Since politics is more ideological and policy oriented, I expect to find more ideological platforms in these states, as the parties strive to point out the differences between their agendas and those of the opposition party. In traditionalist states, there is generally low voter turnout, and elites have historically dominated politics and party organizations. While this may lead to less ideological platforms, most traditionalist states are in the South, where the GOP has built a strong following by appealing to racial and religious conservatives (Carmines and Stimson 1989; Layman 2001). Moreover, as the Southern Grassroots Party Activists Project has shown, Southern Democratic activists are now as nearly liberal as many of their Northern counterparts (McGlennon 2004). Individualist states, by contrast, should have more moderate platforms. In these states, politics is mainly about winning elections and distributing the spoils of office. As Mayhew (1986) noted, these are historically strong organizations, and it is difficult for ideological activists to enter and control the state party organization. These states are also the least likely to have platforms, indicating to some extent the lack of importance that issues and philosophical differences play in party politics in individualist states.[7]

The Results

Table 5.2 shows the regression results for the Republican and Democratic state parties. Importantly, for both parties, median state public opinion is not related to the party's ideology—and is actually in the wrong direction (i.e., more liberal citizens cause more conservative platforms; see models 1 and 3). In contrast, activist opinion is significantly related to state party ideology for Democratic platforms and is at least in the correct direction for each Republican model. The negative coefficients in each model mean that the more liberal activists become, the more liberal the state party platform becomes, while more conservative activists lead to more conservative platforms for both parties.

Since the claim that public opinion does not influence party ideology is a strong one, I performed another test using a different measure for mass public opinion. In the second set of models (2 and 4), I used the percentage of self-identified liberals (for Democrats) and conservatives (for Republicans) in a state. It may be that the use of median public opinion would not take into account states in which opinion is ideologically bipolar. As the second models show for each party, however, this is not the case. Importantly, state public opinion, measured two different ways (by mean public opinion and the percentage of citizens in a state that are self-identified liberals or conservatives), does not appear to have any systematic effect on platform ideology.[8]

The political culture dummy variables are modestly related to each par-

Table 5.2   OLS Regression of State Party Platform Ideology

	Republican Platforms		Democratic Platforms	
	Model 1	Model 2	Model 3	Model 4
Median Public Opinion	−.35		−.06	
	(.48)		(.24)	
Percent Conservative		.62		
		(.79)		
Percent Liberal				−.30
				(.57)
Activist Opinion	−.17	−.16	−.16*	−.18*
	(.14)	(.13)	(.09)	(.09)
Party Competition	−.56*	−.56*	.61***	.64***
	(.33)	(.33)	(.25)	(.25)
Moralist	−.11*	−.11*	.08	.07
	(.06)	(.06)	(.05)	(.05)
Traditionalist	−.12	−.12	−.04	−.05
	(.09)	(.09)	(.06)	(.06)
Turnout	.01	.01	−.01**	−.01*
	(.00)	(.00)	(.00)	(.00)
Constant	.45	.27	.76	.85
	(.58)	(.50)	(.32)	(.37)
Adjusted R	.13	.14	.25	.26
N	30	30	37	37
F	1.75	1.77	3.01	3.07

Note: Cell entries are unstandardized regression coefficients with standard errors in parentheses.
* significant at $p < .10$
** significant at $p < .05$
*** significant at $p < .01$

ty's platform ideology. In moralist states, Democratic platforms are more liberal and Republican platforms are more conservative. The coefficient of −.11 in models 1 and 2 for Republican platforms can be interpreted such that, for a typical state Republican platform that is one hundred sentences long, there will be about eleven more conservative sentences in moralist states compared to nonmoralist state cultures. In each model, turnout reduces platform ideology. The negative coefficient in the Democratic models and the positive coefficient in the Republican models means that when turnout increases, state party platforms become more moderate. The result can be interpreted to mean that a 1 percent increase in turnout leads to a .01 decrease in platform polarization. Since turnout ranges from 29 percent to 61 percent, this seemingly small effect can be significant. Moreover, this correlation is expected; in states where there is greater turnout, parties should be more attentive to public opinion (Hill and Leighley 1993; Brown, Jackson, and Wright 1999).

Importantly, party competition—in all of the specifications of the model—is significantly and positively related to party ideology. The greater the level of party competition between the state parties, the more conservative the Republican platform becomes and the more liberal the Democratic platform becomes. Figure 5.2 compares the ideological polarization of the platforms, or the difference between the ideological score of Republican and Democratic platforms where both state parties have written a platform, to the degree of party competition in each state. The graph shows a clear relationship between party polarization and competition; the more competitive the parties in a state are, the more ideologically distinct each party's platform is. Wisconsin, Washington, Oregon, and Minnesota are all competitive and their parties are sharply polarized, while Idaho, Utah, and Hawaii are all moderate states with low levels of polarization. In fact, only Indiana's parties appear to be acting as Downs's theory would predict.

Why would this cause parties to become more polarized? Key (1956) argued that in such states, parties tend to be competitive, registration laws are more open, and parties must therefore present distinct sets of proposals

Figure 5.2   State Party Competition and Platform Polarization

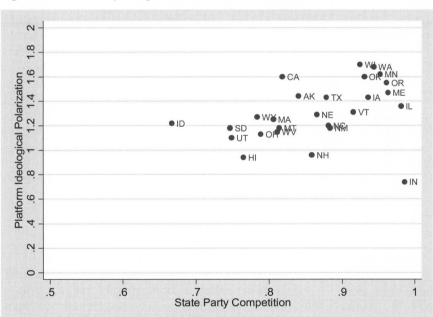

Source: Author's analysis: Bibby and Holbrook (2004).

Note: Platform ideological polarization (y-axis) measures absolute difference in the ideological scores of Republican and Democratic platforms in states where both parties had platforms; state party competition ranges from low (.5) to high (1.0).

to voters in order to win elections. Several studies of legislative politics have found evidence for this counterintuitive hypothesis; increasing competition, at both the district level and for control of the legislature, increases party-line voting in the legislature (Rosenthal 1990). Miller and Stokes (1963) and Gulati (2004) argue that legislators rely heavily on their constituencies, which does not mean the average voter in a district but rather a core group of supporters who reinforce or bias a legislator's perception of what his or her constituents think. Rosenthal (1990) and Aldrich and Battista (2002) point out that the more balanced the parties are in the state legislature, the more salient the party labels become, causing legislators to vote along party lines.

It may be that the presence of an ideological alternative heightens the incentive for activists to become involved in party politics. As Layman (2001) and Carmines and Stimson (1989) show, a change in a party's position on a set of issues sends strong signals to the electorate and to other activists about each party's position on the issues. Layman (2001), for example, analyzed national party platforms between 1972 and 1992 for the relative content each party devoted to social, religious, and cultural issues and found that each party's platform devoted progressively more attention to these issues. By 1992, the party platforms expressed very polarized views on moral issues. As religious conservatives became more influential within the Republican Party, cues were sent to more secular activists, and in a two-party system, this meant becoming more active within the Democratic Party (Layman 2001, 110–27). In fact, increasing conservatism among state Republican platforms is associated with increased liberalism among state Democratic platforms ($r = -.45$). Where Democratic state platforms are very liberal, Republican platforms are very conservative, as in Wisconsin, Washington, and Oregon, while in states where the Democratic Party is relatively conservative, the Republican Party is relatively liberal, as in Indiana, Hawaii, and New Hampshire. Only a few states—Utah, West Virginia, and North Carolina—come near fitting the pattern of a conservative Republican Party with a relatively conservative Democratic Party.

Conclusion

The results indicate that platform content is not random. In fact, the relationship between party competition, activist polarization on religious issues, and state political culture indicates that the platforms are related to important systematic, institutional factors. Importantly, in each specification, the polarization of activists is significantly and positively related to party polarization. This provides strong evidence of the importance of party activists in driving party agendas and the ideological positions of the parties. The consistency of the relationship across different models indicates that there is in fact a strong relationship between the two variables.

The results presented in this chapter should be interpreted cautiously. For each dependent variable, the sample sizes are very small, and so the results can easily be influenced by a few outliers or changes in the specification of the models. Moreover, the lack of organizational variables (such as caucus vs. primary states) means that the model may be underspecified in identifying how party organization influences the ideology of the platforms (Usher 2000). Finally, I have chosen to measure the ideology of the party-as-organization and, perhaps not surprisingly, found that activists do in fact have more ideological views than the general public or even than the party rank and file (Abramowitz, McGlennon, and Rapoport 1986). It may be that with a full set of platforms over an extended period of time I would find more influence for the general public on party ideology, as an analysis taking into account temporal changes in both public opinion and party ideology may reveal a stronger link than the cross-sectional analysis used here (Gray 1976).

Yet, as shown in multiple specifications, variance in state party platform ideology is explained by systematic factors. Party competition, turnout, activist opinion, and state political culture all exert strong influences on party ideology. The influence of party activists, it would appear, distorts the relationship between median state public opinion and platform ideology. The consistency indicates that there is an important divide between the views of those writing the platforms and citizens statewide.

The revitalization of modern parties may be at a cost of broader citizen representation. Party organizations are designed to represent the views of party activists. The results indicate that parties are constructing agendas that do not reflect the views of state citizens. Parties are able to do so because the consequences of diverging from the median opinion in the state are not as severe if both parties are engaged in the polarization. One of the key claims of the Downsian (1957) theory is that voters punish parties or candidates for moving away from the political center by rewarding their competitors. If both parties, however, move to the ideological poles without a corresponding shift in median public opinion, then neither party is at risk of such punishment.

The fact that public opinion is not related to party ideology provides insight into the nature of modern party organizations. As Beck (2003) has recently argued, American politics is characterized by two majorities, one passive and the other highly ideological. Public opinion surveys appear to confirm this point. Rather than seeing a uniform increase in attachment to the parties, surveys reveal an increasingly bipolar pattern of partisanship. While the number of citizens who strongly identify with either major party increased from 24 to 33 percent between 1976 and 2004, the proportion of weak party identifiers decreased from 39 to 28 percent at the same time that the percentage of independents who lean toward one major party or the other increased from 22 to 29 percent (American National Election Studies). This suggests that while the partisanship of some in the electorate has been activated by the polarization of the parties, other voters have become less attached.

Politics in many ways today is a self-selected activity. There can in fact be wide disparities between what the general public believes and what those participating in politics believe. Ideological polarization between the parties is consistent with Schattschneider's and the 1950 APSA Committee on Parties' view that American parties with distinct ideological and policy positions would improve representation within the United States (Shea 2003). As Shea and Beck point out, however, significant disparities between the views of the general public and party activists can lead to lower feelings of political efficacy, lower levels of turnout, and decreased trust in the political system. Indeed, as the model of party polarization showed, there was a significant relationship between platform polarization and state electoral turnout such that there is higher turnout in states where the parties are less polarized. What this chapter has shown is that party agendas, as represented by party platforms, are unrepresentative of the views of most citizens across the states.

Notes

1. I coded sentences using a computer content analysis program, which identifies sentences as liberal or conservative based on the appearance of certain key words from an ideological dictionary I created (see Coffey 2005 for details on the exact coding scheme). The essential idea is that words have significant political and policy meanings, and their appearance in speeches and platforms indicates a greater likelihood that a sentence advocates a particular ideological point of view. The dictionary was created using Laver and Garry's (2000) dictionary from British and Irish party manifestos, as well as words appearing disproportionately in either the Republican or Democratic 1996 and 2000 party platform or in five selected gubernatorial State of the State speeches in 2000 (Alabama, New Mexico, New York, Vermont, and Washington), which were chosen for party, regional, and demographic variation. The dictionary was occasionally modified to include new words when analyzing the platforms. The use of a computer program increases the reliability of the analysis by consistently coding large quantities of text. However, sentences can be miscoded because words have multiple meanings depending on the context in which they are used. As a result, I manually reviewed every sentence in each platform. While this substantially increased the work for content analysis, the gain in validity far outweighed the loss in the reliability. Importantly, the manual review means that ultimately the coding of the sentences was not dependent upon the accuracy of the dictionary. Rather, the dictionary was a tool to make the coding more efficient, while the manual review ensured that the coding scheme was valid. Finally, two independent coders manually reviewed a 10 percent sample of the platforms, and the percentage agreement for the coding of all sentences was 77 percent.

2. Racheter, Kellstedt, and Green (2003) coded the 2002 Iowa platform as containing seventy-three conservative planks and no liberal planks, which compares favorably to my score of −.63, which is also very conservative.

3. An independent sample's t-test shows that the difference in means between the party platform scores is significantly different from zero at p < .01.

4. The updated Erikson, Wright, and McIver data set is available at http://socsci .colorado.edu/~mciverj/wip.html.

5. I have created a measure of party polarization taking the absolute value of the difference between the Democratic Party platform score and the Republican score for all states with two platforms. Since the number of cases is small (26) and the regression results are generally similar to those shown in table 5.2, the polarization score has not been modeled.

6. The data for the Party Elite Studies (1992–2004) were made available by John Jackson and John Green.

7. Of the thirty-four state parties where the dominant political culture is moralist, thirty have platforms (88 percent). By comparison, only 59 percent of individualist state parties (20 out of 34), and 56 percent of traditionalist state parties (18 of 32) have platforms. The average ideological score for Democratic platforms is .72 in moralist states, .62 in traditionalist states, and .62 in individualist states. The average Republican platform score is −.66 in moralist states, −.72 in traditionalist states, and −.55 in individualist states.

8. One problem with the analysis is the potential correlation between activist opinion and state public opinion. The concern is that the lack of a significant coefficient for median public opinion is a statistical artifact and does not represent a meaningful lack of influence for mass public opinion in terms of state party ideology. The correlation of the mean of state public opinion and Republican Party activist ideology is −.71; for Democratic activists and state public opinion, it is −.23. The high correlation combined with the relatively small data set suggests that multicollinearity may be present at least in the Republican model. In order to test for this, I ran separate models using state public opinion and activist opinion. There are, however, no substantive differences in the results when the variables are used separately. Moreover, a matrix of the bivariate correlations shows that none of the correlations for the other variables exceeds .80, which is commonly used as cutoff value for testing for the presence of multicollinearity (Berry and Feldman 1985, 44).

Part II

Party Resources

6

Committees and Candidates

National Party Finance after BCRA

Diana Dwyre, Eric Heberlig, Robin Kolodny, and Bruce Larson

The 2004 elections were the first run under the new federal election campaign law, the Bipartisan Campaign Reform Act of 2002 (BCRA). The new law was meant to end the flow of unregulated soft money to political parties and to increase disclosure about campaign activities by political parties and interest groups. While BCRA was not meant to be a wholesale change in campaign finance regulation, reformers hoped that it would mean that less money would be spent in elections through political parties, that elected officials would be less reliant on big donors, that competition might increase, and that campaigning would be "fairer" to candidates without party and interest group issue advocacy advertising.

Here, we examine several important issues in contemporary campaign finance through the rubric of BCRA. First, we ask about the contemporary state of campaign money via political parties. What do we know about party fundraising after BCRA? Did BCRA succeed in getting "big money" out of politics? Second, we analyze the increased support for party organizations from candidates, particularly sitting members of Congress. If this trend was an unintended consequence of BCRA, what are its implications for the political process? Third, we assess the current situation of competitive elections in the United States and ask whether campaign money has helped or hindered this basic tenet of representative democracies. Fourth, we look at the current pattern of party expenditures to ask whether they are effective in helping the parties reach their goal of controlling governmental institutions.

What Money Is in Party Politics?

Conventional wisdom holds that Republicans have a significant fundraising advantage over Democrats. When we correct the data for inflationary effects (by converting all the amounts to $2,000), we find that in 2004, Democrats significantly closed the gap with Republican fundraising overall (see figure 6.1). Given the traditional Republican money advantage, this finding is extremely significant, as the innovations in fundraising Democrats achieved in 2004 could reshape the nature of electoral competition. This election cycle showed that the Republicans' capital-intensive edge was not so daunting and that the Democrats' labor-intensive edge was indeed replicable by the Republicans.

We disaggregate the six national committees' receipts in constant dollars and find that the Democratic National Committee (DNC) *surpassed* the Republican National Committee (RNC) in receipts in 2003–2004. This was the big story of the 2004 elections (Corrado 2006). The congressional committees (the National Republican Senatorial Committee [NRSC], Democratic Senatorial Campaign Committee [DSCC], National Republican Congressional Committee [NRCC], and Democratic Congressional Campaign Committee [DCCC]) were another matter entirely, with three of the four not achieving parity with their overall fundraising in 2000 (hard and soft money combined; see figure 6.2). Only the NRCC was able to exceed previous 2000 fundraising levels, and it did that by a significant amount—$25 million in hard money. In fact, in the post–soft money environment, the DNC, RNC, and NRCC were able to surpass their previous combination of hard and soft money receipts with hard money only. However, the NRSC, DSCC, and DCCC were not even able to achieve parity with their past combined totals.

Figure 6.1   Overall Party Fundraising Trends

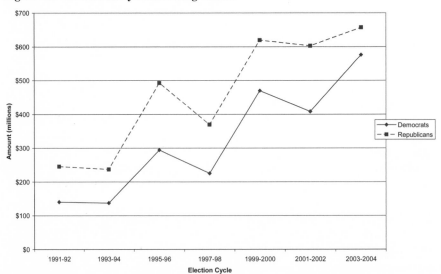

Figure 6.2 National Committee Receipts

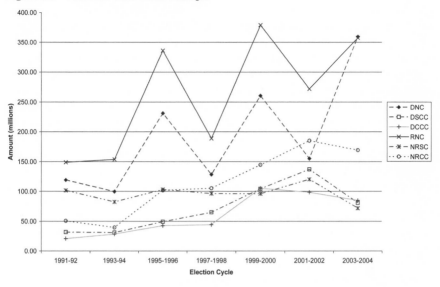

New Rules for Party Fundraising

The sudden loss of soft money after BCRA meant that the parties had to raise much more hard money in order to merely maintain their previous level of fundraising. This new campaign finance environment created incentives for entrepreneurial thinking. Necessity was indeed the mother of invention: all the party committees implemented stepped-up and new fundraising efforts, and they all performed beyond expectations—even the three that failed to replace the banned soft money.

In addition to the soft money ban, BCRA made other changes that were favorable to party fundraising: it raised the hard-money individual contribution limits and, for the first time, indexed those limits to inflation. Congressional reformers recognized that the ban on soft money might have a detrimental effect on party fundraising and that the contribution limits had not been increased since the 1970s, so that the value of the maximum donation had diminished significantly over time. Before passage of BCRA, an individual contributor could give $20,000 in hard money per year to a national party committee. This amount counted against an individual's annual aggregate contribution limit of $25,000 per year for all hard money contributions, including those to candidates and political action committees (PACs). Under the new law, an individual may contribute $25,000 per year to *each* party committee, and there is a separate sublimit within the new aggregate individual contribution limit of $95,000 per two-year election cycle of up to $57,500 for all contributions to party committees and PACs, with the remainder ($37,500) being an individual's total allowed contributions to candidates (see table 6.1).

The new law actually encourages individual contributors to give to the parties by stipulating that $20,000 of the total $95,000 aggregate limit for individuals can be given only to political parties (Magleby, Monson, and Patterson 2005, 13). This incentive seems to have worked. Contributions at the maximum amount constituted a larger proportion of party hard money receipts than in past election cycles for all of the national party committees. For instance, 12.4 percent of the DNC's individual contributions were at the maximum amount in 2004, up from 9.8 percent in 2000; similarly, 17.4 percent of the RNC's individual contributions were maximum contributions, up from 6.5 percent in 2000 (Federal Election Commission 2005a). Of course, some of these individuals may have contributed large sums of soft money before and thus may have given even more before BCRA. Nevertheless, the party-friendly structure of the rules channeled some of that lost soft money to parties in a more open and controlled manner.

Parties raised more in small contributions as well. All of the national party committees raised more from individuals in 2004 than in past elections, and the Democratic committees in particular saw a surge in small contributions of less than $200 (labeled "unitemized" contributions in the Federal Election Commission records). In 2003–2004, the DNC raised $166 million in unitemized contributions, well above the $38 million they raised

Table 6.1   New Contribution Limits under BCRA—Beginning January 1, 2003

Individuals	• Contributions to candidates: $2,000* per election (was $1,000) • Contributions to multicandidate committees (PACs): $5,000 (unchanged) • Contributions to state, district, and local party committees: $10,000 (combined) per year (was $5,000) • Contributions to national party committees: $25,000* per year (was $20,000) • Overall limit on contributions from one person: $95,000* every two years (was $25,000 per year); within this limit, however, only $37,500 may be contributed to candidates, and no more than $37,500 to other committees that are not national parties
Party Committees	• National party committees: up to a total of $35,000* to Senate candidates per six-year campaign (was $17,500) • All other contribution limits remain the same ($5,000 per election for House candidates)

Source: Federal Election Commission n.d.

Note: * Indexed for inflation; increases will be implemented during odd-numbered years starting in 2005 and will be in effect for a two-year period. See Jackson, Bigelow, and Green 2003 for a full discussion.

for 2002 and the $60 million raised for 2000. Likewise, the RNC increased the amount it raised in small chunks, collecting $157 million for 2004, up from $103 million for 2002 and $91 million for 2000 (Federal Election Commission 2005b).

New Approaches to Party Fundraising

The national party committees used a variety of approaches to raise more hard money under the new fundraising rules. They asked current contributors for larger contributions; tapped partisan grassroots supporters for contributions; found new contributors, especially via the Internet; and hit up their own officeholders and candidates to contribute to their party. Both parties invested heavily in new computer technology for direct mail, Internet fundraising, and voter mobilization. The DNC spent about $15 million on such efforts. Its huge database of potential party contributors and voters was dubbed "Demzilla" by party operatives, and the RNC established a similar data program called Voter Vault.[1]

The Internet proved to be an effective fundraising tool for the party committees, and one that involved very little cost, thus retaining nearly the full value of each contribution. While there is no reliable information on how much the parties raised from the Internet, it is safe to assume that at least some of the increase in small contributions came from increased online donating. The parties' websites were set up to accept contributions, and they developed large e-mail lists of party supporters to solicit them for contributions directly and at a much lower cost than traditional direct mail or telemarketing fundraising. Of course, the parties still raised money the old-fashioned way—with mail solicitations, phone calls, and events—and these efforts benefited greatly from the larger and more sophisticated lists of contacts developed by the parties with the aid of advanced computer management systems.

The parties also stepped up their large contributor programs. The DNC established the "Presidential Trust" and enlisted some big-money fundraisers, the "Patriots," to raise at least $100,000 for the Democratic nominee.[2] The RNC invited the Bush team's "Rangers" (who raised $100,000 for Bush) and "Pioneers" (who raised $200,000) to become "Super Rangers" by raising at least $300,000 for the party.[3] Since BCRA permits individual contributions to a party committee of up to $25,000, raising these large sums for the party was quite a bit easier than raising large amounts for a candidate directly, which could be collected in maximum increments of only $2,000.

The Capitol Hill committees continued their programs that rewarded big contributors with access to party leaders. The NRSC's "Majority Makers" gave $25,000 (the maximum) to the party committee and received an invitation to a private reception featuring President George W. Bush at Senate Majority Leader Bill Frist's Washington-area home.[4] The DSCC invited "allied lobbyists and consultants" (not the PACs they represent) to be on its "Majority Council" by making a $25,000 contribution from their personal funds in exchange for monthly meetings with Senate Democratic leaders.[5]

A largely unanticipated source of increased funding for the parties was their own officeholders and candidates. While the parties have long asked their officeholders to contribute to the common goal of attaining or maintaining majority status (Kolodny 1998), the House and Senate party committees enhanced these efforts for the 2004 election. The law allows candidates and former candidates and officeholders to transfer an unlimited amount from their own campaign accounts to a party committee. Party leaders recognized this huge fundraising potential of their own colleagues. The 2003–2004 DCCC chairman, Rep. Robert Matsui (D-Calif.), remarked that "money from members is particularly important, because there [are] no costs of fundraising. . . . When a member gives a dollar, that entire dollar is spent on candidates, whereas with direct mail, there's the cost of stamps and printing" (Carney 2004, 2170). This last fundraising avenue has significant implications for democratic accountability in American elections. Therefore, we will investigate it in some detail.

Individual Candidates as Donors and Parties' Collective Electoral Goals

In 2004, parties expected their congressional members—incumbent officeholders—to pay what are sometimes called "dues" to the relevant party campaign committee. The prescribed amount depended on the officeholder's seniority, committee posts, fundraising history, and leadership positions. For example, the DCCC announced in early 2004 that it expected its 186 safe incumbents to transfer part of the $87 million in their campaign accounts to the campaign committee;[6] it collected $18.3 million dollars from Democratic House members, up from $11.3 million in the previous election cycle. The NRCC received $20 million from its members, up from $13.8 in 2002. The Senate campaign committees did not levy formal dues, but their members nonetheless gave more generously in 2004 than in 2002. Representatives and senators gave more to their party committees in the 2004 election cycle in part because of BCRA's increase in individual contribution limits (from $1,000 to $2,000 per election), which made it possible for them to collect more from individual contributors to their own campaigns.

The increase in contributions to party committees by incumbent members of Congress in the 2004 election cycle is part of a broader trend in the redistribution of campaign funds that began prior to the passage of BCRA. Members of the House increased their total contributions to candidates and party organizations from $27.3 million in 1996 to $73.6 million in 2004, an increase of 170 percent. Senators redistributed fewer dollars but increased their giving even more rapidly than House members, by nearly 250 percent, from $8.1 million in 1996 to $28 million in 2004. Contributions from presidential candidates do not follow the same pattern—or seemingly any pattern. While giving $67 million in 1996, they decreased their donations to $30 million in 2000 and $38.8 million in 2004.

Total contributions by members of Congress grew dramatically between the 1996 and 2004 election cycles as party margins remained narrow and party leaders pressured members to contribute to the party's collective electoral efforts (Kolodny and Dwyre 1998; Heberlig and Larson 2005). Party leaders increasingly sought to exploit Federal Election Commission regulations allowing federal candidates' personal campaign committees (PCCs) to transfer unlimited sums of unobligated hard money to national party committees (11 CFR 1113.2). In contrast, contributions from PCCs to other candidates are limited to $1,000 per election, and contributions from leadership political action committees (LPACs) are limited to $5,000 per election.

To assess the effect of BCRA, we turn to a detailed analysis of contributions by chamber. Figure 6.3, which presents contributions by House members, shows steady growth of all types of contributions, except contributions from LPACs to the party congressional campaign committees (CCCs), which remain modest compared to other types of contributions. Of greatest interest are the contributions from PCCs to CCCs, which—absent any regulatory

Figure 6.3   Redistribution of Campaign Funds by House Members, 1996–2004

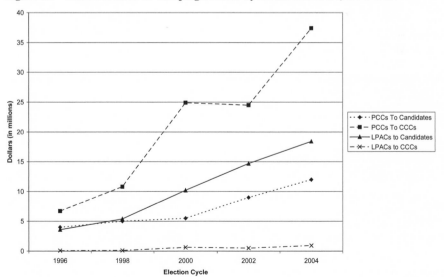

limits—have increased more rapidly than contributions to candidates from PCCs or LPACs. Furthermore, contributions from PCCs to CCCs level off in 2002, then spike upward again in 2004 after the implementation of BCRA, which deprived parties of soft money and prompted them to seek new sources of hard money in large sums.

One would think that such a large increase in hard money contributions to the CCCs would impose substantial fundraising burdens on members of the House. Although it may, members of the House merely shifted the allocation of their party contributions (data not shown). In 2002, House incumbents gave $45.4 million to local, state, and federal party organizations, with $24.5 million (54 percent) going to the CCCs. Their contributions to local, state, and federal party organizations actually declined slightly in 2004, to $41.6 million. At the same time, however, their giving to the CCCs increased to $37.4 million. The CCCs now consume 90 percent of House members' contributions to party organizations. House members helped the CCCs replace lost soft money with hard money at the expense of the state and local party organizations that had received this money in the past.

The redistribution of campaign funds by senators, like their House colleagues, has also increased steadily over the past decade. Senators traditionally have contributed the plurality of their funds to other candidates through LPACs. Though senators' LPAC contributions increased apace in 2004, sena-

Figure 6.4   Redistribution of Campaign Funds by Senators, 1996–2004

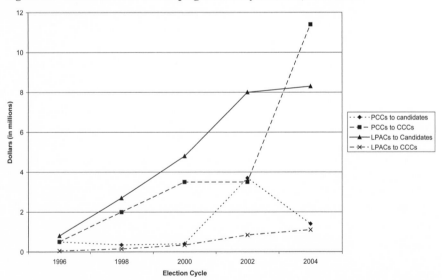

tors dramatically increased their contributions to the Senate CCCs through their PCCs. This spike in contributions to the CCCs mirrors the same increase in House contributions to CCCs. Though senators, unlike House members, increased their giving to local and state party organizations from 2002 to 2004 ($2.7 million to $4.7 million, the proportion of their overall party contributions going to the CCCs increased from 58 percent to 71 percent—similar to the trend among House members. Senators, however, appeared to shift PCC contributions away from candidates ($3.8 million in 2002 to $1.4 million in 2004) in order to increase their giving to CCCs (see figure 6.4). Like House members, senators are increasingly taking advantage of their ability to give unlimited contributions from their PCCs to national party committees, and in 2004, senators gave generously to help their party's CCCs replace soft money banned by BCRA.

Furthermore, the percentage of representatives and senators who redistributed any campaign money continued to increase from 2002 to 2004, continuing the trend across the previous decade (from 80 percent in 1996 to 95 percent in 2004 in the House; from 25 percent in 1996 to 86 percent in 2004 in the Senate). The percentage of members contributing to the CCCs increased more dramatically (58 percent to 95 percent in the House; 18 percent to 90 percent in the Senate) than the percentage contributing to candidates, confirming the shift in the party orientation of giving. Senators illustrate these changes most dramatically. Senators' participation rates had been level for several election cycles after 1998, with senators preferring to contribute to other candidates rather than the CCCs by more than 20 points in most election cycles. However, the proportion of senators contributing to the CCCs jumped dramatically from 61 percent in 2002 to 90 percent in 2004, surpassing the proportion who contributed to other candidates. The increased proportion of members contributing shows that the larger dollar amounts contributed are not merely the result of party and committee leaders contributing more, but of greater participation by the entire party caucuses.

An additional observation regarding participation rates is that a lower proportion of senators than House members have traditionally contributed, though senators nearly closed this gap in 2004. The typically higher levels of giving in the House suggest the greater strength of House party leaders relative to Senate leaders and the greater value of majority party control to House members than to senators.

Following BCRA, the story of redistribution activity is largely one of continuity. Contributions and the percentages of members contributing continued to climb, as they had across the previous election cycles. The critical change that BCRA has likely induced is greater giving to the CCCs as the parties sought to replace soft money with large hard money contributions. Members of the House complied by shifting contributions from state and local party organizations to the CCCs. And since there is some evidence that individual contributors are more likely to give to a candidate than to a party in order to reap the benefit of a personal connection to an officeholder (Francia et al. 2003), legislators can raise money more easily than parties, which can offer only the collective benefits of party loyalty and majority status.

The parties' presidential nominees also transferred large amounts to party committees in 2004, most of it from excess primary funds. John Kerry's campaign gave $23.6 million to the DNC, $3 million to the DCCC, and $3 million to the DSCC (Federal Election Commission 2005a).[7] Al Gore gave $1 million to the DCCC, $1 million to the DSCC, and $4 million to the DNC, most of it leftover from his 2000 presidential campaign. The Bush reelection campaign transferred $26.5 million to the RNC, $1 million to the NRCC, and $1 million to the NRSC (Federal Election Commission 2005b).

But with no other party leaders, such as a Speaker or floor leader, to coordinate their activities for the collective good of the party and to provide incentives for pro-party behavior, presidential candidates are idiosyncratic in their use of funds to assist other candidates and party organizations (ranging from the Clinton campaign's contribution of $5 million to Steve Forbes's contribution of $38 million, both in 1996). Though the contributions of individual presidential candidates vary considerably, the amounts can be substantial. In the presidential elections, the contributions of a few presidential candidates were more substantial than the contributions of all 100 U.S. Senate incumbents. As the leaders of the party ticket, presidential candidates overwhelmingly contributed their funds to party organizations, 99.5 percent, rather than to party candidates. In contrast, House members gave 77 percent of their contributions and senators 64 percent of theirs to party organizations across the five election cycles between 1996 and 2004.

Furthermore, presidential candidates may provide their most valuable assistance not by redistributing campaign funds directly but rather by appearing at candidate and party fundraisers and campaign rallies (Holbrook and McClurg 2005; Jacobson, Kernell, and Lazarus 2004). In 2004, moreover, Kerry and especially Bush engaged in substantial joint fundraising activities that helped their parties. The Bush campaign, for example, used joint fundraising committees in 2004 to help channel substantial sums of campaign money into the campaign accounts of nearly thirty Republican House and Senate candidates.[8]

Where Did the Money Go?

In 2004, the six national party committees spent a total of $1.2 billion, more than twice the $545.7 million spent in 2000 (Federal Election Commission 2005a). The Republicans spent $646 million (almost twice their 2000 spending) and the Democrats $570.5 million (approaching three times the figure in 2000). The DNC had the largest increase, a more than threefold increase to $389.8 million, while the RNC just doubled its expenditures to $382.6 million. The Capitol Hill committees showed similar increases: the DSCC more than doubled to $88.3 million and the DCCC nearly doubled to $92.4 million; the NRCC also nearly doubled to $184.7 million, while the NRSC increased by just half to $78.7 million. Clearly, BCRA did not restrict spending nor slow its rate of increase.

Spending to support candidates is the most directly relevant portion of party expenditures, and in 2004 such spending totaled $378.6 million. Here, the Democrats outspent the Republicans $218.6 million to $160 million. The Democratic advantage came from $120.5 million in independent expenditures by the DNC. In contrast, the RNC spent $18.3 million in independent expenditures, also chiefly in the presidential campaign. However, the RNC spent more than twice as much as the DNC in generic party ads, $45.8 million to $18.6 million. These expenditures were in addition to the coordinated expenditure $16.1 million for the presidential race (the maximum allowed by law). Expenditures by the Hill committees were more even. The DSCC spent $23.8 million compared to $28.6 million for the NRSC. Meanwhile, the DCCC spent $39.7 million and the NRCC $51 million. Here, too, independent expenditures ($122.3 million) were the largest source of candidate support, dwarfing coordinated expenditures and direct contributions combined ($20.8 million). Indeed, direct contributions to candidates were a tiny fraction of total candidate support (just $2.7 million in total).

On the expenditure side, one of the most significant effects of the BCRA was to change the avenue of party assistance from candidate-oriented issue advocacy to independent expenditures. Parties can still help their candidates by making direct contributions and coordinated expenditures in their races, but these types of spending have severe limits. Before BCRA, parties made issue advocacy advertisements, which were paid for with a mix of hard and soft money. Although these ads restricted the type of campaign language parties could use (that is, no "magic words" such as "vote for," "vote against," "support," or "defeat" could be spoken or written), they could be paid for in a way that allowed parties to use generous amounts of unlimited soft money donations mixed with hard money. BCRA eliminated soft money as a fundraising stream for the parties, making issue advocacy a less attractive choice for the political parties. Without the ability to use easy-to-raise soft money, parties could use only hard money for unlimited independent expenditures. However, this category of spending does allow parties to use the magic words and explains why issue advocacy was entirely abandoned.

Money for independent expenditures is raised by the parties in limited, fully disclosed hard money donations, but independent expenditures allow parties to spend in unlimited amounts. The only restriction is that parties may not coordinate their efforts with the candidate they intend to help. For this reason, parties stayed away from independent expenditures in previous elections, even though they have been allowed to make them since 1996. The law's original authors did not mean for parties to have the use of unlimited independent expenditures (making instead a unique category of limited "coordinated" expenditures for parties), but parties won this role in the first of two important Supreme Court rulings discussed below.

Colorado I

In *Colorado Republican Federal Campaign Comm. v. Federal Election Commission* (518 U.S. 604 [1996]), known as *Colorado I*, the Colorado Republican Party spent money to help a yet-to-be-named Republican U.S. Senate candidate defeat Democratic candidate Tim Wirth. Because the ad was really anti-Wirth and because the Republican primary had not yet been held and hence no nominee selected, the party claimed this expenditure could not be coordinated with the candidate's campaign and therefore was independent. Further, the party challenged the notion that there should even be coordinated expenditure limits, arguing that the very basis of a political party is different from any other political donor, as they are trying to promote a slate of candidates and not trying to lobby for particular votes or policy outcomes. In *Colorado I*, the Supreme Court agreed that parties could engage in independent expenditures. However, it remanded the argument about parties and unlimited coordinated contributions to the lower courts. The restrictions against coordination proved burdensome to the national party committees, and they declined to make use of independent expenditures, with the exception of a brief experiment by the NRSC in 1996. Issue advocacy advertising under the soft money regime was preferable, as it did allow some information sharing with the campaigns and central party organizations.

Colorado II

In *Federal Election Commission v. Colorado Republican Federal Campaign Committee* (533 U.S. 431 [2001]), known as *Colorado II*, the Court upheld the constitutionality of coordinated expenditure limits on parties, arguing that to take the limits off would invite wealthy donors to contribute to parties with instructions that their contributions go to particular candidates—a corruption of the party conduit (thus also called the "corrupt conduit" idea).[9] The argument for the 5–4 majority opinion was that evidence of a past tally system by one of the six national party committees, the DSCC, in which the party organization kept track of donors' wishes regarding how their donations should be redistributed, was extrapolated to mean that taking the limits off coordinated spending would be the same as taking real contribution limits off wealthy donors (as if making a check out to a party committee would have implicit or explicit assumptions about the specific candidate or target of such a donation).

The majority opinion also addressed two other corollary arguments of importance. First, it acknowledged, as the Court had previously argued in *Buckley v. Valeo* (1976), that independent expenditures were not as helpful to candidates as coordinated expenditures and could even be harmful to them. The majority opinion quoted from *Buckley*:

> Independent expenditures may well provide little assistance to the candidate's campaign and indeed may prove counterproductive. The absence of prearrangement and coordination of an expenditure with the candidate or his agent not only undermines the value of the expenditure to the candidate, but also alleviates the danger that expenditures will be given as a quid pro quo for improper commitment from the candidate.[10]

Does the Court prefer that party spending end up being counterproductive to the candidate? The Court's focus on the corrupting influence of donors is so intense as to preclude the harm that may come to the quality of democratic discourse by preventing parties from coordinating with their candidates. There are numerous examples of independent party campaigning (through both issue advocacy and independent expenditures) that have introduced themes unimportant to the candidates or made factual errors about candidates or their opponents.[11] We would argue that these rushed, though well-intended, efforts harm not only the parties as viable electoral organizations but also perceptions of candidate competence and integrity (as voters normally do not distinguish among campaign appeals by source) and ultimately citizen interest in the political process.

The second problem in this reasoning, briefly considered by the Court, is the matter of large contributions or transfers from incumbent members of Congress or from prosperous nominees back to the party organizations. The parties argued that their coordinated expenditures amounted to very little compared to donations from incumbent members. The idea was that parties are at least as dependent on their officeholders for funds as on outside donors. But the majority opinion in *Colorado II* argued,

> The Party again discounts the threat of outflanking contribution limits on individual and nonparty groups by stressing that incumbent candidates give more excess campaign funds to parties than parties spend on coordinated expenditures. . . . But the fact that parties may do well for themselves off incumbents does not defuse concern over circumvention; if contributions to a party were

not used as a funnel from donors to candidates, there would be no reason for using the tallying system the way the witnesses have described it. (sec. 5)

The Court does not answer the issue it addresses in *Colorado II* concerning the implications of party reliance on incumbent candidates for democratic governance. Instead, it moves back to its broader concern about parties as conduits for wealthy contributors.

Independent Expenditures in 2004

While party observers often lament how weak the parties seem to be (a debatable contention, to be sure), the prohibition on significant coordination with candidates during the campaign season is an extreme impediment to strong parties. Party organizations that have maximized the use of funds for independent expenditure investment, as the NRCC has, have also witnessed a growth in internal party cohesion in the legislature. While we do not contend that one behavior causes the other, the two are clearly correlated.

In a previous work (Dwyre and Kolodny 2006), we looked carefully at the spending in congressional races in 2004. Because independent expenditures, unlike issue advocacy, are fully disclosed, we can appreciate the magnitude of party investment in competitive races and compare it to the very modest effect of coordinated expenditures (see table 6.2). In House contests, sixty-one candidates received total party spending of $500,000 or more. This figure includes both coordinated and independent expenditures. Since the limit for coordinated spending was $73,000, most of the spending was done independently of the candidates—without their knowledge or consent. Interestingly, we found that seventeen of these candidates were outspent in their own races by national party organizations.

An analysis of Senate races yielded similarly surprising findings. In eight out of nine races considered competitive in 2004, the party committees

Table 6.2   Party Coordinated and Independent Expenditures, 2000–2004 (in millions of dollars)

	1999–2000		2001–2002		2003–2004	
Party Committee	*Coordinated Expenditures*	*Independent Expenditures*	*Coordinated Expenditures*	*Independent Expenditures*	*Coordinated Expenditures*	*Independent Expenditures*
DNC	13.5	0	0.35	0	16.1	120.3
DSCC	0.13	0.13	0.18	0	4.4	18.7
DCCC	2.6	1.9	1.8	1.2	2.4	36.9
RNC	23.7	0	14.1	0.5	16.1	18.3
NRSC	0.000172	0.27	0.55	0	8.4	19.4
NRCC	3.7	0.55	0.45	1.3	3.2	47.3

spent between $1 million and $4 million in independent spending on behalf of their candidate. That parties did not exceed candidate spending in any of these races suggests only that Senate races are extremely expensive. In several instances, parties spent close to half what their candidates did.

The other big story was how the RNC and DNC spent independent expenditures on behalf of their presidential candidates. These committees were not previously allowed to spend independent expenditures, but were given explicit permission to do so in Federal Election Commission rules related to BCRA. The DNC made extensive use of this spending opportunity, using more than $120 million to help John Kerry's campaign. The RNC did not use independent expenditures that much, only $18 million, but instead used a type of "generic" or "hybrid" spending in conjunction with President Bush's reelection committee to allocate an additional $48 million to its candidate's campaign (Dwyre and Kolodny 2006).

The State of Electoral Competition

Despite the record amounts of money the parties have poured into federal elections, the level of competition has not increased in congressional races. Indeed, the number of House and Senate races considered competitive has declined significantly since 1992, as table 6.3 shows (J. Campbell 2003). And the real action took place in only twelve states that were considered to be battlegrounds in the last presidential election. One might expect that the parties, more than other types of contributors, would be inclined to spread the wealth among candidates and thus make more races competitive, giving themselves a better chance of attaining majority status or enhancing their control of a chamber. Yet the parties have not behaved that way.[12]

Prior to the 1980s, the congressional campaign committees generally op-

Table 6.3   Competitive Congressional Races, 1992–2004

Election Year	Competitive House Seats	Competitive Senate Seats
1992	103	17
1994	152	14
1996	174	20
1998	58	15
2000	43	13
2002	48	13
2004	35	9

Sources: CQ Weekly Report (October 24, 1992): 3340, 3342, 3358–59; (October 22, 1994): 2998–99, 3006; (October 19, 1996): 2955–56, 2964; (October 24, 1998): 2870–71, 2873; (September 23, 2000): 2182; (October 26, 2002): 2790, 2794; (October 23, 2004): 2502, 2506.

erated as incumbent protection organizations, giving the majority of their funds to incumbents, most of them in safe seats (Kolodny 1998; Dwyre 1994). As the Republicans began to make some real gains in the House and the Senate (due in part to the realignment in Southern congressional elections), the stakes grew higher and both parties began to distribute their resources more strategically. That is, they directed funds to those candidates in the most competitive contests rather than to safe incumbents who really did not need the money (Dwyre 1994). As the number of competitive races dwindled (see table 6.3), party money went to fewer House and Senate contests.

It is rational for the parties to invest in those races where they have a real chance of making a difference, if their resources are limited. Yet party resources have grown (even under the new BCRA restrictions), and the parties are still not investing in the second-tier races. Instead, they are pouring even more into the handful of races and states deemed truly competitive. Since the parties are not spreading their resources around more widely, they have done little to enhance the level of competition in federal elections. Indeed, since many PACs and big individual contributors follow the parties' lead, they too are directing their resources to those same few close races, leaving hundreds of candidates who might otherwise have a chance starving for cash.

Conclusion

In this chapter, we have established that parties' fundraising abilities and expenditures were not hurt by BCRA as much as some feared (and some, like the RNC and DNC, even prospered) and that competition in national elections continues to decline despite the high levels of money present in the system. The political parties are clearly becoming more aggressive players in the electoral arena. Members of Congress are increasingly cooperating to elect fellow partisans by providing financial assistance to candidates and party committees. Moreover, rather than allocating money on their own, members are increasingly turning over campaign money to the party CCCs, which allocate funds to competitive campaigns (Damore and Hansford 1999; Herrnson 2004). Thus, member contribution activity is increasingly targeted at gaining or preserving majority control and the enhanced power that such control creates for all members of the party. Stronger congressional parties have led to more centralized efforts to coordinate and control party fundraising efforts among incumbents. BCRA has intensified these trends. It did not reduce the flow of money into congressional campaigns. Rather, the parties raised more money than ever, and members of Congress redistributed more than ever to the parties. Parties had come to rely on unlimited soft

money in the 1990s. With such funds banned by BCRA, the parties successfully exploited the ability of incumbents to help replace soft money with
hard money. Members of Congress had increasingly redistributed campaign
money as they responded to the pitched battle for majority control in the
1990s. But BCRA gave them an additional reason to share their campaign
wealth. The evidence we have presented shows a clear shift toward contributions to the CCCs by members of both the House and the Senate in 2004.

Other important consequences of BCRA, we argue, are that forcing parties to act independently of their candidates instead of in a coordinated manner does not promote good democratic discourse and that the arguments for
prohibiting parties from talking to their candidates are problematic. As there
continue to be calls for further reform of the federal campaign finance system (e.g., to regulate the activities of the 527 independent groups), we expect
that some in Congress, especially the party leaders, might call for taking the
cap off of party coordinated expenditures on behalf of candidates as a more
rational way to channel money in federal elections than independent expenditures. Some on the Supreme Court seem open to such a change. Moreover,
if it can be shown that coordinated spending would allow parties and their
candidates to efficiently pursue majority status and perhaps therefore to increase the number of competitive congressional races (even if this is merely
a by-product), then perhaps even reform-oriented interest groups such as
Common Cause and the League of Women Voters might get behind such a
change in policy. We expect that both of the major parties would prefer unlimited coordinated over unlimited independent expenditures.

Further research covering more election cycles is needed to analyze
more fully the relationship between party spending and competition. Of
course, the parties will continue to target the most competitive races. But
with the ability to coordinate with their candidates, and thus to have more
reliable information and fewer wasted and ineffective efforts, the parties may
become motivated to spread their resources more widely.

Notes

1. Paul Farhi, "Parties Square Off in a Database Duel; Voter Information Shapes Strategies," *Washington Post*, July 20, 2004.

2. Sharon Theimer, "Democrats Start Presidential Fund," *Associated Press Online*, January 31, 2003.

3. Jonathan Kaplan, "RNC Offers 'Super Ranger' Status," *The Hill*, May 18, 2004.

4. Sharon Theimer, "Bush Raises Cash for Senate GOP Members," *Associated Press
Online*, March 2, 2004.

5. Alexander Bolton, "Meet the Leader, Only $25K: Senate Dems Sell Lobbyists Ac-
cess for the Maximum," *The Hill*, April 29, 2004.

6. Erin P. Billings, "Buoyed DCCC Raises Money Goal," *Roll Call*, June 22, 2004.

7. Paul Kane, "Kerry Transfers Surplus Money," *Roll Call*, September 22, 2004.

112   *Diana Dwyre, Eric Heberlig, Robin Kolodny, and Bruce Larson*

8. In contrast to 2004, when the Bush campaign conducted its joint fundraising operations mostly with federal Republican candidates, its joint fundraising efforts in 2000 were conducted almost exclusively with state and local GOP committees. Gary Jacobson (2006) argues that only one competitive congressional race, that of the U.S. Senate race in Kentucky on the Democratic side, was underfunded enough that more party investment could have made a difference in the outcome.

9. This is the argument behind the September 29, 2005, indictment against Rep. Tom DeLay (R-Texas) for evading Texas campaign finance law.

10. *Federal Election Commission v. Colorado Republican Federal Campaign Committee* (2001), 00–191, June 25, 2001; section II of Majority Opinion.

11. For example see the "Dictum without Data," study published by the Center for the Study of Elections and Democracy at http://csed.byu.edu/publications.html.

12. One can make the case that competition in presidential elections has increased somewhat since 1992. But as with congressional races, the national parties have increasingly concentrated their funds in a few battleground states.

7

Surviving BCRA

State Party Finance in 2004

Raymond J. La Raja, Susan E. Orr, and Daniel A. Smith

On December 10, 2003, the U.S. Supreme Court upheld the bulk of the Bipartisan Campaign Reform Act of 2002 (BCRA). In *McConnell v. Federal Election Commission*, the Court let stand nearly all of BCRA's Title I, which banned parties from using "soft money" for "federal election activity." This activity, for which only regulated hard money could be used, includes voter registration within 120 days of a federal election, voter identification, get-out-the-vote (GOTV) efforts, and electioneering communications mentioning federal candidates. In banning party soft money, BCRA not only altered the strategies and activities of national parties but also, by extension, those of state parties. With state parties no longer permitted to solicit or transfer soft money for federal activity, some observers questioned whether they would be able to survive under BCRA.

In this chapter, we assess how state parties have responded to the new campaign finance regulatory environment indirectly imposed upon them by federal law. After providing a glimpse at the expectations of observers leading up to the implementation of BCRA, we briefly detail the total contributions and expenditures of the one hundred Democratic and Republican state parties in the 2003–2004 election cycle. We then break down the aggregate spending patterns of state parties, examining their federal account activity in the most recent cycle. Finally, we scrutinize the financial and organizational durability of Democratic and Republican state parties in two states under the new campaign finance regime, comparing over time their federal and non-federal (also known as "state") accounts. In doing so, we are able to shed light on how BCRA's sanctions have affected state party finances and activities, changed the relationship between state and national parties, and altered the overall strength of state parties.[1]

State Parties under BCRA

Prior to the passage of BCRA, many state parties were the beneficiaries of—and in the eyes of some, dependent upon—soft money (Bibby and Hol-brook 1996). Under the Federal Election Campaign Act of 1971 (FECA), not only did state parties raise sizable amounts of soft money for federal campaigns on their own but they also received soft money transfers from the national parties for electoral activities. In order to take advantage of financial incentives under FECA that permitted hard-soft dollar splits on coordinated spending between the national and state parties (Dwyre and Kolodny 2002), the national parties often exchanged soft dollars for more valuable hard dollars raised by state parties.

Though some observers thought state parties would be able to offset the loss of soft dollar transfers, others questioned whether they would be able to respond in the post-BCRA era. Defenders of the new law argued that state parties were becoming mere money-laundering conduits, "used by national party officials as vehicles for implementing their newly developed strategy of federal electioneering under the guise of issue advocacy [television ads]" (Mann 2003, 27). Others argued that state parties prior to BCRA had been able to maintain their autonomy, and as such they would not suffer because they were never heavily dependent on the national parties for their financing (Morehouse and Jewell 2003a). Still others anticipated dire consequences for state parties under BCRA, claiming that the ban on party soft money might diminish the strength of state parties and party competition, especially where state parties were weak fundraisers. These weaker state parties benefited from national party soft money, which helped incorporate them into national campaigns (La Raja 2002, 183). Some even predicted that state parties would "become underfinanced, ineffective bystanders as other groups drive both issues and candidates" (Bowler 2003). With the national parties no longer permitted to transfer soft money to influence the activities of state parties, state parties might have financial disincentives to participate in federal campaigns (Stoltz 2003; La Raja 2003a, 2003b, 2003c).

Contribution and Expenditure Patterns of State Parties

In the 2004 election cycle, state parties raised a total of $723 million (combined federal and state accounts). The total was marginally less than the $823 million raised in 2002 and the $802 million in 2000. In the aggregate, when transfers from the national parties are subtracted from the pre-BCRA contribution totals of the state parties, state parties actually raised more federal dollars from individuals and political action committees (PACs) in the 2004 cycle ($445 million) than previously (Armendariz and Pilhofer 2005; La Raja 2006).

Table 7.1 details the 2003–2004 contribution and expenditures totals for the major state parties in all fifty states. Three Democratic state parties (New Jersey, California, and Florida) each raised in excess of $20 million federal and state dollars, with the New Jersey Democrats raising in excess of $28 million. Republican parties in five states (New York, Ohio, Pennsylvania, California, and Florida) raised more than $20 million during the period, with the Republican Party in Florida topping $50 million in contributions. Over half (58) of the state parties dipped into the red during the cycle, with Democrats in California overspending by more than $12 million and the Ohio GOP spending nearly $10 million more than it raised.

Federal Expenditures of State Parties

In terms of federal account expenditures, the one hundred major state parties spent as much on nonmedia activities under BCRA as they did four years earlier. Remarkably, they did this using about 85 percent hard money, in contrast to 2000 when half their contributions were in the form of soft dollars. There are important differences, however, between Republicans and Democrats and between battleground and nonbattleground states. In the first year after the implementation of BCRA, Republican state parties appear to have been in better shape financially than Democratic parties. Moreover, Democratic parties in nonbattleground states experienced significant declines in spending, suggesting that the national parties concentrated resources more than ever in battleground contests during the 2004 election.

Media Spending

The most dramatic change from the previous presidential election was that state parties no longer sponsored broadcast advertising in federal elections. In 2004, they spent nominal sums on television and radio advertising, compared to the 2000 election when the Democrats and Republicans spent $139 million and $97 million, respectively (see table 7.2). Almost all the advertising by state parties in 2000 came in the form of "issue ads"—paid for, in part, with soft money—which were tailored to help candidates without invoking electioneering slogans. BCRA effectively put an end to this practice by banning soft money that national parties raised and then transferred to state parties to pay for these ads. Instead, national committees paid for advertising directly in 2004, mostly through "independent" expenditures that were not coordinated with their presidential candidates.

Table 7.1   Contributions and Expenditures to State Parties, 2003–2004 Election Cycle, Combined State and Federal Accounts

State	Contributions		Expenditures	
	Democrats	Republicans	Democrats	Republicans
Alabama	$2,228,607	$1,150,753	$1,828,730	$2,062,699
Alaska	$4,266,936	$1,244,623	$4,747,438	$2,202,951
Arizona	$7,868,469	$5,847,710	$8,569,642	$3,855,934
Arkansas	$2,943,251	$1,637,127	$3,395,048	$1,444,130
California	$24,871,666	$29,493,501	$37,230,327	$28,517,361
Colorado	$5,740,980	$4,317,091	$5,127,778	$5,570,696
Connecticut	$1,688,552	$2,342,066	$1,939,843	$2,832,104
Delaware	$2,001,607	$1,651,491	$1,905,091	$1,582,113
Florida	$21,372,089	$50,920,376	$28,826,259	$39,999,847
Georgia	$6,228,851	$7,696,974	$6,147,029	$10,162,738
Hawaii	$1,038,010	$2,252,666	$1,120,111	$2,393,955
Idaho	$513,331	$747,980	$369,266	$638,171
Illinois	$12,267,926	$13,012,475	$12,627,788	$13,633,786
Indiana	$13,483,330	$12,968,497	$14,818,593	$13,625,773
Iowa	$11,653,703	$8,440,876	$7,821,188	$7,542,518
Kansas	$2,559,692	$618,137	$2,753,500	$756,729
Kentucky	$3,290,669	$5,955,769	$4,298,292	$6,663,057
Louisiana	$7,342,891	$4,158,138	$6,883,952	$4,313,624
Maine	$3,294,134	$2,829,943	$3,157,699	$3,071,361
Maryland	$1,346,095	$2,558,404	$1,758,031	$2,752,634
Massachusetts	$2,466,860	$5,044,456	$2,309,896	$5,358,005
Michigan	$16,038,229	$18,886,710	$11,451,416	$12,513,758
Minnesota	$10,857,185	$8,014,688	$12,050,827	$12,951,060
Mississippi	$450,550	$4,000,027	$593,053	$3,810,117
Missouri	$19,218,962	$17,969,958	$21,195,442	$18,019,525
Montana	$2,502,121	$984,479	$3,407,429	$1,167,296
Nebraska	$1,079,490	$1,369,485	$612,295	$1,147,048
New Hampshire	$4,882,164	$2,696,147	$5,645,423	$1,550,671
New Jersey	$28,347,364	$10,564,637	$22,890,214	$11,018,319
New Mexico	$3,878,665	$2,095,993	$3,415,008	$2,385,103
New York	$16,184,698	$22,870,163	$10,982,433	$17,394,286
North Carolina	$14,567,938	$3,109,030	$14,695,828	$5,256,104
North Dakota	$2,812,329	$668,196	$2,063,507	$1,907,874
Ohio	$15,964,691	$25,302,904	$19,429,790	$35,178,063
Oklahoma	$4,940,918	$2,433,460	$5,312,208	$3,212,378
Oregon	$7,434,057	$6,301,120	$7,691,021	$4,540,139
Pennsylvania	$18,219,464	$26,163,070	$17,693,603	$22,958,551
Rhode Island	$257,139	$373,166	$435,943	$362,673
South Carolina	$3,022,456	$2,905,922	$2,962,866	$3,341,184
South Dakota	$2,524,836	$4,220,940	$2,282,389	$6,451,900
Tennessee	$6,645,989	$3,250,576	$8,362,960	$4,797,546
Texas	$3,863,263	$6,701,574	$4,002,354	$10,863,930
Utah	$721,803	$1,296,841	$925,775	$1,636,490
Vermont	$1,174,131	$446,210	$985,615	$563,407
Virginia	$6,500,605	$4,412,126	$5,440,565	$5,902,805
Washington	$17,350,707	$9,962,844	$18,203,345	$9,459,027
West Virginia	$1,823,046	$2,329,813	$1,931,433	$2,050,387
Wisconsin	$9,080,806	$8,458,743	$11,655,924	$6,881,854
Wyoming	$251,800	$1,486,756	$236,278	$1,164,552

Source: Center for Public Integrity, http://www.publicintegrity.org/partylines/default.aspx

Table 7.2   State Party Spending in Presidential Elections, 1992–2004 (in millions of dollars)

	1992	*1996*	*2000*	*2004*
Republicans				
Media	0	26	97	1
Mobilization & Grassroots	7	16	39	71
Administrative	32	53	103	122
Unidentified	2	4	6	4
Total	*41*	*99*	*245*	*198*
Democrats				
Media	3	73	139	3
Mobilization & Grassroots	12	17	51	62
Administrative	36	54	107	108
Unidentified	3	7	32	6
Total	*54*	*150*	*329*	*179*

Source: Federal Election Commission (coded by authors).

Grassroots Campaigning and Mobilization Efforts

BCRA also sought to encourage state parties to focus on grassroots campaigning. The new campaign finance law carved out an exception to the soft money ban for state and local parties that allowed them to spend a limited amount of nonfederal money on party-building activities. The so-called Levin Amendment permitted state and local parties (where state laws permitted) to collect contributions in amounts up to $10,000 that could be used for grassroots activity if combined with hard money. In the end, local and state parties did not take advantage of the Levin Amendment—spending less than $3 million in Levin funds for the cycle—as it proved too complicated to implement.

Among state party committees, Republicans gained significant ground on Democrats in terms of spending on mobilization of voters (see table 7.2). While Democrats outspent them in 2000, Republicans surged ahead in 2004, devoting $71 million to mobilization and grassroots efforts compared to $62 million for Democrats. The differences can be explained by the divergent strategies of the two parties. The Democratic Party pursued a dual strategy of using state parties and 527 organizations to mobilize voters in battleground states. State parties spent hard money, while the 527s relied chiefly on soft money to pursue their GOTV goals. This division of labor reflected concerns by Democratic strategists at the national level that the party could not compete effectively against Republicans in the states with only hard money. Thus, 527s sought to complement Democratic efforts in battleground states.

According to the Center for Responsive Politics (2004), the largest 527 organization, America Coming Together (ACT), spent at least $80 million on voter mobilization to help Democrat John Kerry. Partisan donors wishing to support their favored candidate came to understand a simple heuristic: hard money goes to state parties and soft money to 527s (Weissman and Hassan 2006). Progressive 527 organizations appeared to concentrate on voters in the suburbs, while state parties focused on traditional Democratic bastions in urban areas. It is unclear how this division of labor developed, particularly since coordination between state parties—which operate under federal hard money rules—and 527s—which operate primarily with soft money—is illegal under BCRA. The lack of direct coordination between Democratic parties and 527s may have hampered partisan efforts to mobilize voters. Another problem was that duplicative GOTV operations probably increased administrative costs for the party and its supporters.

Republican partisans worked mostly through the state party structure to mobilize voters in 2004. Building on the strategy developed in the 2002 election, they exploited a massive voter database, which linked party staff with volunteer networks in neighborhoods. Led by the RNC, the party mined consumer data, hunting license registrations, and magazine subscriptions to identify likely Republican donors and voters. Their system, known as "Voter Vault," built a database of 175 million names and integrated a Web-based grassroots organizing tool that allowed campaign volunteers to establish their own "precincts." Much of this work was coordinated with state and local parties.

Armed with these voter profiles, the national and state parties inundated likely Republican voters with direct mail and phone calls. The increase in these two activities was particularly striking. Republican state parties spent almost $50 million on direct mail in 2004, while they spent less than half that amount ($22 million) in 2000. Similarly, they more than doubled their spending on phone banks from $3.6 million in 2000 to $8.6 million in 2004, building on a trend they started at least a decade earlier. Not to be outdone by traditionally strong Democratic field operations, Republicans also doubled expenditures on field canvassing to $18 million in 2004. Paradoxically, while expenditures on voter contacts increased, party staff costs declined. In 2004, Republican state parties spent $33 million on staff in 2004, which was $10 million less than in 2000. Staff costs may have decreased due to outsourcing voter contact activity or because parties achieved productivity gains by relying more heavily on volunteer networks.

Democrats experienced greater declines in staff costs than Republicans, spending $30 million in 2004 on salaries, benefits, and related costs compared to $69 million in 2000. This is one indication that the size of Democratic campaign organizations may have shrunk, in part due to their dual strategy of using 527s. In key battleground states, 527s recruited talented campaigners early in the process before state parties had their wheels turning for the presidential campaign. Nonetheless, Democratic state parties managed to hold their spending steady in a number of areas. Relying on campaign tactics developed in previous presidential elections, they organized "coordinated campaigns" that emphasized canvassing with paid staff and volunteers in heavily Democratic areas. Spending on field operations was $15 million, about the same as in 2000. Similarly, they spent the same amount on phone banks ($6 million) as the previous presidential election. Democrats, however, increased spending on direct mail, from $36 million to $43 million.

The Democrats also significantly augmented office-related expenditures, from $33 million to $68 million (including utilities, travel, equipment, rent, and computers). Most likely a significant portion of Democratic spending was related to amassing and managing a large database. Like the RNC, the DNC wanted to exploit information technology to reach targeted voters. The DNC system combined a voter file called DataMart with another database called Demzilla, which compiled information about donors, activists, volunteers, and local party leaders. Assembling these databases required massive amounts of data collection. State parties may have played an important role in putting together the databases, which might account for the surge in office-related expenses (Reich 2005).

State Party Spending in Battleground States

One important effect of BCRA on state parties was that it concentrated spending more in battleground states. In most presidential elections, the parties pursue an Electoral College strategy that focuses on the large swing states. In 2004, the concentration of funds in battleground states was even greater than in 2000. Table 7.3 compares spending on voter mobilization in the same ten battleground states between 1992 and 2004. These states were chosen because the outcome of the presidential contest in 2000 and 2004 was five percentage points or less between the rival candidates. In 2000, Democrats spent nearly half their funds on voter mobilization in these ten states and the other half in the remaining forty states. In 2004, however, they spent 59 percent of their voter contact funds in these same battleground states. Republicans also concentrated efforts more in battleground states. In 2000, they spent 35 percent of funds in these ten states, while in 2004 this portion increased to 43 percent.

It is difficult to determine whether the new campaign finance law encouraged parties to concentrate voter mobilization activity in selected states. Going back to at least 1992, parties were moving toward a strategy of greater concentration of campaign efforts in swing states. In the past decade, with

Table 7.3   State Party Expenditures on Voter Mobilization (in millions), Battleground vs. Nonbattleground States, 1992–2004

	Nonbattleground	*Battleground*	*% Battleground*
Republicans			
1992	5	2	27%
1996	11	5	32%
2000	25	14	35%
2004	40	31	43%
Democrats			
1992	9	3	23%
1996	12	5	29%
2000	26	25	48%
2004	25	37	59%

Source: Federal Election Commission (coded by authors).

Note: "Battleground" is defined here as the same ten states in which the major party candidates finished five or fewer percentage points apart in both 2000 and 2004. These states are Florida, Iowa, Michigan, Minnesota, New Hampshire, Nevada, Ohio, Oregon, Pennsylvania, and Wisconsin.

the help of technology, parties have enhanced their capacity to identify likely partisan voters in key contests throughout the nation.

Under BCRA, it may be true that parties are less inclined to "waste" hard money on states that are not critical to an election, since hard money is more difficult to raise than soft money. An analysis of national party hard money transfers to state parties in 2004 shows that the RNC and DNC gave more of their money to expected battleground states than in the past. Party leaders in Washington may have instructed donors to focus on these same battleground states when giving hard money. Any of these behaviors may have contributed to a greater imbalance in voter mobilization activity in competitive and noncompetitive states, but it cannot be attributed definitively to BCRA.

State Party Spending in Nonbattleground States

A more detailed analysis of the forty nonbattleground states reveals another post-BCRA pattern. States with campaign finance laws that permit unlimited contributions to the parties fared worse under the new federal system than states that had regimes with contribution caps (in some form) that were similar to BCRA. In other words, soft money states did not appear to make the transition to BCRA as well as hard money states. For Democratic state parties in nonbattleground, soft money states, total nonmedia spending in federal elections declined significantly between 2000 and 2004. These sixteen Democratic state parties spent $87 million in 2000, but only $38 million in 2004. In contrast, states with laws limiting party fundraising experienced an increase in party spending. These twenty-four states spent $25 million in 2000 and roughly $52 million in 2004. These differences suggest that BCRA may have a differential impact on state parties depending on how much state laws vary from BCRA hard money limits. In states where the party was accustomed to raising soft money for state elections, the Democratic organizations appear to have had greater difficulty campaigning in federal elections under BCRA.

For Republicans, the transition to BCRA did not appear as difficult for soft money states. In states with no limits, the parties spent slightly more in 2004 than in 2000. However, in states where the campaign finance laws appeared more similar to BCRA, Republican parties increased their spending even more, from $31.9 million to $53.4 million. It appears, then, that BCRA might have contingent effects on state parties, hurting Democratic organizations more than GOP state parties. Among Democratic parties, the difficulties appear greater in states with few limits on party fundraising.

State Party Activities in Colorado and Florida

As the aggregate findings reveal, a state's electoral and campaign finance regulatory environments are key considerations when assessing BCRA's fiscal and organizational impact on state parties. To understand the potential contingent effects of BCRA, we examine the impact of BCRA on state parties in two states, Colorado and Florida. The parties in the two states make good comparative cases, as both states had competitive federal elections between 2000 and 2004, with Republicans having a slight edge, but where party financing in one (Florida) is unconstrained and in the other (Colorado) it is heavily regulated.

State Electoral Environment and Campaign Finance Regulations

With respect to Florida's electoral environment, the first three electoral cycles of the twenty-first century are ripe for comparison, providing consistency over time as well as useful variations. In 2000 and 2004, Florida was not only a battleground state for the presidency; it also had competitive U.S. Senate races both years. The 2002 midterm election featured an uncompetitive gubernatorial race. In all three cycles, nearly all of the seats in the House of Representatives were won by margins of 55 percent or greater.

Colorado's electoral milieu during the period of study was more varied than Florida's. While the presidential contests in 2000 and 2004 were not competitive, with President Bush taking the state both years, the state had highly competitive U.S. Senate races in 2002 and 2004. Like Florida, Colorado had a less-than-competitive gubernatorial race in 2002, but the state did have a few competitive House races over the three election cycles.

Florida's campaign finance regulations concerning political parties remained unchanged over the three election cycles. Florida has virtually no source or size limits on contributions that can be made to state political parties. Parties registered in the state may receive unlimited contributions from corporations, unions, PACs, and individuals, as well as from national and local political parties. The state's lax contribution requirements to parties, combined with the state's sizable population and importance in the Electoral College tally, have enabled its Democrats and Republicans to become among the top state party fundraisers in the country (Morehouse and Jewell 2003a, 163).

In Colorado, campaign finance regulations were abruptly altered by Amendment 27, a constitutional amendment ballot initiative passed in 2002 that capped contributions to state parties at $2,500 for individuals and PACs, but permitted larger, "bundled" contributions (up to $12,500 annually) to state parties from restricted "Small Donor Committees." The amendment strictly prohibits contributions to state (and local) parties that are earmarked for a candidate committee, but allows unlimited intraparty transfers among the state and national parties. Immediately after its passage, some political observers anticipated that Amendment 27 would severely constrict the fundraising abilities of the state parties, with donors bypassing state parties and contributing instead to 527s with the tacit blessings of party officials.[2]

BCRA's Effects on State Party Contributions

We anticipate that federal parties may reduce their transfers to state parties because they are no longer allowed to take advantage of favorable hard-soft dollar funding ratios. Given the electoral milieu outlined above, it would seem that Florida parties with their high-profile Electoral College status are in a better position than Colorado's to attract transfers from the federal parties post BCRA, as such dollars, being more difficult to raise than the soft dollars used for transfers prior to BCRA, will no doubt be allocated very strategically. Simultaneously the state parties would be expected to see increases in contributions to their state accounts as donors take advantage of the higher contributions limits under BCRA. However, as Florida parties received large influxes into their state accounts prior to BCRA by way of soft dollar transfers, they may struggle to maintain their pre-BCRA state account contribution levels. Parties in Colorado received less soft dollar transfers and thus should see little impact on their state account contributions because of BCRA; Amendment 27, though, should reduce state account contributions.

Contributions to Florida State Parties

It appears that BCRA did not substantially hurt the ability of state parties in Florida to raise money, although it did affect how much they received in transfers from national parties, especially for Democrats. In the post-BCRA 2004 cycle, the Florida Republican Party maintained its federal and state account contributions when compared to the 2000 cycle. As figure 7.1 shows, the state GOP raised a total of $50.9 million in the 2004 cycle, down slightly from the $54.1 million it raised for the 2000 elections. In the 2004 cycle, 72 percent of total party funds were raised by the state party. The balance of $14.2 million was transferred from the national parties to the state party's federal account (hard money only), which demonstrates that the national Republican parties continued to invest heavily in key swing states under BCRA. In the 2004 cycle, the state party raised nearly $27 million in nonfederal (state account) contributions, which was marginally more than in 2000 (not counting the $13.3 million in soft dollars transferred from the national parties). Clearly, the expectation that a large-state party such as the Florida GOP—which seemed hooked on soft money transfusions in 2000 (Barber 2004)—would suffer under BCRA is not the case. In the 2002 gubernatorial cycle, the vast majority of the funds raised by the state GOP went into the party's state account, including some $11.7 million it received in soft money transfers from the national parties (Dunbar 2002). Only $4.2 million (7 percent) of the $60.1 million in total contributions in 2002 went into the state party's federal account. Overall, then, while BCRA appears to curtail soft money transfers, the party has maintained funding for its state account and increased contributions to its federal account.

The Florida Democratic Party, as figure 7.1 shows, consistently trailed (by roughly half) the aggregate campaign contributions made to its Republican counterpart. The total amount of money raised by the Democrats in the 2004 cycle ($21.4 million) was half the total raised during the 2000 cycle ($42.6 million). The party did not receive any federal party transfers in 2004, perhaps due to the national party's complicity in directing donors to contribute to "extra-party" 527 organizations operating in Florida. It is clear that the Florida Democratic Party under FECA was much more dependent on infusions of soft money from the national parties than the GOP was, although its hard money in 2004 was tenfold that of 2000. During the 2002 midterm election, the state party raised more money for its state account (nearly $28 million) than during either presidential cycle.

Contributions to Colorado State Parties

Keeping in mind the electoral backdrop in Colorado and changes in state campaign finance, the impact of BCRA, though apparent, is less clear. The

Figure 7.1 Florida Republican and Democratic Parties, Total Contributions, 2000–2004

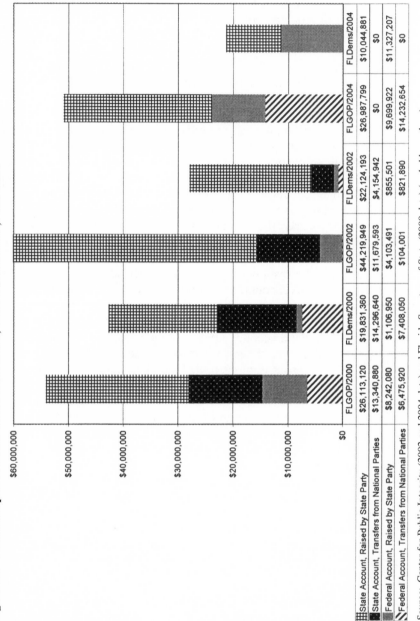

	FLGOP/2000	FLDems/2000	FLGOP/2002	FLDems/2002	FLGOP/2004	FLDems/2004
State Account, Raised by State Party	$26,113,120	$19,831,360	$44,219,949	$22,124,193	$26,987,799	$10,044,881
State Account, Transfers from National Parties	$13,340,880	$14,296,640	$11,679,593	$4,154,942	$0	$0
Federal Account, Raised by State Party	$8,242,080	$1,106,950	$4,103,491	$855,501	$9,699,922	$11,327,207
Federal Account, Transfers from National Parties	$6,475,920	$7,408,050	$104,001	$821,890	$14,232,654	$0

Source: Center for Public Integrity (2002 and 2004 data) and Florida Secretary of State (2000 data) (coded by authors).

compounding effect of the two financial regulations changes appears to have caused almost all contributions to be directed to the state parties' federal accounts. In the 2004 cycle, the Colorado GOP raised considerably more hard dollars than it did four years earlier. As figure 7.2 shows, the party raised $3.8 million for its federal account in 2004, roughly 91 percent of the party's total contributions. During the 2000 cycle, by contrast, contributions to the party's state account made up 63 percent of the $3.1 million in total contributions. There were indications in 2000, though, that the state GOP was well positioned to raise federal hard dollars under BCRA, as the party on its own raised 98 percent of the $1.1 million for its federal account that cycle. During the 2002 midterm cycle with a gubernatorial contest, a tight Senate race, and several House races in play, the Colorado GOP raised considerably more money ($14.1 million) than in either of the presidential elections. It received hefty transfers in hard and soft money from the national party in this final cycle before the soft money ban.

The pattern of campaign contributions to the Colorado Democrats over the three election cycles is somewhat different. During the 2004 cycle, the state party raised 1.4 million, roughly $600,000 less than the amount raised four years earlier (see figure 7.2). As with the state GOP, 95 percent of the funds the Democrats raised in the 2004 cycle were deposited into the party's federal account. The party raised a paltry $247,924 for its state account in 2004, some $229,116 less than in 2000 and roughly one-tenth of the $2.7 million it raised in 2002. Unlike the state GOP, which showed it could easily raise federal hard dollars, the Colorado Democrats appeared still very much dependent on the national party's transfers of hard dollars. During the 2004 cycle, 75 percent ($3.5 million) of donations made to the Democrats' federal account were national party transfers. On its own, the party raised just $1.4 million federal dollars, less than one-third of its overall contributions. This is in sharp contrast to 2000, when the party raised $1.5 million by itself in hard and soft dollars, accounting for four-fifths of its total contributions. During the 2002 cycle, the party's fundraising was quite similar to the GOP's, with the Democrats raising a total of $11.2 million.

Contributions Summary

With higher allowances for hard money contributions under BCRA, the state parties apparently concentrated their efforts on raising federal dollars. The Florida state parties, especially the Democrats, were able to increase contributions to their federal accounts, offsetting to some degree the loss in soft money transfers. However, it is clear that the national Democratic Party organizations, particularly the DNC, abandoned the state Democratic Party in 2004, relying instead on 527 organizations to do grassroots outreach and

Figure 7.2   Colorado Republican and Democratic Parties, Total Contributions, 2000–2004

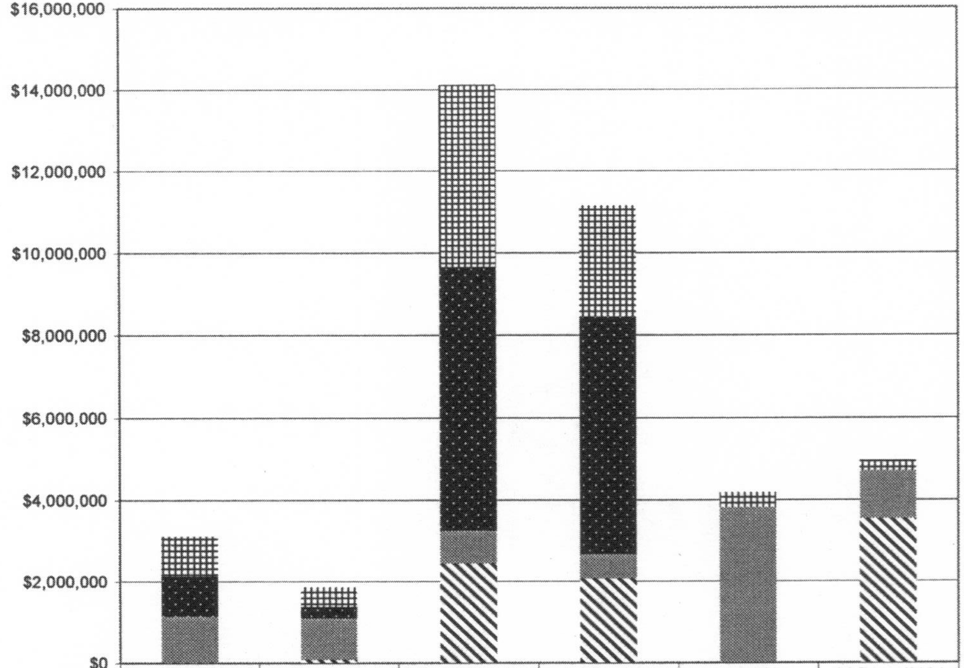

	COGOP/2000	CODems/2000	COGOP/2002	CODems/2002	COGOP/2004	CODems/2004
State Account, Raised by State Party	$972,700	$477,040	$4,460,599	$2,708,318	$377,017	$247,924
State Account, Transfers from National Parties	$996,300	$278,960	$6,407,164	$5,771,139	$0	$0
Federal Account, Raised by State Party	$1,121,120	$1,015,680	$798,965	$604,699	$3,812,062	$1,175,015
Federal Account, Transfers from National Parties	$22,880	$88,320	$2,447,250	$2,073,024	$0	$3,535,547

Source: Center for Public Integrity (2002 and 2004 data) and Colorado Secretary of State (2000 data) (coded by authors).

mobilize partisans. Judging by Kerry's lackluster performance in Florida, the Democrats' dual strategy—with the state party raising hard money and the 527s soft money—did not work well. In contrast, the GOP national committees transferred more than $14 million in hard money to the state party in 2004, suggesting that Republicans were intent on building a grassroots mobilization effort in Florida. While the decline in contribution levels to the parties' state accounts in Colorado was due, in part, to Amendment 27, BCRA provided the state parties with an incentive to raise federal dollars. Nonfederal money for state-level campaigns, in contrast, is seemingly being raised by nonparty vehicles, such as 527s and nonprofits.[3]

BCRA's Effects on State Party Expenditures

In line with the findings at the aggregate level, we would anticipate that media spending by state parties will decline in the post-BCRA era. Similarly, we would expect to see significant increases in candidate support expenditures as well as administration (since salary expenses are included in administration). Due to the shift in contributions generally toward larger funds in federal accounts, we would anticipate that a significant proportion of expenditures will draw from federal account funds, indicating a continued engagement with federal campaigns on the part of state parties.[4]

Expenditures by Florida State Parties

In Florida there is considerable evidence that spending patterns of state parties were affected by BCRA. In the 2004 cycle, Republicans spent $38.4 million, almost $11 million less than in 2000. Figure 7.3 reveals that the party spent far less on media expenditures and considerably more on administration and candidate support, which includes GOTV efforts, party "hoopla" (signs, buttons, etc.), and direct mail. In terms of candidate support and party administration, a different trend emerges. In the 2000 cycle, total spending on candidate support was roughly 21 percent of the party's overall spending. In the 2004 cycle, spending by the party on candidate support nearly doubled to $19.7 million, accounting for 49 percent of the party's total expenditures. The party spent more than $6.5 million on administration in 2000; in the post-BCRA 2004 cycle, administration costs roughly doubled, eating up 27 percent of the party's overall spending.

Given the end of soft money transfers and the increase in allowable federal dollar contributions under BCRA, the ratio of expenditures from the Florida GOP's federal and state accounts appears to have changed. In 2000, 26 percent of the party's total outlays flowed from the federal account; by 2004, the proportion had increased to 48 percent. The GOP increased the proportion with respect to the three major categories of expenditures, the

Figure 7.3 Florida Republican and Democratic Parties, Total Expenditures, 2000–2004

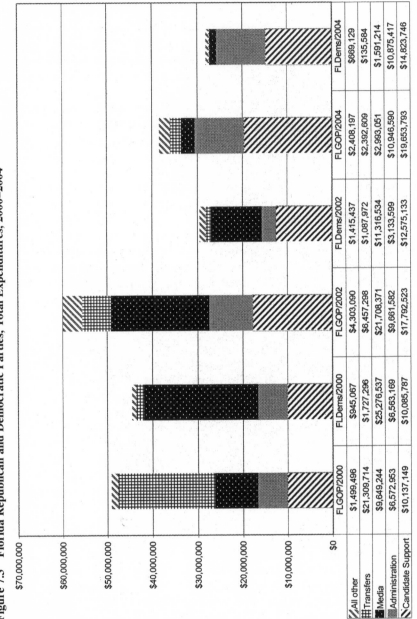

	FLGOP/2000	FLDems/2000	FLGOP/2002	FLDems/2002	FLGOP/2004	FLDems/2004
All other	$1,499,496	$945,067	$4,303,090	$1,415,437	$2,408,197	$669,129
Transfers	$21,309,714	$1,727,296	$6,457,298	$1,087,972	$2,392,609	$135,584
Media	$9,649,244	$25,276,537	$21,708,371	$11,316,534	$2,993,051	$1,591,214
Administration	$6,572,953	$6,563,169	$9,661,582	$3,133,599	$10,946,590	$10,875,417
Candidate Support	$10,137,149	$10,085,787	$17,792,523	$12,575,133	$19,653,793	$14,823,746

Source: Center for Public Integrity (2002 and 2004 data) and Florida Secretary of State (2000 data) (coded by authors).

GOP increased the proportion of its federal account spending on candidate support and administration in 2004 but ended almost entirely any federal account spending on media. Despite the pronounced decline in federal account spending on media, the increases in federal spending on candidate support and administration demonstrate that the state party was still actively participating in federal campaigns. It is likely that the state party was "federalizing" its activity so that it could continue to conduct voter mobilization under the new "federal election activity" rules.

It is important to note the significant decline in transfer payments made by the Florida GOP over the three election cycles. In the 2000 cycle, the state party transferred $21.3 million to the national parties, accounting for 45 percent of the party's total disbursements; in 2002, the amount fell to $6.5 million, and by 2004 it was only $2.4 million. The dramatic decline in intraparty transfers across the two presidential elections was due to BCRA, as the law eliminated the practice of swapping valuable hard dollars collected by the state parties for soft dollars raised by the national parties.

The trends in spending patterns of the Florida Democrats closely parallel those of the GOP. Total expenditures dropped to $28.1 million in 2004 from $44.6 million in 2000. Once BCRA went into effect, the party's expenditures on media declined, but spending on candidate support and administration increased. In 2000, candidate support was 23 percent ($10.1 million) of the party's overall spending; by 2004, it rose to 54 percent ($14.8 million). Figure 7.3 shows how the party's federal account expenditures on media in 2004 decreased as a proportion of total media spending and declined in real dollars.

Expenditures by Colorado State Parties

There is considerable variation in the expenditure patterns of the two state parties in Colorado, as figure 7.4 reveals. Because of Amendment 27, though, it is difficult to discern to what extent the effects are a result of the new state campaign finance regulations at the state or federal level. In contrast to the Florida state parties, overall spending by the two Colorado parties was significantly higher in 2004 than four years earlier, due in part to the two competitive House races in 2004 and the absence of a Senate race in 2000. Expenditures by the Colorado GOP in 2004 increased to $4.7 million, 37 percent more than the party spent in 2000. Spending by the Colorado Democratic party more than doubled over the four years, from $1.5 million to nearly $4 million. Spending by Colorado parties in 2002 surpassed that of the two presidential cycles because of the gubernatorial election and the contested Senate race. Colorado Republicans spent more than $16.7 million in 2002, with the state Democrats spending roughly half that amount.

Similar to the parties in Florida, those in Colorado increased the propor-

Figure 7.4 Colorado Republican and Democratic Parties, Total Expenditures, 2000–2004

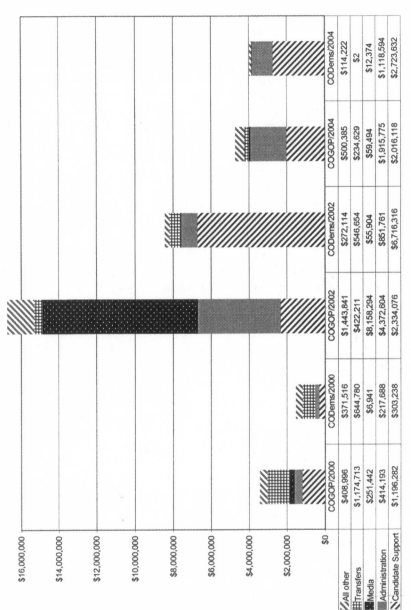

	COGOP/2000	CODems/2000	COGOP/2002	CODems/2002	COGOP/2004	CODems/2004
All other	$408,996	$371,516	$1,443,841	$272,114	$500,385	$114,222
Transfers	$1,174,713	$644,780	$422,211	$546,654	$234,629	$2
Media	$251,442	$6,941	$8,158,294	$55,904	$59,494	$12,374
Administration	$414,193	$217,688	$4,372,604	$851,761	$1,915,775	$1,118,594
Candidate Support	$1,196,282	$303,238	$2,334,076	$6,716,316	$2,016,118	$2,723,632

Source: Center for Public Integrity (2002 and 2004 data) and Colorado Secretary of State (2000 data) (coded by authors).

tion of spending allocated to administration compared with the previous presidential election. Neither state party spent much on media in any cycle, the sole exception being the GOP in the 2002 midterm election. Overall expenditures (combined state and federal accounts) on media in the two presidential cycles comprised less than 7 percent of expenditures for both parties. It is likely that the spike in media expenditures by the state GOP in 2002 ($8.2 million) was driven by national party transfers to assist the competitive U.S. Senate and Seventh Congressional District races (Smith 2004). Spending on candidate support by both parties increased over the two presidential cycles, with the Democrats leading the way. In the 2002 midterm cycle, the Democrats devoted more than four-fifths of their expenditures ($6.7 million) to candidate support, spending less than 1 percent on media; Republicans, in contrast, spent a modest amount ($2.3 million) on candidate support and more than half of their total outlays on media.

Expenditures Summary

Expenditures by the four state parties during the pre- and post-BCRA periods shed light on the issue of state party organizational strength. In both states, the parties are spending less on media and more on administration (including salaries for staff) under BCRA, which differs from the aggregate-level findings. The parties are spending more on candidate support under BCRA, with a consistent proportional increase in money coming from their federal accounts. In Colorado, the impact of Amendment 27 appears to have pushed the parties to draw more heavily on their federal accounts, as the revenue of their state accounts has declined considerably. It is possible that Colorado and other states with more restrictive laws on party financing may actually benefit from the more generous funding levels for state parties under BCRA.

Conclusion

Under BCRA, state parties were able to augment their voter mobilization strategies, continuing a trend that developed in the 1990s. They deployed expensive new technologies to identify and contact likely partisan voters. With the ban on national party soft money, state parties no longer sponsor issue ads, which were carried out under the direction and resources of the national committees. State parties, however, continue to receive transfers of hard money from the national parties—especially the Republicans—to support state party mobilization efforts, though these amounts are targeted more heavily to battleground states than in the past.

Republicans state parties have made the transition to BCRA better than the Democrats. They raised more money and outspent them on voter mobilization activities in 2004. Democrats, however, pursued a dual strategy that relied heavily on outside 527s to campaign for the Democratic presidential nominee. If 527 organization activities are included, Democratic partisans may have outspent Republicans. Democrats, however, probably suffered from their inability to coordinate these activities.

In assessing the impact of BCRA on state parties, an important distinction is whether the party organization operates in a battleground state. It appears that state parties in battleground states were equally active in 2004, if not more so, than in the previous presidential election. In nonbattleground states, however—especially where state campaign finance laws allow soft money—the parties fared worse. This was particularly true for Democratic organizations, which have been more reliant on soft money than their Republican counterparts. The use of Levin funds—which was supposed to allow parties to use soft money for grassroots activity—was not exploited, primarily because of complex Federal Election Commission accounting regulations.

As the two case studies make clear, the fundraising and organizational capacity of state parties is largely conditioned by the electoral context and campaign finance regulations of each state. On the revenue side of the equation, when there are competitive federal races, the parties are able to raise sufficient hard dollars to offset the loss of national soft money transfers, though the Colorado Democrats showed less ability to do so. The ban on soft money in federal elections appears to have had a negligible effect on the ability of the Florida GOP to raise money for its state-level campaigns, as Morehouse and Jewell (2003a) anticipated, but it has had more serious consequences for Florida Democrats. State party coffers have declined with the end of soft money transfers from the national parties, but state parties seem to have survived BCRA, collecting more hard dollars for their federal accounts. Data from the 2006 midterm cycle will certainly help to evaluate these tentative conclusions.

On the expenditure side, the case studies reflect the national patterns. Under BCRA, state parties have decreased expenditures on media and virtually eliminated hard money swaps with the national parties. In contrast, they have increased their spending on candidate support and administration. There is little evidence that state parties in battleground states have removed themselves from federal campaigns under BCRA. In the 2004 cycle, most state party spending on candidate support, which includes targeting and mobilizing voters, flowed from the parties' federal accounts, which is likely an artifact of the new "federal election activity" requirements. Although it is still too early to draw firm conclusions after one post-BCRA election cycle, the spending patterns of state parties seems to be tied as much to a state's electoral context and campaign finance regulations as to changes brought about by BCRA.

Ascertaining the fiscal and organizational strength of state parties under BCRA is a difficult and somewhat subjective enterprise. The shift away from media spending by state parties in the 2004 general election might indicate that nonparty organizations are in a better position to set the campaign agenda, at least when federal candidates are on the ballot. Overall media spending in the 2004 cycle did not decline dramatically. Instead, media expenditures moved from parties (state and national) to nonparty organizations (Weissman and Hassan 2006; Boatright et al. 2006; Armendariz and Pilhofer 2005). The incentives for national party leaders to use nonparty committees instead of state parties for media may weaken the organizational ties between national and state parties. Yet, as the national data and case studies show, state parties under BCRA increased their spending on candidate support and administrative costs, perhaps indicating that some organizations are stronger, particularly in battleground states.

Among the many important questions in anticipation of the next election are whether Republicans will increase their advantage over Democratic state parties and whether Democrats will continue to pursue a dual strategy, relying on both 527s and state party hard money to mobilize voters. Much depends on decisions made by the Federal Election Commission regarding the status of 527 organizations and whether they will be regulated like PACs, which would compel them to use hard money. Another concern for Democrats is whether the national and state parties will inherit the voter data and campaign expertise of 527s such as ACT. Finally, it is worth considering the relative health of the national and state parties. The national parties broke all records for raising hard money, but while state parties held their own collectively, it cannot be said that they fared as well as their national committee counterparts. It remains to be seen whether they can raise hard money from national constituencies that may prefer to give to federal candidates and national committees in Washington. Further research should explore whether the constraints of hard money fundraising for federal elections affect the breadth of state party activities in state elections, especially where state laws differ considerably from BCRA, and in nonbattleground states.

Although it still is too early to fully comprehend how the landscape for state parties has changed under BCRA, the federal law should have contingent effects on the finances and organizational strength of state parties. As was the case with FECA, the electoral and campaign finance regulatory contexts of a state need to be considered when examining BCRA's effect on state parties. During election cycles when states lack competitive presidential, Senate, or House races, the national parties may politely ignore state parties, as our findings suggest. But when there are competitive federal elections to contest, the national parties will continue to be involved in those states in the post-BCRA era. We hesitate to conclude, as Malbin (2006) does, that BCRA has not had "a major effect on the activity . . . or on the financial health of the state parties." Rather, our findings suggest that BCRA has had a *contingent effect* on the campaign finance and organizational capacity of state parties.

Notes

1. Data for this chapter are drawn from state party campaign finance reports filed with the Federal Election Commission (FEC), the Center for Public Integrity (CPI), and the state elections authorities of Colorado and Florida. We thank Bob Biersack of the FEC, Agustin Armendariz of the CPI, and Derek Willis of the *Washington Post* for providing data and helpful insights. Data were coded by the authors into the various categories of contributions and expenditures.

2. Peter Blake, "GOP Jumping Merrily through Fund-Raising Loophole," *Rocky Mountain News*, December 20, 2003.

3. Ibid.

4. Expenditure categories include spending on Media, Administration, Candidate Support, Transfers, and All Other, which includes fund-raising, political contributions, and other or undetermined spending.

8

Rally 'round the Flag

When Interest Groups Invite Themselves to the Party

David B. Magleby, J. Quin Monson, and Kelly D. Patterson

Interest in the 2004 election ran high. The razor-thin margin of President George W. Bush's 2000 election, dissatisfaction in some quarters with his domestic and foreign policies, and his low approval ratings all seemed to indicate a tight race in 2004. The anticipated closeness and intensity of the race led participants from both sides of the political aisle to investigate and adopt new strategies that would help them to achieve a victory. By July 2003, the America Votes (AV) coalition was officially formed, consisting of thirty-two progressive interest groups who each anted up $50,000 for a seat at the table to work together on voter education and mobilization efforts during the 2004 election cycle. Though united in motive, AV and its members did not confine themselves to a particular electoral jurisdiction or a specific message. The scope and breadth of their cooperation resulted in an organization that rivaled a political party's ability to affect elections on a broad scale.

The creation of AV was widely publicized, but was only part of a broader effort to revitalize progressive politics. Responding to favorable political circumstances and recent changes in the campaign finance regulatory environment, a group of prominent political donors provided the funds for new organizations that became part of AV, including America Coming Together (ACT) and the Media Fund.[1] This up-front funding made it possible to retain the services of a group of talented and experienced professionals, many of whom had worked for the Democratic Party or individual Democratic candidates.

The activities and impact of AV raise questions about the conditions necessary for the emergence and effectiveness of such a coalition. While a handful of its largest member organizations, such as ACT and the Media Fund, engaged in most of the electoral activity, our focus is on the AV coalition itself. We seek to understand why and how it undertook its coordinated activities. First, we examine what the literature says about the conditions under which we expect interest groups to cooperate, and then we extend these insights to the electoral arena, where a slightly different set of incentives and benefits foster cooperation. We next describe the formation of AV and the motivations members expressed for joining this coalition. Finally, we compare the scope of this coalition's activities to the efforts of political parties and comment on the long-term prospects for AV or other similar interest group coalitions.

Interest Group Coalitions: Lobbying and Campaigning

Interest group scholars have theorized about the conditions under which individuals join interest groups. Generally, this work relies on theoretical explanations developed by Mancur Olson in his work *The Logic of Collective Action* (1965) or by Robert Salisbury (1969) in his work on exchange theory. Olson and Salisbury posit that individuals need to receive particular benefits in order to participate in groups. Otherwise, there is a strong tendency for individuals to want to "free ride" on the efforts of others. The research places the selective benefits that individuals can receive into three distinct categories: material, solidary, and expressive. Groups need to offer at least one of these particular incentives in order to overcome the individual's incentive to free ride. There are numerous examples of these kinds of benefits. Material benefits include such things as T-shirts, reduced life insurance premiums, or any other sort of discrete benefit an individual may desire. Solidary benefits refer to the relationships that individuals can enjoy in association with others of like mind through such interactions as group meetings or newsletters. Expressive benefits, or what Clark and Wilson (1961) label "purposive incentives," pertain to policy or ideological goals of the participants. Individuals wanting to receive such benefits from a group must do so at a cost, whether monetary or otherwise.

The insights of Olson's and Salisbury's research have also been extrapolated to interest group coalitions (Almeida 2005; Hula 1999). Just as scholars have sought to uncover the reasons why individuals combine to form interest groups, they have also sought to understand the conditions under which separate interest groups combine into coalitions to pursue a particular goal. Essentially, each interest group must assess the various costs and benefits of joining a coalition in much the same way that an individual must weigh the benefits and costs of joining in and participating with a group. Thus, the types of incentives that entice individuals to participate in an interest group can also serve to bring organizations together in a coalition.

The interest group literature has identified several different types of benefits that normally fall under one of the three main headings mentioned above. For example, a material benefit that a group may derive from joining a coalition may be lower operating costs. When costs can be shared, a group has a material incentive to participate in a coalition. A group can also enlist in a coalition to promote solidarity, mainly through sharing information from other groups. This solidary benefit, in turn, can translate into achieving a group's purposive goals, when the additional information gleaned from collaboration helps the group to achieve its policy goals more easily. The group may also recognize the long-term strategic advantage from sharing information with other groups well positioned in the policy environment. With a policy environment that can often be large and complex, individual groups often realize they need assistance from others to effectively and meaningfully affect public policy.

Though coalitions can form relatively quickly under desirable circumstances, there are constraints on the formation of some kinds of coalitions. Groups are more likely to select partners that share a similar ideology (Almeida 2005). This means that coalitions with a broad range of ideological partners will be rare. There is also differentiation of workload once the coalition forms. Not all groups join the coalition at the same time, with the same resources, or with the same motivation (Hula 1995). These differences basically ensure that each group will bear a slightly different burden or have different responsibilities as the coalition seeks to achieve its goals. Even with such complexities, however, groups regularly form coalitions for the purpose of lobbying.

We can apply these insights from the world of interest group lobbying to the world of campaigning. There are several reasons why campaign coalitions may form. First, groups can share the costs of campaigning. If groups have similar motivations and goals in the electoral arena, then there are good reasons to pool resources. Voter registration and voter identification projects lend themselves to cooperative efforts to save costs. Second, groups can receive strategic information from collaboration. In a complex campaign environment, groups may not always know the best places or ways to expend their resources. A coalition can provide the individual member with information and advice, minimizing duplication of effort and increasing efficiency. For example, polling can be designed to address the needs of cooperating groups because there is usually significant overlap in the concerns of related groups. Third, lobbying for legislative votes is similar to "lobbying" for popular votes. In both cases, groups seek to identify and persuade "swing voters" through targeting specific messages (Patterson and Singer 2002). With the right level of coordination, all members of the group are likely to persuade more voters. Finally, groups may form coalitions to campaign so that they can elect individuals whom the coalition can more easily lobby after the campaign is over. All interest groups should desire to see elected officials who are more sympathetic to their policy positions, and campaign efforts may establish an even greater link between their campaign and their lobbying efforts.

We also recognize that there are hurdles groups must overcome to cooperate in a campaign environment. It is one thing for groups to collaborate in a legislature; but it may be something entirely different for groups to collaborate during an election. First, campaigns involve several sorts of unique activities, including voter registration and identification, campaign communication, database management, voter mobilization, and possible litigation. These activities are considerably more complex and costly than simply persuading a few select representatives or senators through direct contact or grassroots lobbying. Second, campaigning and lobbying are different because coordinating so many campaign activities across electoral jurisdictions may create insurmountably high transaction costs. Third, unlike an extended lobbying effort that could span several years, elections occur in a relatively short time frame; the nominees are normally selected only a few months before the general elections. This abbreviated time frame can make it even more difficult for groups to meet and decide on how to allocate resources. In both settings, interest groups may be unsure of their financial resources, but it is our sense that campaign budgets have more uncertainty than lobbying budgets. Finally, the goals in a campaign environment differ from those in a policy environment. An electoral coalition may really claim success only if a particular candidate wins office, whereas in a policy environment, a lobbying coalition can achieve a degree of success by slowing down the policy, seeking major amendments, or producing incremental outcomes.

Yet in spite of such obstacles, we find that interest groups in the 2004 presidential campaign assembled a formidable coalition for the purpose of educating and mobilizing voters against President Bush. They shared an ideological framework, vehemently disapproved of the policies of the Bush administration, exchanged pertinent information, and developed technologies and contacts that they believed would be useful in future electoral contests. Just as the coalition-building literature on interest groups predicts, a mix of material, solidary, and expressive benefits inspired the creation and maintenance of a campaign coalition that seemed to be similar in size and scope to a political party.

Recent research categorizes the coalition that emerged in 2005 as a "shadow party" and argues that it is evidence for the idea of "party networks" (e.g., Skinner 2005). While the coalition relied on former party workers and sought to help a particular candidate, it is still too early to conclude whether the conditions and incentives in 2004 can consistently foster coalitions that merit the title of "shadow party." In part because of the decentralized and candidate-centered structure of U.S. elections, the various participants often have conflicting goals (Magleby, Patterson, and Thurber 2002). Our research here focuses on the possibility that different incentives can produce large campaign coalitions that resemble parties but remain outside a formal party structure.

Campaign Coalition Building: The Formation of America Votes

AV was created in July 2003 for the purpose of increasing voter registration, education, and participation in electoral politics; it claimed to represent twenty million Americans (America Votes 2003). Table 8.1 contains a list of

Table 8.1 America Votes Coalition Members during the 2004 Election

Organization	Total 527 Expenditures
AFL-CIO	$6,494,316
AFSCME	$24,505,616
America Coming Together (ACT)	$78,040,480
American Federation of Teachers	$347,083
Association of Community Organizing for Reform Now (ACORN)	—
Association of Trial Lawyers of America	—
Brady Campaign to Prevent Gun Violence[a]	—
Clean Water Action	$231,796
Defenders of Wildlife Action Fund	$533,390
Democracy for America	$603,771
Democrats 2000 (21st Century Democrats)	$1,256,559
EMILY's List	$8,100,752
Environment 2004, Inc.[b]	$1,167,762
Human Rights Campaign	—
League of Conservation Voters	$5,749,006
Media Fund	$54,494,698
Million Mom March[a]	—
MoveOn.org Voter Fund	$21,346,380
Moving America Forward[b]	—
Music for America	$1,507,324
NARAL Pro-Choice America	—
NAACP National Voter Fund	—
National Education Association	$3,906,333
National Jewish Democratic Council	—
National Treasury Employees Union/Treasury Employees Democracy in Action	—
Partnership for America's Families	$2,936,666
Planned Parenthood Action Fund	$595,288
Service Employees International Union (SEIU)	$46,726,713
Sierra Club	$6,261,811
USAction	—
Voices for Working Families	$7,202,695
Young Voter Alliance (Young Democrats of America)	$723,781

Source: Center for Public Integrity, http://www.publicintegrity.org/527/db.aspx?act = activity2003
Notes: Since the 2004 election, the Alliance for Retired Americans (not listed above) has joined America Votes.

[a] The Brady Campaign and Million Mom March joined America Votes together.
[b] Group has disbanded since 2004 election.

the thirty-two AV members during the 2004 election cycle, along with the total expenditures of AV member organizations who filed as Section 527 groups with the Internal Revenue Service (IRS) as reported in data compiled by the Center for Public Integrity. Groups without spending totals listed are most likely 501(c) organizations, for which expenditure data on their 2004 election activities will not be available until they file with the IRS in 2006. Each AV member paid $50,000 to join.[2]

The table helps illustrate several points about the coalition. First, the coalition included groups with widely varying budgets and issue agendas, including environmental groups, gun control lobbies, labor unions, and unaffiliated political committees. Second, the overall 527 expenditures of AV, approximately $2.8 million during the 2004 cycle, pale in comparison with the total combined spending of the coalition members of at least $273 million.[3] Our focus here is on AV as the hub of all of that spending. While AV could not mandate how members spent their money, there was an effort at unifying and coordinating the message. Two AV members, ACT and the Media Fund, spent about $133 million, or 49 percent of the total AV 527 spending. Because of their large expenditures relative to the other AV members, it is easy to confuse the activities of AV, ACT, and the Media Fund. Furthermore, AV and ACT shared office space, and their staffs interacted on a daily basis throughout the campaign. Functionally, AV served as the umbrella to coordinate the activities of the coalition members; ACT and other smaller groups concentrated on voter registration and mobilization; and the Media Fund and others handled broadcast advertising. Because of this tight coordination, we aggregate the spending of AV coalition members under the AV banner.

Cecile Richards, a veteran labor political organizer and daughter of former Texas governor Ann Richards, helped create America Votes and served as the organization's president. Early on in the election cycle, Richards explained that the purpose of AV was to coordinate the efforts of various 527 groups and make sure the groups avoided wasting money and manpower.[4] The creation of the AV coalition marked an unprecedented effort to unite some of the largest grassroots political organizations to coordinate events, pool resources, and share information in a disciplined manner.[5] AV sought to coordinate a vast get-out-the-vote (GOTV) effort, including television ads, door-knocking, canvassing, direct mail, and phone banks. Indeed, some compared AV to a shadow party with a large membership in every battleground state (Magleby, Monson, and Patterson 2005), or as one observer put it, "Richards' job is to run, what amounts to, the war room of the unofficial campaign, enforcing cooperation and accountability among groups" (Gwynne 2004, 114). AV's efforts were unprecedented in scale for an interest group, amounting to the equivalent of a full-blown presidential campaign.

Measured by both hard and soft money, it approached the size of the campaign waged by Al Gore in 2000 (Gwynne 2004).

The innovative idea behind AV was to "utilize the strong strategic abilities and large membership bases of the groups to break new ground in electoral politics."[6] As we stated earlier, groups needed to be serious to participate in AV because they were asked to pay $50,000 to belong to the organization. This membership fee helped to cover the organizational costs of AV and to begin the process of assembling a database that would allow its members to more effectively contact and mobilize voters. Members would also receive strategic information on message delivery and access to polling data. The unique concept behind AV was that groups would raise and spend their own political money, just as they had done in the past, but now their expenditures would be coordinated with other groups in the AV coalition (Gwynne 2004).

Incentives to Join AV

The difficult part of building a coalition of any size or level of effectiveness rests in providing the necessary incentives for organizations to join and to participate. The groups that joined the AV coalition did so for a variety of reasons. We use the categories developed in the interest group literature to understand how the AV coalition formed and operated.[7]

One important factor was the legal environment of the campaign. The Bipartisan Campaign Reform Act (BCRA) prohibits organizations from engaging in what is called "express advocacy"—calling for the election or defeat of a specific candidate—unless they spend hard dollars for that purpose. However, the Federal Election Commission (FEC) did not impose the same limitations on 527s as on other political committees, permitting them to raise unlimited contributions from individuals. Section 527 organizations were banned from using corporate or union treasury funds for BCRA-defined broadcast electioneering communications within thirty days before a primary or sixty days before a general election. Organizations registered under Section 527 are permitted to raise large sums of unregulated money to promote voter education and turnout, but are prohibited from coordinating activities or sharing information with a candidate campaign or party committee. BCRA lifted ground activity limitations for 527 groups consequently creating an added importance for groups to invest in voter registration and mobilization, targeted mail and phone calls, and internal communications.

Within this regulatory framework, members of the AV coalition had a strong expressive goal in mind when they embarked on their endeavor: educate citizens about the deleterious effects of President Bush's administration, then register and mobilize them to vote. The seed money for AV and some of the other groups in the coalition came from donors who explicitly desired to see Bush defeated in the 2004 election.[8] Indeed, George Soros, one of the leading donors to America Coming Together (ACT), created a controversy when he made the defeat of President Bush his highest priority.[9] However, several groups also cared about publicizing their issue positions and identifying potential voters who agreed with them. Jim Jordan, a political consultant to ACT, stated that his organization "wants to elect Democrats at all levels. . . . It is an organization that is geared to electing Democrats up and down the ticket."[10]

Cathy Duvall, the national field director for AV, said that the organization "wants to win." She also mentioned that it wanted to make the organization viable for a longer period of time and to help to nurture community leadership—but winning elections was at the top of the list. Harold Ickes, president of the Media Fund, pointed out just how difficult it is to "take down [a] sitting president" and that it requires "single-minded focus with a purpose."[11] In fact, the difficulty of this task helps to explain why the AV coalition concentrated on the presidential race and excluded congressional races. Furthermore, a look at the members of the AV coalition shows that the members all shared a progressive orientation toward politics. The environmental, abortion rights, and other groups all believed that the policies of the White House and the Republican-controlled Congress hurt their causes.

Ideological goals often do not have the strength to bring and keep groups together. The structure of AV clearly anticipated the need to offer other benefits to participating members. And while groups paid $50,000 to join the coalition, many concluded that they received substantial material benefits in return. Members of the coalition most frequently mentioned access to the voter file as a reason to participate. AV purchased voter registration lists and worked to create a voter file that would make contacting potential supporters more efficient and effective. The voter file also contained information from the membership lists compiled by the specific interest groups. Most groups regarded the list sharing as a significant enhancement to the voter file. Interest groups intensely value and protect their membership lists because such lists are their most precious resource. However, the additional information in the voter file made it possible for groups to divide up geographic regions and reduce overlap.[12]

Steve Rosenthal, the director of ACT, said that the same people getting lots of mail over and over again—sometimes on the same day—was one of the reasons it was so important to create AV.[13] In addition, the detailed information in the file meant that groups could tailor specific messages to voters. Groups doing a canvass could check the voter file to see if the individual had already been contacted by a particular group and what message had been received. This trend of tailoring messages to voters has been discussed elsewhere (Magleby, Monson, and Patterson 2005). All of the groups believed the voter list enhanced their ability to communicate effectively with potential voters.

It would be difficult to overstate the importance of the voter file. AV contained five separate interest groups that dealt with environmental issues alone (the League of Conservation Voters, the Sierra Club, Defenders of Wildlife, Clean Water Action, and Environment 2004). Only Environment 2004 did not plan to stay around after the election. These groups often eye each other warily because they compete for some of the same members and resources. As Cecile Richards shrewdly observed, "A lot of these groups sat on huge lists, an asset. If these assets could be merged into a coalition, it would provide a real opportunity to do more at the grass roots" and engage in "more retail-style politics." Eventually, all of the groups were able to set aside at least some of their competitive instincts to create a rich and diverse voter file to which they could all gain access. Cathy Duvall estimates that 80 percent of the groups in AV "ponied up membership lists." To be sure, some of the information in the list was restricted, and not all information contained in the group's membership list was appended to the larger voter file. Yet the creation of the voter file produced a significant benefit that all groups enjoyed. Some AV members told us that the quality of data and accuracy of the AV list was disappointing,[14] and even Richards admitted that there were "all kinds of glitches" with the database as a result of inexperience with a task of this magnitude.

The groups also gained the benefit of information provided by political polls. Smaller interest groups that could not afford to do their own polling particularly appreciated this benefit. Whenever any group commissioned a poll, it offered space on the poll to members of the AV coalition. ACT, a prominent member of AV, commissioned most of the polls. Thus, the groups all had access to polling data relating to the campaign and to the effectiveness of the messages they disseminated. Richards said that "America Votes exposed the participating groups to more information, allowing them to fine-tune their mail, phone, media, and rap at the door. All groups, for example, could watch focus groups online in D.C. as they were being conducted in Tampa."

The polling information was also widely shared among AV members through weekly briefings. This strategic information allowed all the groups to test and refine their messages and proved to be a tangible benefit that all groups consumed. For example, when pollster Cornell Belcher identified an effective way to discuss the Yucca Mountain nuclear waste issue in Nevada, a conference call was convened so that he could present the findings to all AV members active in Nevada.[15]

Richards summarized the importance of this shared polling in two ways. First, in the past there had been an excess of polling, and it was underutilized. Second, speaking of interest groups generally, she said each is loath to give up on its issue and tries to make the issue important in the election instead of trying to find out what is important to voters. With AV coordinating the polling and message delivery, this changed. She added, "For the first time, progressives were able get over this and meet voters where they were."

This interaction also meant that groups now had a weekly opportunity to reinforce friendships. AV facilitated the creation of the solidary benefit that the interest group literature says coalitions need to produce in order to ensure the longevity of the coalition. As Padrag Mehta, AV's deputy political director, observed, "The groups in the coalition have now started to meet independently and to form relationships they didn't have."[16] The opportunities to learn from cooperation and to develop working relationships are powerful incentives to create and maintain a coalition.

Many of the groups we interviewed cited specifically the benefits they derived from cooperation. Richards observed that "many of these groups had worked in a silo. There were a lot of inefficiencies." But when a group such as AV can bear many of the administrative costs for bringing groups together, the groups have an even stronger incentive to collaborate with each other, even if they have naturally been rivals. They can share costs and eliminate many of the inefficiencies that occur when groups in a similar policy area all try to contact the same voters. Mehta noted, "There is a need for a group like AV to coordinate. It helps small and large groups: large groups learn about innovations and can take a fresh look at what they do; small groups gain access to resources they wouldn't normally have." They all gain from the elimination of redundant or wasteful allocation of resources in the campaign environment.

Are You Big Enough and Strong Enough?

The coalition assembled under the AV banner included some of the best-known and most experienced members of the interest group pantheon. There is one question that remains: how effective can such a formidable coalition be in the electoral arena? Coalitions of interest groups have had some success in defeating ballot initiatives (Magleby 1984), but how would they do in candidate elections? Interest groups are not supposed to enjoy widespread success in the electoral arena, especially when compared to political parties. Some groups enjoyed success doing "issue advocacy" against and sometimes for candidates, but most of these same groups also invested heavily in parties (Magleby 2000, 2003; Magleby and Monson 2004). Political parties have the organizational and financial means to influence elections on a broad scale, and in the past interest groups assisted parties by funding them. Indeed, the differentiation that E. E. Schattschneider (1975) makes between an interest group and a party depends in large part on the scale of the electoral operation that each is able to maintain. Furthermore, political scientists often differentiate political parties from other types of political organizations by their goals. Parties try to elect individuals to office, and any other goal a party has depends on its ability to succeed in the electoral arena (Aldrich 1995; Schlesinger 1994).

Interest groups play a different role. While some groups do participate in the electoral arena and supplement what parties do, most others seek to influence policy by other means as well (Key 1967). Interest groups are constrained in their electoral activities by legal barriers and by their own organizational mission, and those constraints were strengthened by BCRA (Cigler 2002, 2006). For example, interest groups can advocate election or defeat of a candidate with broadcast advertising only if they use "federal" or "hard" dollars for that purpose. Hard dollars must be raised in smaller amounts, often making it difficult for the group to raise enough money to make a difference. Furthermore, the hard money contributions must be disclosed— something not all donors desire. Interest groups also seek to influence policy and have means at their disposal other than elections. It sometimes does not make sense to allocate precious resources to electoral activities when the prospects for success appear remote. Interest groups do have political action committees that donate directly to candidates, but this activity does not require the same organizational structure necessary to mount major campaigns to register, mobilize, or persuade voters.

These constraints make it very difficult for coalitions of interest groups of any size or consequence to form and influence the fortunes of candidates. Yet, this is precisely what the AV coalition seemed to accomplish. Table 8.2 contains a comparison of the campaign activities of the AV coalition and its subsidiaries to the campaign activities of the two major parties in five presidential battleground states: Florida, Ohio, Missouri, Iowa, and New Mexico. We included estimates of spending on radio and television as well as a count of the number of unique pieces of mail distributed by the AV coalition and the two major parties in these states.

The sheer size of the spending in the battleground states leaps off the table. Huge sums of money and resources were poured into these states by both parties and the AV coalition. The Republican and Democratic parties spent comparable amounts on television in all of the states except for Missouri (where the Republicans believed they had a decisive advantage and did not devote nearly as much as the Democratic Party; Jones et al. 2005). Surprisingly, the AV coalition, mostly through the Media Fund and MoveOn.org, spent nearly as much on television in these states as each of the major parties. While its spending did not keep pace with the major parties in Florida, Iowa, and New Mexico, it actually outspent the two major parties in Missouri and the pivotal state of Ohio. The media efforts of the major parties and AV in Ohio demonstrated that all of the key political organizations be-

Table 8.2 Broadcast Spending and Unique Advertisements of Political Parties and America Votes

Type of Communication	Florida	Iowa	Missouri	New Mexico	Ohio
Democratic Party					
TV	$22,602,573 (29)	$3,632,132 (24)	$2,882,188 (39)	$2,431,140 (34)	$17,330,089 (22)
Radio	$519,261 (8)	$18,988 (—)	$123,947 (—)	$153,048 (2)	$567,774 (3)
Nonbroadcast	64	23	38	43	207
Republican Party					
TV	$21,551,615 (17)	$2,630,716 (16)	$420,623 (26)	$2,482,669 (24)	$15,410,719 (11)
Radio	$427,157 (13)	$25,620 (—)	$63,444 (—)	$63,570 (1)	$147,248 (11)
Nonbroadcast	106	42	16	45	126
America Votes Coalition					
TV	$15,623,219 (9)	$2,568,393 (11)	$4,621,056 (21)	$1,654,086 (19)	$20,752,164 (23)
Radio	$534,148 (9)	$39,620 (—)	$126,647 (—)	$111,845 (1)	$174,210 (7)
Nonbroadcast	179	39	87	149	214
America Votes Subsidiaries*					
TV	$12,959 (—)	$117,561 (1)	$225,651 (3)	$44,417 (1)	$1,003,138 (7)
Radio	—	$14,620 (—)	$4,650 (—)	$20,987 (—)	$126,875 (3)
Nonbroadcast	15	7	36	—	17

Source: David B. Magleby, J. Quin Monson, and Kelly D. Patterson, "2004 Campaign Communications Database" (Center for the Study of Elections and Democracy: Brigham Young University, 2005). Television spending is compiled from Campaign Media Analysis Group data. Radio spending is compiled from ad-buy data collected at a sample of radio stations. For both broadcast media, the number of unique advertisements is shown in parentheses. Nonbroadcast communications include direct mail, e-mail, print ads, personal contacts, and telephone calls and were collected from a reconnaissance network of informants. See Magleby, Monson, and Patterson 2005 for a complete description of the methodology.

Note: In blank cells, a dash reflects only the absence of collected data and does not imply the organization was inactive in that medium.

* The AV subsidiaries are union affiliates of the union federation members, as well as state-level affiliates of national organizations. For this table, they include the Communications Workers of America, Stronger America Now, National Air Traffic Controllers, the American Federation of Government Employees, the United Automobile Workers Union, Working America, Women's Voices, Women's Voices, Women Vote, the Florida Education Association, and the Ohio Education Association.

lieved the fate of the election hinged on that state. The AV coalition also outspent the major parties in radio advertising in all of the battleground states except New Mexico and Ohio, where the Democratic Party spent more.

The AV coalition, true to its mission, saved its most impressive performance for the ground war. Table 8.2 also displays the number of nonbroadcast communications, including direct mail, e-mail, print advertising, personal contacts, and telephone calls. In all but one of the states, Iowa, the AV coalition distributed more nonbroadcast communications than either of the major parties. Only in Iowa did the Republican Party exceed the AV coalition in ground-war communications. In Florida, AV nonbroadcast communications reached 179 unique pieces; in Missouri it was 87; and in the critical state of Ohio, AV sponsored a whopping 214 ground-war communications. AV promised a massive effort in the ground war and delivered an effort that rivaled anything accomplished by the two major parties.

In addition, AV launched Election Action Days—two hundred separate events in sixteen battleground states (Skinner 2004). The series officially began in New Hampshire with the Fifty Million Women Count on September 18, symbolizing the fifty million women who were eligible to vote but did not cast ballots in the 2000 election. AV continued to organize volunteer mobilization events every weekend afterward leading up to Election Day (Skinner 2004).

In the final analysis, it was estimated that "AV organizations mobilized a total of over 100,000 paid and volunteer campaign workers for collaborative GOTV activities in 13 battleground states by sharing targeted lists, campaign materials and infrastructure" (Skinner 2004). Tens of thousands of people were canvassing, phone banking, poll watching, or driving voters to the polls. Many of those involved said they had never before worked for a political campaign.[17] By most measures, the effort of AV to contact, register, educate, and eventually mobilize voters compared favorably in scope and intensity with what the two major parties undertook. The early publicity given to ACT and AV reinforced a sense that the Democratic Party had "outsourced" its GOTV to these groups. Aided by record-setting fundraising, however, much of it late in the election cycle, the Democratic Party did undertake significant GOTV activity (Magleby, Monson, and Patterson 2005, 27).

Table 8.3 displays the range of groups and activities in the battleground state of Ohio. Communications were collected from sixteen of the AV coalition members, plus two AV subsidiary organizations. Following a pattern typical of other states, ACT dominated the nonbroadcast communications in Ohio, leading the way with twenty-seven unique pieces of mail. But the AV activity in Ohio was shared by a broad range of groups. As described earlier, AV would work with state organizations to develop common plans and goals in an effort to reach the widest possible audience (America Votes 2003). Though AV helped coordinate efforts, the coalition "explicitly sought to cap-

Table 8.3   Nonbroadcast Communications by America Votes Coalition Members in Ohio, 2004

	E-mail	Mail	Newspapers/ Magazine	Phone Calls
America Votes Coalition				
AFL-CIO	—	11	2	1
AFSCME	—	6	—	—
America Coming Together	32	27	—	5
America Votes	—	—	—	1
American Federation of Teachers	—	4	—	—
Human Rights Campaign	—	3	—	1
League of Conservation Voters	—	3	—	—
Media Fund	—	—	2	—
MoveOn.org	50	3	—	2
NARAL Pro-Choice America	12	2	—	—
National Education Association	—	11	1	1
NJDC Victory Fund	—	1	3	—
Planned Parenthood Action Fund	—	3	—	—
Sierra Club	—	19	1	3
21st Century Democrats	—	1	—	1
United Food and Commercial Workers International	—	2	—	—
America Votes Subsidiaries				
United Automobile Workers Union	—	6	2	—
Working America	—	9	—	—

Source: David B. Magleby, J. Quin Monson, and Kelly D. Patterson, "2004 Campaign Communications Database" (Center for the Study of Elections and Democracy: Brigham Young University, 2005). This is a subset of the data presented in Mockabee et al. 2005.

Notes: Data represent the number of unique or distinct pieces or ads by the group and do not represent a count of total items sent or made. This table is not intended to portray comprehensive organization activity within the sample races. All state and local chapters or affiliates have been combined with their national affiliate to better render the picture of the organization's activity. In blank cells, a dash reflects only the absence of collected data and does not imply the organization was inactive in that medium. See Magleby, Monson, and Patterson 2005 for a complete description of the methodology.

italize on the strengths of its members" (Magleby, Monson, and Patterson 2005, 29). It expected its coalition members to take the lead in mobilizing their own members. "When planning a large canvass, groups would share membership lists and volunteers to reduce overlap and to produce a more systematic effort. Regions and states would be divided up, depending on the strength of the AV members in those areas" (Magleby, Monson, and Patterson 2005, 29).

While the AV coalition amassed and expended resources on par with the major parties in the presidential race, it did not participate on the same scale in congressional races outside the battleground states. By contrast, the major parties participated actively not only in the presidential campaign but also in House and Senate races across the United States. In several House races alone, the National Republican Congressional Committee and the Democratic Congressional Campaign Committee spent hundreds of thousands of dollars to persuade individuals to vote for their candidates. The difference in the scale of activity for the AV coalition and the political parties is important. Parties were involved on all levels, including state and federal elections. AV was a force only in the presidential election. Political parties enjoy a unique status as an organization because of their ability to influence elections on such a broad scale (Schattschneider 1975). AV up until now has not demonstrated the same breadth of commitment.

It is unclear whether the funds and incentives to maintain this coalition even at the presidential level will persist in future election cycles. As of this writing, the signals are mixed. ACT, AV's largest member, scaled back most operations in August 2005 to evaluate its future.[18] Yet during the first six months of 2005, ACT's nonfederal account raised $4,433,907 and spent $6,623,303. Meanwhile, over the same period, AV raised $330,000 and spent $563,233, taking in contributions from EMILY's List, the League of Conservation Voters, the Service Employees International Union, the Sierra Club, and the Media Fund. Whether AV and company will be back for another election cycle or not, one commentator recently referred to this type of activity as "the first serious challenge to the industrial age structure of the modern political party. . . . [George] Soros and [Peter] Lewis showed Democrats, and more than a few Republicans, that there was a new way of doing business, and it didn't require fealty to an inefficient party apparatus" (Bai 2005, 12).

Conclusion: Incentives Now and in the Future

We began this essay by discussing the conditions that led to the creation of the America Votes coalition. Groups had incentives to create a coalition to campaign in the 2004 presidential election. First, the groups shared an antipathy toward the policies of the Bush administration. Second, AV and some of its members also received an infusion of cash from wealthy donors, which permitted them to bear the costs of coordinating the activities of the coalition's members. Furthermore, the changes in the campaign finance law also helped. As one staff member said, "AV found a hole and exploited it."[19] In other words, BCRA, as interpreted by the Federal Election Commission, allowed the groups to engage in this sort of activity.

Once the coalition formed, it continued to provide incentives to members. Members received access to polls, advice on strategic information, and the opportunity to interact with other groups. As the literature on coalition formation predicted, groups specialized in the particular tasks to which their organizations were best suited.[20] The high degree of cooperation and specialization in the AV coalition propelled it to amass and distribute campaign resources in amounts comparable to what political parties do.

However, it is not clear whether conditions will permit a coalition of this size and breadth to persist in its efforts to participate effectively in campaign activities. When President Bush is no longer in office, much of the antipathy may dissipate. Some members of the coalition wanted it to be less partisan, while others hoped the coalition could become even more partisan.[21] The inclinations and abilities of some groups may create tensions in the coalition. Furthermore, a major unanswered question is whether the individuals who initially funded the coalition and gave it several million dollars will do so in the future. Despite the amount of work accomplished by AV, Bush still won reelection.

In the future, coalition members may choose to invest their resources in more traditional forms of interest group activity, or they may move back toward congressional elections where they can pick and choose the races in which they want to make a difference. This ability to select races only highlights the differences between an interest group and a political party. The major parties seek to influence a much larger number of races. Many members of the AV coalition have expressed dissatisfaction with the Democratic Party, but they may realize that it makes little sense to create an organization that in some ways parallels what that party does. It is not yet clear whether the donors who funded AV and its member organizations in 2004 will continue to fund 527s outside the party apparatus or will move to remake the Democratic Party (Bai 2004b). Whatever happens to AV in the future, the organization overcame several hurdles in the 2004 election cycle to create a coalition that exhibited many of the properties of a political party.

Notes

This research is part of a larger project supported by a grant from the Pew Charitable Trusts. We gratefully acknowledge the research assistance of Betsey Escandon, Kristina Gale, Betsey Gimbel Hawkins, Richard Hawkins, Yale Layton, Emily McClintock, John Baxter Oliphant, Nisha Riggs, Paul Russell, and Brandon Wilson.

1. Glen Justice and Jim Rutenberg, "Advocacy Groups and Campaigns: An Uneasy Shuttle," *New York Times*, September 8, 2004. There are several notable examples of professional staff moving between the Democratic Party and AV or its member organizations reported by Justice and Rutenberg. Jim Jordan was John Kerry's campaign manager and then handled communications for AV. Bill Knapp was a media adviser for Kerry and later did advertising work for the Media Fund. Harold Ickes, who founded the Media Fund and worked with ACT, was also a member of the executive committee of the Democratic National Committee. Pollster Stan Greenberg served as an informal adviser to the Kerry campaign and later did polling for ACT, the Media Fund, and MoveOn.org. Zack Exley advised MoveOn.org on its Internet operations and later ran the Kerry campaign website. Attorney Bob Bauer advised the Kerry campaign and then worked for ACT.

Cathy Duvall, AV's national field director, estimated that three-quarters of the AV staff had worked on failed presidential campaigns, including her work earlier in the cycle for Richard Gephardt (interview by Kelly Patterson and Quin Monson, Washington, D.C., August 18, 2004).

2. Curiously, some groups appear to have paid the $50,000 membership fee but were not listed as AV members. An examination of the 8,872 forms filed by AV with the IRS shows that this list includes American Family Voices and Stronger America Now.

3. This figure only includes the 527 activity of AV coalition members as compiled by the Center for Public Integrity. Because the figure does not include the spending by PACs or by 501(c) members of the AV coalition, the actual total election-related spending by AV members is much higher than this.

4. Thomas Edsall, "Money, Votes Pursed for Democrats," *Washington Post*, December 7, 2003.

5. Interview of Linda Lipson, legislative liaison, Association of Trial Lawyers of America, by David Magleby and Betsey Gimbel, Washington, D.C., June 3, 2004.

6. Dale Russakoff, "Democracy-to-Go," *Washington Post*, October 24, 2004.

7. During the 2004 election cycle, we interviewed thirty-five individuals who worked for AV coalition members or consulted with them on election strategy. Our interviews included AV staff as well as all of the major coalition members, including ACT, the Media Fund, the League of Conservation Voters, the AFL-CIO, the Service Employees International Union, and MoveOn.org. We also monitored the activities of AV members in battleground states. The interviews and the campaign data help to explain why organizations joined the coalition and allow us to gauge the extent to which the organizations specialized in particular campaign activities.

8. Major donors and consultants were brought together for a meeting by George Soros in July 2003, at which Soros first pledged substantial financing to ACT and other AV members (interview of Michael Vachon, political director for George Soros, by David Magleby and Kristina Gale, Washington, D.C., November 8, 2004).

9. At one point Soros said, "I have come to the conclusion that the greatest contribution I can make to the values that I hold would be to contribute to the defeat of George W. Bush" (Leslie Wayne, "And for His Next Feat, a Billionaire Sets Sights on Bush," *New York Times*, May 31, 2004). Earlier he had said that defeating President Bush was "the central focus of my life" (Laura Blumenfeld, "Soros's Deep Pockets vs. Bush," *Washington Post*, November 11, 2003). In the end, Soros contributed $23.7 million to various 527s and spent $2.3 million on independent expenditures (interview of Vachon, November 8, 2004).

10. Interview of Jim Jordan by Kelly Patterson and Betsey Gimbel, Washington, D.C., July 6, 2004.

11. Interview of Harold Ickes by David Magleby and Betsey Gimbel, Washington, D.C., September 16, 2004.

12. Telephone interview of Cecile Richards by David Magleby, Kelly Patterson, and Quin Monson, December 28, 2004.

13. Interview of Steve Rosenthal by David Magleby and Betsey Gimbel, Washington, D.C., December 17, 2004.

14. Telephone interview of Wes Boyd, cofounder and president MoveOn.org, by Kelly Patterson, Quin Monson, Kristina Gale, and Richard Hawkins, December 14, 2004; interview of Mark Longabaugh, vice president of political affairs, League of Conservation Voters, by David Magleby and Betsey Gimbel, Washington, D.C., November 10, 2004.

15. Interview of Richards, December 28, 2004.

16. Interview of Padrag Mehta by Kelly Patterson, Washington, D.C., June 7, 2004.

17. Russakoff, "Democracy-to-Go."

18. Glen Justice, "Democratic Fund-Raiser Unit Is Curtailing Most Operations," *New York Times*, August 4, 2005.

19. Interview of Mehta, June 7, 2004.

20. When no group could perform a certain function, a group would assume that task. For example, the New Democrat Network agreed to take on the task of advertising to Hispanic voters (interview of Simon Rosenberg, director, New Democratic Network, by David Magleby, Betsey Gimbel, and Kelly Patterson, Washington D.C., December 15, 2004).

21. While legal hurdles do not permit the group to become more partisan, some members of the coalition have what is called "MCFL status," which would allow them to spend some forms of soft money when other 527s cannot. MCFL stands for Massachusetts Citizen's for Life. In 1986, the U.S. Supreme Court heard the case of *Federal Election Commission (FEC) v. Massachusetts Citizen's for Life, Inc.* (479 U.S. 238). As a result of the Court's ruling, groups with MCFL status are allowed to accept unlimited individual contributions and spend them during the sixty-day period before a general election when BCRA bans other communications using soft money. Groups with MCFL status are nonprofit, nonstock corporations formed with the intent to advocate or promote specific issues. MCFL groups are allowed to use treasury funds in connection with any public office election as long as they do not accept money from any corporation for such purposes. Four organizations are known to have MCFL status: Planned Parenthood, NARAL Pro-Choice America, the League of Conservation Voters, and Defenders of Wildlife.

9

Deaniacs and Democrats

Howard Dean's Campaign Activists

Scott Keeter, Cary Funk, and Courtney Kennedy

Howard Dean, a physician and four-term governor of Vermont, was an improbable candidate for president of the United States. He was from a small state with a reputation for political eccentricity and had no national political experience. Nevertheless, he mounted an impressive campaign for the nomination of the Democratic Party, leading the field in the preelection polls and up until the Iowa caucuses. Given the polarization of the electorate and the "anybody but Bush" attitude of many Democrats, Dean might well have been competitive in November. Indeed, few would have predicted after his demise as a presidential candidate that he would become the party's national chairman in 2005.

Dean not only became a serious national figure, but his campaign left a strong imprint on the political world. It assembled a network of more than a half-million active supporters and contributors, raised in excess of $20 million in mostly small donations online, and demonstrated the power of the Internet as a networking and mobilizing tool in politics. Thus, one important political legacy of Dean's candidacy is that it established a model for a twenty-first-century grassroots campaign. In his memoir of the nomination contest, former Dean campaign manager Joe Trippi said of the populist Internet supporters, "The only reason the Dean campaign even got close enough that it mattered was because of those people" (2004, 179). Despite their importance, relatively little is known about the campaign foot soldiers—the so-called Deaniacs—who donated time, money, and other resources in hopes of seeing Dean win the nomination.

In this chapter, we present a multidimensional profile of the campaign activists nationwide who helped propel Dean to such improbable prominence. We begin by examining the activists' demographic characteristics and political orientation, as well as their self-reported motivations for supporting Dean's candidacy. We then consider where Dean activists fit within the larger Democratic Party. Finally, we assess the activists' vision for the future direction of the party and its role, relative to other political organizations, in advancing progressive causes.

This analysis is based on data from a unique survey conducted by the Pew Research Center with a random sample of 11,568 activists drawn from the online database of those who had contributed money or otherwise worked on behalf of Governor Dean.[1] The survey was conducted in two waves: one before the election (September 13–October 12) and a second afterward (November 18–December 14). Further details about the survey are provided in an appendix at the end of this chapter.[2]

Who Are the Dean Activists? Who Came and Why?

The Pew study corroborates the view that the Internet played a critical role in the Dean campaign. Fundamentally, however, Dean's candidacy was made viable not by the technology but rather by the issue-driven supporters who *used* the technology to create a movement of political and cultural significance. In that spirit, this section focuses on the foot soldiers of the Dean campaign. We explore who these activists were, how they viewed the political landscape, and what motivated them to mount one of the most surprising movements in recent political history.

Activism and Political Junkies

In many respects, Dean activists resembled other political activists on the Left and Right. They were more interested and engaged in politics, more ideological, and better educated than the average citizen or their fellow partisans. As befits a population heavily involved in politics, Dean activists were heavy news consumers and relied on a wide array of sources—the Web, newspapers, radio, and, to a lesser extent, television. Nearly as many said they regularly get as much news from the network and cable news websites as from the news broadcasts themselves. And 58 percent said they regularly listen to National Public Radio, compared with just 16 percent of the general public.

Moreover, their activism extended beyond just the Dean campaign (see table 9.1). Dean activists were heavily involved in other political and social causes. Nearly eight in ten (77 percent) had signed petitions for something other than the Dean campaign. About half (51 percent) had boycotted a product or company. A similar number, 48 percent, had participated in a protest, demonstration, or rally for an unrelated cause. This contrasts starkly with the general population in 2004, of which just 4 percent had participated in a protest or demonstration in the past year on a national or local issue (American National Election Studies 2004).

Table 9.1   They Really Were Activists

Dean activists who performed the following actions:

During the primaries

Gave money to any candidate	85%
Attended a Dean campaign event	47
Contributed to online chats/blogs	33

During general election campaign

Voted in November 2004	99%
Gave money to the Kerry campaign	66
Sent campaign e-mails for Kerry	54
Attended a Kerry campaign event	40

Source: Pew Research Center survey.

Drawn by the Issues and the Campaign

Dean's supporters were attracted to his campaign by issues (see table 9.2). This fact is true of most activist campaigners. In the case of Dean's followers, a majority (66 percent) cited the war in Iraq as one of the two most important issues. But two other issues that had defined Dean's time as governor of Vermont also resonated with his supporters: health care (34 percent) and fiscal responsibility (24 percent). In addition, the economy and jobs (19 percent), the environment (11 percent), and gay and lesbian rights (9 percent) were also mentioned by significant numbers of supporters.

The transcendent quality of issues is illustrated by the remarkable similarity of the responses from supporters across the demographic spectrum.

Table 9.2   Most Important Issue in Decision to Support Dean

		Age Group		
	All	*15–29*	*30–49*	*50+*
War in Iraq	66%	57%	64%	71%
Health care	34	35	31	35
Fiscal responsibility	24	21	26	24
Economy/jobs	19	17	20	20
Environment	11	11	12	10
Gay/lesbian rights	9	21	10	4
Education	5	11	5	3
Terrorism	4	4	4	5
Abortion	4	7	4	2
International trade	1	2	—	1
Other	13	8	13	14

Source: Pew Research Center survey.
Note: Respondents could select up to two issues.

For example, despite some differences in political attitudes between age groups, younger and older Dean supporters were motivated by a similar set of issues—with the notable exception that gay and lesbian rights were cited by fully one-fifth of the youngest supporters but far fewer of the older Deaniacs. Predictable differences appear in certain subgroups: for example, the least affluent were somewhat more likely to cite the economy and jobs, and younger women were much more likely to cite abortion rights.

While many Dean activists were seasoned veterans of earlier electoral battles, the Dean campaign attracted a sizable number of political newcomers (see table 9.3). More than four in ten Dean activists (42 percent)—and 66 percent of those under age 30—said this was their first presidential campaign. Of the majority with some previous campaign experience, most (36 percent of the total) said they were more involved in the Dean campaign than in prior races, compared with 21 percent who were about as involved or less involved than in the past.

Demographic Distinctiveness

Dean activists were a distinctive group within their own party (see table 9.4). Campaign supporters were equally likely to be men or women. As a group, they were much more racially homogenous than the general public or people who identify with the Democratic Party. More than nine in ten Dean activists (92 percent) were white and just 1 percent were African American (2 percent were Asian and 4 percent described themselves as being of another race or multiracial). By comparison, the public is 79 percent white, as are about two-thirds of national Democrats (68 percent). More than one in five Democrats (22 percent) are African Americans.

Dean activists tended to be not only significantly better educated but also

Table 9.3   Count Me In

	All	15–29	30–49	50+
		Age Group		
Sought out campaign involvement on their own	79%	78%	72%	77%
Campaign experience				
First presidential campaign	42	66%	48%	28%
Not first campaign	57	34	51	71
More active in this one	36	23	32	44
Less active	5	3	5	6
Same	16	8	14	21
No response	1	—	1	1

Source: Pew Research Center survey.

Table 9.4   Dean Activists: White, Well-Educated, Wealthy

	Dean activists	All Dems	General public	Liberals
Race				
White	92%	68%	79%	83%
Black	1	22	11	6
Other/no answer	7	10	10	11
Income				
$75,000+	45%	18%	21%	41%
$50,000–74,999	20	13	15	15
$20,000–49,999	26	35	34	32
<$20,000	6	22	17	12
Age				
Under 30	18%	18%	21%	28%
30–44	26	28	30	29
45–64	42	33	32	32
65+	14	20	16	10
Education				
College grad	79%	25%	26%	49%
Some college	17	22	24	26
HS grad or less	4	53	50	25
Religion				
Protestant	21%	53%	55%	36%
Catholic	13	27	24	23
Jewish	7	3	2	8
Other	21	5	6	11
No religion	38	10	11	22
Sexuality				
Gay, lesbian, or bisexual	12%	6%	4%	NA

Sources: Dean activist figures from Pew Research Center survey of 11,568 Dean activists conducted September–December 2004; figures for Democrats from Pew surveys conducted January 2004–February 2005; general public figures, except religion and sexuality, from U.S. Census Bureau *Annual Social and Economic Supplement*, March 2003, with religious affiliation data from Pew surveys fielded January 2004–February 2005; figures for Liberals (n = 359) based on Pew Research Center 2005 Typology Study; sexuality data for general public from NEP exit poll November 3, 2004. DK/Refused category was omitted, therefore data does not add up to one hundred.

wealthier than other Democrats. Nearly a third of Dean activists (29 percent) reported a family income of more than $100,000 per year, nearly triple the proportion who fall into this bracket among all Democrats (10 percent). An overwhelming majority of the Deaniacs were college graduates (79 percent), and 41 percent had earned a graduate or professional degree. Just a quarter of all Democrats and 26 percent of the general public are college graduates.

Surprisingly, the age profile of Dean activists is similar to that of other Democrats and the public. While news coverage of the Dean campaign focused on his youthful support, the Dean activists were not especially young; just 6 percent were under 23 and 12 percent were 23–29, compared with 8 percent and 10 percent among Democrats nationally.

Dean activists were much more secular than the party as a whole. A relatively large proportion of Dean activists (38 percent) had no formal religious affiliation. Far fewer Democrats (10 percent) and members of the public (11 percent) express no religious preference. Only about a third of Dean activists were affiliated with either the Catholic or Protestant religious traditions (34 percent). One in five Dean activists (21 percent) identified themselves as Unitarians, nondenominational Christians, Buddhists, Muslims, or another religion. Moreover, just 24 percent of Dean activists described themselves as a "religious person." Far more (68 percent), however, said they think of themselves as a "spiritual person."

Where Do Dean Activists Fit in the Democratic Party?

Howard Dean once quipped that he represented the "Democratic wing of the Democratic Party." Dean's followers are more precisely described as part of the liberal wing of the Democratic Party. Across a range of issues— especially military and national security matters, social and cultural issues, and the role of government in solving societal problems—the Dean activists hold much more liberal positions than does the average Democrat in the general public. Their liberalism stands out even when compared with delegates to the 2004 Democratic convention, who themselves were significantly more liberal than rank-and-file Democrats (see the *New York Times/CBS* delegate survey). Roughly eight in ten Dean activists (82 percent) described themselves ideologically as liberal, compared with 41 percent of the convention delegates and 27 percent of national Democrats.

When viewed from another angle, however, the liberalism of the Dean activists doesn't appear to be that different from the subset of liberals within the Democratic Party. As such, they do not constitute a new faction within the party, but rather a more vigorous and high-profile expression of an existing faction.

To better understand how Dean's campaign supporters fit within the Democratic Party, we compared them to a group classified as "Liberals" in the Pew Research Center 2005 Typology Study.[3] The liberal classification is not simply ideological self-identification but is based on a cluster analysis of values across a wide range of topics. From a total of nine typology groups in the general public, three were composed primarily of Democrats: Liberals, Conservative Democrats, and Disadvantaged Democrats. Liberals constitute a small plurality of the Democratic electoral base. Among all who identify themselves as Democrats or Democratic-leaning independents, 34 percent are classified as Liberals, 30 percent as Conservative Democrats, and 20 percent as Disadvantaged Democrats; the remainder are classified in other typology groups.

The typology's Liberals are similar demographically to Dean activists; both groups are largely white, are highly educated, and earn high incomes relative to the general public. Liberals also hold remarkably similar positions to Dean activists on a range of social and cultural issues. Both groups show strong support for gay marriage and acceptance of homosexuality in society, support for government assistance to the poor and environmental protection, and a positive view of immigrants in U.S. society.

This is not to say that the two groups are perfect matches. Dean activists are more positive than Liberals about government effectiveness but are more pessimistic about the degree to which elected officials care about their views. And, while both Deaniacs and Liberals are nearly unanimous in their belief that using military force in Iraq was the wrong decision and in their belief that diplomacy is the best way to ensure peace in the world, other views on military policy are less in sync. Deaniacs are less likely than Liberals to say that the preemptive use of military force is sometimes justified. Views about the how well the war in Iraq is going and what to do with the troops from the time of the survey forward also showed some differences between groups, although some of this may be due to real differences in Iraqi war developments and the different timing of the surveys.

Thus, the Dean activists were clearly drawn primarily from the liberal wing of the Democratic Party. Some version of the Liberal Democratic group has been found in every Pew typology study conducted since 1987. Thus, the Dean activists represent a new manifestation of a long-standing segment of the Democratic Party's base. But Deaniacs were to some degree a unique group because of the key role the Iraq war played in their motivation to participate in the campaign.

How Liberal Are They? Unified Opposition to the War in Iraq

Nearly all Dean activists believe that the decision to use military force in Iraq was wrong (see table 9.5). And there are far fewer hawks among the Dean activists than among Democrats nationally. Nearly all Dean activists (96 percent) believed that diplomacy, rather than military strength, is the best way to ensure peace. Only about a fifth of the Dean activists (19 percent) said military force is often or sometimes justified against countries that may seriously threaten the United States but have not yet attacked, while 21 percent would entirely rule out such preemptive military action. In comparison, both Liberals and Democrats in general are more likely to say that preemptive force is at least sometimes justified (45 percent of all Democrats say this, as do 33 percent of Liberals).

Table 9.5   Views on the Use of Force

	Dean activists	All Dems	General public	Liberals
War in Iraq				
Right decision	1%	21%	49%	11%
Wrong decision	99	71	44	87
No answer/Don't know	—	8	9	2
What is the best way to ensure peace?				
Military strength	3%	15%	30%	6%
Diplomacy	96	76	55	88
No answer/Don't know	1	9	15	6
Is preemptive force justified?				
Often	1%	9%	14%	1%
Sometimes	18	36	46	32
Rarely	60	28	21	44
Never	21	21	14	23
No answer/Don't know	—	6	5	—

Sources: Dean activist figures from Pew Research Center survey of 11,568 Dean activists conducted September–December 2004; figures for Democrats (n = 641) from Pew Research Center survey taken December 2004; figures for Liberals (n = 359) based on Pew Research Center 2005 Typology Study; general public (n = 2000).

The activists were more divided on the question of what to do in Iraq at the time of the survey. Compared with national Democrats, the Dean supporters in September 2004 were actually more supportive of keeping troops in Iraq until the situation stabilized (44 percent said this, compared with 33 percent of Democrats in an August 2004 poll).

Younger and older Dean activists saw eye-to-eye on many issues: the government's efficacy, keeping churches out of politics, the importance of racial discrimination as a reason for racial inequality, the importance of the social safety net for the poor, the value of immigrants, and especially the view that corporations make too much profit. On military matters, though, the older activists who came of age in the 1960s were significantly less supportive of keeping troops in Iraq (34 percent vs. 61 percent among the younger group) and less likely to say that the use of preemptive military force is sometimes justifiable (13 percent vs. 31 percent).

Libertarian Sentiment, at Least on Social Issues

On social issues, Dean activists stood out for their strong support for gay marriage. They shared a near-universal belief (96 percent to 4 percent) that homosexuality should be accepted, rather than discouraged, by society (see table 9.6). In contrast, support for gay marriage was far less common among

Table 9.6 Social and Cultural Issues

	Dean activists	All Democrats	Liberals
Books with "dangerous ideas" ...			
Should be permitted in public school libraries	98%	54%	85%
Should be banned from public school libraries	1	41	13
No answer/Don't know	1	5	2
Homosexuality should be ...			
Accepted by society	96%	58%	92%
Discouraged by society	4	36	5
No answer/Don't know	0	6	3
Immigrants today ...			
Strengthen the U.S. because of hard work and talents	87%	47%	76%
Are a burden because they take jobs, housing, health care	12	43	15
No answer/Don't know	1	10	9
Churches should ...			
Keep out of political issues	69%	45%	NA
Express views on politics	30	51	NA
No answer/Don't know	1	4	NA

Sources: Dean activist figures from Pew Research Center survey of 11,568 Dean activists conducted September–December 2004; figures for Democrats from a Pew survey conducted in December 2004 (n = 641) except churches issue from a Pew survey conducted in August 2004 (n = 237); figures for Liberals (n = 359) based on Pew Research Center 2005 Typology Study.

Democrats in the general public (43 percent favor and half oppose), and a majority of black Democrats (59 percent) believe that homosexuality should be discouraged. Liberals in the Pew Typology Study, however, were similarly lopsided in their support for gay marriage; eight in ten Liberals favored gay marriage, while just 15 percent opposed it.

While there was a majority among Dean activists in support of legalizing gay marriage, those under age 30 did so more strongly; 71 percent strongly favored legalizing gay marriage, compared with 46 percent among those 50 and older. Younger activists also were much more apt to mention gay and lesbian issues as a key reason they joined the campaign (21 percent vs. 4 percent; see table 9.2). Older Dean activists were also less likely to say homosexuality should be accepted by society, though most do accept it.

On other social issues, Deaniacs were just as liberal. They were nearly unanimous in their opposition to censoring "dangerous" books from school libraries. Fully 98 percent of Dean activists said public school libraries should be able to carry any books they want; just 1 percent said that public school libraries should ban books that "contain dangerous ideas." The idea of banning such books draws much more support among all Democrats (41 percent).

Most Dean activists (69 percent) said that churches should keep out of day-to-day social and political matters, but a sizable minority (30 percent), including nearly a quarter (24 percent) of those with no religious affiliation, said churches should weigh in on the issues of the day. The difference between the activists and other Democrats is narrower on this question than on some other social issues.

Nearly three-quarters (74 percent) of Dean activists believed that racial discrimination is the main reason many blacks can't get ahead, but a majority (52 percent) of Democrats nationally say that blacks are "mostly responsible for their own condition." A similar chasm separates the opinions of Dean activists and national Democrats on immigration. Fully 87 percent of activists said immigrants are strengthening the country, while national Democrats are split: 43 percent consider immigrants a burden, while 47 percent think immigrants strengthen the country.

Pro-Government Solutions

Compared with rank-and-file Democrats, Dean activists are more supportive of government solutions to important national problems (see table 9.7). While three-quarters of Dean activists felt that the government often does a better job than people give it credit for, nearly half of Democrats nationally (47 percent) disagree, instead believing that government is almost

Table 9.7   Views on Government

	Dean activists	*All Democrats*	*Liberals*
Government . . .			
Is almost always wasteful and inefficient	25%	47%	45%
Often does a better job than people give it credit for	75	42	48
No answer/Don't know	6	11	7
Stricter environmental regulations . . .			
Are worth the costs	96%	NA	NA
Cost too many jobs and hurt the economy	3	NA	NA
No answer/Don't know	1	NA	NA
Poor people . . .			
Have it easy because of government benefits	5%	24%	11%
Have hard lives because benefits don't go far enough	93	64	80
No answer/Don't know	2	12	9

Sources: Dean activist figures from Pew Research Center survey of 11,568 Dean activists conducted September–December 2004; figures for Democrats (n = 641) from a Pew survey conducted in December 2004; figures for Liberals (n = 359) based on Pew Research Center 2005 Typology Study.

always wasteful and inefficient. Liberals tilt just slightly toward the more positive view of government by 48 percent to 45 percent.

Fully 96 percent of activists want the government to step in to protect the environment even if it hurts business profits and results in the loss of some jobs. With respect to poverty, an overwhelming proportion of Dean activists (93 percent) think government benefits do not go far enough to help poor people live decently. Liberals are similarly inclined to think government benefits don't go far enough to help the poor (80 percent say this) but a more modest majority (64 percent) of Democrats agree.

Where Would Dean Activists Take the Democrats? Leftward Ho!

One crucial test of the Deaniacs' relevance to the future of Democratic politics came in the November 2004 presidential election. While they found in Howard Dean a Democratic candidate they trusted, there was no guarantee that Dean supporters would shift their allegiance to John Kerry in the general election. Kerry was, after all, Dean's strongest rival throughout the run-up to the Democratic primaries and caucuses. Given the Dean activists' opposition to the war, Kerry's vote to authorize the use of military force in Iraq was especially problematic.

Despite this, Dean's activist supporters overwhelmingly—if somewhat unethusiastically—supported Kerry (see table 9.8). Throughout the general election campaign, most Democratic voters consistently characterized their vote as being against George W. Bush rather than for Kerry. This also was the case among Dean activists—69 percent said their vote was against Bush, compared with just 30 percent who said it was a vote for Kerry.

Given their strong liberal tendencies, it is perhaps surprising that only 1 percent of Dean activists threw their support behind Ralph Nader, the out-

Table 9.8   From Dean to Kerry, Reluctantly

	Dean activists	*Democratic voters*
Presidential vote		
For Kerry	97%	89%*
For Bush	—	11
For Nader	1	0
Other/Didn't vote	2	—
Among Kerry voters, vote was . . .		
A vote for Kerry	30%	41%**
A vote against Bush	69	53
No answer/Don't know	1	6

* NEP exit poll; **Pew Research Center Survey Oct. 1–3, 2004; ***Oct. 15–19

spoken independent candidate and longtime crusader for progressive causes. The activists' deeply held political values, such as opposition to the Iraq war, support for social justice, and antipathy toward corporate interests, would seem more at home in the platform articulated by Nader than the Kerry campaign. Based on issues alone, Nader seemed the natural candidate to rekindle the activists' spirits in the aftermath of Dean's defeat in the Democratic primaries.

Nevertheless, fully two-thirds of Dean activists expressed an unfavorable opinion of Nader, with a sizable proportion (30 percent) saying their opinion of him was *very* unfavorable—perhaps because they remembered Nader's impact in the 2000 election, where he captured far more votes in Florida than the margin of Bush's victory there.

Dissatisfaction with Democratic Leadership

While the activists stuck by the Democratic Party's presidential nominee, they were critical of the party in a number of respects. Dean activists overwhelmingly faulted Democratic leaders for going too easy on the president. More than five out of six (86 percent) said the party was not critical enough of President Bush and his policies. Just 12 percent said Democratic leaders had criticized Bush the right amount. With respect to the Iraq, relatively few activists (19 percent) said that Democratic leaders voted for the war because the leaders thought it was the right thing to do. Instead, the vast majority of activists (80 percent) believed Democratic leaders voted for the war out of reluctance to stand up and oppose Bush.

Most Dean activists did not think the party had done well in advocating for its traditional constituencies or for liberal positions in 2004. Just 19 percent rated the party's efforts in promoting progressive/liberal positions as good or excellent; most believed the party had done only a fair (45 percent) or poor (36 percent) job in this area. Dean activists also voiced disappointment with the party's efforts as an advocate for traditional Democratic positions. Fewer than a quarter of Dean activists (21 percent) said the party had done an excellent or good job of standing up for such things as protecting the interest of minorities, helping the poor and needy, and representing working people.

Critical assessments of the Democratic Party put the Dean activists in step with liberal Democrats across the nation. Pew's political typology shows that Liberals are more negative than other subsets of Democratic or Democratic-leaning clusters when evaluating the party. Like Dean activists, less than one-quarter (23 percent) of Liberals said party performance in this area had been excellent or good. Democrats nationally were a bit more favorable toward the party as of March 2005, though not overwhelmingly so. In that survey, 33 percent of Democrats nationwide gave the party excellent or good marks; that figure is down significantly since from before the election (49 percent in July 2004).

The Future of the Democratic Party

Given their numbers, their highly visible role in the 2004 campaign, and their generally strong commitment to political activity, the attitudes of Dean activists toward the Democratic Party will help shape the party's future direction. The Dean activists are highly critical of the Democratic Party in a number of areas. But they are not ready to give up on it—rather, they want it to reflect to a much greater degree their own liberal and progressive positions (see table 9.9).

Despite the Democrats' lack of bottom-line success in the last three elections (2004, 2002, and 2000), only a small fraction of activists thought the Democratic Party should die off and be replaced by an entirely new political party. But maintaining the status quo was also seen as unacceptable; just 8 percent of Dean activists wanted the party to remain more or less the same. The Dean activists expressed the most support (67 percent) for the Democratic Party responding, instead, by adopting more liberal or progressive positions.

These attitudes contrast sharply with the opinions of both Democratic officials and rank-and-file Democrats. A Gallup poll of Democratic National Committee members in February 2005 showed that, by more than two to one (52 percent to 23 percent), they want the party to become more moderate rather than more liberal. That view is shared by Democrats nationally; in a January 2005 survey, Gallup found that 59 percent of Democrats wanted the party to take a more moderate course.

Extraparty Advocacy for Progressive Issues

While Deaniacs want the Democratic Party to move to the left, they do not completely trust the party to take the lead in promoting their views. Only 38 percent identified the Democratic Party as the best vehicle to advance

Table 9.9   Dean Activists Favor Shift to the Left

Dean activists' preference for the future of the Democratic Party:	
Reflect more progressive/liberal positions	67%
Reflect more centrist positions	13
Die off and be replaced by new party	11
Remain the same	8
No answer	1

Source: Pew Research Center survey.

progressive and liberal causes. Nearly as many (36 percent) cited privately funded advocacy groups, the so-called 527s, and 13 percent thought a new political party would be most effective.

Nonetheless, 527s were not universally loved. A majority of Dean activists (55 percent) approved of the role 527s have played in elections, but 41 percent disapproved. According to Byron York, organizations such as 527s that arose after the adoption of new campaign finance rules "actually *increased* the influence of big money in politics. By giving directly to 'independent' groups rather than to the party itself, big-ticket donors could influence campaign strategy and tactics more directly than they ever had previously" (2005, 7).

Still, a clear majority of Deaniacs (72 percent) think the major liberal philanthropists such as George Soros, Peter Lewis, and Andy Rappaport are helping rather than hurting progressive and liberal causes (see table 9.10). Financially, at least, the philanthropists have been helpful. Federal campaign finance records from 2004 show that the largest portion of funding for pro-Democratic 527s came from just five people,[4] and their collective contribution surpassed the $75 million in federal funds that John Kerry received to run his postconvention campaign (York 2005).

Conclusion

Howard Dean's candidacy for the 2004 Democratic presidential nomination serves as a reminder that the right mix of candidate, issues, and effort can mobilize grassroots supporters. The Dean campaign succeeded beyond its own hopes and expectations in mobilizing about half of a million people to take action in support of the campaign; this was a clear grassroots success, with many supporters getting involved in presidential campaigns for the first time. In contrast to some news media depictions of a campaign dominated

Table 9.10   Dean Activists' Views on the Impact of Liberal Philanthropists

Dean activists' views of the impact of liberal philanthropists such as George Soros, Peter Lewis, and Andy Rappaport on:

	Progressive or Liberal Causes	Democratic Party	U.S. Political System
Mostly helping	72%	57%	51%
Mostly hurting	6	10	14
No impact	16	26	28
No answer	6	7	7

Source: Pew Research Center survey.

by college-age firebrands, the majority of Dean's campaign supporters were well over 30. They were nearly unanimous in their opposition to the war in Iraq and to President George W. Bush's policies more generally.

Dean campaign supporters' views across a range of issues are to the left of the general population and of Democrats as whole but look roughly comparable to those of one of the three major subgroups within the Democratic Party, the Liberals, as classified in the Pew Research Center's 2005 Typology Study. Liberals are the largest wing of the Democratic electoral base. The newly flexed muscle of the Dean campaign supporters will play an influential role in shaping the future of the Democratic Party, regardless of whether they remain associated with a future Dean campaign or align with other liberal candidates and causes within the party.

Looking ahead to 2008, the behavior of the Dean activists and the larger group of liberals from which they are drawn will have an important impact on the Democratic Party's electoral fortunes. In 2004, antipathy to George W. Bush unified and energized all factions of the Democratic Party, despite a lack of enthusiasm for its presidential nominee. Without Bush heading the Republican ticket in 2008, this unity may be harder to achieve. Intraparty disputes over how liberal or conservative a candidate to nominate will be more prominent, and the liberal wing will arguably play the largest role in the outcome, given its size and the monetary resources it commands. Even so, the ideological leanings of the 2008 party nominee cannot be predicted for certain. Party centrists fear that the nomination of another liberal candidate will doom the Democrats' chances of regaining the White House. If the war in Iraq is no longer dominating the political scene as the nomination process gets under way, Dean activists and their fellow liberals may be willing to accept a more centrist presidential nominee if their desire to recapture the White House convinces them that this is necessary.

Appendix: About the Surveys

The activists participating in the study were randomly selected from the Democracy for America (formerly Dean for America) volunteer database. Only active members of the campaign were eligible for participation.[5] Democracy for America contacted these activists by e-mail on behalf of the Pew Research Center for the People and the Press. Respondents were directed to a website managed by the Pew Research Center, where they could complete the survey. Interviews were completed between September 13 and December 14, 2004.

There were two separate samples: one group was interviewed in September and again after the election; a separate sample was interviewed only after the election. The September survey drew 3,925 respondents, for a response rate of 13 percent. Slightly more than half (51 percent) of those responding to the September survey also completed the postelection reinterview. In the second sample, 19 percent of those invited to participate completed the survey.

Although the response rates in the study were relatively low, auxiliary information in the Democracy for America database enabled us to compare the survey respondents with all Dean activists in terms of campaign activity. We found only two substantive differences between the sample of respondents and the entire database, and we have reason to believe that neither resulted in a significant bias in the sample. Younger activists may have been slightly underrepresented in the study, and people who participated in the poll were more likely than the average activist to have contributed money to the campaign. Despite the latter difference, the study participants and the entire pool of activists had similar levels of campaign involvement on other measures of activity, including membership in MeetUp for Dean and membership in Commons. On measures within the survey itself, those who contributed money tended to hold the same views on major political issues, the party, and the campaign as those who did not make a contribution. Weighting the data so as to correct for the underrepresentation of younger activists and the overrepresentation of contributors suggested that the error due to nonresponse was minimal. Consequently, the analysis presented in this chapter is based on the sample of respondents without weighting. Further details about the methodology are available from the authors.

Notes

1. Governor Dean and his political organization, Democracy for America (formerly known as Dean for America), generously provided the Pew Research Center for the People and the Press with access to their database, from which Pew drew a random sample. Democracy for America then sent an e-mail message to those who had been selected, requesting that they participate in the survey. Respondents completed the survey on a website created by Pew. In order to protect the confidentiality of the respondents, Pew had no access to the names and addresses in the database. Democracy for America officials did not view the completed interviews and did not know who chose to participate in the survey. Neither Dean nor his organization had any control over the drafting of the questionnaires for this study or the content of this report.

2. The Pew Research Center first released results from this study in an April 6, 2005, press release, "The Dean Activists: Their Profile and Prospects." The release, which includes complete toplines from the surveys, is available online at http://people-press.org/reports/display.php3?ReportID = 240. An earlier version of this paper, which also includes a more complete discussion of the importance of the Internet for the Dean campaign, was presented at the 2005 annual meeting of the American Association for Public Opinion Research (Keeter, Funk, and Kennedy 2005).

3. For more details on the Pew Research Center 2005 Typology Study and the method used to classify liberal Democrats, see http://wheredoyoufit.org. Nine value dimensions were

used to create the typology: foreign policy assertiveness, religion and morality, environmentalism and regulation, social welfare, immigration, business sentiment, financial security, antigovernment sentiment, and individualism. Each value dimension is based on combined responses to two or more survey questions. Each of the questions used a "balanced alternative" format that presented respondents with two statements and asked them to choose the one that most closely reflects their own views. To measure intensity, each question was followed by a probe to determine whether or not respondents felt strongly or not about the choice they selected. As in past typologies, a measure of political attentiveness and voting participation was used to extract the "Bystander" group, people who are largely unengaged and uninvolved in politics. A statistical cluster analysis was used to sort the remaining respondents into relatively homogenous groups based on the nine value scales, party identification, and self-reported ideology.

4. The five biggest donors to Democratic 527s were George Soros, Peter Lewis, Stephen Bing, and Herbert and Marion Sandler (York 2005).

5. "Active members of the campaign" were defined as those having made a financial contribution or engaged in at least one substantive activity, such as attending a MeetUp for Dean.

Part III

Party Activities

10

Machine Politics for the Twenty-First Century?

Multilevel Marketing and Party Organizations

Peter Ubertaccio

The organizational activities of the Republican Party since the 2000 election suggest a new future for party organizations in the United States. Republicans used the techniques of multilevel marketing (MLM) companies to strengthen their grassroots organizations, energizing both activists and voters. These techniques may provide the institutional support for fundamentally transformed parties at the grass roots. Writing about the 2004 Bush campaign in Ohio, Matt Bai claimed to be witnessing "the emerging portrait of politics in a new century" (2004a, 44). This emerging party organization extends naturally from the demise of traditional parties, with their history of local autonomy and dependence on patronage, and the rise of consultant-based organizations that rely heavily on candidate-centered marketing strategies.

Political scientists have long viewed party activists and regular, grassroots members as a defining characteristic of the American party system. Party scholarship has highlighted the weakness of party organizations and the loose affiliation of citizens to parties. The authors of the American Political Science Association's (APSA) report "Toward a More Responsible Two-Party System" (1950) called for a more active party membership as one component of a strengthened party organization that would complement a new focus on party programs. The difficulty of that enterprise was demonstrated by Eldersveld (1964), who found that relatively few Democratic and Republican precinct captains were actually engaging in "critical" activities: party registration, canvassing, and Election Day efforts. Taking the authors of the APSA report to task for neglecting to specify concrete steps to achieving its goal, Mileur suggests that "political parties are products of their environments—legal, historical, and cultural—and their reconditioning requires confronting these factors squarely" (1992, 169).

The present political environment, with a closely divided electorate mirrored in the partisan division in Congress and close presidential elections, is increasingly amenable to the tactics of MLM. And these tactics may represent yet another step toward the kind of party organization the APSA authors envisioned (see Green and Herrnson 2002 for other evidence of this trend), perhaps in the form of "franchise" parties discussed by R. Kenneth Carty (2004). Because the Republicans developed MLM as an explicit strategy in the 2002 and 2004 campaigns, this chapter will focus on their efforts.

Multilevel Marketing Techniques

The leading name in multilevel marketing is Amway. The parent company of Amway is Alticor, the president of which, Dick De Vos Jr., is a candidate for the Republican nomination for governor in Michigan in 2006. De Vos's father, Richard De Vos, founded Amway in 1959, and the company had 2004 sales in excess of $6.2 billion. The De Vos family has long had an affiliation with GOP politics, and Dick De Vos's wife was the former chair of the Michigan Republican Party. The formal entrance of the De Vos family into elective politics is only the latest evidence of the synergy between MLM and the GOP.

Amway's sales plan is exceedingly simple. According to the company's website:

> It allows you to build your business through retailing products and sponsoring other people who, in turn, can retail products and offer the business opportunity to others. By passing your sales and marketing knowledge to your developing team, you not only build your own business network but also enable others to build one of their own.[1]

MLM emphasizes a team approach to profit making and business organization. Kleeneze, a major British MLM firm, explains the approach this way:

> By introducing (sponsoring) other people into the business, you are entitled to extra profits, based on the turnover of your group. This is the network marketing side of the business and the higher your group turnover, the more money you will make. Believe it or not there are people earning over £10,000 per month via this method.[2]

Tupperware describes its team-driven approach similarly:

> As your recruits build you become an Associate Manager, hosting an average of five Demonstrations per week. On top of your Demonstrator rewards you will receive monthly bonuses for your team achieving sales targets, and for your first 6 months we support you with our New Manager Development Program.[3]

Entrepreneur.com published an article on the success of MLM that makes clear the utility of this approach to party politics. The key components are:

1. Mentorship: "Practice what they teach. [To succeed,] you need to be willing to listen and learn from mentors. The way this industry is structured, it's in the best interests of the [veterans in your company] to help you succeed, so they're willing to teach you the system. Whatever [your mentor] did to become successful, it's very duplicatible, but you have to be willing to listen and be taught and follow those systems" (Smith 2005).
2. Hierarchy: "The higher-ups. It can be called various things, but the general term is the 'upline,' meaning the people above you. How supportive are they? Do they call you? Do they help you put a plan in place? Are they as committed to your success as they are to their own? You should be able to relate to [the people in your upline] and be able to call them at any time to say 'I need some help.' How much support there is from the people above you in the company is very important" (Smith 2005).
3. Recruitment: "Take up the lead with your downline. There's a term in the network marketing industry called 'orphans'—when somebody is brought in and then the person who brought them in is just so busy bringing in other people that they don't spend the time to teach and train [the new person]. You should be prepared to spend at least 30 days helping a new person come into the industry—training them, supporting them and holding their hand until they feel confident to be able to go off on their own. You really need to ask yourself, are you willing to do that? Are you able to do that? This is really about long-term relationship building. It's not about just bringing people into the business and just moving forward. It's about working with these people and helping them to develop relationships" (Smith 2005).

Far from the quaint Tupperware parties in the 1950s, MLM emerged in the twenty-first century as a multibillion dollar enterprise. The company's success is due in no small measure to its pitch. An analysis in the alternative online magazine *EnergyGrid* declared, "The reason why MLM can work so well is that people are much more likely to fall for a sales pitch from a friend or relative, or a stranger in a home setting, than they are from a stranger in a shop or market, or an advert in a paper, magazine or on the Internet." In fact, MLM techniques have become such a powerful wealth creator that major corporations have developed their own network marketing client companies. Citigroup's Primerica is a leading marketer of life insurance and financial products, while Colgate-Palmolive operates Princess House, a direct marketer of household goods.

Applying MLM to Party Organizations

The goals of the Republican Party after the 2000 election mirrored those of a multilevel marketing company: to find an effective way to register and turn out more voters at the grass roots (Racicot 2004). To this end, the GOP instituted the 72-Hour Task Force in 2002. This program was designed to increase the number of Republican voters by contacting them three days before the polls opened on Election Day in 2002 and 2004. In its implementation, the 72-Hour Task Force drew heavily on MLM techniques to create a new organizational level of activism, the grassroots network, complete with "upline" and "downline" participants who could reach voters effectively.

Dan Balz described these efforts as "a throwback that both Democrats and Republicans have rediscovered as an antidote to television ads."[4] But this "throwback" was applied with modern marketing techniques. For example, the Republican National Committee (RNC) ran experiments to test the claims of MLM firms. According to Franke-Ruta and Meyerson (2004), in 2002 as an experiment, "four volunteers were pitted against a professional telemarketing firm, each with an identical script and separate lists of voter names. The four volunteers got almost 5 percent more people to the polls than the pros." As Ken Mehlman noted, "The most important thing you can do in politics is give someone a personal contact from a credible source. Not just a personal contact from a paid person on the ground, but someone in their church, their gun club or the PTA."[5]

Volunteers were recruited by national, state, local, and collegiate party organizations at rallies, at meetings, and through the Internet. The new recruits were assigned to localities in which they would network. All such volunteers reported to an RNC marshal who would organize them into units of two or three individuals. Each unit was assigned a specific task: operating phone banks, canvassing precincts, or assisting with campaign rallies. The training involved in this approach was rigorous, often occurring over period of months and often targeted at specific goals of expanding the GOP coalition and registering new voters.

In some respects, this type of organizational harnessing of activism came naturally to Republicans, which had long used marketing techniques for party building, such as the innovative use of direct mail in the late 1970s and early 1980s (Herrnson 1988). And it fit with the personal experiences of GOP operatives such as Karl Rove and Blaise Hazelwood at the RNC. Hazelwood was quite cognizant of the fact that MLM tactics applied older concepts of party organizations to the modern era of marketing campaigns.

As Balz pointed out soon after the 2002 elections, "In some ways, Hazelwood was a natural to oversee the 72-Hour Project. . . . She began door-to-door canvassing as a 10-year-old in Arizona when her father was running for precinct committeeman, and she learned firsthand the value of human contact, meticulous organization and volunteer muscle in political campaigns."[6]

Get-out-the-vote drives were not the only traditional party activities updated by MLM. A new type of patronage has infiltrated these organizations. In his analysis of the role of money in Colorado's Seventh District race of 2002, Daniel A. Smith documented the use of campaign "volunteers" recruited through state and national party organizations:

> Aided by a $250,000 soft money contribution from the RNC, the state party's ninety-six hour program paid "volunteers" $200 for their efforts and included 114 Oral Roberts University students bused in from Oklahoma. During literature drops, the students were seen talking on cellular telephones provided by the party and driving cars courtesy of a John Elway dealership. The NRCC [National Republican Congressional Committee] also spent $14,559 in hard money to target Latinos in a late surge of "robo-calls" staffing [Democratic candidate] Feeley's legislative and lobbying record. (2004, 193)

Republican Bob Beauprez won the district by 121 votes. Smith credits the victory to the coordinated campaign plan of the national party organizations and the party's financial backing and adds the concern that "the parties' outside money contributed to the widening disconnect between the constituents residing in the district and the candidates who tirelessly campaigned to represent them" (Smith 2004, 198).

Other less selective incentives were employed as well, such as receiving a signed picture of the president or tickets to Bush reelection events in 2004. The *Washington Post* reported that "tickets to Bush events, distributed by the Republican Party, go only to those who volunteer or donate to the party or, in some cases, sign an endorsement of the GOP ticket and provide names and addresses."[7] In fact, the Bush campaign received a good deal of criticism for restricting attendance to its campaign rallies and events. Civil liberty groups and political opponents decried what was viewed as either extreme security measures or hostility to open and free political discourse or both. But viewed from the lens of MLM, the practice was a way in which to reward downline workers with a tangible benefit for their organizational prowess.

In contrast to the concern raised by Smith, Bai's analysis of MLM tactics in the 2004 Ohio presidential campaign paints a different portrait of the role of the national parties. Campaign manager Ken Mehlman was one of the preeminent architects of what was referred to as "the Plan." Local parties and campaign organizations were to work in consultation with the national party and the Bush campaign to set goals for the volunteer aspect of the reelection effort. Said Mehlman, "The lessons of reality TV are that people are into participatory activities. . . . They want to have influence over a decision that's made. They don't want to just sit and passively absorb. They want to be involved, and a political program ought to recognize that" (Bai 2004a, 45–46).

The Republican effort to coordinate the activity of thousands of volunteers and use them to target voters is a new twist on traditional party mobilization. Bruce Newman's 1994 study of political marketing details the transition of an older "party concept" of campaign strategy, where patronage and a "lifetime of party affiliation" play a crucial role in a candidate's success, to a "marketing concept" of strategy. In the latter, "strategy originates from the voter and begins by breaking down the electorate into distinct and separate segments of voters." Using the techniques of political consultants, once segmentation has been achieved, "the candidate creates an image for himself and uses that to position himself. The strategy is then executed through information channels based on the results of marketing research and polling" (Newman 1994, 38).

The party approach to Newman's candidate-centered strategy broadens the techniques to include party and national campaign organizations. Where Smith sees a worrisome trend of interference and disconnect, Bai sees the layers of party and campaign organizations working together in a consultative fashion. "Rove and Mehlman gleaned a critical lesson from the 2002 Congressional and 2003 gubernatorial elections . . . the way to build a grassroots movement is to get one volunteer to recruit several other volunteers, and so on, so that the organization is constantly growing, feeding off itself" (Bai 2004a, 47).

The process of mobilizing voters is left in the hands of local volunteers, called Bush team leaders. For example, Bai (2004a) was introduced to Todd Hanks, the Delaware County, Ohio, Bush campaign chair. Bush won Delaware County with 66 percent of the vote in 2000, so it was a solidly Republican county where Bush needed to win big to offset expected Democratic gains in the urban areas of the state. In order to keep Ohio in the GOP fold, Hanks was committed to maximizing the Republican vote. As a downline participant, Hanks was recruited and kept in the organization in the same way someone is recruited and kept in an MLM company. Despite his strong political preference for Bush, "Hanks readily admitted that his ultimate goal is to rise through the ranks of local and even state politics," wrote Bai. "For Hanks, the Bush campaign offers a chance to recruit a 'downline' of new volunteers who will, ideally, remain loyal to him in future campaigns— including his own" (Bai 2004a, 68). The old-style, patronage-based machine has thus been replaced by the pyramid goals of multilevel marketing organizations.

The organizational capacity of MLM exceeds in sheer numbers the limited scope of the consultant-driven candidate organizations from which it grew. The traditional party organizations of the early twentieth century, with their dependence on party bosses, local autonomy, and patronage, gave way in the 1970s and 1980s to new candidate-centered organizations separated from the normal party structure. These candidate-centered entities were dominated by a professional staff of consultants and pollsters and only tangentially related to their party organizations, which had become large funnelers of money to candidates. The Richard Daleys of an earlier era gave way to the James Carvilles of modern electoral politics. The tried and true methods of these traditional organizations were pushed aside by the new communication techniques. In the late twentieth century, "The campaign's theme and message are communicated through television and radio commercials, through direct mail pieces, and increasingly through campaign websites," Dennis Johnson (2001, 13) has written. "Those communications are developed and honed through the use of sophisticated research analyses, especially survey research, focus groups, and dial meter sessions." In an important sense, MLM merges old-fashioned grassroots methods with sophisticated modern messages.

The Bush "Brand" and MLM in 2002

The Republicans' use of MLM techniques was a rational response to their critical need to increase voter turnout in the wake of Bush's loss of the popular vote in 2000. Garance Franke-Ruta and Harold Meyerson noted in the *American Prospect* that Rove's prediction that Bush would win 50–51 percent of the popular vote in 2000 was off by a crucial two percentage points. As the RNC's political director, Hazelwood, "had research showing that union households in 1998 and 2000 were turning out to vote at rates much higher than their percentage in the population. Evangelicals, meanwhile, were underperforming, putting Republicans at a distinct disadvantage in the final seventy-two hours of a race, when union mobilizations led by the AFL-CIO were having a strong impact in turning out households that would vote Democratic" (Franke-Ruta and Meyerson 2004). Thus was the MLM of parties put into action.

This new approach was implemented in the 2002 midterm elections, and it had three prongs. The first was financial, and Bush used the summer months to raise record amounts of money for Republican candidates while focusing on get-out-the vote drives and defending the record of his party during the fall months leading up to the election. This financial effort was by all accounts quite successful (Magleby and Monson 2004).

The second prong was the use of Bush's leadership to unite the Republican Party. The "Bush leadership," specifically his wartime record post 9/11, was the focal point of the strategy. In the spring of 2002, a GOP pollster called this development the "Bush brand." The branding was in part a product of "Bush's sky-high approval ratings" that have had the effect of extending his popularity far "longer than normal, making him the GOP symbol." Having a product to sell is, of course, critical to any marketing technique, especially for MLM where the personal contact of the sales force is on the line. Wrapping a presidency in the cloak of party is both unusual by contemporary standards and fraught with political uncertainty. In this regard, Bush's involvement in the party was not dissimilar to that of his predecessors, but was more intense and comprehensive. Arguably, the terrorist attacks of 2001 created a wave of public support for the president that allowed him to reverse the historical course and demonstrate the strength of a strong executive as party leader. In any event, the Bush "brand" was essential to the success of the MLM techniques.

Unlike most of his predecessors, Bush took an active, if at times behind-the-scenes, role in promoting particularly strong GOP candidates in state primary elections. The White House very publicly let it be known that it supported Norm Coleman in Minnesota, Jim Talent in Missouri, Greg Ganske in Iowa, and Richard Riordan for the gubernatorial nomination in California. These efforts were not always successful—as when California Republicans spurned the presidential advice, choosing William Simon as their nominee and losing a surprisingly close election to incumbent Gray Davis—but they worked more often than not.

After fielding a strong ticket in most states, the president returned to his chief of state role. As the early glimpses of his campaign speeches indicate, Bush called upon the American people to assist him in fighting the war on terror and to protect homeland security by electing good people to Congress. And Bush handled party politics differently from recent presidents, who practiced the "politics of triangulation," scoring personal victories at the expense of their party fortunes. A good example was the willingness of the White House to get involved in the selection of the congressional leadership. Senate Majority Leader Trent Lott's praise of Strom Thurmond's segregationist presidential campaign in 1948 gave the White House an opportunity to assert Bush's dominance. In response, the White House engaged in an effort to bring about Lott's removal and install its favored candidate, Senator Bill Frist of Tennessee.[8]

Once the financial and leadership elements were in place, the third prong of the Republicans' MLM approach was organizational—the implementation of MLM techniques in the party and campaign. The key organizational units in battleground states became the living room of upline managers and downline recruits. "The big thing that brings them [campaign volunteers] all together is viral activity," claimed Ken Mehlman (Bai 2004a, 47). Because the goal of this vibrant grassroots organization was to reach as many voters as possible during the final seventy-two hours of the campaign and get them to the polls, human interaction and organization of efforts were at a premium.

Finally, Bush returned to the campaign trail, being the best upline salesman for the Bush brand. He was relentless in these efforts, visiting forty states and more than a hundred congressional districts on behalf of Republican candidates in 2002. During the last five days of the 2002 campaign, Bush participated in seventeen key candidate events. The *Washington Post* reported that "the work paid big dividends on Election Day, when a surge of Republican voters in states such as Florida, Georgia, North Carolina and Missouri overwhelmed the Democrats and turned what many had called one of the most competitive midterm campaigns in history into a substantial Republican victory."[9] The GOP won 73 percent of the seventeen key races where Bush had personally campaigned, some by a margin of just 1 percent of the vote. The relatively low turnout in the 2002 election assuredly assisted the GOP, particularly because the turnout of GOP voters increased 4 percent nationally over turnout in 1998.

The success of the 2002 campaign provided the evidence Republican Party leaders needed of the effectiveness of not only Bush as party leader but also the MLM of parties. Indeed, by 2004, Bush's efforts as party leader bore fruit because of the organizational MLM techniques on the ground. According to Bush's chief strategist Matthew Dowd,

> We were able to win some close races that we probably wouldn't have won unless we had learned from what we had learned in 2000 through the 72-Hour Task Force and done some things. I mean, we put a lot of stuff in place in Georgia, where we had some surprising victories in the Senate and the governor's race. We put some stuff in place in Minnesota, where [former Vice President Walter] Mondale was supposed to win and ended up losing to Senator [Norm] Coleman. Missouri. So there were some spots that we did some stuff that I think we pulled some races out. We had good candidates, but also, we had such good tactics. But having a president with a 60 percent, 59 percent job approval helps.[10]

MLM in 2004

Bush and the Republicans faced a similar strategic problem in the 2004 campaign and set out to implement MLM techniques on an even larger scale. The 2004 election also presented the Bush campaign with a greater challenge than its 2002 efforts on behalf of congressional candidates. The president's public approval rating had dipped to 41 percent in May as concerns over the war in Iraq and the nation's economy mounted, and Democrats had a high degree of unity in their preference to have Bush removed from power. Bush would have to rely strongly on his own base, rather than winning over independents or Democrats, and that reliance would focus on particular states such as Ohio. It was in that state that MLM was most crucial. Evidence of the heightened emphasis on MLM is found in a series of PowerPoint presentations put together by Karl Rove. According to Byron York, the Rove presentation was "unintentionally made available" to Democratic strategists at the outset of the campaign. In fact, knowledge of this document was a major inspiration for the grassroots innovations among Democrats in 2004, including America Coming Together (York 2005).

The Rove document uses the language of MLM, including key phrases such as "Back to People Power" and "The results were conclusive—It Works!" It also borrows heavily from MLM techniques:

- "If you need votes from a constituency, go after them in a serious and targeted way."
- "Don't wait for outside groups to turnout voters, do it yourself."
- "Customize mail and phone programs to individual voters and their concerns."
- "Make all voter contact motivational, visually appealing."
- "Fight for this vote like you mean it."
- "Devote resources."

The GOP "Plan" in 2004 developed grassroots organizations in all fifty states, but with special emphasis on sixteen "battleground states," using the lessons of 2002 and the 72-Hour Task Force. The top of the upline managers were at the campaign headquarters in Arlington, Virginia, overseeing regional coordinators and state-level coordinators; these three levels were paid campaign officials. Beneath the state-level coordinators were the downline managers and participants—county, city, and precinct officials—who were volunteers. By Election Day, this cooperative operation had more than one million volunteers nationwide and was described as a "national party machine" (Milkis and Rhodes 2005).

The Ohio version of this organization was described as follows:

> To conduct the ground war, the GOP constructed an extraordinary grassroots organization that reached into every region of the state. Based on roughly 150 field staff and involving some 12,000 local party officials, it recruited more than 85,000 volunteers. The overall effort also included a full-time registration coordinator, fifty field personnel dedicated to registration, and ten coordinators working with churches. These activists were recruited from social and political networks and the Bush web site, which generated six different kinds of "team leaders." The success of these efforts relied on detailed information about voters, clear goals, and a high degree of accountability for results. (Mockabee et al. 2005)

The first step in implementing the Plan was to recruit Bush team leaders, and a major part of this effort was six issue-based "coalitions":

> The coalition program looked to identify prominent individuals with credibility within a specific coalition or formal leaders of coalition groups. . . . Party personnel were charged with hosting regular conference calls with key leaders to invest them in Republican efforts and to motivate them on issues they care about. Events, in particular, were targeted—Republican representatives were present at every gun show, state fair, Veterans of Foreign Wars convention, Christian music festival, business expo, anti-tax rally, and fish fry they could find. (Shaw 2004)

According to the Plan, "The first thing is to determine where the most important voting blocs/coalitions are that need to be penetrated and maximizing in order to achieve victory. It is important to prioritize to be effective." This was followed by the movement to "target coalition groups on issues that they care about and that will motivate them to vote. Some of these groups include: social conservatives, agriculture, Catholics, Sportsmen, etc. Targeting these groups can increase Republican turnout 4 percent." (East 2004)

The final element was to draft a countywide plan of action: "Now all that is needed is to put all the information gathered in one plan and one timeline. This is critical. A plan lets everyone know what is expected of them and the timeline allows volunteers to plan ahead and save the dates on their calendars." This effort was similar in design to the MeetUp phenomena of the 2004 election, used to great effect early in the campaign by the Howard Dean campaign. But MLM techniques advanced by the GOP promised greater results and organizational clarity.

The upline managers set specific goals for the downline participants, including recruiting volunteers, organizing campaign events, and registering and contacting voters. Participants at every level of the organization were held accountable for meeting these goals. Just as importantly, the Bush campaign provided highly targeted messages for the volunteers to deliver. This "micro-targeting" was produced by extensive and sophisticated research. As Dan Balz and Mike Allen reported:

> The Bush operation sniffed out potential voters with precision-guided accuracy, particularly in fast-growing counties beyond the first ring of suburbs of major cities. The campaign used computer models and demographic files to locate probable GOP voters. Once those people were identified, the RNC sought to register them, and the campaign used phone calls, mail and front-porch visits—all with a message emphasizing the issues about which they cared most—to encourage them to turn out for Bush.[11]

The net result of the MLM techniques was greater attention to the grass roots and more viral activity among potential Bush voters in 2004. According to State Senator Jane Earll of Erie County, Pennsylvania, compared to past campaigns, "There are more campaign people around, more coordination, more ground troops and grass-roots organizing."[12]

After the 2004 election, RNC chairman Ed Gillespie e-mailed his followers with the good news:

> 1.2 million volunteers made over 15 million contacts, knocking on doors and making calls in the 72 hours before the polls closed. 7.2 million e-activists were contacting their family, friends, co-workers. The RNC registered 3.4 million new voters, enlisted 1.4 million Team Leaders, and contacted—on a person to person basis—30 million Americans in the months leading up to and including Election Day, and in the final 72 hours we met 129 percent of our door-knocking goal; and met 120 percent of our phone-calling goal. (East 2004)

Of course, President Bush was deeply involved in the 2004 campaign, and the Republicans lavished extensive resources on television advertising and other high-tech activities (Ceaser and Busch 2005). However, the grass-roots operation made a critical difference, such as tipping Ohio into the Republican column and delivering the presidency to Bush (Mockabee et al. 2005). A good example is the case of Todd Hanks, the Bush team leader in Delaware County, Ohio, described earlier: although Bush won the county by the same percentage—66 percent—as in 2000, the actual number of Bush voters increased dramatically due to the expanded turnout. The *Columbus Dispatch* reported that Democratic counties saw turnout increase up to 24 percent over 2000 in some places, and Republican counties exceeded those numbers: "Delaware County led the way with a 43 percent voter increase over 2000, followed by Warren with 34 percent, Union with 31 percent and Pickaway with 26 percent."[13] Republican consultant Barry Bennet explained the focus on traditional GOP voters: "They live in counties that are so Republican that their vote never really mattered before. . . . We just went in and maximized our vote. We called, mailed, knocked on doors and they came out."[14]

Many observers were impressed by these results, which suggested a historical comparison. The *Los Angeles Times* reported:

> In some ways the technologically driven outreach is a throwback to the days of the urban political machines, when ward heelers knew how to get out the vote in their part of the big city. After decades of less efficient direct mail and cold calls, the technology has evolved to the point that millions of residents living in battleground states are getting as much personal attention as a 1940s Democrat did in Chicago.[15]

Along the same lines, Bai commented, "To watch [the Bush volunteers] recruit new voters and volunteers in exurban town houses, cajoling one neighbor at a time, is to imagine how it might have looked to see the Democratic ward bosses organize their tenements in the days of Tammany Hall" (2004a, 126). He concluded, "The comparison suggests a vision of the future: win or lose, a lasting political organization could well be the legacy of the Bush pyramid. It's not unrealistic to think that these new precinct-by-precinct county organizations in fledgling communities all over America may endure long after Karl Rove has retired to lead seminars at a Texas university" (126).

Conclusion

The Republican application of MLM techniques to party organization paid off with party victories in 2002 and 2004. Significantly, Republican Party affiliation in the electorate has not changed since the election of Bush, hovering around 31 percent of the population, with Democrats declining from 36 percent to 33 percent (Harris Interactive 2005). MLM has not served to increase the number of Americans who are members of the GOP, but the processes are in place to maximize their role on Election Day. If the Republicans continue to fund MLM operations, they hold out the possibility of providing the organizational apparatus necessary for a sustained increase in GOP turnout.

The unique role played by Bush and the use of MLM in 2002 and 2004 suggest that, however fleeting the Bush "brand" is in the early part of the new century, a new model of presidential-party interaction and the multilevel marketing of such may transform party organizations. Bush's efforts as party leader and the integration of national Republican themes to local party organizations and campaigns is a remarkable turnaround for a party that had witnessed three electoral landslides at the presidential level under Eisenhower, Nixon, and Reagan but watched its fortunes founder in other races.

Bush's decision to pursue a party strategy does not yet qualify the GOP as a "franchise party" that would resemble the responsible party organizations proposed by the APSA authors (1950). As Carty explains:

> Franchise systems exist to couple the efficiencies of scale and standardization with the advantages of local participation in ongoing operations and delivery of the organization's product. Typically, a central organization, recognizable by its common brand, determines the product line and sets standards for its production and labeling, designs and manages marketing and advertising strategy, and provides management help and training as well as arranging for the supplies needed by local outlets. (2004, 10)

However, a strong presidential "brand" and MLM techniques could move the major party organization in that direction.

Democratic Party strategists studied the remarkable success of the GOP and formulated an MLM strategy of their own. In the aftermath of their 2002 loss, they unveiled Project 5104, "which denotes the DNC's goal of winning 51 percent of the national vote in 2004." Using a "comprehensive database that features economic, demographic, and consumer data on about 158 million voters nationwide" (Mercurio 2003). Ruy Teixeira commented, "The labor movement will match this expanded turnout initiative with its 'Partnership for Working Families,' which will target not just union voters, but also non-union liberals and Democratic-leaning voters in the party's 158 million-voter database" (2003). Similarly, the America Votes coalition of interest groups—and in particular, America Coming Together—deployed a small army of paid canvassers and volunteer activists to register and mobilize voters in 2004 (York 2005). However, these efforts suffered from a lack of coordination in practice and fell short of the GOP efforts in key battleground states, such as Ohio (see chapter 8).

Despite the Democrats' setbacks, former chairman Terry McAuliffe and current chair Howard Dean have moved their party in the direction of MLM due to the strategic success of the GOP. The true test of the institutionalization of MLM tactics will be whether the major parties find the evidence of 2002–2004 so compelling that they continue to use them and in the process reinvigorate grassroots party organizations.

Notes

1. "The Amway Sales Plan," http://www.amway.com/en/busopp/the-amway-sales-plan-10096.aspx.
2. "Team Building—The Power of Network Marketing," http://www.kleeneze2003.co.uk/teambuilding.htm.
3. "Career Path," http://www.tupperware.com.au/dir063/webtupp.nsf/pages/careerpath.
4. Dan Balz, "Getting the Votes—And the Kudos," *Washington Post*, January 1, 2003.
5. Morton Kondracke, "Registration Wars in Ohio, Florida Produce a Draw," *Roll Call*, October 28, 2004.
6. Ibid.
7. Dan Eggen, "Policing Is Aggressive at Bush Events," *Washington Post*, October 28, 2004.
8. Elisabeth Bumiller, "Divisive Words: Behind the Scenes," *New York Times*, December 21, 2002.
9. Balz, "Getting the Votes."
10. Interview of Matthew Dowd by PBS *Frontline*, January 4, 2005, available at http://www.pbs.org/wgbh/pages/frontline/shows/architect/interviews/dowd.html.
11. Dan Balz and Mike Allen, "Four More Years Attributed to Rove's Strategy," *Washington Post*, November 7, 2004.
12. Tom Raum, "Bush Making Gains in Battleground States," *Las Vegas Sun*, September 14, 2004.
13. Joe Hallett and Jonathan Riskind, "Ohio Results Defies Conventional Wisdom," *Columbus Dispatch*, November 4, 2004.
14. Ibid.
15. Joseph Menn, "The Race for the White House," *Los Angeles Times*, October 28, 2004.

11

The [Un]coordinated Campaign

The Battle for Mahoning County, Ohio

Melanie J. Blumberg, William C. Binning, and John C. Green

In 2004, both the Democrats and Republicans waged extraordinary campaigns to secure Ohio's twenty-one electoral votes, and the presidential contest was settled in the Buckeye State by some 118,000 votes out of 5.7 million cast (Mockabee et al. 2005). Compared to the 2000 campaign, the Democrats and their allies enjoyed a larger net gain in campaign resources. In 2000, George W. Bush had carried the state by an unexpectedly small margin after the Gore campaign shifted the bulk of its resources to Florida in the final weeks (Blumberg, Binning, and Green 2003). That close result, plus President Bush's perceived weaknesses four years later, led the Democrats to believe it was possible to wrest Ohio from the Republican column (Green 2004).

As a consequence, there were impressive innovations in the Ohio "ground war" in 2004. However, the campaign suffered from a lack of coordination that made these innovations less effective than they otherwise could have been. Indeed, this "uncoordinated" campaign helps explain why John Kerry narrowly lost Ohio despite the extraordinary campaign on his behalf. In large part, these problems stemmed from difficulties typical to presidential campaigns, but the new campaign finance laws created problems as well. This chapter explores these issues in Mahoning County, Ohio.

Mahoning County and Democratic Campaigns

Mahoning County is one of the Democratic strongholds in Ohio (it includes the old steel city of Youngstown), typically producing majorities for Democratic presidents far above those in other urban areas and the state as a whole. For example, in 2000, Gore won the county by 63 percent, seventeen points higher than his statewide margin. From the mid-1930s until the mid-

1970s, a Democratic machine dominated Mahoning County politics. A classic "party-in-control," it lingered until 1994, when a group of reformers calling themselves Democrats for Change took over the party (Binning, Blumberg, and Green 1996). These reformers introduced a modern "party-in-service" to candidates (see Aldrich 1995), which included President Bill Clinton. In 1992 and 1996, both the remnant of the machine and the reformers ran effective get-out-the-vote (GOTV) efforts on behalf of Clinton, with the latter far exceeding state expectations (Blumberg, Binning, and Green 1999). By the late 1990s, the original leaders of Democrats for Change had left party politics and had been succeeded by less prominent reformers. This shift in leadership weakened the local organization, and partly as a consequence, the 2000 presidential campaign was less effective (Blumberg, Binning, and Green 2003).

The mechanism for these grassroots campaigns in the 1990s was the "Coordinated Campaign," an innovation of the Democratic National Committee (DNC) in the 1980s (Corrado 1996). The underlying goal of the Coordinated Campaign was to provide services that were too costly for candidates to do individually, a prime example of which was voter registration and GOTV programs (Bibby 1990). To this end, the Coordinated Campaign sought to integrate the party organizations, combining the financial resources of the national committees (including party "soft money") with the political knowledge and volunteers of state and local committees.

In principle, the Coordinated Campaign was aimed at electing Democrats at all levels of government. However, its primary focus was presidential elections, where the Democrats had done poorly despite continued success in congressional, state, and local races (Margolis and Green 1993). Put another way, the Democrats wanted to harness their subnational electoral strength to win the White House. In this regard, the Coordinated Campaign had mixed results (Trish 1994; Heldman 1996), and Ohio was a good example: although Clinton won Ohio in 1992 and 1996, the Republicans dominated state elections in the 1990s. By 2004, Democratic operatives and allies were again ready to innovate.

One innovation was America Votes, a coalition of liberal interest groups designed to better coordinate grassroots activities in the 2004 campaign (see chapter 8). The coalition partners included groups long involved in Democratic campaigns, such as labor unions, which ramped up their grassroots efforts. But other groups were newly founded, the most important of which was America Coming Together (ACT). It was designed to deploy a sophisticated grassroots operation to register and mobilize voters, using paid canvassers, modern information technology, and efficient organization (Skinner 2005). Although ACT was run by well-known Democratic activists (and part of the "shadow Democratic Party"), it was entirely independent of the rest of the Democratic campaign effort. The most important reason for this separation was financial: ACT was largely funded with "soft money," funds once raised by party committees with the help of their candidates, but newly banned under the Bipartisan Campaign Reform Act of 2002 (BCRA). Legally, ACT could use such funds for "nonpartisan" grassroots activities, but it could not coordinate its efforts with party organizations or the presidential campaign. Other features of the new campaign finance laws also inhibited coordination among other elements in the Democratic campaign as well (Malbin 2003).

The net result was an extraordinary level of resources available for the ground war in 2004, but with a much lower level of coordination than in past campaigns. It is worth reviewing each of the major elements in this "uncoordinated" campaign in Mahoning County.

ACT in Mahoning County

Ohio was one of the states targeted by ACT, and its operation was under way by late 2003. Shortly thereafter, Bill Padisak, a vice president of the Service Employees International Union (SEIU), was hired to run ACT's Mahoning Valley operation (including Mahoning and Trumbull counties). Amply funded, the ACT program had three phases. The first was a voter registration drive that lasted three months in summer of 2004 and registered approximately 10,000 voters in Mahoning County. Padisak recruited and trained sixty paid canvassers, many of whom were Youngstown State University students. They were provided with Palm Pilots, walking lists, and scripts and were sent out to walk precincts, mostly in low-income urban areas, in the late afternoon and early evening and on weekends. Using voter data provided by the National Committee for an Effective Congress (NCEC), the canvassers worked in teams of ten, with typically thirty canvassers per day. The canvassers used the Palm Pilots to identify targeted voters and also to collect new voter information. This information was eventually added to the NCEC database for future use.

The second phase was a voter-canvassing effort that began after the voter registration rolls closed, based on the updated NCEC targeting data. Here, the paid canvassers and volunteers implemented a "CKCC" (card, knock, call, card) program, with the goal of contacting all likely Democratic voters four times; Palm Pilots were used to show commercials to prospective voters. These grassroots efforts were complemented by ACT telephone banks and direct mail, which were run at the state level (see Mockabee et al. 2005). Part of this effort was an absentee vote program among senior citizens, which delivered four thousand absentee ballots in Mahoning County.

The third and final phase was the GOTV effort, culminating with Election Day activities. The canvassers targeted twenty thousand "progressive" and "interested" voters, concentrated in heavily Democratic precincts. This focus on "base" precincts was a scaled-back version of an original plan that included "persuadable" precincts as well. Instead, ACT decided to concentrate its resources. Padisak was originally told to hire six hundred canvassers for Election Day, but when it became clear Ohio was a toss-up, he was instructed to double his efforts. He hired 1,250 workers and rented 250 vans to transport the canvassers out into the neighborhoods (but not to take voters to the polls, a traditional party activity). ACT's Mahoning County Election Day payroll was $175,000. The canvassers were organized into teams of six with a supervisor, and each team made three passes in targeted areas on Election Day: a note was put on the door, then a door hanger was put on the knob, and, finally, a canvasser knocked on the door.

All told, ACT's activity in Mahoning County was impressive. There were, however, a number of problems. First, there were the inevitable problems associated with starting a new operation from scratch. There was also some question about the quality of the paid canvassers, especially on Election Day.[1] The biggest problem was targeting the same precincts as other Democratic groups. This resulted from the required lack of coordination between ACT and other organizations required by the federal campaign finance laws, a requirement Padisak observed scrupulously.

Labor and Mahoning County

ACT was not the only grassroots innovation in 2004. Organized labor reinvigorated its grassroots effort with a ten-point program called Take Back Ohio. The state was divided into ten zones; Mahoning, along with four other counties, was in Zone 1. In late February 2004, Debbie Bindas, an official with the American Federation of State, County, and Municipal Employees (AFSCME), was released from her work responsibilities to serve as the Zone 1 coordinator. By the first week in March, the operation was in high gear. Initially, there were two full-time workers and one part-time worker administering the Zone 1 program. The staff increased to ten by July and reached its full complement of thirty-five a month before the election, drawn from eleven states and a wide variety of unions.

The first task was to update the union leadership list, which necessitated contacting the 497 locals in Zone 1. Once this information was obtained, Bindas made sure that every local had a coordinator, who was responsible for recruiting fellow union members to volunteer. All volunteers received training on how to become "communicators" to sell the Kerry-Edwards ticket to the labor constituency. All told, it is estimated that labor recruited several hundred volunteers in Mahoning County.

Take Back Ohio involved new tactics. For example, the traditional literature drops, where volunteers hung candidate information on house doors, were a thing of the past. Volunteers were mandated to do one-on-one contacts with *all* AFL-CIO affiliated members. *Every* union member was on a home visit list: if the volunteer did not find the member at home, he or she was contacted at work within twenty-four hours of the attempt. These efforts were complemented by work-site leaflets, direct mail, and union publications (see Mockabee et al. 2005).

Like ACT and its Palm Pilots, Take Back Ohio went high-tech. Bindas had bar-coded lists with every union member's name and address. When the volunteer found someone at home, the union member was asked to identify the one issue most important to him or her. The response was recorded, the sheet was scanned into database, and the union member was sent literature from the Washington office. The volunteers registered and reregistered every person because the unions did not want to take the chance that some were not registered properly, such as not having changed their address at the Board of Elections.

As Election Day neared, Take Back Ohio did telephone banking, concentrating on undecided voters. During the last two days of the campaign, labor volunteers fanned out across the area to get out the labor vote. The GOTV contacts were concentrated in areas with union households, typically heavily Democratic precincts. Most observers agree this effort was impressive and that labor was quite effective in mobilizing its own constituency. However, ACT and other elements of the Democratic campaign focused on these areas as well. The campaign finance laws prevented Take Back Ohio from coordinating with other elements of the Democratic campaign, but long-standing relationships with the Democratic Party reduced the inefficiency somewhat (for example, Bindas was an Ohio Democratic state central committeewoman).

The Mahoning County Democratic Party

In 2004, the local Democratic committee was a weaker organization than it was in 1996 and 2000. The local party chair, Lisa Antonini, had been the director of operations under the Democrats for Change and had taken the post with the blessing of the original reform leaders. However, she faced a number of new challenges. First, Antonini had limited personal resources. Unlike the original chair of the reformed "party-in-service," she worked full-time for the county treasurer, which precluded her from devoting significant time to party business. This lack of time limited her ability to maintain regular contact with the party faithful. In the service party, many precinct committee members participated for social or expressive reasons rather than material incentives, such as patronage jobs, and required a great deal of personal attention. In addition, many of the original reform activists had lost interest in the party as time passed. As a consequence, the party's activist corps and volunteer base were attenuated.

The activist corps was also dispirited. A local scandal and the conviction of nearly eighty officeholders and attorneys had left political enthusiasm at low ebb. Under these circumstances, the local party had difficulty raising money, compounding its personnel problems. In addition, Antonini's leadership skills were questioned when the party lost the juvenile court judgeship, a position that controlled more than a hundred scarce patronage jobs. Governor Bob Taft had appointed a Republican judge to fill an unexpected vacancy, and the local party was forced to let the appointed judge run unopposed in 2002. In 2004, the juvenile court race was perceived by many party insiders as a referendum on Antonini's effectiveness as party chair. Accordingly, she put the local party "in service" to the Democratic juvenile court candidate. All other races were given lower priority—including the presidential campaign.

In sum, the local Democratic Party was not the asset to the 2004 presidential campaign that it had been in previous elections, when it was the "point of the spear" in the Coordinated Campaign. The local party lacked volunteers and finances and was distracted by a critical local contest. The new campaign finance laws provided an additional barrier to participation in the presidential race. Antonini felt constrained by the complicated federal rules on what she could do or spend on behalf of the Kerry-Edwards ticket.[2] The result was that the local party did little direct presidential campaigning. Its efforts were limited to working the polls, providing voters with rides on Election Day, and coordinating the GOTV efforts in downtown Youngstown.

The Coordinated Campaign in Mahoning County

One of the unexpected results of the new campaign finance laws in 2004 was the extensive funds raised by the Kerry campaign during the primary season and by Democratic Party committees throughout the year (Malbin 2006). As a consequence, the Ohio Coordinated Campaign was especially well funded (Mockabee et al. 2005). However, it was very slow to develop, with two distinct phases.

In late spring 2004, the Kerry campaign began to assemble an Ohio organization, appointing John Poersch as director of the Coordinated Campaign, the same post he held in the 2000 presidential campaign. By May, Rick Barga was appointed Mahoning County field director. Although from Ohio, Barga was an outsider to Mahoning County and had worked for Kerry in other states.[3] The local party chair, Antonini, was irritated because she was not consulted before naming a field director, a common practice in previous Coordinated Campaigns (Blumberg, Binning, and Green 1999, 2003). Initially, Barga had limited contact with Antonini and the local party.

Barga attempted to recruit local volunteers and immediately ran into difficulties. He initially relied on information given to him by the 1996 regional field director, a local resident. This outdated information was almost as useless as the local party's "worthless" database. By late July, Barga had already gone through the precinct committee list twice and netted only thirty volunteers. He lost two workers when they learned they would not be paid: he had not heard of "street money," which is a common practice for campaign workers in Mahoning County. An intern in charge of staffing the telephone bank during the early part of the campaign indicated that she was having difficulty getting even two people a night to make calls. When Barga complained about the lack of party assistance to the 2000 field director, Danny Thomas (a local resident), Thomas replied that "there was none to give." Despite the Kerry campaign's hefty finances, early money was not abundant in the Mahoning County operation.

Meanwhile, Barga had numerous disagreements with state party officials and Kerry campaign operatives. They disagreed over event arrangements and messages, such as automobile fuel efficiency standards in an area where one of the largest employers was General Motors. The Kerry campaign, in particular, ignored local concerns. An egregious example occurred when Kerry visited the old Sheet & Tube steel factory to show how Ohio's economy was collapsing under Bush policies. The only problem was that the mill had closed during the Carter administration twenty-seven years earlier.

There was a parallel African-American outreach effort that was at best confusing and at worst inefficient. State Representative Sylvester Patton Jr. was in charge of the local Ohio Legislative Black Caucus (OLBC), with two paid staffers, but the DNC sent A. Robert Brown to Youngstown to oversee its own African-American outreach program. Thomas said it was a like a comedy, with Patton going out the back door of campaign headquarters and Brown coming in the front door. These outreach efforts fell far behind those of previous campaigns.

These difficulties appear to have been common across the Buckeye State. One veteran Democratic operative, Joe Grandmaison, said the Ohio campaign was as bad an operation as he had ever seen. He reported, "I have been in a lot of campaigns, and I can't even discuss the Ohio operation without getting frustrated." The situation was addressed at the beginning of October when Jim DeMay, the Ohio director of the 1996 Coordinated Campaign, was deployed at the state headquarters. Shortly thereafter, Barga was fired as the Mahoning County field director.[4] As with the initial appointments, these changes were made without consulting the local party officials. Antonini and Barga finally came to a meeting of the minds, and she hired him to help coordinate local races.

The second phase of the Coordinated Campaign began approximately three weeks before the election. Thomas was recruited to help organize the GOTV effort, and two outside operatives arrived as well: Nancy Richardson, a former education adviser to Massachusetts governor Michael Dukakis and a former Youngstown resident, and Cheryl Losser, a DNC official with extensive GOTV experience.

Richardson described the second phase of the Coordinated Campaign as "one with multiple power and management centers." She managed one center at the party headquarters in downtown Youngtown, including telephone banking, African-American canvassing, and other Election Day activities. She also handled booking hotel rooms for the candidates and their staff, finding accommodations for volunteers, and making sure everyone was fed. Antonini and Barga added another center, coordinating inner-city precincts. Losser ran a third center, an office in the suburbs, and coordinated non-African American precincts.

The largest resource problem continued to be the lack of local party volunteers. Richardson found it extremely difficult to "energize people in a dying area" to work for the party, and in addition, ACT and Take Back Ohio had siphoned away many volunteers. This problem was eventually alleviated by the continuing influx of outsiders. Grandmaison, a director of the Export-Import Bank and veteran operative, came to Ohio with a dozen friends from Washington, D.C., nine days prior to the election as part of a "Road Trip to Victory." This contingent revived the telephone bank operation, located in the offices of a law firm in downtown Youngstown. One week prior to the election, busloads of "Kerry Travelers" arrived, and more volunteers came in private cars.

In addition, elected officials came from across the country. Assemblyman Joe Nation arrived from California with three staff members. Representative John Olver from Massachusetts came with approximately six staffers and Representative Joe Serrano from New York sent two people, including his chief of staff. An assistant secretary of agriculture from the Clinton administration also appeared, as did Ohio congressman Ted Strickland's aide, Chad Tanner, who was put in charge of press relations.

Richardson likened it to an "Internet start-up with teams assuming roles that were needed at the time, creative ideas bubbling up, [and] no particular hierarchy in the end, but everyone working toward one goal." However, there were continuing "personnel problems" at the three management centers. In addition to the tension between the local party chair and Coordinated Campaign staff, Losser angered many volunteers who were unwilling to deal with her take-charge personality. According to Richardson, "Joe [Grandmaison] was a master at smoothing ruffled feathers." In retrospect, Richardson said the "the [multiple] offices may have saved the campaign." Because the "personalities" had a difficult time coexisting, it was probably best to separate them, and everyone "had a place to go and work."

And there were continued tensions with state headquarters. A good example occurred on Election Day. Grandmaison was contacted by "some kid in Columbus" who said he would be calling the office every thirty minutes to find how many people were given rides to the polls and if there were any problems. Grandmaison told him, "I will give you the numbers now, because I'm going to lie to you anyway." He explained that the young staffers lacked experience: "They just do it by the numbers. They don't understand. There's no reasonableness. There's no judgment. It's like they are in charge of the German army."

Finally, there was ongoing friction with the presidential candidate. According to Grandmaison, the Coordinated Campaign was "impossible" when it came to arranging campaign visits by the candidate and surrogates. Local activists complained that events were poorly planned and executed, and that local notables were often offended. Perhaps the low point was Kerry's well-publicized goose hunting trip in October. The event was disorganized and subjected the candidate to ridicule.[5] Similarly, the many Kerry surrogates who visited Mahoning County were often deployed ineffectively.[6] According to David Skolnick, the political reporter for the Youngstown *Vindicator*, "most of the special events and campaign itself were anything but coordinated."

Richardson reported that plentiful funds became available once the Kerry campaign determined that Ohio was a targeted state, and the Mahoning field operation finally came together at the end of campaign. The local operation eventually mustered several hundred volunteers from one source or another. Many out-of-town volunteers went door-to-door, "knocking and talking" rather than doing the traditional literature drops. Another hundred volunteers worked the telephone bank, and the output expanded to ten thousand calls per day.

The state headquarters sent a list of swing voters that was reworked by the local operation. Priority 1 precincts had a low turnout and high Democratic Performance Index (DPI); Priority 2 precincts had 65 percent turnout and high DPI; and Priority 3 precincts had 75 percent turnout and high DPI. These were many of the same precincts targeted by other groups. Unlike 1996 (Blumberg, Binning, and Green 1999), the campaign did not work all precincts in the county. Here, too, the new campaign finance laws were an impediment to communication with the other elements of the Democratic campaign.[7]

On October 31, Kerry spoke to an estimated twenty thousand people packed into Warren's Courthouse Square, joined by former senator John Glenn, local congressmen Tim Ryan and Ted Strickland, retired admiral William Crowe, and singer Bon Jovi.[8] This was the proverbial shot in the arm the campaign needed, and it reached a classic fever pitch on Election Day.

The Results

These multiple campaign efforts produced a record level of voter registration, expanding the rolls by some sixteen thousand over 2000. In fact, it appeared that the entire voting-age population of the county was registered at least once, if not more often: according to the Mahoning County Board of Elections records, there were 195,092 registered voters on Election Day, but the 2000 U.S. Census counted only 186,928 people over 18 years old living in the county. The local election officials offered a variety of explanations for this discrepancy, including names not having been purged from the rolls.[9]

The multiple GOTV efforts paid off, as well: turnout rose by six percentage points to more than 67 percent of registered voters. Kerry garnered 13,857 more votes than Gore did in 2000. He won Mahoning County with 63 percent of the two-party vote, fourteen percentage points better Kerry's statewide performance of 49 percent. As impressive as these results were, Kerry obtained almost exactly the same percentage of the two-party vote as Gore had in 2000. Indeed, Bush gained an additional 8,252 ballots in Mahoning County. Put another way, Kerry failed to make up any ground on Bush's 2000 margin of victory in this Democratic bastion. This story was pretty much the same across Ohio: Kerry was able to reduce 2000 Bush's vote margin by just 46,000 votes—which could be accounted for by the absence of Ralph Nader from the 2004 ballot (Green 2004).

Mahoning County experienced a number of balloting problems on Election Day, although not the kinds of legal challenges that were anticipated.[10] These problems generated charges that the election was "stolen," but there is no evidence to support this claim. According to Grandmaison, Kerry's defeat can be attributed to the Democrats' ineptness rather than to fraud or Republican shenanigans. A DNC report supports this perspective: "The statistical study of precinct-level data does not suggest the occurrence of widespread fraud that systematically misallocated votes from Kerry to Bush" (Democratic National Committee Voting Rights Institute 2005, 10).

Many factors contributed to these close results, one of which was the poor coordination of the Democratic campaign efforts. This problem is well illustrated by the fact that all the major groups targeted the same heavily Democratic precincts while other precincts were passed by. Some of the problems are commonplace in presidential campaigns, including friction between presidential campaigns and party officials, a lack of party integration, and local party organizational problems. However, these challenges had been met in recent presidential campaigns, and in 2004 there were extraordinary resources available. Indeed, ACT, Take Back Ohio, and the Kerry campaign did impressive work that went a long way toward remedying the internal weaknesses of the Ohio party organizations. But they were unable to provide a critical resource: teamwork.

One reason for the lack of teamwork was the new campaign finance rules under BCRA. ACT, Take Back Ohio, the Kerry campaign, and the Ohio Democratic committees were prohibited from communicating with each other—and there is good reason to believe this prohibition was followed. This meant that the campaign would be "uncoordinated," with unfortunate consequences: the "outsourcing" of traditional grassroots party operations to ACT was inefficient; the strength of traditional party allies, such as labor, was not effectively harnessed; and critical resources were concentrated in the most transient of political organizations, a presidential campaign. In 2004, party organizations also obtained new resources (see chapters 6 and 7), but the impact on the Ohio Democratic state and local parties was limited.

Notes

We wish to thank Rick Barga (interviewed on June 25, 2004, August 4, 2004, and February 11, 2005), Debbie Bindas (May 19, 2005), J. Joseph Grandmaison (August 17, 2005), William Padisak (December 6, 2004), Nancy Richardson (June 2, 2005), David Skolnick (July 8, 2005), and Danny Thomas Jr. (May 26, 2005) for sharing their experiences and insights with us.

1. One ACT participant remarked, "It seemed like the campaign was just hiring warm bodies rather than take the time to hire quality, educated canvassers. Most of the canvassers were only interested in the money."

2. Not all local chairs drew the same conclusions, however. For example, in neighboring Trumbull County, the local party was more engaged in the presidential campaign. Clearly, there was considerable confusion about the new campaign rules.

3. David Skolnick, "Kerry Campaign Fires Area Coordinator," *Vindicator* (Youngstown, Ohio), October 5, 2004.

4. Ibid.

5. David Skolnick, "Kerry's Goose Hunting Is for the Birds," *Vindicator*, October 22, 2004.

6. Sean Barron, "Celebrities Roll into Boardman to Educate and Register Voters," *Vindicator*, October 4, 2004.

7. The Coordinated Campaign had some trouble complying with the complexity of the new campaign finance rules. For example, telephone calls initially said they were calling on behalf of the "Kerry-Edwards campaign." The use of candidates' name in this regard is illegal. The campaign corrected this mistake when it was brought to its attention, subsequently using the appropriate "Victory 2004" name.

8. David Skolnick, "Kerry Rallies the Vote," *Vindicator*, October 31, 2004.

9. David Skolnick, "County Shows More Voters than Eligible Are Registered," *Vindicator*, October 19, 2004.

10. The Coordinated Campaign trained almost two hundred people to watch for voting irregularities and to be prepared for legal challenges at the polls.

12

Organizational Strength and Campaign
Professionalism in State Parties

David A. Dulio and R. Sam Garrett

Despite a steady stream of research on the strength of party organizations, some important ways in which parties are involved in campaigns remain unexplored. Much of the existing work on party strength appeared in the 1980s, a period when political consultants were establishing a strong presence in campaign politics, including work with party organizations. Observers soon discovered consultants, and a lively debate followed over whether consultants and parties are adversaries or allies. There is a growing consensus among political scientists that parties and consultants are allies, meaning that each group helps the other provide services and win elections. But the relationship between parties and consultants remains controversial. Although party elites—those running and employed by political parties—often value consultants, sometimes party activists do not. In this chapter, however, we find evidence that behind the scenes, weak and strong state party organizations forge relationships with political consultants, even if activists sometimes criticize consultants for usurping the party. Some of the circumstances surrounding the 2005 election of Howard Dean as Democratic National Committee (DNC) chairman illustrate the tension between parties needing consultants to build viable organizations but also limiting their public reliance on consultants.

This chapter explores the connection between campaign consultants and party organizational strength at the state level in the early twenty-first century. Relying on surveys of state party officials performed by John Aldrich and his colleagues (Aldrich, Gomez, and Griffin 1999) and James A. Thurber (2002), we have created a dichotomous measure of state party organizational strength and examined how different parties evaluate and utilize political consultants. In keeping with recent scholarship, we find that political consultants do not weaken political parties, and in fact, parties and consultants perform complementary roles in the campaign process. We determine that consultants provide help in areas where parties are less effective in assisting their candidates. And while we find that weaker parties are more in need of the services consultants perform, even strong parties make extensive use of these services.

Political Consultants, Political Parties, and Organizational Strength

Political consultants are a relatively new set of actors in American campaigns. By the 1980s, political consultants had become major strategic players in many campaigns at the national and state levels (Dulio 2004; Herrnson 2004; Sabato 1981; Thurber and Nelson 2000). Consultants are now used extensively to provide specialized services, including polling, fundraising, direct mail, media production, opposition research, and press relations (Dulio 2004; Herrnson 2004).

Unfortunately, consultants were largely excluded from the research on party strength published during the 1980s. This omission may reflect the debate among political scientists over whether consultants are good or bad for parties. Some scholars subscribed to the *adversarial* view of party-consultant relationships, seeing consultants as a negative influence on party organizations (Agranoff 1972; Petracca 1989; Rosenbloom 1973; Sabato 1981). Put simply, as consultants grow stronger, parties weaken (Kolodny and Logan 1998; Abbe and Herrnson n.d.). Consultants encouraged candidates to develop short-term strategies to win elections, especially downplaying their candidates' party affiliation. For example, Magleby, Patterson, and Thurber (2002) argue that parties and consultants should be seen as the agents of two sets of principals: parties and candidates. While consultants seek to serve both sets of principals, at times the desire to win elections will override the party's goals of winning legislative majorities and coordinating issue agendas. This results in weaker ties between candidates and party organizations, as well as between candidates of the same party.

In fact, many scholars have linked party decline with the rise of candidate-centered politics (Sabato 1981). This was true for several reasons. During the "golden age" of political parties at the end of the nineteenth century, "an individual candidate's 'organization' was often little more than a loyal following within the party" (Herrnson 2004, 69). Political parties and their loyal band of cronies played significant roles in orchestrating House and Senate campaigns until the mid-twentieth century. However, by the 1950s few candidates could depend on parties to win nominations and elections on their behalf, as more open primary systems weakened party elites' control over the nomination process. Moreover, changes in campaign finance law, especially the enactment of the Federal Elections Campaign Act of 1971 (FECA), seemed at first to seriously weaken parties. In the 1980s political action committees (PACs) exploded in importance, as favorable campaign finance laws encouraged candidates to seek PAC donations. The overall effect of these changes appeared to make party labels less irrelevant, as citizens more frequently split their tickets, incumbency rates increased, and divided government became a regular part of state and national politics (Fiorina 1996; Wattenburg 1998).

Countering the adversarial view is a growing consensus among scholars that parties and consultants do not have an adversarial relationship. According to this *allied* view of party-consultant relationships, the two sides enjoy a symbiotic connection (Kolodny and Logan 1998; Abbe and Herrnson n.d.; Kolodny 2000; Dulio and Thurber 2003). Party organizations continue to be relevant precisely because they have developed a division of labor with consultants. Consultants manage some electioneering tasks—for example, polling, media production, and direct mail—that parties cannot do as efficiently. Meanwhile, party organizations perform other tasks, such as research and voter mobilization, which consultants cannot do as well (Abbe and Herrnson n.d.; Kolodny 2000; Dulio 2004; Dulio and Thurber 2003).

At the same time that the role of consultants in politics has been growing, numerous studies have also shown that party organizational strength at the state and national levels has increased considerably over the previous two decades (Cotter et al. 1984; Aldrich 1995, 2000; Jewell and Morehouse 2000; La Raja 2003a). As Aldrich argues, one reason some scholars still see parties as being in decline is because of a substantial change in the way parties are organized. The nineteenth-century "party-in-control" in which the party held a "monopoly of resources" (Aldrich 1995, 269) has given way to the "party-in-service" in which parties seek to assist candidates in their development of personal campaign organizations.

We argue that consultants are a major part of this new type of party system. This allied view of the party-consultant relationship has led to the inclusion of consultants in research on party organizations. It is this nexus that we explore here.

Data and Expectations

To assess the impact of organizational strength on the use of campaign professionals in state parties, we turned to two unique data sets. Both are surveys of state party officials, with each focusing on one aspect of the relationship between parties and consultants. First, in 1999, John Aldrich and his colleagues Brad Gomez and John Griffin conducted the State Party Organizations Study at Duke University. They conducted a mail survey and received sixty-five responses from state chairs across the nation.

The second survey we employed was conducted in 2002 by James Thurber and his colleagues at American University's Center for Congressional and Presidential Studies (CCPS).[1] The CCPS study explores state party use of political consultants during the 2002 elections, including why parties hire consultants, whether state parties would recommend that their candidates hire consultants in the next election cycle, and the division of labor between consultants and parties in modern campaigns. Respondents included executive directors and other party elites responsible for hiring consultants (e.g., political directors, communications directors). The CCPS survey, conducted by telephone, included eighty-seven respondents in the final sample.[2]

We combined the data sets by matching the party affiliation and state of the respondents from each data set. Not all responses from the Aldrich survey matched the responses from the Thurber survey. For instance, the CCPS study had responses from elites in both the Democratic and Republican parties in Alaska, while Aldrich received a response only from the Democratic state chair. After sorting through the responses and eliminating the cases that were unavailable, fifty-six cases were included in our analysis.

We do not believe that either the different survey methods (mail for Aldrich and phone for CCPS) or the different time frame (1999 for Aldrich and 2002 for CCPS) pose any significant problems, because the two data sets address different questions and were used for two different purposes in our study. The Aldrich data were used solely to create a list of "strong" and "weak" state party organizations; the more recent CCPS data were used solely to investigate the role and use of consultants in state parties.

To analyze the differences between organizationally strong and organizationally weak state parties in their reliance on outside political consultants, we first needed to create a measure of organizational strength. There is no universal operationalization of political parties' organizational strength. In general, however, organizational "strength" refers to a party's ability to compete at the ballot box. Hershey notes, for example, that in addition to traditional measures of party strength such as the size of a state party's budget and staff, "there are other ways to measure party strength. A strong party would work effectively to register voters, tell them about party candidates, and get them to the polls on Election Day. It would be successful in filling its ticket with viable candidates" (2005, 48).

However, most works—including the two we rely on for the underpinnings of this chapter—use quantified indices of party strength. Gibson and colleagues (1983, 198)—the forerunners to Aldrich's survey, which is central to this chapter—measured party strength using three dimensions: bureaucratization, recruitment, and programmatic activity. Bureaucratization refers to the formal party structure and includes the size of the party staff and budget and levels of professionalization. Recruitment includes activities related to enlisting and funding candidates, while programmatic activity measures the role of parties in mobilizing voters, conducting polls, and providing services to candidates.

We relied solely on the Aldrich data to build a multiple-measure index of party strength. Most of those variables are used in Aldrich's own measures of party strength. We omitted others included in his assessment from our calculation of party strength, however, because they either closely or explicitly dealt with activities that outside consultants would provide. Our revised party strength index included:

- whether the chair was full- or part-time
- whether the state party offices operated out of the chair's home, business, or separate building
- whether the chair was salaried
- if the state party contributed to various campaigns (governor, U.S. House, U.S. Senate, state house, state senate, or other state constitutional or local office)
- if the party employed an executive director
- how active the party was in recruiting candidates in races around the state
- if the state party engaged in activities with county party organizations, such as sharing mailing lists or conducting joint fundraising programs, get-out-the-vote (GOTV) drives, or registration drives

Each of these variables was converted to a dichotomous 0–1 variable (although many were already dichotomous in the original Aldrich data set). The fifteen variables we used were then aggregated to create an overall party strength index. State parties that scored a 10 or higher on this index were coded as strong, and those scoring 9 and lower were coded as weak.[3] The results are listed in table 12.1.

We believe there are competing expectations that might explain any differences in the ways that strong and weak political parties utilize political consultants. For instance, it might be that strong state parties employ professionals more than their weaker counterparts because they have the structure and budget to do so. Alternatively, perhaps weaker state parties look to consultants more than stronger ones because weak parties need more help to be competitive than strong parties do. Building on the prior work discussed above, we also examined state party elites' attitudes on whether their relationships with consultants are allied or adversarial.

Party Elites' Attitudes about Campaign Professionalization

Before assessing how state parties with different levels of organizational strength utilized consultants, we examined how state party elites viewed the roles of parties and consultants generally. This continues previous work that has shown that party elites generally believe that consultants are increasingly

Table 12.1 Selected State Party Activities Used to Create Strong/Weak Party Variable

State Party	Full-time state chair	Office facilities operated out of separate facilities or chair's home or business	Salaried chair	Does party contribute monetarily to federal, state, or local campaigns?	Full-time executive director	Active involvement in recruiting gubernatorial candidates	Active involvement in recruiting other state constitutional office candidates	Active involvement in recruiting U.S. House candidates	Active involvement in recruiting U.S. Senate candidates	Active involvement in recruiting state legislative candidates	Active involvement in recruiting county and local candidates	Party shared mailing lists with county party organizations	Party conducted joint fundraising programs with county party organizations	Party participated in joint get-out-the-vote drives with county party organizations	Party participated in joint registration drives with county party organizations	Total activities
Alabama Republicans		✓		✓	✓	✓	✓	✓	✓	✓	✓	✓	✓		✓	11
Alaska Democrats		✓		✓	✓	✓	✓			✓				✓		5
Arizona Democrats		✓		✓	✓	✓	✓	✓	✓	✓		✓		✓	✓	9
Arizona Republicans		✓		✓	✓	✓	✓	✓		✓		✓		✓		11
Arkansas Democrats		✓		✓	✓	✓	✓	✓		✓		✓		✓		9
Arkansas Republicans		✓		✓	✓	✓	✓	✓	✓	✓				✓		10
Colorado Republicans		✓		✓	✓		✓			✓				✓		7
Connecticut Democrats		✓								✓				✓		5
Florida Democrats		✓		✓	✓	✓	✓		✓	✓		✓		✓	✓	11
Florida Republicans	✓	✓	✓	✓	✓		✓	✓		✓		✓		✓	✓	10
Hawaii Democrats		✓	✓	✓	✓	✓	✓			✓		✓		✓	✓	6
Hawaii Republicans		✓		✓	✓	✓	✓	✓	✓	✓	✓	✓	✓	✓	✓	13
Idaho Democrats		✓		✓	✓					✓				✓		6
Illinois Democrats		✓		✓	✓					✓				✓		5
Illinois Republicans	✓	✓	✓	✓	✓		✓	✓	✓	✓		✓		✓	✓	9
Indiana Republicans	✓	✓	✓	✓	✓	✓	✓			✓	✓	✓	✓	✓	✓	9
Iowa Republicans	✓	✓		✓	✓		✓			✓		✓		✓	✓	15
Kansas Republicans		✓	✓	✓	✓		✓		✓	✓		✓	✓	✓	✓	7
Kentucky Democrats		✓	✓	✓	✓		✓			✓		✓		✓	✓	7
Kentucky Republicans		✓		✓	✓					✓				✓		5
Louisiana Democrats		✓	✓	✓	✓	✓	✓	✓	✓	✓	✓	✓	✓	✓		9

	Total
Maine Democrats	8
Maryland Republicans	9
Massachusetts Democrats	3
Minnesota Democrats	7
Minnesota Republicans	10
Mississippi Republicans	9
Missouri Republicans	7
Montana Democrats	6
Montana Republicans	7
Nebraska Democrats	10
Nebraska Republicans	7
Nevada Democrats	4
New Hampshire Republicans	10
New Jersey Democrats	7
New Jersey Republicans	8
New York Democrats	10
North Carolina Democrats	5
North Dakota Democrats	10
Ohio Democrats	14
Ohio Republicans	12
Oregon Democrats	7
Pennsylvania Democrats	12
Rhode Island Democrats	4
Rhode Island Republicans	8
South Carolina Democrats	9
South Carolina Republicans	8
Tennessee Democrats	9
Utah Democrats	12
Utah Republicans	5
Vermont Republicans	12
Virginia Democrats	12
Washington Democrats	13
Wisconsin Democrats	9
Wisconsin Republicans	6
Wyoming Democrats	11

Source: John H. Aldrich, Brad Gomez, and John D. Griffin, State Party Organizations Study, 1999, State Party Chair Questionnaire (calculations by authors).
Note: All state party organizations that completed valid questionnaires from both the Aldrich study and the CCPS study are included in the table; those parties not included here did not respond to one or both studies.

involved in elections at all levels (Dulio and Thurber 2003; Dulio and Nelson 2005). Here, we find some interesting trends and differences between strong and weak state party organizations. Table 12.2 reports party operatives' mean responses on the question of whether the role of both parties and professional consultants has increased or decreased. At every level, more party operatives in states with strong organizations report that party roles have increased, as seen by their higher mean ranking. In terms of differences across levels of organizational strength, the smallest difference was at the local level (3.75 for strong parties compared to 3.72 for weak organizations). Putting aside the parties' roles in primary elections for a moment, local parties also received the lowest mean ranking for both strong and weak organizations, indicating that the local level is where the fewest party operatives saw an increase in party power.

The greatest differences between operatives' views in strong and weak parties appear at the national level (mean rating of 4.05 vs. 3.75) and in primary elections (4.06 vs. 3.26), with operatives from strong parties more likely to indicate that the parties' role had increased significantly in recent years in both areas. In contrast, operatives in both strong and weak party organizations saw that parties' roles at the state level have increased as well (mean rankings of 4.10 and 3.83). Reinforcing this point is the fact that operatives in both types of organizations reported their highest mean ranking

Table 12.2 State Party Elites' Views of the Role of Parties and Consultants, by Organizational Strength

Has the role of the following increased or decreased?[a]

	Weak Parties	Strong Parties	All Parties
Political parties at the local level	3.72	3.75	3.73
Political parties at the state level	3.83	4.10	3.93
Political parties at the national level	3.75	4.05[b]	3.86
Political parties in primary elections	3.26	4.06[c]	3.53
Political consultants at the local level	3.69	3.45	3.61
Political consultants at the state level	4.08	3.60[d]	3.91
Political consultants at the national level	4.15	3.89[e]	4.06
Political consultants in primary elections	3.94	3.84	3.91

[a] Mean rankings based on a scale of 1–5, where:
    5 = increased very much
    4 = increased somewhat
    3 = stayed the same
    2 = decreased somewhat
    1 = decreased very much
[b] difference of means test, $p = 0.11$
[c] difference of means test, $p = 0.002$
[d] difference of means test, $p = 0.014$
[e] difference of means test, $p = 0.16$

here. These high rankings for state parties must be viewed with some caution since the data come from state party employees.

Very different results were found when party elites were asked about the role of political consultants at different levels of campaigns. In every instance, fewer respondents from strong party organizations said that the role of consultants had increased. Once again, only a small difference between operatives from strong and weak party organizations was found at the local level (mean ranking of 3.45 vs. 3.69 for strong and weak parties, respectively). Furthermore, the lowest mean ranking for consultants' roles occurred at the local level for operatives from both weak and strong organizations. We should also not be surprised by this result, given that professional consultants have not become as dominant in local elections as they have in higher-level races.

At the state level, however, there are significant differences between strong and weak parties (3.60 for those from strong parties and 4.08 from weak parties). More operatives from weaker state parties reported that consultants' roles had increased. Perhaps this result reflects the fact that these parties do not have the resources they need to assist their candidates as much as they might like, and as a consequence, consultants have become major players in their party's state campaigns. Elites in strong party organizations, on the other hand, may not see the same kind of impact from outside consultants due to the parties' greater institutional capacity.

On average, operatives from both strong and weak party organizations see the greatest increase in consultants' presence at the national level (mean ratings of 3.89 and 4.15). Given the ubiquitous nature of professionals in campaigns for Congress and the White House, this finding is not surprising. Overall, the mean scores on the role of consultants were all more than 3.5—showing a greater role for consultants at all levels. This evidence reveals that state party operatives perceive that consultants have a pervasive influence in modern campaigns.

Prior work has also shown that party operatives in the states believe that there are some services that candidates demand during a campaign that are better provided by professional consultants than by parties, but that there are other services that are better provided by parties (Dulio and Thurber 2003; Dulio and Nelson 2005). Generally, these tasks fit into a two-category division of labor: consultants are regarded as better suited for message creation and delivery (polling, media, and direct mail), while parties are better at providing labor-intensive services and staff resources (opposition research, GOTV, and fundraising).[4] Party elites also believe that parties maintain a strong role in providing campaign management or strategic advice.[5] Given the differences between strong and weak party operatives on the role of consultants, there may also be differences on the division of labor between consultants and parties. Table 12.3 addresses this possibility.

Table 12.3   State Party Elites' Views of the Level of Consultants' Services, by Organizational Strength

Have consultants taken over provision of the following electioneering services?[a]

	Weak Parties	*Strong Parties*	*All Parties*
Campaign advertising	3.17	2.85[b]	3.05
Fundraising	2.44	2.45	2.45
Get out the vote	1.83	1.75	1.80
Polling	3.22	3.00[c]	3.14
Opposition research	2.56	2.55	2.55
Direct mail	2.80	3.00	2.88
Management or strategic advice	2.50	2.53	2.51

[a] Mean rankings based on a scale of 1–4, where:
  4 = strongly agree
  3 = somewhat agree
  2 = somewhat disagree
  1 = strongly disagree
[b] difference of means test, p = 0.08
[c] difference of means test, p = 0.13

First, there is no difference between those in strong or weak party organizations when it comes to their general attitude on whether consultants are better able to provide some services than are parties. They agree with equal vigor—more than 60 percent of operatives in each group said that there are some services that consultants provide that parties cannot.[6]

Second, in the areas of fundraising, field operations and GOTV efforts, and opposition research—the areas that consultants and parties agree are best provided by parties—there is also little or no difference between those from strong or weak organizations (see table 12.3). In addition, the low aggregate responses, especially for GOTV efforts, reflect the feeling that operatives from both strong and weak party organizations say that consultants have not replaced parties in these areas. In a finding that is consistent with prior work, party elites from both strong and weak parties also were skeptical that consultants had taken over in the area of management and strategic advice. As Dulio and Thurber (2003) argue, party operatives still believe they have something to offer in the area of management and strategic advice.

In the areas of polling and campaign advertising, there were significant differences between elites in strong and weak party organizations, with those from weak parties more likely to say that consultants had taken over for parties in these areas. However, we should be careful to say that even though they had a lower mean rating, operatives from strong party organizations did not fully reject the idea that consultants had taken over the provision of these services, either. One area where we may have expected this pattern was direct mail, but there was a small difference in the opposite direction.

Campaign Professionalism in Strong and Weak Parties

There are at least two ways that state parties can involve professional political consultants in campaigns: they can recommend specific consultants to their candidates, and they can pay for their services directly (either for candidate use or their own purposes). It is well established at the national level that political parties are not shy about recommending consultants to their candidates (Herrnson 1988; Sabato 1981). However, we know less about the importance of this practice at the state level. When asked about recommending consultants to candidates, state party operatives reported the practice was nearly universal. In both strong and weak party organizations, 80 percent or more of the respondents said that they recommend outside consultants to their candidates. We believe that one reason these figures were not closer to 100 percent is the presence of competitive races in the states. In states without serious competitive races, party organizations, be they strong or weak, may not feel the need to recommend outside consultants— their candidates will likely either coast to victory and not need as much help in their campaign, let alone in identifying professionals, or never be in the running as token opposition and not even think about hiring professionals. Clearly, however, state parties are heavily involved in funneling consultants to their candidates through recommendations.

What kind of consultants do state party operatives recommend to candidates? Overall, huge majorities of operatives from both strong and weak party organizations say they would recommend pollsters (87.5 percent and 92.3 percent, respectively), media consultants (93.8 and 100 percent), and direct mail specialists (81.3 and 92.3 percent) to their candidates. This pattern is not surprising, since all these services are central to message creation and delivery, the very kind of services where consultants are viewed as dominant. The parties—especially weak state parties—choose not to provide these services in-house presumably because they do not have the infrastructure to do so.[7]

However, an interesting and large difference between strong and weak party organizations appears on recommending fundraising consultants. A full 73 percent of party operatives from weak party organizations say they would recommend a fundraiser to their candidates, compared to only about 44 percent of those from strong party organizations. While fundraising is an integral part of what political parties do—both to fill their own coffers and to help their candidates—weaker state party organizations are less well equipped in this area. For weak parties, fundraising is therefore just another service that they do not have the resources to provide, making consultants the only real alternative.

Party elites were also asked about which factors influence their decisions to recommend particular consultants to candidates. Specifically, they were asked about seven attributes of the consultant: ideology, win/loss record, experience in that particular state, fees and affordability, experience in the particular type of race, past record on ethical issues, and experience working for state or national parties. The order of the mean ratings (see table 12.4) provides some indication of the impact of party strength on consultant recommendations. For instance, the highest mean ranking for weak party organizations was on the importance of the consultant's experience in the state. By contrast, this was only the sixth-highest rating for operatives from strong parties. The highest mean rating for strong party organizations was the consultant's experience in the particular type of race, followed closely by fees or affordability. These factors were tied for third in the ratings of weak party organizations. We believe that these figures are a clear signal that the operatives from weak state parties are referring candidates to consultants who have a track record in their states because the party alone cannot provide the same quality of advice to candidates. Interestingly, although in these cases consultants are clearly replacing parties, the party-consultant relationship is not necessarily adversarial. Indeed, it appears that weak parties are willingly reducing their roles in campaigns. In doing so, they are ironically allied with political consultants.

In addition to consultants' experiences in the particular type of race, assessment of their past ethical conduct was also important to operatives in both strong and weak party organizations—but was more important for weak

Table 12.4 State Parties' Criteria for Recommending Consultants, by Organizational Strength

How important are the following factors in recommending consultants to candidates?[a]

	Weak Parties	Strong Parties	All Parties
Experience in the state	4.25	3.50[b]	3.98
Past record on ethical issues	4.19	3.79[c]	4.05
Experience in the type of race	4.00	4.00	4.00
Fees or affordability	4.00	3.95	3.98
Ideology	3.72	3.60	3.68
Win/loss record	3.58	3.60	3.59
Previous experience in another state or national party	2.94	2.95	2.95

[a] Mean rankings based on a scale of 1–5, where:
  5 = extremely important
  4 = very important
  3 = somewhat important
  2 = not very important
  1 = not at all important
[b] difference of means test, p = 0.001
[c] difference of means test, p = 0.04

parties. This pattern may also reveal the importance of consultants as allies to weak organizations. It is interesting to note the relative lack of importance of consultants' experience working for a state or national party organization: this factor had the lowest mean ranking by operatives from both strong and weak party organizations. This result is surprising given the fact that prior research has shown that parties act as training grounds for consultants (Kolodny and Logan 1998; Thurber, Nelson, and Dulio 2000) and that consultants with party experience get more party business (Kolodny and Logan 1998).

When examining the hiring practices of state political parties, we again see evidence of the pervasiveness of consultants in today's campaigns. State party elites were asked whether or not they planned to hire the same four types of consultants noted above—pollsters, media consultants, direct mail specialists, and fundraisers—in the 2002 cycle. There are no substantive differences between strong and weak party organizations with regard to pollsters or direct mail specialists; in both cases, large majorities said they "probably" or "definitely" would hire these types of consultants (88.9 and 83.4 percent for pollsters and 94.4 and 88.6 percent for direct mail specialists among strong and weak party organizations, respectively). Again, this speaks to the division of labor noted above: parties are not as engaged in message creation and delivery in modern campaigns, relying instead on consultants.

In terms of the parties' hiring of fundraisers, there is a small difference between strong and weak party organizations. Strong party organizations likely have the staff and resources to do as much fundraising as they need without much outside help. This may also be the case with weak party organizations, but it might also be the case that weak parties simply do not raise enough money to warrant the help of an outside professional. However, the absence of a large difference in this case is not because of the near-unanimous response that parties would hire this type of consultant but rather the parties' relative lack of interest in hiring a fundraiser. Here, only about one in three party organizations (both strong and weak) said that they "definitely" would hire a fundraiser.

One curious result is the party operatives' response to the question of whether they would hire a media specialist in 2002. Overall, fewer operatives said their organizations would hire a media consultant (70.6 percent would "probably" or "definitely" hire one) compared to pollsters (85.2 percent) or direct mail specialists (90.6 percent). With the cost of media buys always increasing, it is not likely to be cost-effective for state parties to engage in their own media campaigns when compared to in-house production of direct mail. However, there was a large difference between strong and weak party organizations in this regard: operatives from weak party organizations were more likely to say their organizations would hire a media consultant than those from strong parties (80 percent to 50 percent). This result is exactly the opposite of what we might expect. It is not likely to be the case that strong parties do not need the services of media consultants because they have the in-house capacity to produce television ads, since even parties at the national level have moved away from providing this service. It is also unlikely that weak party organizations could hire a media consultant and then buy airtime required to put the spot on the air, given their smaller budgets.

It could be that this result is a function of the 2002 election cycle. Perhaps those operatives from weak state party organizations that said they would hire a media specialist were expecting financing from outside sources, such as the national parties, for consulting fees and airtime. Indeed, weak party organizations with high-profile competitive races—for the U.S. House, U.S. Senate, or a governorship—could reasonably have expected such aid. By the same logic, it may also be that those operatives from strong party organizations that said they would not hire a media consultant may have lacked competitive races.

We can begin to better understand the results on hiring decisions by examining factors behind the decision as well as for whom the consultants would perform services (the party, its candidates, or both). Considering the latter first, there was agreement between strong and weak party organizations on the ultimate beneficiaries of the consultants' work. In polling, media, and direct mail, sizable majorities of operatives from both kinds of states said that the consultants they hired would work for both the party and its candidates. Meanwhile, between one-quarter and one-third said that consultants would work exclusively for the party, and very few said that they would work exclusively for candidates. Media consultants are a slight exception. More state party elites said that the media consultants they hired would work solely for a candidate—11 percent of those from weak parties and 14 percent from strong parties reported this arrangement. As for fundraisers, the majority of operatives from both kinds of parties said that the fundraisers would work only for the party, and the rest said that they would work for both the party and its candidates (not one party operative said the fundraiser they hired would work exclusively for a candidate). This finding is curious given the preponderance of evidence that parties do not turn to outside professionals for help in fundraising. Of course, relatively few party operatives said that their organization would hire a fundraiser in the first place, and this question was asked only of those who said they would do so.

We can get more of an indication about party hiring practices by looking at some of the reasons party operatives report for hiring consultants. These data are presented in table 12.5. There are several reasons state parties may want to hire outside consultants. For instance, they might find it more economical to pay consultants for a small amount of work that needs to be done

Table 12.5   Factors in State Parties' Decisions to Hire Consultants, by Consultant Type and Organizational Strength

How important are the following factors in deciding whether or not to hire an outside consultant?[a]

	Weak Parties	Strong Parties	All Parties
Pollsters			
Party does not perform that service	4.00	3.38[b]	3.78
Party likely to be directed by national party	2.93	2.56	2.80
Allows party to save on staff salary	2.70	2.56	2.65
Direct mail			
Party does not perform that service	3.71	2.73[c]	3.39
Party likely to be directed by national party	3.19	2.24[d]	2.85
Allows party to save on staff salary	2.61	3.00	2.75
Media			
Party does not perform that service	3.54	3.38	3.50
Party likely to be directed by national party	3.04	2.75[e]	2.97
Allows party to save on staff salary	2.61	2.75	2.64
Fundraiser			
Party does not perform that service	2.35	2.25	2.31
Party likely to be directed by national party	2.72	2.58	2.67
Allows party to save on staff salary	3.06	2.83	2.79

[a] Mean rankings based on a scale of 1–5, where:
  5 = extremely important
  4 = very important
  3 = somewhat important
  2 = not very important
  1 = not at all important
[b] difference of means test, p = 0.04
[c] difference of means test, p = 0.005
[d] difference of means test, p = 0.001
[e] difference of means test, p = 0.12

rather than to invest in the infrastructure and staff needed to produce the same service in-house. Parties might also be encouraged by the national party organization to hire consultants, or state parties simply may not perform that service. Here again, we see some complementary evidence for the existence of an "allied" division of labor between parties and consultants.

In the cases of pollsters and media consultants, operatives from both strong and weak party organizations indicate that the most important reason for hiring a consultant is that their organizations do not provide this particular service. The mean ratings for weak (4.00 for pollsters and 3.54 for media specialists) and strong (3.38 for both) parties far outpaced the reason with the second-highest mean rating, namely, that the national party was likely to pay for the service. The third reason, to save the cost of staff salaries, was even less important. Here, the pattern of rankings for both strong and weak party organizations was the same. However, all the average ratings from strong party organizations were significantly lower than those from weak parties, indicating that fewer operatives in those states saw *each* factor as important.

As for hiring direct mail consultants, the fact that their party does not provide that particular service was again the highest mean reason for weak party organization operatives, while strong party organization operatives had much lower rankings. Indeed, more operatives from strong party organizations said that cost savings on staff were the biggest reason for hiring a direct mail specialist. There is an important regularity behind these patterns: both strong and weak party operatives find that they need consultants because they do not provide certain services to candidates. As one might expect, this pattern is the strongest in the weak party organizations.

The story is much different, however, with regard to fundraising consultants. There were no differences between strong and weak parties in the order of importance of the different factors or the importance of individual factors. For instance, the fact that their organizations did not perform this particular service was the least important reason for hiring a fundraiser or any other consultant. The highest mean rating for fundraisers (which was relatively low, compared to the other factors) was to save money on salaries.[8]

Conclusion

This chapter has examined the relationship between campaign consultants and state party organizational strength. We find additional evidence of the view that political parties and consultants are allies in electioneering. In fact, party officials look to consultants for help in areas where they cannot effectively help their candidates. This pattern holds for both organizationally strong and weak parties. However, weak parties may turn to consultants for help slightly more often because of their lower levels of resources. These data reveal additional evidence of a division of labor between consultants and parties that helps achieve the goal of winning elections.

Overall, we find that strong state party organizations share the national parties' view that consultants are important resources, skilled at providing polling, media, and direct mail. In contrast, weak party organizations often turn to consultants to make up for their lack of resources. Interestingly, while strong state parties, like the national parties, do not generally emphasize consultants' roles in fundraising, weak state parties have little choice but to use consultants as fundraisers.

Of course, the relationship between parties and consultants does not occur in a vacuum. Ultimately, elections are decided by a relationship between candidates and voters, which parties and consultants often mediate. Given the multifaceted nature of modern party organizations, however, the use of consultants can produce tensions between party professionals and party activists because, to some extent, each has a different set of goals. The use of consultants threatens to exacerbate these tensions.

For example, even after his dramatic defeat as a 2004 presidential candidate, Democrat Howard Dean reconnected with a nationwide grassroots base to be elected DNC chairman in early 2005. DNC leaders reportedly chose Dean in the hopes that he could reinvigorate state parties in the same manner that had "propelled President [George W.] Bush to a victory in pivotal Ohio, thanks to a strong state party and a network of local volunteers."[9] Democratic state party leaders in so-called red states found Dean's message particularly attractive. After reportedly receiving only $12,000—of $400 million raised nationally—from the DNC during the 2004 cycle, for example, Nebraska Democratic state chairman Steve Achelpohl complained, "There are a lot of unhappy people [among Democratic state chairs] like me who have been disappointed by the unconscionably small piece of the pie we've been allocated."[10] Democratic officials in other states echoed similar sentiments.

Dean responded by promising to strengthen state parties, saying that doing so "is a central part of our plan to make the Democratic Party competitive in every race, in every district, in every state and territory." Dean also drew a sharp distinction between party activists—long recognized as the lifeblood of strong parties—and political consultants, which, as we have shown, can have a significant connection to party strength. Moments after his election as chairman, "a thousand party diehards sprang from their chairs" when Dean declared, "Strength does not come from the consultants down, [it] comes from the grassroots up!"[11]

Although our findings strengthen the claim that state parties and consultants are allies, consultants are not always popular, even if they make parties stronger. As Howard Dean's rhetorical style demonstrates, while parties and consultants are often allies, party activists—another pillar of party strength—might prefer to believe that parties and consultants are adversaries. Like most matters in American politics, the debate over party strength and consultant relationships is impassioned but not absolute.

Notes

This paper represents the views of the authors. It does not necessarily represent the views of the Library of Congress, the Congressional Research Service, or any other institution with which the authors are affiliated. The authors thank John H. Aldrich and James A. Thurber for generously providing data.

1. The CCPS survey was administered by Harris Interactive. Thurber's co-researchers were David A. Dulio and Candice J. Nelson.

2. More information on the CCPS survey is available from the authors of this chapter.

3. This is admittedly an arbitrary cutoff for what defines "strong" or "weak" parties. However, we have confidence in the cut point because it is a conservative one—rather than, say, the median value—that includes a relatively small number of state parties (in the final analysis, we had twenty state parties in our "strong" category and thirty-six in our "weak" category). In addition, we had a limited theoretical foundation from which to work.

4. This division of labor reflects the "allied" vision of party-consultant relationships discussed previously.

5. However, using in-depth qualitative data, Garrett (2005, chaps. 4–5) finds that political professionals of all stripes say that parties generally play a limited role in providing strategic advice.

6. In these differences, it is interesting to note that those from weak state parties illustrate views similar those of professional consultants; see Dulio and Nelson 2005 for consultant data.

7. In each instance reported in table 12.3, more state party operatives from weak party organizations than from strong parties said that they would recommend these consultants.

8. Recall that few state party elites said that they would hire a fundraiser at all.

9. Dick Polman, "Dean's Victory Marks Historic Shift in Party," *Philadelphia Inquirer*, February 13, 2005.

10. Don Walton, "State Dems Seek More from National Party," *Lincoln Star Journal*, February 1, 2005.

11. Polman, "Dean's Victory."

13

Local Parties and Mobilizing the Vote

The Case of Young Citizens

Daniel M. Shea and John C. Green

By all accounts, American party organizations are strong and vibrant at the beginning of the twenty-first century. The national committees have never been stronger in organizational terms, and the state committees are by and large viable organizations (Bibby 1990), while local party committees have gained some new organizational vitality as well (Frendreis and Gitelson 1993). But such organizational prowess begs an important question: how effective are these strong party organizations at connecting with the citizenry? On this score, some scholars have expressed some serious doubts about the significance of organizational strength, noting these improvements occurred during a period of weak partisanship in the public and relatively low levels of turnout (Coleman 1996; Shea 2003). This question is particularly relevant when it comes to the future: What are the party organizations doing for the next generation of partisans? That is, what are parties doing to connect with young citizens and mobilize them to vote?

In this chapter, we investigate these questions with a study of local party organizations and the youth vote (18–25 years old). It appears that many local party committees have the capacity to mobilize young voters and are heavily engaged in the electoral process. However, local party leaders are not especially *interested* in the youth vote—despite agreeing that youth disengagement is a serious problem and believing that local parties can make a big difference in bringing the youth into the electoral process. We argue that local parties have the potential to play a major role in mobilizing the youth and thus revitalizing political participation in America. Real innovation in this regard would allow strong and vibrant party organizations to live up to their promise as instruments of democracy.

The Youth Vote and Party Politics

From the 1960s to 2000, there was a steady decline in citizen participation in politics (Rosenstone and Hansen 1993; Putnam 2000). Shrinking voter turnout was one indicator of the problem—surely the most recogniz-able—but other modes of political behavior such as sending letters to elected officials, helping a candidate or a party, wearing a campaign button, and talking about politics with family and friends have declined as well. According to the American National Election Studies, the number of Americans "very much interested" in political campaigns has dropped by nearly 40 per-cent since the 1960s. This withdrawal from politics is both perplexing and troubling.

The problem is especially pronounced among younger Americans, espe-cially those 18 to 24 years old. In 1972, the first election in which 18-year-olds had the right to vote, 50 percent did so. In subsequent elections, the figure dropped roughly 30 percent. And in the 1998 and 2002 midterm elec-tions, this figure fell below 20 percent. A recent study of younger Ameri-cans, commissioned by the Center for Information and Research on Civic Learning and Engagement (CIRCLE), found that while attitudes toward gov-ernment may have improved in the wake of 9/11, the number of young Americans willing to take part in our political system has continued to shrink. Only about two-thirds of the 18- to 25-year-olds in the CIRCLE sur-vey had registered to vote, a decline from two years before, and 49 percent of the overall group (15- to 25-year-olds) said that voting was "a little impor-tant" or "not at all important" to them. Many other indicators in this study, and in numerous other studies, have suggested the same thing: younger vot-ers were turned off by politics. This departure of young citizens from the electoral sphere during the past few decades has profound implications for the quality of American democracy (Galston 2001; Patterson 2003).

But then, much to the surprise of all manner of observers, youth voting increased dramatically in 2004. Surely this was part of the overall surge in voting in the close and fiercely contested 2004 campaign. But while overall turnout expanded by about 6 percent, it increased most among the youngest voters. Whereas just 36 percent of 18- to 24-year-olds voted in 2000, some 47 percent did so in 2004. This changed represented a stunning eleven per-centage point increase—about double the rate of increase among any other age group. Although the youth still voted at a lower rate than older Ameri-cans, the gap at the polls narrowed.

Is this dramatic change just a short-term phenomenon occasioned by the special circumstances of 2004, including the candidates and controversies of the moment? Or does it represent a long-term increase in engagement of young citizens—and perhaps the citizenry at large? Full answers to these questions won't be known for some time, of course, but a brief review of the conventional wisdom on youth participation is helpful.

The most common explanations for the low levels of youth voting focus on the character (and deficiencies) of the individual citizen. The decline of participation is due to changes in attitudes, especially among younger

Americans, who are seen as apathetic and self-centered. They are also seen as ignorant of their duties as citizens, in part due to poor civic education in high school.[1] The solution to this problem has been to change youth attitudes. For instance, many high school and college programs have been developed to promote students' interest and knowledge of politics. MTV's *Rock the Vote*, which emerged in 1992 and was reenergized for the 2004 presidential contest, is prominent example. And there has been no shortage of hectoring of the youth by their more civic-minded elders.

Certainly there is some validity to this perspective, but it is not much help in explaining the sudden increase in youth voting in 2004. After all, there is no evidence of a sudden change in the attitudes or knowledge of young citizens in this particular election.

A less common approach has been to focus on political elites, candidates, public officials, and campaign professionals. Here the main culprit is "new-style political campaigns," which have focused on negative campaigning, extensive fundraising, and the precise targeting of voters, compounded by sensational media coverage of politics. This style of politics alienates many voters, but especially the youth. The solution to this problem has focused on changing the style of campaign and campaign coverage to more effectively engage younger citizens. Efforts to develop codes of conduct for campaigns, campaign finance reform, and improved media coverage are good examples.

Once again, while these proposals certainly have merit, they don't help much in explaining the sudden increase of youth voting in 2004. After all, a rash of reforms did not suddenly change the new-style campaigns—and in fact, 2004 was in many ways the epitome of it.

A final approach has received relatively little attention—the role of organizations dedicated to mobilizing citizens to vote. Simply put, there has been a decline in this most basic of democratic functions, and the key culprits in this regard have been the local political parties, once the dominant electoral organizations in the United States (Milkis 1999; Putnam 2000). This decline was partly in *capacity* to mobilize the vote—local parties became weaker in both absolute and relative terms, losing out to candidates, interest groups, and higher-level party organizations. But there was also a decline in the *interest* in voter mobilization as local parties became adjuncts to the new style of campaigning and the organizations that practice it. Writing in the *Atlantic Monthly*, Don Peck captured this last point well: "In recent decades parties have moved away from grassroots mobilization efforts, which reach out to nonvoters, to focus on 'switching' independents that have a strong history of voting" (2002, 48). Young voters were especially affected by this change.

The solution to this problem is to reinvigorate mobilizing institutions, especially local political parties. This perspective may help explain the dramatic change in the 2004 vote, because there was a sudden and dramatic expansion of mobilizing institutions in the 2004 campaign. The Republicans built an extraordinary grassroots program within their party organizations (see chapter 10), and on the Democratic side, liberal interest groups and labor unions instituted large and innovative grassroots activities (see chapters 8 and 11). The growth of the Internet as a tool, as demonstrated especially by Howard Dean's primary campaign (see chapter 9), and the efforts of Christian conservatives in opposition to same-sex marriage (Abramowitz 2004) are additional examples of this expansion. All these efforts may have reached young voters, but there were also a large number of special programs aimed at the youth vote, both within and outside of party organizations (Shea and Green 2006, appendix).

If reinvigorated institutions were crucial to the 2004 vote, then maintaining these institutions and their activities in the future will be critical to maintaining a high level of youth participation beyond 2004. Here local party organizations may be especially important. After all, they have a permanence that other organizations lack and, like other party organizations, a long-term interest in voter mobilization. Scholars have long noted that voter participation was highest when local political parties were vibrant. In 1942, Schattschneider observed, "Once party organizations become active in the electorate, a vast field of extension and intensification of effort is opened up, the extension of the franchise to new social classes, for example" (47). There is some evidence that local party organizations have been growing stronger over the last several decades, and this strength has been associated with higher turnout (see, for example, Frendreis, Gibson, and Vertz 1990; Frendreis and Gitelson 1993, 1999; Frendreis et al. 1996). Our questions are these: do local party organizations have sufficient capacity to mobilize young voters, and do they have an interest in doing so?

The Study

This chapter is based on a telephone survey of a random sample of Democratic and Republican local party chairs drawn from the thousand most populated counties across the country. According to the 2000 census, these counties contain 87 percent of the American population, so this sample covers the local parties most capable of influencing the electorate. The survey was conducted between October 1 and November 10, 2003, producing a total of 403 Democratic and 402 Republican responses, with a cooperation rate of about 50 percent. The responses were found to deviate only slightly from the geographic and demographic characteristics of the original sample of counties; the data were weighted to correct for these modest differences.

Each interview lasted roughly thirty minutes and included batteries on organization strength, party activities, and the political environment as well as extensive questions on youth mobilization. This study was supported by a grant from CIRCLE to research the current and potential connections between local party organizations and the youth. (For early reports of this project, see Shea and Green 2004.)

Local Party Capacity

What kind of organizational capacity do local parties have in the early years of the twenty-first century? Several studies conducted in the 1990s suggest that many local parties were strong organizations and had become stronger over time (Frendreis and Gitelson 1993, 1999). Our survey produces similar findings, as can be seen in table 13.1, which lists several basic features associated with organization strength (see Cotter et al. 1984).

Overall, about three-fifths of the parties surveyed maintained a party headquarters during campaign season, a basic organizational feature on which the Democrats and Republicans were very similar. Almost the same proportion reported having a website, evidence of using modern campaign technology; here the Republicans were more modestly more active. However, less than two-fifths of the organizations maintained an office year-round even when campaigns were not under way; here, too, the Republicans were modestly better off. Only one-quarter of the parties had a full-time chair. Most of the chairs interviewed had other occupations, often in government or politics. Finally, very few local parties had paid staff—overall, just

Table 13.1 Organizational Features of Local Party Committees, 2003

	Democrat	*Republican*	*Both*
During the campaign, did the party have a . . .			
Headquarters	63.1%	60.6%	61.9%
Website	57.6	64.3	61.0
Year-round office	34.8	41.5	38.1
Full-time chair	26.2	23.8	25.0
Paid staff	6.5	9.0	7.8
Proportion of parties that, of the above, had . . .			
None or one feature	36.2%	30.8%	33.4%
Two features	37.9	42.8	40.3
Three features	20.0	18.8	19.4
Four or five features	6.0	7.8	6.9
Additional measures of organizational strength			
Committee positions filled (mean)	65.6%	67.6%	66.6%
Mean annual budget	$37,464	$40,838	$39,151
Mean per capital budget	$221	$242	$232

7.8 percent. There was no statistically significant difference between the major parties in terms of the full-time chairs or paid staff.

These findings fit well with previous research on the organizational strength of local parties, and in some cases, these figures are higher. For example, in Frendreis and Gitelson's 1999 study, about 4 percent of the county committees boasted full-time staff, while we found roughly twice that amount. It could be that local party strength has continued to grow. However, such conclusions must be viewed with great caution because of the differences in samples surveyed in these studies.

A simple additive index of these organizational features provides a crude measure of the distribution of local party strength. Overall, one-third of these committees reported none or just one of these attributes. These would appear to be weak organizations; the Democratic committees were a bit more common in this category. Another two-fifths of these committees reported two of the organizational features; the Republican committees were a bit more common in this mid-range category. Finally, the remaining quarter of the parties had three or more of these attributes. Democrats and Republicans were equally common in this category of strong organizations.

Two additional measures of organizational strength are located at the bottom of table 13.1. The first is the mean percentage of the party committee offices that were filled, usually precinct committeemen and committee-women. Since such local party officials tend to be party activists, this is a crude measure of the volunteer labor force available to local committees. Here the overall mean is an impressive two-thirds of the seats filled. As one might imagine, there is considerable variation in this figure, but the major parties did not differ significantly in terms of these resources. The final entry in the table is the average budget for the local parties measured on a per capita basis (to control for the great variation in population). Here the mean party's budget was about $230, with an average yearly budget of about $40,000. The Republican committees were a little wealthier than the Democrats, but not dramatically so.

What activities do the local parties undertake with these resources? Table 13.2 reports responses on the mean percentage of the committee's total effort directed at five types of activity: get-out-the-vote (GOTV) activities, campaign services to candidates, campaign events, voter registration, and noncampaign activities (such as regular fundraising and social events).

Consistent with past research, GOTV activities ranged first, on average accounting for 30 percent of the local parties' efforts. Three activities essentially tied for second place, averaging between one-sixth and one-fifth of the committees' total effort: campaign services to candidates, campaign events, and voter registration. Of course, some of these activities may be connected to GOTV efforts, such as the mailing of party slate cards to voters and holding rallies right before the election. Finally, only about one-tenth of commit-

Table 13.2   Local Party Activities, 2003

	Democrat	*Republican*	*Both*
Mean distribution of local party effort			
GOTV activities	31.0%	30.1%	30.6%
Campaign services	17.4	19.6	18.5
Campaign events	17.8	19.2	18.5
Voter registration	17.5	15.3	16.4
Noncampaign activities	11.1	11.0	11.1
Percentage receiving aid from . . .			
State party	53.0%	52.3%	52.6%
National party	13.0	12.4	12.8
Local party agreement with the following statements			
Local party relies on volunteers, not consultants	75.9%	76.1%	76.0%
Campaign consultants are allies of parties, not adversaries	59.8	72.1	65.9
Local party is heavily involved in campaigns	60.4	66.3	63.3
Primary goal of party is to win elections, not to develop partisanship	58.1	66.3	62.2

tees' total effort on average was directed toward noncampaign activities. It is interesting to note that there was no significant difference between the Democrats and Republicans in terms of the relative distribution of activities.

These party committees report receiving some aid from their state and national party committees, much of it directed at GOTV activities. Overall, just over half of the committees reported receiving state assistance. However many fewer reported national committee assistance—just 13 percent. It could be, of course, that national support came through state parties and was carefully targeted to competitive areas.

In this regard, the respondents' views of the Bipartisan Campaign Reform Act of 2002 (BCRA) are interesting, since these reforms banned party committees from raising "soft money," some of which had been used to fund grassroots activities. Indeed, an objection to BCRA was that it would have a negative effect on voter registration and GOTV programs. In response, a special provision was put in the legislation allowing for "Levin committees," whereby local party committees could raise soft money under carefully regulated circumstances (La Raja 2006). In fall 2003, the local party chairs had a largely negative view of the impact of BCRA on local parties. Overall, one-third thought the impact would be negative, and only one-tenth thought it would be positive (with the remainder expecting no significant impact). Here, the Republican chairs were more pessimistic than their Democratic counterparts (38.6 and 26.5 percent, respectively, expected a negative impact). However, only one-tenth of the chairs reported knowing about Levin committees, and only two-fifths said they were "very likely" to take advantage of the provision. On this point, the chairs were prescient: very few Levin committees were established in 2004, partly because of their complex regulations and partly because BCRA did not inhibit party fundraising (La Raja 2006). Indeed, BCRA may not have the negative effect on local committees the chairs feared.

The remaining entries in table 13.2 reinforce the clear emphasis on voter mobilization by local party committees. When asked if their committee largely employed volunteers or campaign consultants to run campaigns, three-quarters of both parties' chairs said volunteers. But when asked if consultants were "adversaries" or "allies" of local party committees, two-thirds overall chose allies, a pattern found in other studies of party leaders (see chapter 12). Here, there was a sharp partisan difference: the Republicans chose the allied response much more often than did the Democrats (72.1 to 59.8 percent). In a separate question, just 6 percent of the chairs reported that campaign consultants were "very important" to their organization; another one-third said "somewhat important." Overall, two-thirds of the chairs reported that their organizations were heavily involved in campaigns, and more than three-fifths believed that the principal goal of the local party was to win elections, as opposed to building party attachment. The Republican chairs had modestly higher scores on these questions than the Democratic chairs.

In sum, it does appear that many local party committees do have the capacity to mobilize voters, including the youth.

Interest in Young Voters

But how interested are local parties in mobilizing *young* voters? Our survey provides a mixed assessment. In order to measure the priority that local chairs assign to youth mobilization, we asked the chairs, "Are there demographic groups of voters that are currently important to the long-term success of your local party?" Almost 88 percent of the chairs could think of such a group. We asked this question three times to allow the respondents to mention a wide variety of groups—which they did.

Overall, just 8 percent of the party chairs mentioned young voters (18–24 years of age) in their first response; an additional 12 percent mentioned young voters on the second try, and 18 percent on the third. In all, local party leaders were given three opportunities to suggest that younger voters are important to the long-term success of their local party, but less than two-fifths did so. In contrast, senior citizens were far more likely to be mentioned: they were named by 21 percent on the first opportunity, 19 on the second, and 10 on the third, for a total of one-half of the party chairs.

There was some variation by party. Republican leaders were nearly twice as likely to mention young voters on the first question (8 percent compared to 5 percent), but Democrats were more likely to mention young voters, on the two follow-ups. In total, 32 percent of Democrats and 26 percent of Republicans mentioned young voters. Although not entirely absent from the political radar screen of the local chairs, the youth were not a prominent focus.

The chairs were then asked if they have developed specific get-out-the-vote programs for young voters. Here, just 41 percent of party leaders said yes (a figure remarkably similar to the 38 percent who mentioned youth as an important group). A follow-up question asked them to describe their program. On closer inspection, we find that a vast majority of these programs might be dubbed "modest" or "traditional." For example, common responses were "Some people in our party have spoken at area schools" or "Our people set up booths at fairs and malls." Only a handful of party chairs mentioned what we might call "significant" activities—programs that require a substantial amount of time or resources. Roughly half of the responses were limited to college programs. "We make contacts with campus College Republicans," noted one; another said, "We work with Young Democrats organizations on college campuses." Moreover, many of the respondents who mentioned that they had programs were unable to provide much specificity. While it is fair to say that these efforts might make a difference, college students are already much more likely to vote than noncollege students, who make up about half of this age group.[2]

One explanation for these findings could be that local party chairs are not especially interested in the youth vote and do not see the lack of youth participation as a problem. But this is not true. When asked if they agreed with the statement "The lack of political engagement by young people is a serious problem," some 88 percent agreed—and 52 percent "strongly agreed." Here the party differences are interesting: 96 percent of Democratic chairs agreed that the lack of youth political engagement was a problem, compared to 82 percent of Republican chairs. This difference may reflect strategic calculation: perhaps some of the chairs concluded that young voters were more likely to be Democratic voters. But even so, large majorities of the chairs saw the lack of youth participation as problematic.

We then asked the respondents a battery of questions on the causes of youth disengagement; the results are reported in table 13.3. According to the party chairs, the major reason for youth disengagement is inadequate education of the youth: 71 percent disagreed with the statement "high schools do a lot to prepare young people for their role as citizens." On this question, Republicans were much more critical of the high schools than the Democrats

Table 13.3   Reasons Given by Local Party Chairs for Youth Disengagement from Politics, 2003

	Democrat	Republican	Both
High schools do a lot to prepare young people for their role as citizens			
Agree	30.6	21.4	26.0
Neutral	2.8	3.0	2.9
Disagree	66.7	75.6	71.1
Young people are turned off by the negativity of campaigns			
Agree	74.6	65.0	69.8
Neutral	6.7	9.0	7.8
Disagree	18.7	26.1	22.4
Media has done much to turn young people away from politics			
Agree	58.2	72.6	65.4
Neutral	7.0	5.5	6.3
Disagree	34.8	21.9	28.3
Candidates ignore the youth vote			
Agree	64.6	53.9	59.3
Neutral	8.0	7.6	7.8
Disagree	27.4	38.5	32.9
Young voters are turned off to politics because of the amount of money involved in campaigns			
Agree	43.4	33.5	38.4
Neutral	10.5	7.1	8.8
Disagree	46.1	59.4	52.8

(75 to 66 percent). Negative campaigning scored a close second, with 70 percent of the chairs agreeing that negative campaigning turns off young voters. The Democratic chairs were more likely to agree with this proposition than the Republicans (75 to 65 percent). And the media get their share of the blame: 65 percent of the respondents agreed that the "media has done much to turn young people away from politics." Here, it was the Republicans who agreed most (73 to 58 percent). Finally, 58 percent of the chairs agreed that "people do not become interested in politics until they reach middle age," an issue upon which there was agreement across party lines.

So, the local party chairs agreed with both the notion that youth disengagement is an individual problem (young people are not well educated and not interested in politics) and the criticism of political elites (negative campaigning, poor media coverage). They did not, however, agree with the proposition that the amount of money spent in campaigns turns off young voters. Overall, 53 percent disagreed with the statement (59 percent of Republicans and 46 percent of Democrats). But the chairs were willing to assign some blame to the political process as well: 59 percent agreed that "candidates ignore the youth vote." Here, Democrats had a more negative judgment than Republicans (65 to 54 percent).

The chairs did express considerable optimism about the possibility of mobilizing young voters. For instance, 87 percent agreed that "young voters will respond to the right candidates and issues." Furthermore, 93 percent agreed that "local parties can make a big difference getting young people involved in politics." On these positive points, there was a bipartisan consensus.

Why would so many party chairs suggest youth engagement is a serious problem and that their efforts have the potential to make a difference, but at the same time be uninterested in mobilizing young voters? For one thing, a local party might consider numerous groups to be of critical importance to their efforts. Minority voters, union members, and women, for example, were frequently mentioned by Democratic leaders, and blue-collar workers and middle-class citizens were often noted by Republic leaders—just to mention a few. Given that younger voters typically make up only 14 percent of the electorate, we might expect political operatives to pay a limited amount of attention to this group. Indeed, perhaps they are giving this group enough attention.

Another reason may be the perceived difficulty of mobilizing young voters. Local party chairs were asked, "In your experience, how difficult has it been to mobilize young voters, 18 to 25 years of age?" Some 46 percent noted that it has been "very difficult" and another 45 percent said it was "difficult." There is some variation by party: 56 percent of the Democrats and 37 percent of the Republicans said youth mobilization was "very difficult." Conversely, only 5 percent of Democrats and 13 percent of GOP chairs said it was "not at all difficult." One interesting caveat to these figures is highlighted by the differences between chairs that report youth programs and those that do not. Only 37 percent of the former reported that mobilizing the youth was "very difficult," while 58 percent of those without such programs gave this answer. This suggests the possibility that youth programs may not be as difficult as commonly perceived.

Conclusion

In sum, local political parties appear to have the capacity to effectively mobilize the youth into the political process. And if present trends continue, this capacity will continue to expand. Indeed, it may well have expanded in the 2004 election, especially in battleground states where strong party and interest group activities, including a large number directed specifically at young people, may have played a decisive role in expanding youth turnout.

However, local party leaders as a group to not appear strongly interested in mobilizing the youth vote. Young citizens are not high on the radar screens of many party leaders compared to other groups, such as senior citizens, who vote at very high rates. And even when youth are a political priority, many local parties appear to have only modest programs to register young voters and get them to the polls. This situation may result from strategic considerations or the difficulty of mobilizing young people. Perhaps local party leaders, given their increased emphasis on helping candidates win elections—rather than cultivating long-term party loyalties—have concluded that it is more profitable to persuade undecided voters than to mobilize a group traditionally on the sidelines. The good news is that local party leaders recognize the disengagement of youth citizens as a serious problem and believe local parties can do something about it. One would surely hope that the dramatic increase of youth voting in 2004 caught their attention.

We believe the time is ripe for local party committees to create innovative programs to reach out to young voters and bring them into the electoral process. Young voters are increasingly up for grabs politically, and in the closely divided electorate, they are a resource that can win elections. The sudden upswing in young voter turnout in 2004, whatever its source, presents local party committees with a golden opportunity. And of course, it is in the long-term interests of political parties to develop positive relationships with young people, who are the middle-aged and older voters of tomorrow. If local parties make good on this opportunity, then the strong and vibrant party organizations of the twenty-first century will live up to their promise as instruments of democracy.

Notes

1. See, for example, a recent report by the Representative Democracy Project, a federally funded partnership among the national Conference of State Legislatures, the Center for Civic Education, and the Center on Congress at Indiana University; numerous studies commissioned by the Center for Civic Education; and several studies by the Center for Information and Research on Civic Learning and Engagement.

2. For a discussion of the "college connection" and voting rates, see CIRCLE information at http://www.civicyouth.org/quick/non_college.htm.

Part IV

Minor Parties

14

The Dynamic of Third Parties
and the Perot Constituency

Twelve Years and Counting

Ronald B. Rapoport and Walter J. Stone

Ask a political scientist why the United States has a two-party system, and you are likely to get an institutional- or policy-based explanation. The winner-take-all system of single-member districts and the Unit Rule in the Electoral College encourage factions to remain in their party rather than striking out on their own. Campaign-finance and ballot-access laws stack the electoral process in favor of the existing parties and against upstart independent candidates or third parties that manage to attract a few votes. Each of these explanations has considerable validity.

However, there is another, more overtly political, explanation for why the American two-party system persists. We call this explanation the "dynamic of third parties." Third-party candidates are most likely to emerge and attract a significant vote share under conditions of "major-party failure" (Rosenstone, Behr, and Lazarus 1996). This failure may be a recession or scandal that implicates both parties or a persistent policy problem such as lingering deficits or a divisive war that neither party has adequately addressed. When a third-party or independent candidate (we use the terms interchangeably) attracts a significant share of the vote in an election, it signals the two major parties that there is a substantial disaffected constituency in the electorate. In response, one or both of the major parties make a bid for the third party's constituency by adopting policy positions designed to attract its support. If the major-party bid is successful, the third party's constituency shifts to that party, taking the wind out of the movement's sails.

As a result, successful third-party movements generally do not last very long. The larger their vote share is, the more tempting their constituencies are to a major party and the more likely a takeover bid is to be vigorous and successful. But another consequence of this bid is change in the major party itself. The effect third parties can have on major-party change has been recognized by scholars for some time. Walter Dean Burnham (1970) and James Sundquist (1983) give third parties a significant place in their explanations of changes in the two-party system. The authors of the most systematic account of the emergence of third parties describe this dynamic of third parties in this way:

> Thus the power of third parties lies in their capacity to affect the content and range of political discourse, and ultimately public policy, by raising issues and options that the two major parties have ignored. In so doing, they not only promote their cause but affect the very character of the two-party system. When a third party compels a major party to adopt policies it otherwise may not have, it stimulates a redrawing of the political battle lines and a reshuffling of the major party coalitions. (Rosenstone, Behr, and Lazarus 1996; cf. Mazmanian 1974, 143)

Figure 14.1 summarizes the logic of the dynamic of third parties.

Although the dynamic of third parties is widely recognized in American political history, its implications have never been examined thoroughly by exploring the impact of a significant third-party movement. In this chapter,

Figure 14.1   The Dynamic of Third Parties

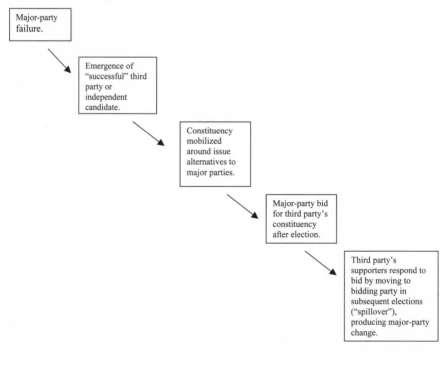

we relate the dynamic of third parties to Ross Perot's independent electoral movement in the 1992 presidential election and to its aftermath in national elections from 1994 through 2004. We summarize an argument developed more fully in our book on the Perot movement and its effects (Rapoport and Stone 2005) and extend the analysis through the 2004 elections. In studying this case, we hope to illustrate the potential impact third parties can have on change in the major parties by revisiting an example most scholars dismissed as of little long-term significance.

Surveys of Potential Perot Activists as Data Sources

Our primary sources of data are surveys of potential Perot activists in 1992 and 1996, with parallel samples of major-party potential activists in 1996.[1] The 1992 survey of potential Perot activists was based on a national sample of callers to Perot's toll-free number. This study was extended into a six-wave panel in which we recontacted respondents in 1994 and subsequent election years. In 1996 we added national samples of Reform, Democratic, and Republican contributors to their respective national parties in the period before the 1996 election season. We also recontacted these respondents in subsequent elections, generating a second long-run panel.

We refer to our respondents as "potential activists" because calling Perot campaign headquarters or writing a (typically small) check to a political party does not constitute activism in a candidate's campaign. Why focus on potential activists for a third-party movement rather than ordinary voters? One reason is convenience and accessibility. Callers to the Perot campaign and party contributors identify themselves as unusually interested in the third-party movement. Ordinary voters for Perot (or any third-party candidate) do not identify themselves as such except in surveys of the entire population of citizens. A random sample of ordinary citizens, even in a year such as 1992 when the third-party candidate was extraordinarily successful, would produce a relatively small number of respondents who voted for the candidate.[2] To study the dynamic of third parties as it plays out in subsequent elections, we must study third-party supporters through time following the election in which the third party appeared. A small baseline sample of voters in the initial election quickly dwindles to meager numbers over any significant period of time.[3]

Our surveys of potential Perot activists do not suffer from the limitations of general population surveys. And potential Perot activists defined in advance were likely to yield a substantial number of actual activists. Indeed, about three-quarters of the 1992 sample engaged in some sort of campaign-related activity for Perot during the spring and summer campaign, before he temporarily dropped out in July. Just over half of the sample was active in some way beyond voting during the abbreviated fall campaign after he reentered.[4] Moreover, we began with a large sample of almost two thousand callers in 1992, which yielded 1,321 respondents to the first wave of the panel. Because we had high response rates to the first and subsequent waves of the panel, we have unique data not only on what motivated activist supporters during Perot's initial campaign but also on what they did in the elections that followed. We thus have unusually complete data on a third-party candidate's core supporters during the election in which the candidate emerged and in the third party's aftermath, allowing us to observe the consequences of a major-party bid.

There are several advantages to studying activists in a third-party movement. Activists mobilize ordinary voters, both by leading opinion and by stimulating others to participate (Beck 1974; Eldersveld 1956; Gerber and Green 2000; Katz and Eldersveld 1961; Rosenstone and Hansen 1993). Indeed, 64 percent of the 1992 sample tried to convince others to support Perot during the spring-summer phase of the campaign. Moreover, Perot's name could not have appeared on any state's presidential ballot without extensive grassroots efforts by volunteer activists to organize and collect ballot petition signatures. Activists are better informed about politics than the average voter, and they are relatively well versed in the choices and issues at stake. As a result, the issue basis of a party or campaign comes into sharper relief by studying activists compared with looking exclusively at voters (McClosky, Hoffman, and O'Hara 1960; Miller and Jennings 1986).

Of greater importance, campaign activists are likely to be especially sensitive to changing opportunities and choices as events unfold (Carmines and Stimson 1989; Jacobson 2000; Miller and Schofield 2003). Third-party activists, for instance, should be more responsive than third-party voters to a major-party bid for their support, and a successful bid would have to appeal to activists as part of its ultimate strategy of attracting voters (Miller and Schofield 2003). Thus, we rely on our activist samples for most of the information we report about the Perot constituency and for evidence on individuals' behavior in elections after 1992. In the larger project, we flesh out the story of the Perot movement and its impact on the major-party system in much more detail (Rapoport and Stone 2005).

The Dynamic of Third Parties and the Perot Movement

We need not tarry over the first two stages of the dynamic of third parties depicted in figure 14.1. There was substantial discontent with both the Republican and Democratic parties before Ross Perot announced his intention to run. Indeed, a significant reason behind support for Perot in the 1992 was the "push" potential supporters felt away from both parties. At the same time, however, people were strongly pulled toward Perot as a candidate. His candidacy exploited (and probably helped stimulate) dissatisfaction with the Democratic and Republican parties, but, as we will show, it had more substance than merely registering discontent.

Perot was also extraordinarily successful in attracting support from activists and voters. His "legions" of volunteers completed the Herculean task of getting his name on the ballot of all fifty states. He won the largest popular vote share since ex-president Theodore Roosevelt ran as an independent in 1912, and his was the first third-party movement to win more than 5 percent in two consecutive elections since the Republican Party emerged in 1856. Thus, by any standard, Ross Perot's electoral movement was significant; the question is whether its significance extended beyond its own successes in 1992 and 1996 and had a lasting impact on electoral politics. For that to have occurred, the conditions described by the dynamic of third parties would have to apply both to the movement in 1992 and 1996 and to the elections that followed.

An Issue Constituency for Perot?

One of the conditions for the dynamic of third parties to work is the existence of a clearly defined issue constituency that supports the insurgent candidate and can be attracted by subsequent major-party appeals. One of the reasons Ross Perot's campaign was dismissed by many observers was the perception that he did not have an issue agenda that unified his supporters and differentiated them from the major-party supporters. Is it true, as *Washington Post* columnist E. J. Dionne put it during Perot's campaign, that "Perot's vote suggests his supporters were bound together only by anger over the nation's economy and a rejection of the two major party nominees"?[5]

A third party's constituency is distinctive to the degree that it differs from that of the major parties, and in turn this distinction is affected by the degree of choice offered by the major parties on the issues in question. When the major parties converge to the same position on an issue or issues and a significant number of people disagree with that position, there is an opportunity for a third party to appeal to the disaffected constituency. A third party could emerge to articulate a distinctive position on the issue or issues of concern, point out the absence of choice between the Democrats and Republicans, and attract significant support. Its success would signal the existence of many supporters of the third party's issue positions, which could set up a bid by one or both major parties. In contrast, when the major parties offer a clear choice on issues, the opportunity for a third party is less propitious, because potential supporters have a greater stake in major-party conflict. There is no reason to expect the major parties to converge or distinguish themselves on every issue, so opportunity for third-party traction may occur on some issues and not on others.

Ross Perot emphasized three issue clusters in his 1992 campaign: balancing the federal budget, reform, and economic nationalism (Rapoport and Stone 2005). On issues related to these dimensions, potential Perot activists were consistently supportive of the Perot agenda. They favored term limits, amending the Constitution to require a balanced budget, and increasing taxes to reduce the deficit, and they backed measures to limit foreign imports and decrease foreign involvement.

In contrast to their support for these "Perot issues," the potential activists could be found on both the liberal and conservative sides of the issues that traditionally divide the major parties. For example, Perot callers were strongly opposed to eliminating the death penalty and they staunchly opposed a constitutional amendment to limit abortions. They favored national health insurance and further government regulation to control pollution, while they adopted conservative positions on two other issues by opposing affirmative action and permitting gays in the military. On the overall liberal-conservative spectrum, they placed themselves on average just to the right of center, but this position reflected a pattern of diverse positions on specific issues rather than a consistently centrist position across the issues (Rapoport and Stone 2005, chap. 4). Indeed, when we compare Perot supporters with major-party activists, the Democratic and Republican constituencies diverge most sharply on the traditional Left-Right dimension, with Democrats taking consistently strong liberal positions and Republicans occupying equally clear positions on the right. On the Perot issues of reform, economic nationalism, and balancing the budget, potential Perot activists were unified in favor of all three and were distinct from the position of both major parties—although they were not as distinct from the major parties as the two parties typically are from each other.

Figure 14.2 depicts the placement of the Perot movement and the two major parties in 1992 on a graph with the traditional Left-Right issues on the horizontal dimension and the Perot issues on the vertical.[6] The advantage Perot had on his key issues was that while Democrats and Republicans were sharply different on the liberal-conservative dimension, they were close to indifferent or in opposition on the Perot issues. Meanwhile, Perot's relatively centrist position on Left-Right issues gave way to a distinctly supportive position on budget, reform, and economic nationalism issues.

This seems about as close to an ideal situation as a third party can hope for in American politics, and it helps explain the historic levels of electoral support Perot enjoyed in the 1992 election. In addition, of course, the 1992 issue map indicates the strong signal sent by the Perot movement—a signal unlikely to be missed by entrepreneurial party leaders seeking to add to their base in a competitive electoral environment.

Figure 14.2   Two-Dimensional Map of 1992 Candidates and Parties

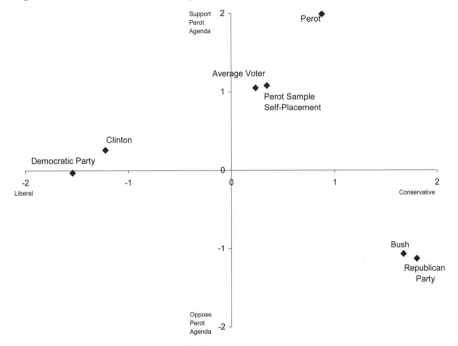

The Major-Party Bid for Perot Supporters

Although the administration of Bill Clinton made an overt bid for the Perot constituency early on, the Republicans were in a much better position to appeal to Perot supporters because they were not in control of any of the major institutions of national government. In addition, they had a natural affinity with Perot on the budget issue (Rapoport and Stone 2005, chap. 7). Despite the fact that some Republican leaders resisted the idea of cozying up to the man whom many blamed for their loss of the presidency in 1992, House Republicans under the leadership of John Kasich and Newt Gingrich made concerted overtures to Perot, especially on the deficit issue.

Clear evidence of a centrally coordinated bid from the Republican Party is found in the Contract with America, a unique attempt by a congressional party to impose a national frame on U.S. House races in the 1994 elections. The Contract was signed by virtually all Republican House candidates and was written with the 1992 Perot constituency expressly in mind (Rapoport and Stone 2005, chap. 7). It was as remarkable for what it left out as for what it included. Included in the Contract were a number of commitments specifically linked to the Perot agenda: on reform issues, term limits, balancing the federal budget, and foreign involvement. On the other hand, the Contract said nothing about the party's commitments to a constitutional amendment prohibiting abortion, which would have been expected if it were designed to appeal to the Republican base, nor did it mention the Republican Party's long-standing commitment to free trade. Overall, the Contract was significantly closer to the Perot agenda, as represented in Perot's book *United We Stand*, than it was to the 1992 Republican platform (Rapoport and Stone 2005, chap. 7).

Interviews we conducted with Republican strategists indicate a concerted effort to identify and contact 1992 Perot voters in the 1994 campaign by concentrating their efforts where Perot won a substantial share of the 1992 vote. According to Dave Sackett, a polling strategist working for the Republican Party, one project identified selected precincts nationwide with high Perot voting. Registered voters who habitually voted in either party's primary were removed, and telephone canvassers contacted the remaining households to identify individuals who had voted for Perot in 1992. All individuals identified as actual or potential Perot supporters in 1992 were directly contacted by telephone, sent direct mail tailored around Perot's issues, and canvassed door-do-door prior to the 1994 elections.[7] Our survey of potential Perot activists indicates these efforts paid off. The more active individuals were for Perot in 1992, the more likely they were to have been contacted by Republican House campaigns in advance of the 1994 elections (Rapoport and Stone 2005, fig. 7.3).

Another way a major party could make a bid in subsequent years is by putting up more experienced candidates who are able to effectively appeal to the third party's former supporters. Experienced candidates may run for the House as a result of national party efforts to recruit them, or they may individually recognize the third party's vote share as representing the same opportunity for them that was seen by national party leaders. Under either scenario, if the size of the Perot vote in a district signaled an opportunity for 1994 Republican House candidates, we should find a clear relationship between that vote and the emergence of experienced challengers. In fact, we do find that experienced challengers were much more likely to run in 1994 in districts where Perot had done well in 1992 than we would expect based on a host of factors ordinarily used to explain why experienced candidates in a party run for the House (Rapoport and Stone 2005, 159–61). There is also a significant relationship between the 1992 district vote for Perot and the amount of money expended on the race by the Republican Party (Rapoport and Stone 2005, 162).

The Perot Constituency's Response

The 1994 elections are important to our thesis, because if the dynamic of third parties is to apply to the Perot case, it must help explain the historic

Republican victory in that year. Prior to the 1994 elections, the Republican Party bid for the Perot constituency. Therefore, our expectation is simple: the Republicans should have benefited from former Perot voters' support in their drive to win control of Congress.

There is a strong relationship between the size of Perot's 1992 vote in districts held by the Democrats before the 1994 elections and the probability that the district would flip to the Republican column in 1994. In marginal Democratic districts where Perot won 5 percent of the vote, the probability that the district would flip to the GOP was only .03, whereas in districts where Perot won 30 percent of the popular vote, the probability it would flip soared to .81.[8]

Based on a simulation of the 1994 elections that employs a multivariate statistical model to explain the Republicans' vote share in each district, we conclude that the GOP owed its majority to the size of the Perot vote in 1992, and that if Perot's share in 1992 had been under about 13 percent of the popular vote, the Democrats would have retained majority control. In sum, therefore, our analysis means that the Republican victory in 1994 was directly attributable to the size of the Perot vote and logic of the dynamic of third parties, which the Republicans exploited well. In contrast to many interpretations of the 1994 elections, the "Gingrich Revolution" owed its success not to a rightward shift in the electorate, but to the Republicans' success in responding to the signal sent by a moderate insurgent candidacy committed to budgetary responsibility, reform, and restraint abroad.

As mentioned, mass public opinion surveys generally are not up to the task of testing our theory. Nonetheless, it is important to our argument to demonstrate a link between behavioral shifts among individuals consistent with the change in fortunes experienced by the Republicans and its source in the Perot vote at the aggregate level. We do this by demonstrating a "spillover effect" from the 1992 Perot campaign to Republican House campaigns in 1994 among activists. A spillover effect would occur if active participation in the 1992 Perot campaign increased involvement in subsequent GOP House campaigns—the greater the activism for Perot, the greater the activism for Republican House candidates in 1994. In addition, spillover from the Perot to the Republican campaigns should depend on contact by the Republicans. We expect a spillover effect because active involvement for Perot should have made individuals more visible to Republican campaigns and because those who were active in Perot's campaign would have been more sensitive to the Republican Party's bid for their support.

Figure 14.3 shows that in our panel of potential Perot activists, there was an effect of activism in the 1992 Perot campaign on active involvement for Republican House candidates in 1994, but only when there was contact from a House candidate's campaign. This effect, in other words, provides a microbehavioral mechanism consistent with the dynamic of third parties because the stronger the bid (the more contact) made to individual Perot activ-

Figure 14.3   Spillover Effect of 1992 Perot Activism on Activity in 1994 Republican House Campaigns by Contact from Republican Campaign

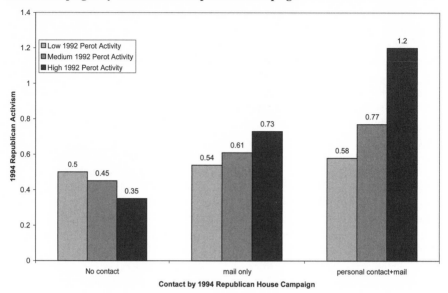

ists, the greater the tendency for them to shift activity to the Republican Party; and the stronger their involvement for Perot, the more the activists moved into Republican campaigns.[9]

We have already seen that the Republican mobilization strategy in 1994 was to identify and contact Perot activists; here we see that effort paid off by stimulating those most involved for Perot to move into the Republican camp. It is likely that the same processes were at work in the electorate as a whole. Moreover, the movement of the most active elements of the Perot constituency to Republican campaigns surely brought many ordinary citizens with them, as activists' convictions and behavior permeated their social, work, and political networks. The evidence, in other words, provides confirmation of individual change consistent with the electoral shift to the Republican Party after the 1992 election and the dynamic of third parties.[10] Additional analysis reveals that spillover into Republican campaigns continued through the 2000 elections and included spillover into the Buchanan and McCain nomination campaigns in 1996 and 2000, respectively.

Continuity in the Perot Constituency through 2004

We have seen that the Republican bid for the Perot constituency was successful in mobilizing former Perot supporters into GOP campaigns, which helps explain the aggregate election outcomes that favored Republicans, especially in 1994.[11] However, we have yet to examine whether the Perot constituency remained committed to its issue agenda in the years after 1992. This is important for two reasons: (1) continuity in the issue commitments of the Perot constituency is essential to Perot supporters' ability to effect change in the Republican Party as they responded to the GOP bid for their support in 1994 and in later years, and (2) continuity may affect the constituency's ability to have a lasting impact on national politics after the Republicans backed away from their bid following the 2000 presidential election. We will examine each of these implications after demonstrating the degree of continuity we find among Perot supporters between 1996 and 2004.

Figure 14.4 presents comparative data from our surveys of major-party and Reform contributors, summarizing the degree of commitment to the Perot agenda in each of four groups of respondents: core Republicans, by which we mean Republican contributors who were *never* active in the Perot movement; Democratic contributors; Reform contributors as a whole; and the subset of Reform contributors who were mobilized into Republican Party campaigns between 1994 and 2000 in response to the Republican bid.

The figure demonstrates that the Perot constituency remained intact and distinct through the 2004 elections in its commitment to the Perot agenda, compared with core Republicans and Democrats. In 1996, Reform contribu-

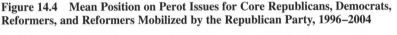

Figure 14.4   Mean Position on Perot Issues for Core Republicans, Democrats, Reformers, and Reformers Mobilized by the Republican Party, 1996–2004

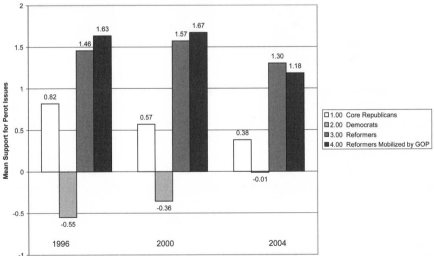

Note: Entries are mean support for Perot issue positions. Issue items are coded on seven-point scales from −3 (strongly oppose the Perot position) through +3 (strongly support the Perot position).

tors who were active in Republican campaigns as well as those Reform contributors who remained outside the Republican Party were strongly committed to the Perot issues. In the same year, Republicans were more modestly supportive of Perot issues, and Democrats were opposed. The same basic pattern holds through the 2004 elections, except that Democrats' opposition to the Perot agenda softened to the point where by 2004 they were indifferent, while Republicans' support was cut about in half. Meanwhile, Reformers maintained relatively strong support for the issues that motivated Perot's campaigns.

Figure 14.4 provides striking evidence of continuity and distinctiveness in the Perot constituency, up to twelve years after Perot's initial campaign. It is perhaps not surprising that Reform contributors as a whole remained strongly committed to the Perot agenda, but there was little difference between them and those drawn into the GOP ranks. And by 2004, both groups of Reformers were sharply more committed to the Perot issues than core Republicans. Moreover, when we break down the Perot issue index into individual issue items (data not shown), Reformers are consistently distinct from core Republicans with the exception of increasing taxes to reduce the deficit.[12]

The Republican Agenda under President George W. Bush

The persistence of the Perot constituency through the 2004 election is potentially of great political significance because the Republican Party, under the leadership of President George W. Bush, has retreated spectacularly from the positions it took in its bid for Perot supporters. Indeed, across the three issue dimensions that define the Perot agenda, the Republicans since the 2000 election have adopted positions and policies opposed to those articulated by Ross Perot and consistently held by his constituency since 1992.

Under President Bush, the United States committed to its most important military venture since Vietnam when it invaded Iraq in 2003. More troubling than the invasion, from the perspective of Perot supporters' long-term policy interests, was the decision to undertake in Afghanistan and Iraq the most extensive nation-building projects since the Marshall Plan after World War II. This commitment is not in keeping with Perot's emphasis on domestic priorities or with his economic nationalism emphasis on limited foreign involvements.[13]

Bush's renunciation of the economic nationalism part of the Perot agenda extended to trade and immigration as well. In contrast to Perot activists' persistent support of limiting immigration, Bush early on offered strong support for an agreement between the United States and Mexico that would "pave the way for many illegal Mexican immigrants—up to 3 million—to remain in the United States and would 'serve as a precedent for other nationalities.'"[14] Although the 9/11 attacks prevented immediate follow-up on this initiative, the administration maintained its guest-worker program, especially for farm workers.

Bush's support for NAFTA and CAFTA, the North American and Central American free trade agreements, remained a linchpin of Republican trade policy, despite the opposition of Perot and his supporters. Indeed, Bush backed down on his only trade policy likely to appeal to Perot's supporters: his promise to impose tariffs on steel imports for up to three years in order to help domestic producers.[15]

Finally, in the areas of the federal budget and reform, Bush's performance was, if anything, even less in keeping with those of Perot and his supporters than it was on other Perot issues. Under Bush and the Republican majorities in Congress, the budget surplus of $236 billion in fiscal 2000 was wiped out and the deficit ballooned to $412 billion in fiscal 2004. As tax revenues declined and spending increased, the prospects for ever-increasing deficits became a prominent aspect of President Bush's legacy.

The most significant reform initiative during Bush's first term dealt with campaign finance in the guise of the McCain-Feingold and Shays-Meehan proposals to limit soft money—positions with overwhelming support from Perot activists. Although President Bush did not threaten a veto, neither did he endorse the bill, saying he would "reserve judgment until he sees the final product."[16] Without Bush's support, only thirty-nine Republicans voted for the House version, and it passed on a close vote. Bush further signaled his ambivalence by failing to arrange a high-profile signing of the legislation and by not inviting Senator John McCain, the leading Republican proponent of reform in Congress, to attend the signing.

In sum, the Bush administration and the Republican Party have effectively reneged on the bid the GOP made for the Perot constituency following the 1992 election. We have seen that the issue commitments behind the Perot constituency remained largely intact through the 2004 election. Does Perot activists' continuing support for Perot issues combined with Republican ambivalence or opposition on those same issues mean that Perot activists withdrew from their previous involvement in the Republican Party in 2004?

In Rapoport and Stone 2005 (fig. 9.1), we showed that Perot callers to the 1992 toll-free number maintained by the Perot campaign were more active in Republican than in Democratic campaigns from 1994 through 2000. In this section, we will examine whether there was a change in relative campaign activity between 2000 and 2004 in response to the Bush administration's policies contrary to the Perot agenda. Our measure of Republican campaign activity is a simple count of the number of activities that respondents performed for Republicans in presidential and House campaigns, as well as for the Republican ticket as a whole. We create identical counts of

Democratic campaign activity in both years and compare them by taking the ratio of Republican to Democratic activity. The advantage of using a ratio is that it controls for different levels of mobilization and activism that occur in both parties in different election years.

Figure 14.5 reports the ratio of Republican to Democratic activities for 2000 and 2004. A score above 1.0 indicates a Republican advantage in activity, below 1.0 greater Democratic than Republican activism. Consistent with our earlier results (Rapoport and Stone 2005), there was substantially more Republican activism than Democratic activism in all campaigns in the 2000 election.[17] In fact, the Reformers were again about half as active in Republican campaigns as they were for Democratic candidates. However, by 2004, there was a radical shift in overall activity. Not only did the Republican advantage disappear in 2004, but there was slightly more activity in Democratic campaigns than in Republican campaigns. In the presidential campaign, there was only 87 percent as much Republican activity as Democratic, a decline in the ratio between 2000 and 2004 of almost 40 percent. Republican House candidates continued to retain a slim advantage over their Democratic counterparts, probably owing to the larger number of Republican incumbents running for reelection, but even here the GOP advantage over the Democrats in House races declined to virtual parity.[18]

Figure 14.5   Relative Major Party Campaign Activity for Reform Contributor Sample, 2000–2004

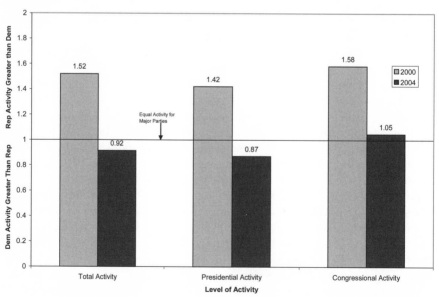

We have seen the spillover that occurred between the 1992 Perot campaign and 1994 Republican House campaigns (figure 14.3). Similar spillover effects occurred to the Republican Party's advantage in 1996 through 2000 (Rapoport and Stone 2005). There is no evidence of spillover from the 1992 Perot campaign into Democratic campaigns during this period. We interpret all of this as evidence of a favorable response by core Perot supporters to the GOP bid that occurred in various ways throughout the 1990s and into the 2000 elections. The question, then, is did the Republican renunciation of the Perot program result in spillover into Democratic campaigns in 2004 for the first time since 1992?

An analysis of relative campaign activity in Republican and Democratic campaigns between 2000 and 2004 reveals that Perot activity was strongly associated with a decline in Republican activity relative to Democratic activity—as the number of activities in the 1992 Perot campaign increased, respondents became *less* engaged in 2004 Republican campaigns, controlling for 2000 activity. For every activity for Perot performed twelve years earlier, our sample shifted by .15 activities away from the Republicans.

The effects of contact by major-party campaigns in 2004 were also strong. But while Democratic contact produced a relative increase in Democratic activism and Republican contact increased activism in that party's campaign, each Democratic contact again had half as much effect as each Republican contact (.329 vs. 216). However, because Republicans contacted Perot supporters more frequently than Democrats did (an average of 2.4 contacts by Republicans vs. 1.8 by Democrats), the net effect of contact for the two parties is about the same. Thus, in 2004 both parties had the opportunity to mobilize former Perot supporters, unlike in previous years when Republicans alone were effective in mobilizing activists for Perot.

Conclusion

Third parties in American politics face a number of barriers to their formation and success in national elections. As a result, serious national third-party efforts are rare, and candidacies that attract a substantial share of the popular vote are rarer still. Nonetheless, despite the institutional and political barriers to third parties, occasionally one emerges that captures a significant vote share. When that occurs, the dynamic of third parties has a chance of producing significant change in the two-party system. A necessary condition for the dynamic of third parties to play out is for the third-party movement to be supported by a constituency with a reasonably coherent issue agenda. An issue-based constituency can then motivate a major-party bid for its support in subsequent elections.

Contrary to the views of many academic and other close observers of

American politics, Ross Perot's followers were united by a common set of issue concerns that differentiated them from major-party supporters. As a result, there was a programmatic basis for the Republican bid, which was successful in attracting a significant portion of the Perot constituency to its cause. Several consequences followed from the success of the Republican bid. First, Republican electoral fortunes changed dramatically for the better. The GOP won majority control of the House and Senate for the first time since the 1952 elections, and they won an excruciatingly close presidential election in 2000, while continuing to hold thin majorities in Congress. The dynamic of third parties, in other words, played out in the post-Perot era by helping to create one of the most competitive and partisan periods in American history. Additions to the Republican Party from the ranks of the Perot constituency also changed the GOP in discernable ways, for example, by shifting the aggregate policy commitments of its activist and congressional ranks in a direction more consistent with the Perot issue agenda (Rapoport and Stone 2005, chap. 10).

One implication of our analysis is that the Perot constituency appeared to be alive and well twelve years after the 1992 election. We should be cautious about exactly how we interpret the idea of a "Perot constituency." We do not think that it necessarily means that former Perot activists and voters would necessarily think of themselves as Perot disciples or still part of his political movement. Indeed, we found that by the 1996 election, when Perot ran a second time, a large percentage of 1992 Perot activists had dropped out of his campaign and evaluated him much less positively. Despite the candidate-centered nature of much of our politics and the fact that Perot epitomized this development in many ways, he nonetheless tapped into and/or helped create a sizable constituency committed to a reasonably coherent issue agenda of reform, deficit reduction, and economic nationalism. Because these commitments still animate the individuals involved, the possibility that the Perot constituency could continue to play a pivotal role in our politics is real.

Despite the fact that the Republican Party took on a more Perot-friendly cast in the 1994–2000 period, after the 2000 election, under the leadership of President George W. Bush, House Majority Leader Tom DeLay, and others, the Republican Party effectively renounced its commitment to the Perot constituency. It has since presided over record-breaking deficits, led the charge to a new and more aggressive form of internationalism, and dragged its feet on reform issues of keen interest to the Perot constituency. As a result, we have seen that, beginning in the 2004 election, former Perot activists have partially withdrawn from Republican campaigns, and they have shown significant signs—again for the first time—of shifting their support to the Democrats.

This leads to a second implication of our analysis, which is that the Bush renunciation of the Perot agenda creates an opportunity for the Democratic Party to bid for its support. Even though Democratic contact with Perot supporters was less than Republican contact, our results from 2004 suggest former Perot supporters shifted strongly toward Democratic activity. Perot supporters in 2004 were ripe for the picking. An entrepreneurial Democratic candidate or leader might well articulate a program that could plausibly appeal to Perot supporters and, as the Republicans did in 1994, target former Perot backers for direct campaign appeals. A strategy of this sort could tip the national electoral balance in the Democrats' favor. Such a leader might point to the balanced federal budget and surplus during the Clinton years, to a more measured form of internationalism built on dissatisfaction with the Iraq experience, and to domestic economic insecurities stemming from a global economy. If so, our data suggest there may be more than a remnant of the Perot movement available for mobilization, waiting in the wings to stimulate a new direction in major-party politics.

Notes

1. Details about the surveys may be found in Rapoport and Stone 2005, appendix A.

2. The 1992 American National Election Study (ANES) panel survey of the U.S. electorate yielded only 128 respondents who reported voting for Perot.

3. The ANES panel included only sixty-one 1992 Perot voters who reported casting a presidential vote in the 1996 election. At that, of course, it was only a four-year panel, whereas our potential-activist panels stretch more than twice that period of time.

4. Only one respondent held a paid position in the campaign; all others who were active were volunteers.

5. E. J. Dionne, "Anger at the Economy Was the Glue Binding Supporters to Perot," *Washington Post*, November 12, 1992.

6. The placements of all three parties and candidates are based upon the perceptions of Perot activists.

7. Authors' interview with Dave Sackett, Alexandria, VA, July 31, 2003.

8. This analysis was carried out on Democratic-held seats where the Democrat won in 1992 with 60 percent or less of the popular vote. The analysis controls for a variety of other explanations for why it might switch to the Republican Party, including the size of the two-party vote share in 1988 and 1992, the experience and spending of both parties' House candidates, the level of support Democratic incumbents gave to President Clinton (as a control for the possibility that voters were reacting against President Clinton's policies), and whether the district is in the South.

9. The analysis controls for previous Republican campaign activism, party identification, and the degree of preference for 1994 House candidates.

10. There is no evidence of spillover between the Perot and Democratic campaigns in 1994, even in the presence of contact from the Democrats. This suggests that the Republican contact was tied specifically to the Perot program, as we have suggested. We also find long-term effects of spillover to the 2000 House campaigns, indicating a remarkable staying power to Perot's effect on Republican fortunes (Rapoport and Stone 2005, chap. 9).

11. See Rapoport and Stone 2005 for an analysis of the impact of Perot on elections from 1996 through 2000. The general point is that the Republican "resurgence" owed its strength

and staying power to the success of the Republican bid, as illustrated here in the 1994 elections. The one national election that the Republicans did not win in this period, the 1996 presidential contest, was nonetheless one in which their candidate, Bob Dole, was helped by the Perot vote.

12. In the 2004 survey, the items composing the Perot index were: limiting immigration, limiting imports, limiting foreign involvement, support for term limits, eliminating soft money contributions to parties, and raising taxes to reduce the deficit. Only on the latter item were core Republicans more supportive than Reformers.

13. Our 2004 survey shows that Reform contributors were much more strongly opposed to the Bush administration's Iraq policy than Republicans, though they were not quite as strongly opposed as Democratic contributors.

14. Frank Davies, "Relief for Mexican Workers a Top Priority" *San Diego Union-Tribune*, August 4, 2001.

15. Richard W. Stevenson and Elizabeth Becker, "After 21 Months, Bush Lifts Tariff on Steel Imports," *New York Times*, December 5, 2003.

16. Greg Gordon and Lawrence M. O'Rourke, "Senate Bars 'Soft Money': Campaign-Finance Battle Moves Next to House," *Minneapolis Star Tribune*, April 3, 2001.

17. In Rapoport and Stone 2005, we report on the 1992–2000 caller panel, whereas figure 14.5 reports results from the 1996–2004 contributor surveys. We use the contributor surveys here because of lower attrition rates in that panel than in the caller study.

18. Essentially the same picture emerges when we restrict the analysis to Reformers who had been active between 1996 and 2000 in Republican campaigns. The decline in the Republican advantage is sharp, although the ratios remain slightly in favor of the Republicans in both House and presidential campaigns.

15

The Declining Significance of Ralph

Christian Collet and Jerrold Hansen

Following a surprising campaign in which many considered him to hold the balance of power between the two major parties, Ralph Nader's third run for the presidency in 2004 was something far less auspicious. Attacked by the Left, strategically promoted by the Right, and shunned by his Green Party base, "Nader-the-Independent" seemingly spent as much time in court vying for ballot access as on the campaign trail competing for votes. His appearances diminished from "Super Rallies" in raucous concert arenas to the sedate confines of university lecture halls. He lacked the money for ads but became the target of ads attacking him. In the end, Nader qualified for nearly three-quarters of state ballots, representing a variety of party labels. But he received less than half the votes he got in 2000 and saw his share exceed the two-party margin in only one state, Wisconsin, which was carried narrowly by Senator John Kerry. Four years prior, the Nader vote was a factor in at least eight states, two of which—Florida and New Hampshire—went infamously to then governor George W. Bush.

Failure is rarely a source of inspiration in political science, perpetual failure even less so. Even the body of literature that concerns itself with those who rarely win American elections—call them "third," "minor," or "alternative" parties and candidates—often concentrates on such movements at their peak rather than their decline (e.g., Rosenstone, Behr, and Lazarus 1996).[1] Nader's run in 2004, however, remains extraordinary if for no other reason than because two-party electoral politics in the twenty-first century is extraordinary—extraordinarily competitive. If much of what we know about alternative politics is true—that significant independents emerge in a climate of major party vulnerability, not strength, "after landslides, not cliffhangers," as Rosenstone and his colleagues put it[2]—we would not have expected a candidate of Nader's stature to come forth in 2004. Yet, with no party structure, a reputation in decline, and the Republicans and Democrats nearly deadlocked in the Electoral College, he did.

In this chapter, we look at this unique and highly controversial presidential run. We begin by unfolding the events of 2004, marking the points of contrast between this and the past Nader efforts in 1996 and 2000. Here we give particular attention to the effect of state ballot-access laws—an issue that, in and of itself, came to dominate the Nader campaign. We then analyze the changes in Nader's constituency by using survey data provided by the Gallup Organization and aggregate data gathered at the state and county level. We conclude by addressing the consequences of Nader's decline and considering its broader implications for multiparty and independent politics in America.

The Anatomy of Descendence: The 2004 Campaign

It seems odd to describe as compelling a presidential campaign that receives 0.4 percent of the national vote, appears on just over two-thirds of ballots, and finishes fourth, fifth, and sometimes even sixth behind other minor party candidates in several states. Yet, in a climate of celebrity fascination as well as tight two-party competition, Ralph Nader somehow remained a story in 2004: the anticandidate, the consumer's crusader defying embittered Democrats and suddenly pragmatic progressives, as well as journalists who seemed to simultaneously dismiss and cover his every move. Perhaps at no time in recent American history has a political figure with so marginal a constituency been so closely watched or so readily feared. Governor George Wallace in 1968 could lay claim to the South. And Ross Perot, leading the polls in early 1992, could claim almost anything due to his wealth. But the Nader 2004 campaign rested solely on *potential*—the mere hypothesis that he *might* affect another dramatically close election by tapping anger simmering over the Bush administration's incursion into Iraq. As Michael Moore's controversial documentary *Fahrenheit 9/11* became a surprise hit in the spring and Vermont governor Howard Dean surged to an early lead for the Democratic nomination, it seemed certain that antiwar sentiment would spill over into the fall campaign. Nader, this time with no party to satisfy, would unquestionably be the most freewheeling critic of the Bush doctrine.

The irony was that when Nader finally announced his intention to mount another presidential run on *Meet the Press* on February 22, 2004, Moore, like Noam Chomsky and other icons of the Left, had long since taken public stands against such a campaign. *The Nation*, as early as December 2002, begged on its pages "Ralph, Don't Run" and, in an open letter to Nader published six days before his announcement, repeated its plea. After Dean dropped out on February 18, he explicitly cautioned his supporters "not to be tempted by independent or third party candidates."

For his part, Nader played down his potential threat to the Left, saying "the liberal establishment" should "relax and rejoice," since his "candidacy is not going to get many Democratic votes." Conservatives and independents disaffected from Bush would be his primary constituency this year, drawn to his clear stances against free trade and corporate crime. "The party-out-of-power members come back into the fold," he told National Public Radio. "It's the party-in-power that has the difficulty on the edges."

A Break from the Greens

Within the Green Party, a long debate has centered on the value of running candidates for the presidency. In some ways, it is reflective of a fundamental paradox facing minor parties in the United States: should they marshal their scant resources in an attempt to grow, even at the risk of losing their philosophical raison d'être? Or should they stay ideologically pure, even at the risk of being electorally stagnant (Collet 2002)? The purism-pragmatism dilemma is a unique one for the Greens, because considerable emphasis is placed on local activism—and because the party has shown success in some towns and cities by running focused, parochial campaigns. "Grassroots democracy" is at the top of their Ten Key Values, even before "ecological wisdom."

So when Nader told the party in a letter dated December 22, 2003, that he would not seek its nomination for the presidency, the news came as a mixed blessing. On the one hand, Nader—who had never registered as Green—was slapping the party in the face and recalling the fears of some who never wanted to become involved in presidential politics in the first place. On the other hand, it was clear he still wanted their support. "The occasion for this letter," he wrote, "is not simply that there are robust contending views about whether to have a Presidential candidate . . . but that . . . it is not feasible within the difficult parameters of state and federal election laws to wait and see what the Green Party will do." Because party rules required the decision to be made by delegates at its national convention the following June, Nader explained that it was too risky to wait; in many states, the requirements for getting on the ballot would require longer preparation.

Nader's semi-withdrawal from the Green nomination quest left an opening for David Cobb, a public interest lawyer who helped to found the Texas Green Party in 1999 and organized the successful ballot-access drive there for Nader in 2000. Cobb's mantra was for the Greens to pursue a so-called safe states strategy: in areas where the major parties were competitive, Cobb would abstain. It was antithetical to Nader's pursuit of being the relevant pivot, but Cobb argued that it would help to keep progressives from tuning the Greens out in the future. Nader, for his part, tried to maintain ties to the party by nominating longtime activist Peter Miguel Camejo as his running mate. In early 2004, Camejo had begun his own campaign for the Green presidential nomination in California, but just before the party convention in Milwaukee began, he joined the Nader ticket.

When the convention met on June 26, the Greens' decision boiled down to three choices: (1) abstain from the presidential race altogether; (2) nominate Cobb; or (3) endorse Nader (Martin 2005). Camejo carried a so-called Unity Resolution that would have allowed Greens to endorse both Cobb and Nader and then allow each state party to use the party's ballot line at their own discretion; it was rejected (Camejo 2005). After the first round of voting, which by party rule is held under an instant runoff system, Cobb received 309 delegate votes compared to 119 for Camejo and 117.5 for Nader. In the second round, Cobb prevailed over "no nominee," 408–308, and won the nomination.[3]

Without the Greens, Nader was still able to qualify for thirty-five state ballots (see table 15.1). Although his campaign was nominally independent, he appeared in eighteen states as the nominee of eight different political parties—ranging from the Reform party (in Colorado, Florida, Kansas, Mississippi, and Rhode Island) to the Peace and Justice party in New York. In four states, he ran under the designation "The Better Life." He qualified as an Independent (or "By Petition") in seventeen, mostly smaller, states (totaling 115 electoral votes). The four states in which Nader was barred entirely included three crucial elements of his influence-oriented campaign: Oregon and Hawaii, which each had given him 5 percent in 2000, and Ohio, which was promising to be the Florida of 2004. Symptomatic of the backlash against his candidacy, these failures distinguish this run from his run in 2000, where the three states in which he failed to qualify—South Dakota, Oklahoma, and North Carolina—were strategically inconsequential. On the bright side, Nader had somehow managed, under extremely difficult circumstances (Winger 2005), to make it onto two-thirds of the state ballots.[4] On the dark side, these states nominated only a little over half of the electors in

Table 15.1   Nader Ballot Status and Electoral College Impact, 1996–2004

	1996		2000		2004	
	States[a]	*EV[b]*	*States*	*EV*	*States*	*EV*
Appeared on state ballots	22	225	44	481	35	278
as a party candidate	19	192	39	435	18	163
as an independent	3	33	5	46	17	115
Certified as a write-in	15	225	4	32	12	222
Failed to qualify	14	88	3	25	4	38

Source: Federal Election Commission.
[a] Number of states in each category, including the District of Columbia
[b] EV = Total number of electoral votes for the relevant states

the Electoral College. In more than two-fifths of the College, as in 1996, voters would have to write in his name.

A Spoiled Image

As Nader became bogged down in legal trenches, his reputation took a further beating. The austerity of his campaign—he raised just $2.5 million in individual contributions—not only fostered a plodding image but also left his growing armada of antagonists free to attack. Several websites launched in response to his candidacy, but TheNaderFactor.com (funded by a group of Democratic activists calling itself the National Progress Fund) was perhaps the most vigorous, using its resources to air spots in battleground states that portrayed a phony "Bush-Nader '04" ticket and linked the candidate to the GOP right wing. A thirty-second radio ad in Oregon, Pennsylvania, and Florida asked listeners, "Remember Florida and the 2000 election? Well, the same right-wing Republicans that are anti-choice and anti-environment are suddenly pro-Nader." In New Mexico and Wisconsin, a television ad from TheNaderFactor.com showed a remorseful Nader voter from 2000 who had concluded afterward that the decision was wrong (Appleman 2004).

The respect that Nader had garnered over decades of leading the cause of consumer advocacy began to seem like ancient history. In a 1976 Roper poll, more than two thousand Americans were asked to identify the characteristics that described Ralph Nader. Topping the list were "dedicated" (checked by 40 percent of the respondents), "honest" (34 percent), and "public spirited" (30 percent).[5] Nader was often mentioned in other surveys as one of the most admired Americans; in both 1972 and 1976, his name was floated as a presidential nominee. As recently as 1989, 70 percent of Americans had a "favorable" view of Nader, according to an NBC News/*Wall Street Journal* poll.[6] His visibility receded through the 1990s, but rebounded in 2000 to enjoy a nearly two-to-one ratio of favorable to unfavorable ratings throughout most of that campaign.

In the interregnum between the Supreme Court verdict on the election in December 2000 and becoming a repeat candidate in early 2004, Nader started to fall into disfavor. This is shown in detail in a series of surveys conducted by Stanley Greenberg for the Democratic-leaning Democracy Corps/Institute for America's Future.[7] Measuring Nader's popularity through 100-point "feeling thermometers," figure 15.1 shows only small increases in his "cold" ratings through October 2000; a plurality were still neutral. But then two large increases in "cold" feelings occurred, the first from May 2001 to July 2002, and the second between May 2003 to May 2004.[8] Nader thus began the 2004 campaign with roughly half of America holding an antipathetic view of him. And as the campaign wore on, public perceptions—seemingly like the candidate himself—hardened. Between

Figure 15.1   Democracy Corps Poll Feeling Thermometers Regarding Ralph Nader, August 2000–November 2004

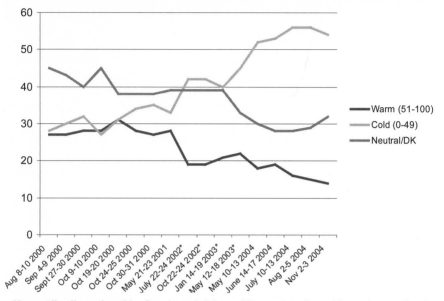

Notes: All polls conducted by Greenberg, Quinlan and Rosner Associates. All samples are of regis-tered likely voters, with the exception of the post–Election Day survey taken on November 2–3, 2004, which is of voters who participated in that election, N varies from 988 to 1,027 for the former, 2,000 for the latter. Data points noted by (*) indicate that the question wording was modified to "Green Party/ Ralph Nader's Party." See note 6 for the actual question wording.

Gallup surveys in March and September 2004, Nader went from 26 to 33 percent "favorable" and from 44 to 48 percent "unfavorable." In the Green-berg polls, he went from 52 percent "cold" in March 2004 to 54 percent on Election Day.

In a deliberate, almost self-fulfilling fashion, Nader thus encountered the twin political pillars of expediency and entrenchment. It was more than a surly Left and the "corporation disguised as a human being" in the White House, as Nader liked to say, that he ran against. It was the very system—a Byzantine structure of laws and rules, made and preserved by the corporate-beholden major parties—that suffocated anyone with the temerity to chal-lenge it on the ballot or in the debate hall. Above all, it was a society driven by money. Journalists began to note that Nader's once inexhaustible energy seemed to diminish as his opponents grew larger; at times, Nader would wield his broadening brush and attack the very culture that put shopping and sports over education and activism. With his popularity in decline, was the public becoming as much his target as the corporations who corrupted them? Independent candidacies had prospered before by telling Americans things they didn't want to hear. But in Nader's case, it seemed the messenger was becoming as bitter as the message. His relevance was still a question mark, though, depending on the closeness between Kerry and Bush—and whether history would repeat itself in Florida, where Nader was on the ballot.

On November 2, the answer came. Bush comfortably won the national vote by more than 3 million; Nader garnered 465,650 votes out of 122,295,345 cast, a microscopic 0.4 percent that put him much closer to Libertarian candidate Michael Bednarik (397,265) than to having any effect on the outcome between the major parties. In only one county—Grand in Utah—did Nader match the 2.7 percent share he earned nationwide in 2000; in a handful of others in the Deep South and Mountain West, Nader actually finished behind Bednarik, and sometimes behind Constitution party candidate Michael Peroutka and Green Party candidate Cobb. It was easily the worst of his three presidential runs, amounting to less than a sixth of the votes he had earned in 2000—and just two-thirds of what he earned in 1996, when he only passively campaigned. What happened?

Individual-Level Analysis: More Conservative, Less Committed

Between 2000 and 2004, some noteworthy changes took place in the Nader constituency (see table 15.2). Relying on data provided by the Gallup Organization,[9] we focus on three. The first is a *social/demographic shift* away from well-educated, non-churchgoing supporters to less-educated, Protestant, occasional churchgoers. The second is a *partisan and ideological shift* from independents, Democrats, and liberals toward moderate and conservative Republicans. The third is an apparent *shift toward lower propensity voters*—the group that had strong intentions to vote in 2000 receded in intensity in 2004.

Looking at table 15.2, we see that Nader made slight gains among women in 2004; his support, however, remained majority male—a contrast with Gore and Kerry, who have relied more on support from women. Nader made further gains among those Americans already known to be a significant part of the Nader coalition: those who are 18–29 years old. Both Nader and Kerry lost married voters, as well as union households. More significant, however, is that Nader appears to have ceded to the Democrat some of the better educated—another key element of his prior campaign. Seventy-one percent of Nader's 2000 constituency had gone to college; four years later, this had declined to 61 percent. By comparison, 69 percent of Kerry backers had gone to college and 44 percent took a diploma—an increase of twelve percentage points from Al Gore's.

Table 15.2 Nader and Kerry/Gore Preelection Supporters

	Nader 2004	Nader 2000	Net Change	Kerry	Gore	Net Change
Gender						
Male	52%	54%	−2	45%	42%	+3
Female	48	46	+2	55	58	−3
Age						
18–29	22%	17%	+5	14%	11%	+3
30–49	40	43	−3	35	40	−5
50–64	25	25	0	29	26	+3
65+	13	14	−1	22	24	−2
Marital status						
Married	44%	49%	−5	49%	51%	−2
Live with partner	9	5	+4	7	5	+2
Widowed	7	6	+1	10	12	−2
Divorced	16	14	+2	16	16	0
Single, never married	21	24	−3	18	17	+1
Union household	16%	20%	−4	19%	22%	−3
Education						
High school diploma	30%	24%	+6	24%	36%	−12
Some college	27	33	−6	25	32	−7
College graduate	34	38	−4	44	32	+12
Religion						
Protestant	42%	28%	+14	45%	40%	+5
Catholic	23	26	−3	26	29	−3
Other	20	22	−2	17	18	−1
None	13	19	−6	11	7	+4
Frequency of church attendance						
Once per week	22%	21%	+1	25%	32%	−7
Almost every week	8	7	+1	11	11	0
Once a month	13	10	+3	14	14	0
Seldom/Never	56	63	−7	49	41	+8
Party identification						
Republican (+ lean)	31%	21%	+10	7%	7%	0
Independent (no lean)	19	26	−7	3	4	−1
Democrat (+ lean)	50	54	−4	90	89	+1
Ideology						
Very liberal	11%	14%	−3	8%	4%	+4
Liberal	20	26	−6	26	23	+3
Moderate	40	38	+2	46	46	0
Conservative	22	16	+6	16	20	−4
Very conservative	4	2	+2	3	3	0
Don't Know	2	4	−2	1	3	−2
High likelihood of voting[a]	62%	80%	−18	86%	84%	+2
(N)	919	591		10,446	8,096	

Notes: Data are pooled from preelection Gallup polls throughout 2000 and 2004. They are unweighted.

[a] The polls asked respondents to assess their likelihood of voting on a 1–10 scale, with 10 being extremely likely. "High likelihood" is defined as those who gave a 9 or 10.

Religion is another area of difference. Naderites in 2000 were distinguished by low levels of religiosity: 19 percent reported they were not affiliated with an organized church and 63 percent said they "seldom" or "never" attended services. Four years later, this declined to 13 and 56 percent, respectively, as the proportion that identified as Protestants increased substantially (from 28 to 42 percent). Kerry may have picked up some of this non-churchgoing crowd as he posted gains in the proportion of those who "seldom" or "never" attend services.

The second important shift revolves around partisanship and ideology. In 2000, 54 percent of Nader supporters identified as Democrats, 26 percent as independents. But as the Kerry/Gore base attracted just a handful of Republicans over two elections (7 percent), Nader's campaign grew from one-fifth (21 percent) to nearly one-third GOP-identifying (31 percent). The proportion of Democrats in his campaign declined to 50 percent, and independents shrank to less than one-fifth (19 percent). Further, consider Nader's loss (and Kerry's gain) of liberals. Those reporting themselves to be very or somewhat liberal were a combined 40 percent of Nader's 2000 backing, just 27 percent of Gore's. But four years later, liberals constituted a larger proportion of Kerry's (34 percent), not Nader's (31 percent), support. As conservatives declined from Gore to Kerry, they became a larger part of the Nader campaign, growing from 18 to 26 percent.

The last area of contrast—and in some ways the most important—is in the likelihood of voting. As the last of seven screening items in their likely-voter model, Gallup asks the question, "If '1' represents someone who will definitely not vote and '10' represents someone who definitely will vote, where on this scale would you place yourself?" To be considered a likely voter, a poll respondent would answer 7 or higher. In table 15.2, we show the percentage of those who gave a response of 9 or 10—the Americans most motivated to cast a ballot. In 2000, 80 percent of Nader backers fell into this high-propensity category—a proportion in the ballpark with Gore's backers (84 percent). But in 2004, as Kerry's share of these voters grew to 86 percent, Nader's fell dramatically to just 62 percent.

Where the 2000 Nader campaign revealed itself as a small but active center-left following, the 2004 version came to resemble the loose, perpetual fragments of major party dissent, the fringe floaters inclined either to abstain from politics or to cast ballots, perhaps on a whim, for anything but the establishment. We can see this in greater detail in the Edison/Mitofsky National Exit poll (data not shown). In many ways, those who went to the polls for Nader in 2004 look more like those who voted for "Other" (that is, an alternative candidate unmeasured or categorized in the survey) than those who backed the Democratic nominee: they are more conservative and give higher approval ratings to Bush and more support for the war in Iraq (although two in three nonetheless opposed the decision to go to war). This is a change from the 2000 election, when Nader voters were decidedly less supportive of establishment policies than Gore voters (Collet and Hansen 2002). Voters for Nader and "Other" in 2004, furthermore, share the twin traits of being late deciders and less likely to say their vote was "for [their] candidate."

At the Aggregate Level

When looking at the aggregate-level returns for Nader in 2004 compared to 2000 and 1996,[10] one can witness demographic continuity in the midst of substantial numerical change.

To get a sense of Nader's decline, one needs to consider first his initial rise between 1996 and 2000.[11] The New England states saw the most dramatic movement in this period, with Nader surging in states such as Rhode Island (from 1.5 to 6.1 percent) and New Hampshire, where he was unqualified in 1996 but took a pivotal 3.9 percent as a Green four years later (Bush defeated Gore there by less than 1.3 percentage points). His growth was steadier in the five Pacific states. In 1996, he was qualified in four as a Green; in Washington, he was on as an independent. Nader went from 3 percent across the region in 1996 to almost 5 percent in 2000, seeing his vote go as high as 10 percent in Alaska and 6 percent in Hawaii. He had grown respectably in California, and Oregon, it seemed, was becoming a crucial stop on the Nader campaign map. His 5 percent there in 2000, it was thought, played a role in the nail biter that saw Gore prevail by 0.4 percentage points.

To say the bloom had worn off Nader's rose would be a poetic understatement, for the declines were profound across the most important constituencies he had established in the two prior elections: in the Pacific, where he had ballot-access problems, his vote dropped by more than five percentage points; in New England, he made the ballot, for the most part, but saw his vote plummet by a similar margin; and in the Mountain states, he also saw an above-average drop. Nader's decline was generally higher in the smallest states (defined as those with three to six electors), such as Vermont and New Hampshire, than in larger ones. And he dropped more precipitously in Gore and Kerry states than in states won by Bush, perhaps further indication of liberal alienation and the tactical efforts to keep him off the ballot. Too, it seems as if Nader may have suffered without the Green Party label. He fell harder in states where he was on as party candidate in 2000 than in states where he had been an independent.

Nader's Legacy

In his last public appearance of the 2004 campaign, Nader met with a small gathering in the dimly lit basement of the Capitol View Library in southwest Washington. He was asked by one journalist whether his candidacy was worth it. "Of course," he replied. "The fight for justice is always worth it. What's the alternative, surrender?" (D'arcy 2004).

In an increasingly rigid and competitive two-party system, Nader's question, though intended as rhetorical, is worth pondering. Nader's 2004 run not only came to symbolize the near impossibility of qualifying for the ballot as in independent in fifty-plus-one states but also the self-fulfilling prophecy of centering a campaign around the ambiguous theme of one's own futile crusade: fighting the system itself. In 1996, and particularly in 2000, Nader deftly tapped into progressive frustration that built during the Clinton years, and he did so under the banner of a growing, futuristically minded—and at that point, largely unknown—Green Party. The message, though critical, remained upbeat. By 2004, having heard the spoiler scenario repeated countless times, Americans were unconvinced that Nader could do anything other than hurt the Democrats. His campaign was, by definition, a negative from the beginning.

As our analysis shows, the younger, single, well-educated liberals that animated Nader's previous runs abandoned him and consolidated behind Kerry. He suffered without Green Party ballot access, particularly in the Pacific states, and saw his vote collapse everywhere—most significantly in the New England and Mountain regions where he had done well (in a relative sense) in 2000. His support became more diverse, including more Republicans and conservatives, but increasingly tenuous: supporters were less inspired by Nader as a person; less inclined to know about, or agree with, many of his issue positions; and most importantly, less likely to vote. In contrast to the movement of progressive "raiders" that seemed to grow naturally out of his 1970s anticorporate crusades, the Nader constituency today is something akin to a disparate, expressive, and possibly perpetuating "other" vote. Nader's predictions of antiestablishment, conservative support proved somewhat accurate, even if the size of that constituency was exaggerated.

From the standpoint of building continued support for fundamental changes in national party politics, the Nader campaign in 2004 will be looked upon as a setback. Despite making an explicit appeal to unify alternatives into a single crusade, Nader eschewed the Greens and disdained their nominating system—and he suffered as a result. He not only lost the opportunity for ballot access in the Pacific and other regions but also undermined his own party-building principles. Like Jesse Ventura, he could be seen as a party wrecker. Like John Anderson and Ross Perot, his once-serious persona was transformed by the American presidential process into a national punch line. And with him, some might argue, went his most relevant issues: the role of money in politics, access to presidential debates, changes to the electoral system.

Was Ralph Nader merely a phenomenon created by an era of historically competitive elections? Or is there a substantive legacy for his three presidential campaigns? At the very least, it may be said that Nader has kept the light on alternative politics in a post-Perot era, where otherwise it might have been overshadowed by intense major-partisanship. However, it may also be said that the light he brought was by 2004 casting dark shadows. Nevertheless, even if his vote seems increasingly unstable and peripheral, our analysis suggests a geographic base remains for any challenger to the major parties—primarily in New England states and in parts of the West. Significant numbers of young voters remained with Nader in 2004 and would seemingly be attracted to him or a viable successor. Further, through his national effort to gain ballot access, he helped to expose to a new voting generation the extraordinary barriers (and undermining tactics) faced by those who want a chance to compete. Losing an election—not to mention a reputation—seems a taxing way to prove the point, but the point was nonetheless made.

Will Nader continue? The answer, in and of itself, seems irrelevant, perhaps as irrelevant as his 2000 campaign might have been if the election were not so excruciatingly close. Future close elections may continue to compel him. Few precedents exist, however, for a four-time minor-party presidential candidate to improve his standing among the American public. The only one to do so was Socialist Eugene Debs in 1912. So the deeper question is not about Nader, but whether *any* alternative candidate of national stature will be willing to endure the process of running for president in such a climate—or to run with a constituency that can only alter an outcome, not win an election. In 1968 or 1992, following landslides, Americans could accept the idea of an outsider throwing a wrench into the system. In 2004, they could not.

Notes

1. There are exceptions (e.g., Green and Binning 2002), including valuable work by Rapoport and Stone (2005) on the movement of minor party activists over time (see also chapter 14).

2. Rosenstone and his colleagues explain, "Third party candidates run to gain votes, not to affect election outcomes. If nationally prestigious candidates were mounting campaigns in an effort to change outcomes, then close presidential elections—when a shift of a few votes to a third party candidate could make a big difference in who wins—would prompt them to run. But just the opposite holds: nationally prestigious [third party] politicians appear after landslides, not cliffhangers" (Rosenstone, Behr, and Lazarus 1996, 201).

3. In personal correspondence dated December 17, 2005, Theresa Amato, Nader's campaign manager, informs us that "many, if not most of the [first round] votes for Camejo and other 'favorite son/daughter' stand-ins were meant for Ralph Nader and most of these voters were released from their pledge to vote for a particular candidate after the first round."

4. The authors thank Richard Winger for his correspondence regarding Nader's ballot-access situation.

5. Roper Report 76-10. Survey taken November 6–11, 1976 (n = 2,002). Question: "Here's another card with a list of words and phrases on it. Would you call off all of them that describe your feelings about Ralph Nader?" Accessed via R-POLL, the Roper Center online database available through LEXIS/NEXIS Academic Universe.

6. Survey taken January 14–17, 1989 (n = 2,025). Question: "In general, do you have a favorable or unfavorable opinion of Ralph Nader?" Accessed via R-POLL.

7. The Democracy Corps polls are of likely registered voters or registrants who had already voted. Question: "I'd like to rate your feelings toward some people and organizations, with 100 meaning a very warm, favorable feeling, zero meaning a very cold, unfavorable feeling, and 50 meaning not particularly warm or cold. You can use any number from 0 to 100, the higher the number the more favorable your feelings are toward that person or organization. If you have no opinion or never heard of that person or organization, please say so. Ralph Nader. Give . . . Ralph Nader a rating, with 100 meaning a very warm favorable feeling, zero meaning a very cold, unfavorable feeling, and 50 meaning not particularly warm or cold."

8. Along with an overwhelming public perception that he ruined Al Gore's chance of keeping the presidency in Democratic control (a debatable topic in academic circles—see, e.g., Burden 2004; Herron and Lewis 2004; Collet and Hansen 2002), there are several smaller events that may have slowly influenced the turn in public opinion on Nader. In mid-2001, James Carville began to openly attack Nader at Democratic gatherings; at the same time, Nader continued to draw thousands to his rallies and generally positive media for the launch of his "Democracy Rising" movement and his book *Crashing the Party*. From 2002, however, his press turned increasingly negative. In June of that year, he was roundly attacked for criticizing NBA officiating and for asking 18-year-old Cleveland Cavaliers rookie LeBron James to take a stand against Third World sweatshops. Such issues, it seemed, fell out of the purview of a presidential candidate during a nonelection season. In January 2003, Al Sharpton and Dennis Kucinich began to campaign for the presidency—in Sharpton's case, explicitly in pursuit of Nader's progressive constituency.

9. The Gallup Organization polled Americans on their presidential vote choice at twenty-six intervals between January 9 and October 31, 2004 (eighty days of interviewing spread over eight months). Pooled, these surveys included interviews with 28,242 adults (18 and over)—among them were 1,049 firm or leaning Nader supporters. The authors thank Lydia Saad of the Gallup Organization for help with these data.

10. Election returns were gathered from uselectionsatlas.org and merged to form a single, usable data set.

11. The divisions are defined as follows: New England = CT, ME, MA, NH, RI, and VT; Middle Atlantic = NJ, NY, and PA; East North Central = IN, IL, MI, OH, and WI; West North Central = IA, KS, MN, MO, NE, ND, and SD; South Atlantic = DE, DC, FL, GA, MD, NC, SC, VA, and WV; East South Central = AL, KY, MS, and TN; West South Central = AR, LA, OK, and TX; Mountain = AZ, CO, ID, NM, MT, UT, NV, and WY; Pacific = AK, WA, OR, CA, and HI.

Part V

Partisanship and the Public

16

The Growing Polarization of American Voters

David C. Kimball and Cassie A. Gross

When Hurricane Katrina hit the Gulf Coast in late August 2005, it left in its wake several long-term challenges for government at the local, state, and national level. However, it took only a few days for people to form opinions about the government's response to the crisis, and those opinions split along predictable partisan lines. A *Washington Post*/ABC News poll conducted on September 2, 2005 (just four days after the hurricane), found that 74 percent of Republicans approved of the way President Bush was handling the crisis, while only 17 percent of Democrats approved.[1] A CBS/*New York Times* poll conducted roughly ten days later found a very similar partisan split in evaluations of the president's response to the hurricane.[2] The highly partisan public reaction to a natural disaster is further evidence of political polarization in the United States.

Surging party polarization in the United States has recently received considerable scholarly attention. There is clear evidence of a growing influence of party and ideology on voting behavior during the last twenty years (Miller 1991; Bartels 2000; Abramowitz and Saunders 1998, 2005; Jacobson 2003; Stonecash, Brewer, and Mariani 2003). As party loyalty among voters has increased, rates of split-ticket voting have decreased. The same trends are evident in common measures: ticket splitting began increasing in the 1950s, peaked around 1980, and then declined substantially. The 2004 election produced the lowest levels of ticket splitting seen since the 1950s and 1960s. Thus, aggregate voting trends clearly point to growing party polarization in the United States.

In this chapter, we examine the political attitudes behind party polarization in the United States. We measure party polarization by examining responses to "feeling thermometer" ratings of political parties and presidential candidates collected in National Election Study (NES) surveys. Using these measures, we find that the 2004 election stands out as the most polarized campaign since NES began using feeling thermometers in 1964. In comparing levels of polarization among different groups of people, we find evidence that party polarization in the United States is an elite-driven development.

Searching for Political Polarization

A current subject of debate is whether the resurgent partisanship in the United States is a result of elite polarization alone or whether the mass public is simultaneously polarizing as well. There is clear evidence of polarization at the elite level. For example, roll-call vote studies indicate that Republican members of Congress have become more unified and more conservative during the last thirty years, while the Democrats in Congress have become more uniformly liberal (Rohde 1991; Poole and Rosenthal 1997). Similarly, the issue distance between Republican and Democratic party activists on social and economic issues has grown during the same period (see chapter 4 in this volume; Layman 2001; Wolbrecht 2002; Cotter and Fisher 2004; Layman et al. 2005).

At the same time, there is some disagreement about whether polarization has also taken place in the mass public. The debate focuses on whether there is a "culture war" in the United States, often summarized in the red state–blue state dichotomy used by journalists and pundits (Hunter 1994; Green et al. 1996; Williams 1997; Layman 2001; Frank 2004; Fiorina 2005; Ansolabehere, Rodden, and Snyder 2005). Much of the scholarly debate has examined whether different groups have moved farther apart in their positions on particular issues. Some argue that most Americans still hold moderate views on a host of economic and cultural issues (Fiorina 2005; Ansolabehere, Rodden, and Snyder 2005). If this perspective is true, then the increased partisanship in voting is simply the result of moderate voters having to choose between more extreme candidates than in the past.

One of the strongest challenges is a study by Fiorina (2005), who claims that mass polarization is a "myth." He argues that partisan, geographical, and social cleavages have not grown much over time and actually have diminished on some issues. Some studies of public opinion have found support for Fiorina's claim that Americans have not moved further apart on many issues (DiMaggio, Evans, and Bryson 1996; Evans 2003; Mouw and Sobel 2001). On the other hand, several studies find growing issue distances between Democrats and Republicans on several types of issues (DiMaggio, Evans, and Bryson 1996; Layman 2001; Fleisher and Bond 2001; Layman and Carsey 2002; Evans 2003). Part of the debate between Fiorina and others is whether Democrats and Republicans have moved *substantially* further apart in their issue positions (Fiorina 2005, 25–32).

Furthermore, other studies find a growing gap between Republicans and Democrats in terms of ideological identification, with Republicans becoming more conservative and Democrats more liberal over time (Abramowitz and Saunders 1998; Jacobson 2000). Still others find growing party differences in public evaluations of parties, candidates, and government institutions

(Fleisher and Bond 2001; Hetherington 2001; Jacobson 2003; Kimball 2005).

While studies of the issue distance between partisans are important, they may miss a psychological aspect of polarization. Political polarization is more than just holding different positions on hot-button issues. Polarization is also accompanied by an us-versus-them mentality, in which partisanship shapes the way people see the political world. As stated in *The American Voter*, "Identification with a party raises a perceptual screen through which the individual tends to see what is favorable to his partisan orientation" (Campbell et al. 1960, 133). This view is consistent with long-standing research emphasizing the importance of group perceptions in party identification and mass political behavior (Campbell et al. 1960; Berelson, Lazarsfeld, and McPhee 1954, 77–86).

Partisans are motivated to perceive events and even facts in ways that support their party (Fischle 2000; Bartels 2002). For example, in the 2004 NES survey, the mean placement of the Democratic Party on the seven-point ideology scale is 3.0 (slightly liberal). However, the mean placement of the Democratic Party by Democrats is 3.4 (between middle-of-the-road and slightly liberal), while the mean placement of the Democratic Party by Republicans is 2.4 (between slightly liberal and liberal). Clearly, the Democratic Party is perceived as more liberal by Republicans than by Democrats.

An example of public opinion on President Bush's policy agenda may be more instructive (Andres 2005). In recent public opinion surveys, respondents were asked about their support for two of President Bush's domestic policy proposals (private accounts for Social Security and school voucher programs). The survey questions explicitly identified President Bush as the source of the proposals. Elsewhere in the same survey, respondents were asked whether they supported private accounts for Social Security and school vouchers without naming President Bush as the architect of the proposals.

The results (shown in table 16.1) indicate that public support for both proposals drops significantly when President Bush is identified as the one proposing them. More specifically, support for the two policies drops substantially among Democrats when the policies are tied to President Bush, while Republican support for the policies is largely unaffected by the change in question wording. For some Democrats apparently, the moment they discover that President Bush is behind a policy proposal is the same moment they decide not to support the proposal. In contrast, Republicans generally have a positive view of President Bush, so their support does not drop after the president's name is attached to the policies. The vast majority of survey questions on public policy matters do not identify the politician or party advocating the policy. Thus, to mainly consider a respondent's self-placement

Table 16.1   Impact of President Bush on Public Support for Policy Initiatives

Policy Proposal	All Respondents	Democrats	Republicans
Support for private Social Security accounts (no Bush mention)[a]	56%	42%	77%
Support for President Bush's Social Security proposals[a]	37	11	74
Support for school vouchers (no Bush mention)[b]	62	55	70
Support for President Bush's school voucher program[b]	45	31	65

Source: Andres 2005.
[a] ABC/*Washington Post* poll conducted March 10–13, 2005
[b] Gallup poll conducted January 2001

on issue or ideological scales may miss some degree to which people exaggerate group differences, thus missing an important aspect of polarization.

Another way to understand the psychological side of partisan polarization is to consider social identity theory, which holds that partisans are motivated to praise their own group, denigrate the opposing group, and exaggerate intergroup differences (Tajfel and Turner 1986). In other words, people tend to believe there are greater differences between groups than actually exist. This insight has a ready application to American politics. Despite studies indicating that most citizens hold moderate positions and that rank-and-file partisans may not be very far apart on many issues, voters may still see their own party as good and the other party as bad. In addition, political campaigns in the United States tend to exaggerate party differences. For example, in the 2004 presidential campaign, the Republican Party spent more than $3 million compiling commercial databases on the consumer habits of Democrats and Republicans. The party conducted surveys to identify "anger points" (i.e., issues that made voters angry) that mirrored President Bush's policy agenda for different consumer groups then used the information to target those groups during the campaign.[3] Targeting consumers on the basis of issues that anger them may be an effective vote-getting strategy, but it is also likely to exaggerate the differences between the two major political parties. The in-group versus out-group perspective of social identity theory has also been used to study partisanship and attitudes toward other groups in the United States (Greene 2004; Bolce and De Maio 1999).

We measure polarization by the correlation between the party and candidate feeling thermometer ratings in National Election Study surveys. Thermometer scales ask respondents to rate an object on a scale ranging from 0 (indicating very cold feelings toward the person or group) to 100 (indicating very warm feelings). Measuring the correlation between thermometer ratings of the Democratic Party and thermometer ratings of the Republican Party, for example, captures the us-versus-them mindset that is an important feature of polarization. In a highly polarized citizenry, we would expect a strong negative correlation between the two party thermometer ratings and between the two presidential candidate thermometer ratings, as people rate their own party positively while rating the other party negatively. In a nonpolarized citizenry, conversely, one might expect no correlation. Finding a negative correlation between different objects on feeling thermometer ratings is actually hindered by a "response-set bias," a tendency for survey respondents to give similar ratings to all groups (Green 1988; Wilcox, Sigelman, and Cook 1989; Weisberg, Haynes, and Krosnick 1995). Thus, correlations between thermometer ratings provide conservative estimates of levels of party polarization.

Many other studies have used thermometer ratings to measure attitudes toward political parties and candidates (e.g., Wattenberg 1998; Bolce and De Maio 1999; Hetherington 2001; Fleisher and Bond 2001; Greene 2004; Fiorina 2005). These studies tend to compare mean thermometer ratings of the same object by different groups of respondents, or they compare the number of group respondents rating a political object positively (above 50) versus the number rating the object negatively (below 50). To our knowledge, Weisberg's studies of presidential elections are the only reports of correlations between thermometer ratings (e.g., Weisberg and Hill 2004; Weisberg and Kimball 1995). In the following section, we use the correlation measure to see whether party polarization has increased in recent elections. We then apply the measure to the 2004 election more closely to see which segments of the public are most polarized.

Trends in Party Polarization

We first examine correlations between thermometer ratings of political parties and presidential candidates in elections since 1964, when NES introduced the thermometer questions. The results (see table 16.2) suggest that party polarization reached new heights in 2004. The 2004 election produces the strongest negative correlation between party and presidential candidate thermometer ratings in the time series. In comparing presidential elections over time, we do not find evidence of a secular increase in party polarization. Polarization increased after the 1970s but then remained fairly level until rising sharply in 2004.

Wattenberg (1998, 158–62) argues that Americans have become more polarized in evaluations of specific political figures (especially President Ronald Reagan) but not in evaluations of political parties. The evidence here tends to suggest otherwise. The elections of 1972 and 1976 (featuring no

Table 16.2   Measures of Party Polarization in Presidential Elections

	Correlation between	
	party thermometers	candidate thermometers
1964	−.37	NA
1968	−.18	−.17
1972	.02ns	−.42
1976	.02ns	−.30
1980	−.23	−.29
1984	−.40	−.53
1988	−.39	−.38
1992	−.27	−.39
1996	−.40	−.42
2000	−.36	−.39
2004	−.47	−.61

Source: American National Election Studies.
NA = not available
ns nonsignificant

correlation between party thermometers and negative correlations between candidate thermometers) support Wattenberg's thesis, and correlations between candidate thermometer ratings are usually stronger than correlations between party thermometer ratings. However, each election since 1980 shows fairly reliable polarization between the two parties.[4] In addition, other presidential candidates after Reagan have generated similar levels of polarization. Finally, the strong correlations in 2004 suggest that President George W. Bush is a more polarizing political figure than either Reagan or President Bill Clinton.

A by-product of increasing party polarization in the United States is more intense feelings about presidential campaigns. Figure 16.1 provides more evidence that the 2004 election stands out as one of the most intensely contested campaigns in recent history. The trend lines in figure 16.1 indicate growing campaign intensity over time. In 2004, 85 percent of NES respondents said they care a good deal about who wins the presidential election, the highest percentage recorded since the NES began asking this question in 1952. Similarly, the 2004 election produced the highest percentage of respondents who see important differences between the parties (76 percent)—the second highest figure, recorded in 2000, is a distant 64 percent. While not pictured in figure 16.1, the 2004 election also produced the highest percentage of NES respondents who participated in campaign activities (Abramowitz and Saunders 2005).[5] Finally, a relatively large portion of voters made up their minds early in the 2004 campaign, and only 30 percent of NES respondents reported making their presidential voting decision after the national party conventions. This is tied for the second lowest such percent-

Figure 16.1   By-products of Partisan Polarization, 1952–2004

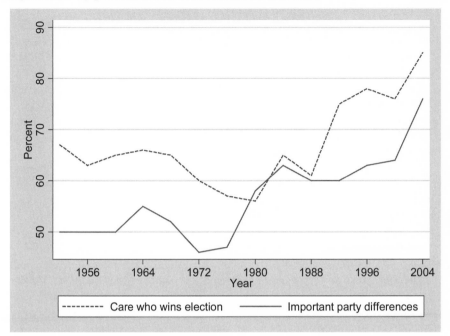

Source: American National Election Studies

age recorded by NES behind the Eisenhower-Stevenson rematch in 1956. Thus, several measures indicate that the 2004 presidential election was one of the most intense, polarizing campaigns of the last fifty years.

Who Are the Most Polarized People?

We next take a closer look at the 2004 election to find groups most likely to view the political world in a polarized fashion. We hypothesize that party polarization in the United States is largely an elite-driven phenomenon. People do not form political opinions in a vacuum. Many citizens tend to follow the opinion leadership of elites (elected officials, pundits, and party and interest group leaders) who share their point of view (Zaller 1992). The growing ideological distance between parties at the elite level has increased the salience of party labels and ideological considerations when citizens evaluate politicians and make voting decisions, in effect "priming" the general public to be more partisan as well (Kimball 2005). Thus, as political parties at the national level have become more unified in ideologically driven disputes, the public has come to see politics in more partisan terms (Hethering-ton 2001; Burden and Kimball 2002; Jacobson 2003).

There is additional evidence suggesting that political elites are leading the charge toward more polarized politics in the United States. Several stud-ies indicate that party polarization at the elite level began in the 1970s (Rohde 1991; Poole and Rosenthal 1997; Layman 2001), while party polar-ization at the mass level lagged behind, not starting until the 1980s (Miller 1991; Abramowitz and Saunders 1998; Bartels 2000; Hetherington 2001; Jacobson 2000). Furthermore, other studies have demonstrated elite leader-ship of public opinion on several important issues (Carmines and Stimson 1989; Brody 1991; Zaller 1992).

If party polarization is driven by political elites, then which citizens should exhibit the highest levels of polarization? Layman and Carsey (2002) found that as elites have become more polarized across issue dimensions (what they label "conflict extension"), party identifiers that are most aware of those differences are the most likely to become similarly polarized across issue dimensions.

We first examine strength of partisan political commitment. We expect that people most committed to a partisan agenda are most likely to mimic elites and view politics through a partisan lens. The results in table 16.3 sup-port this hypothesis. As expected, strength of partisanship is fairly strongly associated with levels of party polarization. Strong partisans are much more polarized in their evaluations of the parties and presidential candidates than are weak partisans and independents. In addition, partisans active in cam-paigning are more polarized than the rest of the electorate. Strong partisans and people involved in many campaign activities produce the highest levels of party polarization among the various subgroups we examine in this chap-ter. Similarly, those who care about the outcome of the presidential election are substantially more polarized than politically apathetic citizens. In fact, those who professed no interest in the presidential campaign produced no evidence of polarization—the correlations between party and candidate ther-mometer ratings are statistically insignificant for this group of politically dis-interested citizens. Those citizens most committed to partisan politics (through campaign activity or their own party identification) produce the highest levels of polarization.

It is worth noting the sizable numbers of people in the strongly commit-ted categories of table 16.3. In 2004, one-third of the NES respondents were strong partisans, while only 10 percent were pure independents. Similarly, 22 percent engaged in high levels of campaign activity (two or more activi-ties). The strongest and most active partisans, therefore, are not exactly a thin slice of the electorate.

We also compare overtly partisan activity to other political activity that is often nonpartisan (see the bottom of table 16.3). We examined two NES

Table 16.3   Party Polarization by Political Commitment in 2004

	Correlation between	
	party thermometers	*candidate thermometers*
Strength of partisanship		
Pure independent	.30	−.28
Independent leaner	−.17	−.51
Weak partisan	−.32	−.47
Strong partisan	−.70	−.78
Campaign activity		
None	−.29	−.50
One	−.51	−.55
Two or more	−.60	−.80
Cares who wins election		
No	−.08[ns]	−.06[ns]
Yes	−.50	−.65
Member of an organization (nonreligious)		
No	−.43	−.57
Yes	−.52	−.68
Worked with others in the community		
No	−.46	−.59
Yes	−.52	−.68

Source: American National Election Study 2004.
[ns] nonsignificant

questions that asked whether respondents worked with others in their community on local issues or whether they belonged to any kind of nonreligious organization (such as a union, school group, or hobby club, for example). While we see that people who work with others in their community or are members of an organization are more polarized than nonparticipants in their views of the parties and presidential candidates, the differences are fairly mild. This suggests that it is a commitment to partisan activity rather than political activity per se that is the stronger predictor of polarization.

If party polarization is elite driven, then we also expect levels of polarization to be highest among citizens who are most attentive to the politics that elites produce. We test this hypothesis by examining some measures of political awareness and interest (see table 16.4). As expected, party polarization is more severe among the highly knowledgeable and highly interested segments of the public.[6] Furthermore, people who see important differences between the political parties are more polarized than those who see no party differences. Thus, party polarization rises among the segment of the general public that is most attentive to politics in the United States.

In another element of the elite-driven theory of party polarization, we

Table 16.4   Party Polarization by Awareness and Mobilization in 2004

	Correlation between	
	party thermometers	*candidate thermometers*
Sees an important differences between parties		
No	−.18	−.49
Yes	−.53	−.64
Political knowledge		
Low	−.36	−.47
Medium	−.47	−.63
High	−.57	−.72
Interest in political campaigns		
Not much	−.25	−.37
Somewhat	−.39	−.56
Very much	−.58	−.70
Contacted by a political party		
No	−.36	−.57
Yes	−.60	−.67

Source: American National Election Study 2004.

expect higher levels of polarization among people who are mobilized by political parties. We examine whether mobilization efforts by political parties may be a source of increased polarization (see table 16.4). As expected, those who have been contacted by one of the political parties indeed are more polarized than those who avoid party contact (particularly in their evaluations of the two parties). This is significant because 45 percent of NES respondents in 2004 reported being contacted by a political party, a substantial increase from previous years. By comparison, for example, only 20 percent reported contact by a political party in the 1992 presidential election. The mobilization efforts of political parties, which have expanded dramatically in recent elections, have likely contributed to the growing polarization of the American public.

We also examine the news media as an elite influence on public opinion. Perhaps party polarization is shaped by these sources of news and other political information, especially by the new forms of media in the United States. For example, some scholars see the Internet as a polarizing force in American democracy because of the user's ability to filter out opposing views (Sunstein 2001; Bimber and Davis 2003). Others suggest that talk radio is a source of political persuasion (Barker 2002) and may polarize the public due to the red-meat content of some talk radio programs.

Indeed, we find higher levels of polarization among people who get campaign information from the Internet and listen to political talk radio (see table 16.5). However, this may reflect self-selective attention to politics among Internet users and talk radio listeners, rather than the independent effects of talk radio and the Internet on the public. We also find somewhat higher levels of polarization among people who get campaign news from newspapers and from television, two staples of the old mainstream media. Thus, it appears that attention to politics through any medium—not just new forms of media—contributes to party polarization.

Finally, we examine several demographic factors to look for other correlates of party polarization in 2004 (see table 16.6). First, we examine the familiar red state–blue state divide, and we find little difference in party polarization between Republican (red) and Democratic (blue) states. Furthermore, party polarization was no higher in the "purple" battleground states of the 2004 presidential election than in the noncompetitive states.[7] Finally, there does not appear to be a strong regional basis for party polarization in the United States. Thus, party polarization is not confined to a particular set of states based on region or partisanship.

In terms of other demographic variables, we find somewhat higher levels of party polarization among women, whites, upper income earners, elderly citizens, and married couples. However, most of these demographic differences in party polarization are not nearly as strong as those associated with political awareness and political commitment (presented above). Further-

Table 16.5   Media Usage Correlates of Party Polarization in 2004

	Correlation between	
	party thermometers	*candidate thermometers*
Listens to political talk radio		
No	− .37	− .53
Yes	− .56	− .70
Saw campaign information on the Internet		
Has no Internet access	− .37	− .55
No, but has Internet access	− .45	− .57
Yes	− .55	− .69
Read about campaign in a newspaper in past week		
Did not read a newspaper in the past week	− .40	− .49
No, but did read a newspaper	− .49	− .62
Yes	− .49	− .65
Attention to campaign on national TV news		
Did not watch national TV news	− .38	− .59
Some, very little, or none	− .44	− .54
Quite a bit or a great deal	− .53	− .67

Source: American National Election Study 2004.

Table 16.6 Demographic Correlates of Party Polarization in 2004

	Correlation between	
	party thermometers	*candidate thermometers*
State partisanship		
Red	−.49	−.58
Purple (battleground)	−.50	−.62
Blue	−.43	−.63
Region		
Northeast	−.44	−.63
North Central	−.54	−.63
South	−.48	−.60
West	−.40	−.58
Gender		
Male	−.41	−.58
Female	−.52	−.64
Race		
Nonwhite	−.26	−.43
White	−.52	−.64
Income		
Bottom third	−.39	−.49
Middle third	−.44	−.63
Top third	−.62	−.67
Age		
18–35	−.39	−.57
36–60	−.47	−.61
Over 60	−.54	−.64
Marital status		
Married	−.54	−.66
Unmarried	−.34	−.51

Source: American National Election Study 2004.

more, several of the demographic measures, including income, age, race, and marital status, may simply be proxies for political activity and proximity to the political system. For each of the demographic comparisons in table 16.6, the subgroup with the highest voter turnout rate produces the highest levels of party polarization. The results in table 16.6 tend to reinforce the conclusion that party polarization is strongly related to political activity and awareness.

Conclusion

In studying political polarization in the United States, it is important to consider the us-versus-them mentality that accompanies diverging positions on important issues. We have attempted to measure this psychological component of party polarization using questions common to the NES battery for several elections. We find that the 2004 election stands out as the most polarized presidential campaign in forty years. This finding is consistent with several studies that have documented growing party polarization in the American public (Hetherington 2001; Abramowitz and Saunders 1998, 2005; Layman 2001). One dissenter is Fiorina (2005, 25), who argues that there is partisan polarization but not "popular" polarization along other lines of disagreement. The resurgence of parties in recent years, however, means that parties are once again the primary organizing force in American mass politics. To look for another type of polarization is to look for a straw man.

In examining sources of party polarization in the United States, we find evidence consistent with the theory that polarization is an elite-driven phenomenon. People tend to follow the opinion leadership of elites who share their political predispositions, and people tend to view politics through more partisan-colored glasses when elites engage in partisan conflict. We find the strongest levels of party polarization among those most committed and attentive to political elites in the United States. In addition, mobilization efforts by the political parties appear to contribute to polarization in the general public. By comparison, we find little evidence that regional differences are sources of party polarization.

Once unleashed, it is difficult to rein in the forces creating party polarization. It might be defused by the emergence of a group of elite political figures who reach across party boundaries, as senators John McCain and Joe Lieberman have done. However, recent history does not offer much encouragement, because politicians who reach out to the other political party often get punished by their own party. Senator Lieberman was soundly defeated when he sought the Democratic nomination for president in 2004. Senator McCain, too, was defeated when he campaigned for the GOP presidential nomination in 2000, and there is tremendous distrust of Senator McCain among Republicans after his attempts to find legislative compromises with Democrats on issues such as campaign finance reform, global warming, and immigration.

Party polarization among the mass public tends to reinforce a political strategy of pleasing the party base. For example, President Bush's nomination of White House counsel Harriet Miers to be a Supreme Court justice was not derailed by Democrats but by Republicans who were uncertain of her qualifications and conservative bona fides. After the Miers nomination was withdrawn, the president responded by nominating Judge Samuel Alito, who holds more firmly established conservative views.

From our vantage point, polarization at the elite level shows no signs of abating. As a result, party polarization among the public will likely continue as well.

Notes

1. Dan Balz, "For Bush, a Deepening Divide," *Washington Post*, September 7, 2005.
2. The poll numbers were retrieved from PollingReport.com, http://www.pollingreport .com/disasters.htm.
3. Thomas B. Edsall and James V. Grimaldi, "On Nov. 2, GOP Got More Bang for its Billion, Analysis Shows," *Washington Post*, December 30, 2004.
4. The weaker correlation between party thermometers prior to 1980 may be a question-wording artifact. Prior to 1978, the NES asked respondents to rate "Republicans" and "Democrats" on the feeling thermometers. Since then, it has asked people to rate the "Republican Party" and the "Democratic Party."
5. Our campaign activity measure is constructed from six items that asked respondents whether or not they participated in specific actions: tried to influence others, attended a meeting, wore a campaign button, donated to a candidate, donated to a party, or other campaign activity.
6. Our political knowledge measure is constructed from eight factual questions in the NES survey (identifying individual political figures, which party is more conservative, and which party controls more seats in the House and Senate). We summed the number of correct responses to the eight items and then collapsed the resulting scale into thirds.
7. We categorize red, purple, and blue states using the same classification as Abramowitz and Saunders (2005). George Bush won the red states by at least six percentage points, and John Kerry won the blue states by at least six points. The margin of victory in the purple states was less than six points.

17

Party Coalitions in the American Public

Morality Politics, Issue Agendas, and the 2004 Election

John R. Petrocik

The New Deal party coalitions were defined by region, religion, national origin, race, and social class. These particular cleavages were not novel.[1] Similar social differences distinguished party supporters in comparable Western European party systems. The distinctiveness of the American parties was in the weakness with which these differences correlated with party preference. Moreover, although Catholics and Protestants preferred different parties, neither party embraced the "religious impulse." The class basis of the party system was extremely weak. The Democratic Party was associated with "average" Americans, while the GOP was linked to the wealthy and big business, but party identification correlated only weakly with measures of social status.

These previously missing social cleavages in American party politics have become prominent within the last twenty years. The religious impulse, expressed in the concern of Republican politicians and activists with moral, ethical, and religion-based issues, has become an increasingly important aspect of interparty debate (Abramowitz 1997). Simultaneously, social class has become one of the strongest correlates of party preference: Republican and Democratic identifiers have become increasingly distinct in their religiosity and social class. The changes have had an effect on the issue agendas of the parties.

Social Cleavages and Party Systems

The key to this connection between groups and parties is the influence of social characteristics and their associated structures on the perceptions, beliefs, and interests of citizens. Social characteristics place us within networks of common experiences that buttress our already powerful tendency to develop social identities (see Tajfel and Turner 1986; Sidanius and Pratto 2001). We think of ourselves as, for example, Irish Catholic, African American, Jewish, Christian, or an average working person. We look at the world through this identity; others are inclined to see us in these terms as well and conduct themselves accordingly. A group's members experience similar advantages, disadvantages, and relationships with others within and outside the group. Such common experiences lead to ever more distinctive beliefs and perceptions. The salience of any social identity varies among individuals and groups but their existence is a virtual constant. When the identity is linked to real and imagined material and symbolic wins and losses, the groups frequently organize into opposing political parties.

Social Groups and Electoral Issues

Political issue conflict is affected because the party-group alignment dictates the issue concerns and policy prescriptions of a party. The linkage is completely recursive: groups support a party because of the policies it promotes; the party promotes certain policies because it draws supporters, activists, and candidates from particular groups. Tangible economic interests are often behind party competition, as when managers and employees are locked into disputes over wages and terms of employment. At other times the conflict is largely symbolic: ethnic self-esteem and cultural beliefs are at issue. Indeed there are probably as many symbolic conflicts as there are material ones in modern societies—and the intensity of the former is at least as great. A party's candidates and leaders may offer policy proposals as public goods in which all will share, but a party's proposals have their origins in the values and interests of their supporters.

Not surprisingly, therefore, a party's vision of the "common good" is often unshared or even opposed by those outside the party. These latter issues tend to arise from the concerns of groups associated with only one party. Democrats, reflecting the prominence of African Americans and other ethnic minorities among their supporters, commonly see serious racial discrimination problems in need of attention by the government. Republicans, with few supporters from minority ethnic groups, tend not to see racial discrimination as particularly pressing. Their attention is much more likely to be drawn to government spending and taxes, reflecting the values and interests of the upscale and business interests that are overrepresented among contemporary GOP supporters.

The specificity of the party's position on any issue depends on the diversity of the party's constituency. A party with a support base that is specific to a small number of groups has, ceteris paribus, a greater likelihood of adopting highly specific and detailed positions on issues, because there is only a small chance that the position will be internally divisive. A diverse coalitional party, by contrast, has a greater likelihood of alienating important coalitional segments with any given (but not every) issue position because of the greater probability that one or more of the groups in the coalition will be opposed. Their positions on issues are often more general, or even nonexistent. Indeed, both parties can broadly agree about some matters as a result of the presence of the affected group in both parties. In the case of the diverse "big tent" Democrats and Republicans, for example, issue specificity is often low, issue differences between the parties are comparatively small, and the issue space—defined as a range of support and opposition within each party for any given issue—can be relatively large (see Carmines and Stimson 1989; Ladd 1970; Petrocik 1981, 1987, 1998; Sundquist 1983).

Religion and Social Class as American Party Cleavages

Religion and social class differences between the parties have been particularly weak. While it is conventional to think of the GOP as the party of business and the middle and upper classes, upscale Americans were only slightly less Democratic (at 53 percent Democrat compared to 39 percent Republican) than those in the bottom half (who were 58 percent Democratic and 33 percent Republican). Divisions between Catholics and Protestants confounded class; national origin and regional cultures divided coreligionists and made it difficult to develop or sustain class or religiously linked party loyalties (see Benson 1961; Kelley 1979; Kleppner 1970; Lipset 1963; Wolfinger 1965). Religious observance was meaningful only within the context of a religion: the most religiously observant Catholics and Jews were the most Democratic, but religious observance per se was unrelated to party preference and voting (see Berelson, Lazarsfeld, and McPhee 1954; Campbell, Gurin, and Miller 1954; Campbell et al. 1960; Lazarsfeld, Berelson, and Gaudet 1944; Lenski 1961; Lipset 1960, 1970; Lubell 1952). Overall, the insignificance of religion and class in shaping party loyalty set the United States apart from the norm (Rose and Urwin 1970).[2]

The New Deal Party Coalitions

Region was the dominant distinction between Democrats and Republicans in the New Deal party system. The regional difference was not a mask for race, religion, or any other social characteristic. Individuals otherwise identical by religion, social class, and so on were significantly more likely to be Democrats if they lived in the Deep South or a Border South state.[3]

Outside of the South, Catholics were significantly more Democratic than Protestants, and Jews were measurably more Democratic than Catholics. But social class had virtually no effect on the Democratic preference of either group. Ethnic loyalties and socialization made their Democratic allegiance "sticky" and resistant through the 1950s to crosscutting class pressures. The only factor that significantly affected the partisanship of these groups to any degree was union membership. Catholics and Jews who lived in union households were more Democratic than those who lived in nonunion households. The effect was larger for Catholics largely because Jews were so Democratic that the influence of union membership was held down by something of a "ceiling effect."

Northern Protestants were the most politically heterogeneous and divided by social differences. Race mattered; blacks were forty-three percentage points more Democratic than Republican, while whites had a fourteen-point Republican bias. Union membership had a big effect on the party identification of white Northern Protestants (hereafter, "WASPs"). Social class influence was a weak overall influence on party preference, but it made a difference among some groups. Upscale WASPs were thirty-five percentage points more Republican than Democratic; less well-off WASPs had a party bias that was only twelve points more Republican.

Table 17.1 organizes the social differences in a way that identifies the discrete social groups that define the elements of each party's coalition.[4] It reports the party bias of each group and the contribution each made to the Democratic and Republican electorate of the 1950s. African Americans are collected as a group because they were measurably more Democratic than

Table 17.1   The New Deal Party Coalitions as of the 1950s

| | *Proportion of U.S.* | | | |
	Population	*Democrats*	*Republicans*	*Party Bias*
Southern whites	16%	26%	7%	− 59
Border South whites	5	6	5	− 29
Jews	3	4	1	− 51
Blacks	9	10	5	− 33
Catholics	13	14	9	− 29
Union households	19	21	15	− 29
Immigrant Southerners	2	1	3	18
Downscale WASPs	14	10	21	12
Upscale WASPs	16	7	30	35
Others	5	2	4	35
Average				− 17

Source: American National Election Studies.

Notes: The party bias is the difference in the proportion identifying as Democratic, less the proportion identifying as Republican. Negative numbers indicate a plurality of Democrats, positive numbers a plurality of Republicans. The other columns are percentages which total 100 percent, with some rounding error.

any comparable group of white citizens—and no other social trait differentiated their partisanship. In addition, reflecting the impact of union affiliation on party preference, Catholics or WASPs from a union household are classified as "union households." Blacks, Jews, and Southern whites were given priority status both because no variable further specified their party identification and because of the substantive political salience of the social groups they represent.

The parties were most divided on the social welfare issues that defined the policy agenda of the New Deal realignment. The mean difference between the party's supporters on racial issues was trivial because Southern whites, a significant element in the Democratic coalition, were as conservative on racial matters as other parts of the Democratic coalition were liberal. Foreign policy issues throughout the period also did little to differentiate Democratic identifiers from Republican partisans.

The diverse and often contrary position of the groups within each party's coalition—but especially the Democrats—mandated campaigns that centered on social spending, social welfare, and role of government issues (Petrocik, Benoit, and Hansen 2003–2004). Welfare issues were a source of party voting and other issues shaped defection rates while simultaneously being responsible for one of the hallmarks of American voters: their low levels of issue voting. Americans were party voters (upwards of 75 percent cast a vote consistent with their party identification for president and Congress), but because their partisanship was poorly related to their attitudes on many matters, they were not issue voters.[5]

The Contemporary Party Coalitions

A substantial relationship among party preference, class, and religiosity emerged by the 1980s. Figure 17.1 shows this change. A slight overall erosion in Democratic strength was dominated by a large shift to the GOP among upscale and religiously observant Americans by the 1980s. Religiosity and class created a party divide in excess of twenty points by the start of the 1990s. Class differences are sharper now (since lower-SES Americans are clearly Democratic), but religiosity is also a substantial current influence on partisanship (see Hout, Brooks, and Manza 1995; Huckfeldt and Kohfeld 1989; Layman 2001; Miller and Shanks 1996; and Stonecash 2000 for similar findings).

A Religious and Class Cleavage

A party difference of more than twenty points exists between observant and less observant Catholics; the class difference in partisanship is forty

Figure 17.1   The Effect of Religiosity and Class on Partisanship
(White Catholics and Protestants only)

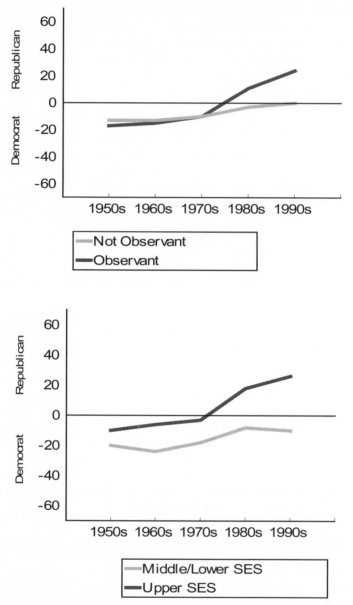

Source: American National Election Studies.

points. Upscale Catholics prefer the GOP over the Democrats by almost fifteen points, while less-well-off Catholics prefer the Democrats over the Republicans by more than twenty points. Today, observant Catholics are slightly Republican overall, while less-religious Catholics are about twenty points more Democratic than Republican (Gilbert 1993; Guth and Green 1992; Jelen 1991; Leege and Kellstedt 1993; Smidt 1993).

Southern whites are a good group with which to observe the change. The sixty-point Democratic plurality that was undifferentiated by social class or religion in the 1950s became a slight GOP bias with substantial religious and class dimensions in the 1990s. Religious and upscale Southern whites changed the most. They made a disproportionate contribution to the increase in the class and religious differences between Democrats and Republicans. Today, upscale Southern whites are about forty points more Republican than Democrat; lower-SES Southern whites are evenly divided. Religiously observant Southern whites identify about thirty points more with the GOP, while those who are not observant are evenly divided in their party preference.[6] The national pattern appears in figure 17.1.

Religion and class effects have not been uniform. African Americans became more Democratic irrespective of religiosity or social class.[7] There is a slight party difference associated with social class and religiosity among Jews, but no longitudinal trend to the difference.[8] With these caveats, markers of class and religiosity differentiated partisanship by the end of the 1990s: upscale, religious, and nonunion Catholics and Protestants were more inclined to the Republicans than their lower-SES, union, and less religiously observant counterparts.

The New Coalitions

Table 17.2 reports the party coalitions that emerged from the changes since the 1970s.[9] Religiously observant whites are 59 percent Republican and 32 percent Democratic and contribute 35 percent of all GOP identifiers. Further, the magnitude of the religiously observant among Republicans (35 percent) makes them the single largest group in the GOP coalition. Their movement into Republican ranks is the largest contributor to the erosion of the Democratic plurality in party identification between the 1950s and the current period. Upscale respondents (identified with the GOP by a margin of 54 to 38 percent) contribute another 17 percent to the Republican coalition. Upscale and religious Americans constitute more than 50 percent of all Republicans; the Democratic electorate receives about 26 percent of its support from these two groups. The Democratic core is the 37 percent who are African American, Hispanic, Jewish, or Asian. The remaining groups make relatively similar contributions to both parties.

Table 17.2   The Contemporary Party Coalitions, 1992–2004

	Proportion of U.S.			
	Population	*Democrats*	*Republicans*	*Party Bias*
African Americans	12%	20%	2%	− 72
Hispanics	8	10	6	− 33
Jews	3	4	1	− 67
Union household	11	14	11	− 15
Low-SES Catholics	4	4	4	− 22
Low-SES WASPs	10	8	10	− 4
No religious preference	12	13	11	− 15
Upscale Catholics	5	5	5	− 4
Upscale WASPs	7	5	12	31
Religious Catholics	8	7	8	5
Religious Protestants	17	9	27	39
Asians/Others	4	3	4	14
Average				− 7

Source: American National Election Studies.

Notes: The party bias is the difference in the proportion identifying as Democratic, less the proportion identifying as Republican. Negative numbers indicate a plurality of Democrats, positive numbers a plurality of Republicans. The other columns are percentages which total 100 percent, with some rounding error.

The 2004 Election

In general, George W. Bush assembled the typical coalition of a winning GOP presidential candidate (see table 17.3). The elements of the party coalitions voted in 2004 much as they have since 1992, and not much differently from each group's voting pattern since the mid-1980s. Bush received substantial majorities from the religiously observant, upper-status whites, and white voters in general. He did poorly among blacks, Hispanics, and Jews; lost voters in union households by a substantial margin (as Republicans frequently do); and essentially split the vote of whites with below-median incomes.

There is some indication that the 2004 vote may have had a Catholic-Protestant dimension. Religious Catholics and lower-SES/nonreligious Catholics were slightly less supportive of Bush than both normally are when Republicans win the presidential election. Bush's support among religious Protestants and lower-SES/nonreligious Protestants was correspondingly higher than his win might have led an observer to expect. All four groups might have been responding to John Kerry's public (albeit low-key) embrace of his Catholic faith. However, some caution is in order here. It is easy to find significance in this Catholic-Protestant difference, but it may be statistical oscillation that indicates nothing of substantive significance. It is worth noting only because religion, religiosity, moral-cultural issues, and social iden-

Table 17.3   Contemporary Party Coalitions and the Presidential Vote, 1992–2004

| | *Percent voting Republican for president in* | | | |
	2004	*2000*	*1996*	*1992*
African Americans	10%	8%	1%	6%
Hispanics	33	35	20	35
Jews	17	8	7	9
Union household	42	39	20	30
Low-SES Catholics	33	59	23	19
Low-SES WASPs	62	50	40	34
No religious preference	52	40	33	45
Upscale Catholics	57	52	46	31
Upscale WASPs	67	61	50	50
Religious Catholics	50	56	54	43
Religious Protestants	76	70	67	62
Asians/Others	74	40	33	54
All voters	*52%*	*48%*	*41%*	*38%*

Source: American National Election Studies.
Note: The relatively low GOP presidential vote among some groups in 1992 reflects Ross Perot's success in 1992.

tifiers seemed to be stimulated by this election a bit more than in recent elections simply because the religious faith of the candidates was a topic for observers, the candidates, and the respective party campaigns.

Issues in the Contemporary Party Coalitions

We expect the government and the political process to spend a considerable amount of energy dealing with issues that arise from the economic and social features of the nation. But what constitutes an issue for government action is clearly in the eye of the beholder. Different groups are differently positioned relative the dynamics of the society, and this tangible self-interest factor shapes what is perceived to be an "important" issue (e.g., agreements that facilitate production overseas by U.S. companies mobilize opposition from those whose livelihoods may be threatened), but material interests are not the only source of conflict.

Ethnic groups that promote bilingual education are often as motivated by a commitment to carve out a place for their culture as they are for educational programs that improve prospects for the success of their children. Campaigns to establish holidays for significant figures within minority groups, the renaming of public facilities, or lobbying that attempts to produce foreign policies desired by the countries from which their families emigrated are typically motivated by ethnic or racial identification.

Religious groups and those with strong religious impulses attempt to influence policies that create a public space that recognizes and promotes values and beliefs rooted in religion. They care about these matters and view the political process and government in these terms.

Measuring Issue Effects

There are several ways to examine the issue effects of the contemporary party coalitions. This analysis focuses on evaluations of the parties and candidates.[10]

First, one would expect that the ties between the parties and the various social groups would be reflected in the comments made about the parties by voters. A simple example: among union members and their family members, an identification of the GOP with business might be expected to elicit references to labor policy as a reason to dislike the Republican Party but like the Democratic Party. If this issue was particularly prominent in the party conflict, it might also emerge as a reason to like the GOP and dislike the Democratic Party among Republican identifiers, especially the most upscale Republicans. This measure may be more information-rich than a series of cross-sectional correlations between the issues of the moment and party assessments, because it is a slightly better indicator of long-term assessments, although the evaluations also reflect immediate concerns of the election at hand.

Second, and this is implied in the previous point, the open-ended evaluations allow one to examine the penetration of issues throughout the electorate. If one side's reasons for liking a party or candidate are offered as reasons for disliking the same party or candidate by the other side, it suggests that a particular issue or group of issues are central elements of the party cleavage and will be prominent in partisan elections. By contrast, an issue that arises among partisans of only one party might be regarded as less central and consequently less likely to be a regular point of contention.

Finally, responses to open-ended questions about problems requiring government action are a particularly demanding test of the degree of politicization of various classes of issues. They allow citizens to proffer, largely without the limitation imposed by the prior expectations of the researcher, what they find to be the most prominent features of the parties and candidates. Compared to closed questions, the open-ended format tends to elicit responses for more salient issues, thereby also permitting the analysis to identify the sources of the issues that provide policy debate. Further, as is the case with the party and candidate evaluations, there are at least two plausible predictions about the sources of the problem mentions. Minimally, one might expect only the groups most likely to care about a problem to mention it (for instance, the religiously oriented might be particularly inclined to mention moral and value issues). But it is possible that the issue would be so identified with a party that it would be mentioned as a problem by many, not just those with a particular investment in it. The salience of these problems can be further assessed by examining their influence on the Bush-Kerry vote. As before, we could observe asymmetry—issues linked to the GOP coalition might matter most to Republicans or the groups most sensitive to an issue. It is also possible that the issues are so endemic to the partisanship of the electorate that that they provide voting criteria on both sides.

Party and Candidate Images in 2004

Four issue categories, representing the bulk of all mentions, are reported in this analysis. The most common comments about the candidates referred to personal qualities (strong, decisive, weak, experienced, and so forth). But the discrete issue comments largely fell into four categories: moral and value references (hereafter also referred to as "cultural issues" or "cultural and moral issues"), social welfare issues, matters dealing with economic policy, and foreign policy and defense (including terrorism). Foreign policy and defense references were the most common comments about the candidates, reflecting, one might surmise, the facts of U.S. military involvement in the Middle East and the national emphasis on terrorism and security. The interesting responses for this analysis are the prominence of cultural and moral references, and that they were more common than social welfare issues.

Party issue evaluations confirm the candidate comments. The noteworthy feature of the party mentions, which differ slightly, is that moral and cultural issues are prominently mentioned as reasons to like *and* dislike both parties, while social welfare issues were a feature of the Democratic Party, and economic policy was identified with the Republicans.

Particularly noteworthy is the differential prominence of the issues in the assessment of the candidates and parties. Cultural issues were a particular strength of Bush. Thirty-five percent offered a cultural or moral issue as a reason to prefer Bush over Kerry, with 19 percent giving it as a reason to like Bush and 16 percent mentioning the issue as a reason to dislike Kerry. About one-third of those mentioning a cultural issue as a reason to like George Bush or dislike Kerry mentioned the issue as a reason to both like Bush *and* dislike Kerry. Kerry, by comparison, was much more likely to be viewed in terms of social welfare concerns: 29 percent offered this type of issue as a reason to like him (18 percent) or dislike Bush (11 percent), but only 7 percent mentioned social welfare issues positively in connection with Bush (with 4 percent finding this a reason to like Bush and 3 percent a reason to dislike Kerry). Economic issue mentions followed a similar pattern. Foreign policy references were also asymmetric and mostly reflected a positive assessment of Bush (probably not surprising for an incumbent president who projected strong leadership in the middle of warlike conditions).

The likes and dislikes of parties that were mentioned are slightly different but illustrate more sharply the issue links to the parties. There is imbalance on issues of social welfare (favoring the Democrats) and economic policy and foreign affairs (favoring the Republicans). But cultural issues are balanced in their mentions of likes and dislikes for both parties. In the aggregate, 34 percent mentioned cultural issues as a reason to prefer the Republicans, with nearly equal proportions offering it as a reason to like the GOP (19 percent) as to dislike the Democrats (15 percent). The proportions for the Democrats were slightly different. Overall 32 percent referred to this type of issue in commenting on the Democrats. Fewer respondents stated it as a reason to like the Democrats (12 percent) than offering it as a reason to dislike the Republicans (20 percent). The data on cultural issues indicate how salient they are as issue cleavages between the parties and show that there is considerable agreement on this issue as an appropriate criterion to evaluate the parties. Most of those who mentioned morality or values as a reason to like Bush also gave morality and value reasons to dislike Kerry—and vice versa.

The social groups that define a party's coalition provide its issue agenda. Table 17.4 focuses on just cultural and social welfare issues, the two that plausibly are the most likely to be linked to the groupings that define the

Table 17.4   Issue Mentions in Evaluations of the Candidates by Coalition Groups

| | | *Type of Positive Mention of the Candidates* | | | |
| | | *Bush* | | *Kerry* | |
	Party Bias	*Cultural*	*Welfare*	*Cultural*	*Welfare*
African Americans	−72	3%	2%	4%	15%
Hispanics	−33	12	4	11	11
Jews	−67	2	0	29	12
Union household	−15	10	5	11	19
Low-SES Catholics	−22	4	3	11	13
Low-SES WASPs	−4	18	2	5	11
No religious preference	−15	5	6	14	13
Upscale Catholics	−4	4	4	16	8
Upscale WASPs	31	12	2	5	4
Religious Catholics	5	27	1	9	20
Religious Protestants	39	32	4	3	6
Asians/Others	14	16	5	3	14
Average	−7	14%	3%	9%	12%

Source: American National Election Studies.

Note: The table reports the proportion of each coalition group that made at least one positive mention of a cultural or social welfare issue in evaluating the candidates.

contemporary coalitions. The table reports the proportion of each coalition group that made at least one positive mention of a cultural or social welfare issue in evaluating the candidates. The table ignores the fact that some groups tended to mention some issues more than once, thereby not producing a complete enumeration of the proportion of all issue mentions that fall into the category. However, this decision doesn't distort the pattern, and it eases the presentation of what would otherwise be extensive tabular data.

Twenty-seven percent of religious Catholics mentioned cultural issues at least once in explaining why they liked George Bush.[11] Religious Protestants were even more likely to do so. If it were not for these groups, the rate of cultural mentions would have been well below 10 percent overall, and given the prominence of these groups in the GOP coalition, the incidence of cultural references within the Republican Party would have been drastically less, because upwards of 50 percent of the positive assessments of Bush and the GOP were contributed by these two groups. Welfare concerns were rarely mentioned as a positive comment about Bush.

John Kerry's assessments are not quite mirror images of references to Bush. Social welfare references are more prominent among reasons to like Kerry, but cultural issue references are slightly more prominent in reasons to like him also. The key difference is that for Kerry they do not come from groups that are religiously defined. The cultural issue "mentioners" are more identified by class and status or, in the case of Jews, with a religious minority traditionally opposed to the religious and values references that are categorized as cultural in these data. The net result is that, between these two issues, the Republican Party's constituency views candidates in terms of cultural issues, while Democratic groups give considerable attention to social welfare issues.

Table 17.5 repeats the preceding breakdown for the comments about the political parties, with similar results. The religiously observant were particularly likely to mention cultural issues and unlikely to mention social welfare issues as one of the things they like about the Republicans. Interestingly, the most Democratic groups—the secular, those from union households, Jews, and low-SES Catholics—also mentioned cultural issues as a reason to prefer the Democrats. The cultural issue mentions of these groups, however, were mirror images of the reasons offered by respondents in the religious groups.

This difference between candidate and party evaluations seems meaningful. Immediate issues, which may be short lived, are likely to have a strong effect on the way individual candidates are evaluated by the electorate. However, the parties are more enduring, and the relative consensus of the electorate—even across the party divide—about the issue reasons for liking one party and not the other is a noteworthy marker of the status of the issue as central to the programmatic divisions of the party system. In this case, the fact that partisans of both parties mention cultural issues more often

Table 17.5 Issue Mentions in Evaluations of the Political Parties by Coalition Groups

| | | Type of Positive Mention of the Parties | | | |
| | | Republican | | Democratic | |
	Party Bias	Cultural	Welfare	Cultural	Welfare
African Americans	− 72	5%	1%	10%	17%
Hispanics	− 33	7	3	7	12
Jews	− 67	5	12	29	12
Union household	− 15	5	2	17	12
Low-SES Catholics	− 22	3	1	19	9
Low-SES WASPs	− 4	7	6	7	15
Secular	− 15	6	3	22	9
Upscale Catholics	− 4	8	5	17	7
Upscale WASPs	31	16	10	22	6
Religious Catholics	5	21	3	9	15
Religious Protestants	39	27	8	11	7
Asians/Others	14	13	9	5	11
Average	*− 7*	*11%*	*5%*	*14%*	*11%*

Source: American National Election Studies

Note: The table reports the proportion of each coalition group that made at least one positive mention of a cultural or social welfare issue in evaluating the parties.

than any of the others suggests that these issues will be prominent in politics and governance.

Issue Concerns and the 2004 Vote

Whether the voters were reporting likes and dislikes about Kerry and Bush or the Democrats and the GOP, those who mentioned cultural, eco-

Table 17.6 Evaluation Dimensions and the 2004 Presidential Vote

| | Candidate Evaluations Bush Vote | | | Party Evaluations Bush Vote | | |
Type of Issue Mentioned	Expected	Reported	Gain/Loss	Expected	Reported	Gain/Loss
Cultural	55%	61%	+ 6	52%	54%	+ 2
Social welfare	36	27	− 9	42	37	− 5
Economic	51	56	+ 5	57	61	+ 4
Foreign/Defense	52	54	+ 2	52	55	+ 3

Source: American National Election Studies.

Note: Table entries are the Republican vote in percentages. For the calculation of the expected vote, see Converse (1966) and Petrocik (1989).

nomic, or foreign policy issues were, ceteris paribus, more likely to cast a Republican vote than those who mentioned a social welfare issue in their party or candidate evaluations (see table 17.6). The expected Republican vote among those who mentioned a cultural issue in evaluating the candidates was 55 percent; the expected vote among those who mentioned a cultural issue in expressing their likes and dislikes about the parties was 52 percent Republican. The differences between the candidate and party expected vote columns reflect, as noted earlier, a difference in the way candidates and parties are viewed. Cultural issue perspectives are a more widely distributed and salient perspective on the parties than they are on the candidates. Bush and Kerry may have differentially prospered (or suffered) from this view of the parties. However, it is noteworthy that the cultural issues shaping candidate evaluations are not candidate specific (and are perhaps transient by virtue of that), but a more enduring aspect of the party systems for the Democratic and Republican parties.

The low expected GOP vote among those mentioning social welfare issues is a second notable feature of the expected vote data. Democratic identifiers were much more likely than Republicans to offer social welfare issues as a reason to like or dislike the candidates or parties, but especially as a reason to like Kerry and the Democratic Party. Consequently, Bush's expected vote among respondents mentioning social welfare issues in evaluating him and Kerry was only 36 percent, and only slightly better (42 percent) when the issue was mentioned as something they liked or disliked about the parties.

A comparison of the expected and reported Bush vote by the type of issue mentioned illustrates the additional impact of these issues. The second and fifth columns of table 17.6 list the reported Bush vote associated with these different mentions; the third and sixth columns report how much that vote exceeded what was expected given the partisanship of the individuals. Bush's majorities among those mentioning cultural issues in connection with him and Kerry exceeded the partisan vote by approximately six percentage points. It exceeded the partisan vote among those mentioning economic and foreign policy issues by five and two points, respectively. The gains from these issues were smaller when these issue mentions are connected with the parties, but his vote exceeded the party baseline there as well—and the baseline party vote (column 4) is very Republican.

Bush's losses were concentrated among those who mentioned social welfare issues in evaluating the candidates or the parties. When social welfare likes and dislikes were offered as evaluations of Bush and Kerry, Bush's vote was only 27 percent (column 2)—a full nine percentage points below a quite low baseline (column 1). Social welfare mentions regarding the parties did not seem to be so concentrated among Democratic partisans, but, as before, Bush's vote was lower, by five percentage points, than the expected 42 percent.

The Issue Agenda of the 2004 Vote

Cultural issues were not at the top of voters' concerns in 2004. In response to a question about what problems were the most important issues facing the country during the preceding year, cultural issues were among the least frequently mentioned. Terrorism topped the list at 37 percent, and the three most frequently mentioned—terrorism, Iraq, and foreign policy in general—were arguably nondomestic and constituted 62 percent of all the problems mentioned in the survey. But cultural and social welfare issues were sufficiently compelling to moderate the effect of these issues on the vote. Lurking (and that may be the apt word) behind this recognition of the prominence of defense and security issues was a set of enduring images of the parties and concerns of voters—which were not front and center in 2004 but nonetheless had a substantial impact on George Bush's reelection.

Table 17.7 stratifies the problem mentions by whether cultural and social welfare evaluations were offered in the "like" and "dislike" mentions of the candidates. The top half of the table contrasts those who mentioned cultural issues with those who did not; the bottom half of the table contrasts those who did and did not refer to social welfare issues. The impact of cultural and welfare issues is impressive. Nominally hurtful (for Bush) issue concerns in

Table 17.7   Campaign Issues, Cultural Issues, and the Presidential Vote

| | Issue mentioned in evaluating candidates | |
| | **Cultural issue** | |
Most important 2004 issue	*Not mentioned*	*Mentioned*
Terrorism	69%	77%
Iraq	29	46
Foreign Policy	53	51
	Social Welfare issue	
	Not mentioned	*Mentioned*
Terrorism	74%	51%
Iraq	35	17
Foreign Policy	57	33

Source: American National Election Studies.
Note: Table entries are the percentage voting for George W. Bush in 2004

2004 were trumped by cultural issue assessments of the candidates. On average, cultural issue mentions increased Bush's vote thirteen percentage points, with increases in Bush's vote among those mentioning terrorism as the major problem faced by the country during 2004. Impressively, even those who mentioned Iraq as a major problem during 2004 were Bush voters when they were also inclined to think of the candidates in cultural issue terms, a result that probably demonstrates that Iraq was mentioned by two very different groups in the electorate: those who supported the overthrow of Saddam Hussein's regime and those who opposed this undertaking.

In contrast, voters who made social welfare assessments of the candidates—compared to those who did not—were strongly inclined to support Kerry regardless of the problems they saw as important during 2004. Voters who thought terrorism was a major problem for the country overwhelmingly voted for Bush. Approximately three-quarters of them voted for Bush if social welfare issues were not part of the candidates' profiles, but Kerry took half of the group who saw terrorism as a major problem but viewed the candidates in terms of social welfare issues. Indeed, as one goes down the second half of the table, Bush's support drops considerably—occasionally to a very nominal level—whenever the voter also views the candidates through the lens of social welfare issues.

Christian Democracy and the American Parties

The mix of sectarian, national origin, and immigrant-versus-native divisions that helped to suppress the link between party conflict and the religious impulse through most of American history has largely vanished. The religiosity of Americans, however, remains high at the same time that new beliefs and lifestyles have competed with traditional, often religiously linked, beliefs. Parallel efforts to reduce the heretofore overt role of religious belief in the public space has also mobilized the religious and the most socially conservative. The mobilization of the religious impulse by the GOP has created a Republican coalition that is highly similar to the coalitions that support Christian Democratic parties through much of the rest of the world. Its impact on American electoral politics is to make cultural and moral issues a centerpiece of party conflict, often able to trump economic concerns and major international events.

Notes

1. In almost every society, party divisions correlate with social characteristics (Alford 1963; Bartolini and Mair 1990; Benson 1961; Converse 1974; Hays 1975; Kelley 1979; LaPa-

lombara and Weiner 1966; Lijphart 1977, 1979, 1989; Lipset 1963, 1970; Lipset and Rokkan 1967; Maguire 1983; Powell 1982; Rokkan 1970; Rose 1974; Rose and Urwin 1969, 1970; Ware 1996). They continue to matter today, and the nascent party systems of Eastern Europe are developing similar social cleavages (see Evans and Whitefield 1993).

2. Consider, for example, Holland, which from the late 1940s until the early 1970s operated a very highly aligned party system. During this period, the five major parties drew their support from very limited groups (see Lijphart 1968). The Catholic People's party (KVP) drew more than 90 percent of its support from religious Catholics, and 75 percent of religious Catholics voted for the KVP—making it the largest of the five major parties. Religious Protestants supported the Christian Historical Union (CHU) or the Anti-Revolutionary party (ARP), the former for theological liberals and the latter for conservatives. The political party link for the religious Protestants was as strong as the party link for religious Catholics. In both cases, more than 70 percent of all CHU and ARP support came from "their" confessional groupings, and greater-than-60-percent majorities of each religious group supported their group's party. The less religious supported the class-based Liberal (VVD) and Labor (PvdA) parties, which drew massively disproportionate shares of their support from the middle class (VVD) and working class (PvdA). This has changed dramatically in the last twenty-five years. See Rochon 1999 and Irwin 1984.

3. The Deep South refers to the states of Virginia, Alabama, Arkansas, Florida, Georgia, Louisiana, Mississippi, North Carolina, South Carolina, and Texas. The Border South states are Kentucky, Maryland, Oklahoma, Tennessee, and West Virginia.

4. The party coalition profile resulted from an asymmetric analysis of variance of party preference. The technique described in Sonquist, Baker, and Morgan (1973) is commonly used by marketers in an attempt to identify the combinations of social characteristics that best explain the variance in some dependent variable—party identification, in this case. The analysis is described in Petrocik 1981 and 1998. Detailed code to construct these groups can be requested from the author.

5. Ultimately, these issue cleavages (and others) became the proximate cause of the erosion of the Democratic plurality as the most disaffected Southern whites moved into the Republican Party in the 1970s and 1980s.

6. Changes among whites in the Border South have been smaller and similar to the patterns observed for Catholics: class differences are quite strong, religious differences more muted, and their aggregate party preference has a distinctive Democratic tilt.

7. However, the difference was small, and it distinguished only Democratic supermajorities. The party bias of the less well off was sixty-eight percentage points Democratic. Upscale blacks gave an eighty-point plurality to the Democrats.

8. Upscale Hispanics were also less Democratic, but again there was no trend to the difference. Religious observance was substantially unrelated to party preference.

9. The contemporary coalition profile is based on the same kind of segmentation analysis used for the New Deal coalitions (see note 4). The analysis merged the 1992, 1994, and 1996 NES surveys. The data sets were weighted so that sample sizes did not allow any one of the years to exert a disproportionate effect on the results. The same variables (region, religion, race, social class, religiosity, and size of place of residence) were analyzed. These resulting groups are, again, exclusive. The partisan homogeneity of African Americans, Hispanics, and Jews made them priority groups irrespective of their social class, union membership, or religiosity. Union membership emerged as a dominant characteristic. Anyone from a household with a union member is in the union category, except for respondents who are Jewish, black, or Hispanic. The religious categories, therefore, are limited to avowed Protestants and Catholics who are not union members. Status difference among Catholics and Protestants is limited to those who are not union members and not categorized among the religious. Detailed code to construct these groups can be requested from the author.

10. These are the standard "master code" party and candidate questions. Respondents are asked whether there is anything they like about a candidate or party (each is identified by name). If they indicate that there is something they like, a follow-up question asks them what it is that they like about the candidate or party. The specific codes assigned to the issue mentions are available on request.

11. This numbers in this table and table 17.5 slightly undercount the references because some 7–10 percent had nothing to say about Bush. Nonmentions of likes and dislikes about the parties was even higher (about 25 percent). However, it seemed better to include those who had no reply to the questions in order to not introduce other distortions. This count algorithm has the virtue of faithfully counting the proportion of each group who made the mention. It is a conservative way of counting and probably has fewer distortions than alternative methods.

18

The Rise of the Ideological Voter

The Changing Bases of Partisanship in the American Electorate

Kyle L. Saunders and Alan I. Abramowitz

In *Partisan Hearts and Minds: Political Parties and the Social Identities of Voters*, Donald Green, Bradley Palmquist, and Eric Schickler (2002) argue that party identification in the United States is based on voters' social identities rather than on a rational assessment of the parties' policies or performance in office. Green and his colleagues make four major claims about the nature of contemporary party identification:

1. Party identification is more stable at both the aggregate and the individual level than most recent scholarship has suggested. Outside of the South, there has been little change in the distribution of party identification in the United States for several decades (52–84).
2. Voters' party loyalties are largely insulated from the effects of current issues such as the state of the economy and the performance of the incumbent president (85–108).
3. Party loyalties exert a powerful influence on citizens' issue positions, evaluations of political leaders, and voting decisions (204–29).
4. Most importantly, party identification is based mainly on identification with social groups rather than a rational evaluation of the parties' ideological orientations or policies (25–51).

According to them, "People ask themselves two questions when deciding which party to support: What kinds of social groups come to mind as I think about Democrats, Republicans, and Independents? Which assemblage of groups (if any) best describes me?" (8).

In proposing this social identity theory, Green, Palmquist, and Schickler explicitly challenge rational-choice explanations of party identification such as those proposed by Downs (1957) and Fiorina (1981). Green and his colleagues view party identification as an emotional attachment grounded in enduring group loyalties rather than as a deliberate choice based on a preference for one set of policy positions over another—a choice that can be modified if parties' policy positions change or new issues arise (Page and Jones 1979; Franklin and Jackson 1983; Carmines, McIver, and Stimson 1987; Luskin, McIver, and Carmines 1989; Franklin 1992).

Like Campbell, Converse, Miller, and Stokes (1960), Green and his colleagues downplay the role of issues and ideology in the formation of party identification. While recognizing that party loyalties can be influenced by dramatic changes in the parties' policy stands or ideological positions, Green, Palmquist, and Schickler argue that such shifts are relatively rare and generally confined to periods of major realignment, such as the New Deal era in the United States. In this regard, social identity theory stands in sharp contrast to ideological realignment theory, which claims that as a result of the growing ideological polarization of the two major parties since the 1980s, Americans have increasingly been choosing a party identification on the basis of their ideological preferences, leading to a gradual realignment of party loyalties along ideological lines (Abramowitz and Saunders 1998; Saunders and Abramowitz 2004).

According to Green and colleagues, even the one exception to the rule of partisan stability in recent American political history—the dramatic realignment of Southern white voters' party loyalties since the end of World War II—was based more on changing perceptions of the parties' ties to social groups than on issues or ideology. They argue that as Southerners began to assume leadership positions in the Republican Party during the 1980s and 1990s, Republicanism came to be seen as a respectable affiliation among white Southerners. According to Green, Palmquist, and Schickler, "As the Republican image improved, Republican identification became increasingly prevalent among all segments of the ideological continuum" (160).

They argue that "the growing correlation between liberalism-conservatism and party [among Southern whites] reflects cohort replacement as older conservative Democrats pass away" (161). With this process of generational replacement largely completed, they claim that "the pace of partisan conversion [in the South] appears to have slowed to the near-standstill characteristic of party identification in the non-South" (163).

Trends in Party Identification

One of the key claims made by Green and his colleagues is that outside of the South there has been little change in partisanship since the 1960s. However, this claim appears to be contradicted by a considerable body of research that has documented changes in partisanship based on such factors as gender (Wirls 1986; Kaufmann and Petrocik 1999), marital status (Weisberg 1987), religiosity (Guth and Green 1990; Layman and Carmines 1997), and social class (Stonecash, Brewer, and Mariani 2003).

In order to test the claim that partisanship outside of the South has been stable, table 18.1 presents data from American National Election Study (NES) surveys on trends in party identification in the United States since the 1960s.[1]

The evidence presented in table 18.1 does not support the conclusion that party identification outside of the South has been stable since the 1960s. Although the most dramatic change has occurred among white Southerners, there has also been a substantial increase in Republican identification among whites outside of the South. During the 1960s, the Democratic Party enjoyed an average advantage of thirteen percentage points over the Republican Party among non-Southern whites. Since 1980, however, this advantage has disappeared: in the 2002–2004 NES surveys, non-Southern whites favored the Republican Party over the Democratic Party by a five-point margin.[2]

Outside of the South, Republican gains have been much larger in certain white subgroups than in the overall white electorate. Table 18.2 presents data from NES surveys on trends in party identification since the 1960s among various subgroups of Northern whites. Because the data for the most recent period are based on only two elections, some caution is warranted in distinguishing long-term trends from short-term shifts such as the recent movement of white women toward the Republican Party. However, there is little question that Republican identification has increased dramatically since 1980 among several groups: men, married voters, Catholics, and the religiously observant.

Among white Catholics, for example, the Democratic advantage, which was forty-two points in the 1960s and thirty-six points in the 1970s, has completely disappeared. In the 2002–2004 NES surveys, Republican identifiers slightly outnumbered Democratic identifiers among non-Southern white Catholics. Similarly, in the 2004 national exit poll, Republican identifiers

Table 18.1   Net Party Identification in the United States by Race and Region

	1962–1970	1972–1980	1982–1990	1992–2000	2002–2004	Change
All respondents	+24	+20	+13	+11	+7	−17
African Americans	+72	+74	+72	+72	+75	+3
Whites	+18	+13	+10	−7	−25	
South	+36	+25	+9	−7	−17	−53
North	+13	+9	−2	+3	−5	−18

Source: American National Election Studies.

Note: Net party identification = percentage of Democratic identifiers and leaners minus percentage of Republican identifiers and leaners.

Table 18.2   Net Party Identification of Northern White Subgroups

	1962–1970	1972–1980	1982–1990	1992–2000	2002–2004	Change
Males	+14	+8	−6	−6	−10	−24
Females	+12	+9	+2	+11	−1	−13
Married	+13	+6	−7	−5	−14	−27
Unmarried	+12	+16	+6	+14	+10	−2
Protestant	−5	−10	−18	−14	−20	−15
Catholic	+42	+36	+17	+13	−2	−44
Jewish	+72	+58	+46	+72	+67	−5
Other/None	+29	+28	+16	+23	+15	−14
Observant	+60	−9	−16	−16	−22	
Nonobservant	+27	+21	+9	+18	+15	−12

Source: American National Election Studies.

Note: Net party identification = percentage of Democratic identifiers and leaners minus percentage of Republican identifiers and leaners.

outnumbered Democratic identifiers by 41 percent to 34 percent among non-Southern white Catholics. The Republican gains in this group are very significant politically because, according to the national exit poll, Catholics comprised more than 30 percent of the white electorate outside of the South in 2004.

Ideology in the American Electorate: Meaning and Measurement

The evidence examined thus far indicates that since the 1970s there has been a substantial increase in Republican identification among whites both outside the South and within the South and that this increase has been quite dramatic among certain subgroups such as Catholics. But why has this shift occurred? Contrary to Green and his colleagues, we believe that ideology has played a major role in producing a secular realignment of party loyalties in the United States since the 1970s. According to this ideological realignment hypothesis, the increasing clarity of ideological differences between the parties during the Reagan and post-Reagan eras has made it easier for citizens to choose a party identification based on their ideological orientations.

Before examining the impact of ideological orientations on party identification, however, we need to demonstrate that members of the public, or at least a substantial proportion of them, *have* meaningful ideological orientations. While the concept of ideology has been defined in many different ways (Gerring 1997), political scientists generally view an ideology as a set of beliefs about the role of government that shapes responses to a wide range of specific policy issues (Converse 1964; Peffley and Hurwitz 1985). Among political elites in the United States, positions on a wide range of economic, social, and foreign policy issues appear to be structured by a single liberal-conservative dimension (Poole and Rosenthal 1991). However, the extent of ideological thinking in the public has been a subject of debate since the publication of Converse's 1964 seminal study of belief systems in mass publics, which suggested that awareness of ideological concepts and use of such concepts by ordinary citizens were quite limited.

Although some subsequent studies have supported Converse's conclusions about the lack of ideological sophistication among the general public in the United States (Axelrod 1967; Bishop et al. 1978; Sullivan, Piereson, and Marcus 1978; Conover and Feldman 1981; Knight 1985; Jennings 1992), other studies have suggested that the ability of ordinary citizens to comprehend and employ ideological concepts depends on the extent and clarity of ideological cues provided by political elites. According to this view, the greater the prevalence and clarity of ideological cues in the political environment, the higher the level of ideological comprehension and reasoning should be among the electorate (Field and Anderson 1969; Nie and Anderson 1974; Nie and Rabjohn 1979; Nie, Verba, and Petrocik 1979; Craig and Hurley 1984; Jacoby 1995). From this standpoint, the increased ideological polarization of the parties in recent years and the increased salience of ideological conflict in the media should have produced an increase in ideological comprehension and reasoning among the American public.

While we do not claim that ordinary citizens in the United States now possess belief systems as elaborate or constrained as those evident among political activists and elites (Jennings 1992; Saunders and Abramowitz 2004), our evidence does point to a substantial increase in the ability of citizens to apply ideological labels to the political parties, an increase in the coherence of citizens' views across different issues, and a growing connection between the ideological labels that citizens choose and their positions on a wide range of domestic and foreign policy issues.

In 1972, when the NES began asking respondents to place themselves and the two major parties on a seven-point liberal-conservative scale, only 48 percent of respondents were able to place themselves on the scale and to place the Democratic Party to the left of the Republican Party. By 1996 and 2004, however, 67 percent of respondents were able to place themselves on the scale and to place the Democrats to the left of the Republicans. These results indicate that public awareness of ideological differences between the parties has increased substantially in the past three decades.

The NES data also indicate that there has also been an increase in the ideological coherence of citizens' policy preferences and in the correlation between ideological identification and policy preferences. Table 18.3 dis-

Table 18.3   Analysis of an Eight-Item Liberal-Conservative Scale, 1984–2004

	1984	1988	1992	1996	2000	2004
Cronbach's alpha	.65	.66	.70	.75	.74	.77
Correlation of liberal-conservative identification with . . .						
Jobs/Living standards	.36	.23	.28	.36	.35	.43
Health insurance	.19	.23	.30	.39	.31	.43
Spending/Services	.24	.33	.32	.38	.46	.42
Aid to blacks	.31	.26	.27	.37	.32	.37
Defense spending	.27	.30	.28	.35	.35	.34
Abortion	.14	.21	.32	.37	.39	.33
Women's role	.19	.23	.28	.31	.32	.32
All seven policy issues	*.44*	*.46*	*.51*	*.60*	*.60*	*.62*

Source: American National Election Studies.
Note: Correlations are Pearson's r. All coefficients are statistically significant (p < .001).

plays a measure of the internal consistency (Cronbach's alpha) of responses to eight items that were included in every presidential election year survey between 1984 and 2004. The eight items include liberal-conservative identification and opinions on seven policy issues: government responsibility for jobs and living standards, government responsibility for health insurance, government services and spending, defense spending, government aid to blacks, abortion, and women's roles. The table also shows the correlation between liberal-conservative identification and responses to the seven policy issues.

The increasing value of Cronbach's alpha over time indicates that citizens' responses to these eight questions have become more internally consistent since 1984. In addition, contrary to the claim that ideological labels have little policy content for most Americans (Conover and Feldman 1981), the evidence in table 18.3 shows that liberal-conservative self-identification was related to preferences on every policy issue in every survey and that this relationship has grown stronger over time. These results indicate that there is an ideological structure to Americans' opinions on policy issues and that ideological self-identification is a valid indicator of the liberalism or conservatism of citizens' policy orientations.[3]

Group Membership, Ideology, and Partisan Change

In order to test the ideological realignment hypothesis, we will first examine trends in party identification among some of the white subgroups that have experienced the largest Republican gains since the 1970s, while controlling for ideological identification. If the ideological realignment hypothesis is correct, we should find that Republican gains have been greatest among conservative identifiers and smallest among liberal identifiers.

The evidence presented in table 18.4 provides strong support for the ideological realignment hypothesis. For every subgroup examined, the increase in Republican identification was much larger among conservative identifiers than among moderate or liberal identifiers. In fact, Republican identification declined among liberal identifiers in every subgroup except Catholics. Among Southern whites, for example, there was a fifty-four-point

Table 18.4   Net Party Identification of Selected White Subgroups by Ideological Self-Identification

	1972–1980	1982–1990	1992–2000	2002–2004	Change
All Whites					
Liberals	+53	+52	+66	+66	+13
Moderates	+20	+10	+11	+12	−8
Conservatives	−29	−44	−54	−67	−38
South					
Liberals	+55	+49	+60	+62	+7
Moderates	+33	+27	+6	+3	−30
Conservatives	−6	−31	−59	−60	−54
North					
Liberals	+52	+53	+68	+68	+16
Moderates	+16	+7	+13	+11	−5
Conservatives	−37	−49	−52	−70	−33
Males					
Liberals	+53	+49	+63	+62	+9
Moderates	+22	+12	+10	+14	−8
Conservatives	−30	−49	−59	−70	−40
Married					
Liberals	+51	+49	+68	+63	+12
Moderates	+20	+11	+8	+7	−13
Conservatives	−31	−48	−56	−69	−38
Catholics					
Liberals	+70	+54	+71	+59	−11
Moderates	+43	+28	+21	+6	−37
Conservatives	−7	−30	−42	−59	−52
Observant					
Liberals	+42	+54	+65	+60	+18
Moderates	+18	+13	+9	+13	−5
Conservatives	−29	−46	−60	−69	−40

Source: American National Election Studies.
Note: Net party identification = percentage of Democratic identifiers and leaners minus percentage of Republican identifiers and leaners.

increase in net Republican identification among conservatives and a seven-point decrease in net Republican identification among liberals. Similarly, among religiously observant whites, there was a forty-point increase in net Republican identification among conservatives and an eighteen-point decrease in net Republican identification among liberals.

The end result of the process of ideological realignment has been a marked increase in the correlation between ideology and party identification. Table 18.5 displays the trend in the correlation between ideology and party identification between the 1970s and 2004 for the entire electorate and for several major subgroups. The correlation between ideology and party identification increases in all groups including Southern and non-Southern whites. In fact, the increase in the correlation between ideology and party identification is just as great for non-Southern whites as it is for Southern whites.

The increasing correlation between ideology and party identification was not simply a result of generational replacement. Table 18.6 presents the results of a cohort analysis of the relationship between ideology and party identification among Northern and Southern whites from the 1970s through the 1990s. Almost every ten-year age cohort shows an increase in the correlation between ideology and party identification over time. For example, among Southern whites who were in their twenties during the 1970s, the correlation between ideology and party identification was only .27. However, among members of the same cohort during the 1990s, the correlation between ideology and party identification was .54. Similarly, among Northern whites who were in their twenties during the 1970s, the correlation between ideology and party identification was only .34, but among members of the same cohort during the 1990s, the correlation between ideology and party identification was .61.

Table 18.5   Correlation between Party Identification and Ideological Self-Identification by Decade

	1972– 1980	*1982– 1990*	*1992– 2000*	*2002– 2004*	*Change*
All Respondents	.35	.39	.49	.58	+.23
African Americans	.14	.14	.24	.23	+.09
Whites	.34	.42	.53	.64	+.30
South	.26	.33	.50	.55	+.29
North	.38	.45	.54	.66	+.28
No College	.26	.27	.34	.49	+.23
College	.47	.54	.65	.71	+.24

Source: American National Election Studies.

Note: Product-moment correlations between seven-point party identification scale and seven-point liberal-conservative scale. All coefficients are statistically significant (p < .001).

Table 18.6 Cohort Analysis of Correlation between Ideological Self-Identification and Party Identification for White Respondents by Decade

Region	Age Group	1972–1980	1982–1990	1992–2000
South	20–29	.27	.28	.54
	30–39	.36	.39	.58
	40–49	.22	.44	.54
	50–59	.21	.40	.56
	60+	.32	.32	.45
North	20–29	.34	.44	.59
	30–39	.37	.52	.57
	40–49	.39	.48	.61
	50–59	.38	.49	.57
	60+	.38	.39	.46

Source: American National Election Studies.
Note: Pearson product-moment correlations between seven-point liberal-conservative scale and seven-point party identification scale. All coefficients are statistically significant (p < .001).

Ideological Realignment versus Partisan Persuasion: White Southerners and Catholics

The evidence examined thus far indicates that the relationship between ideology and party identification became considerably stronger among both Northern and Southern whites who remained in the electorate between the 1970s and the 1990s. However, cohort analysis does not allow us to determine whether ideology was influencing party identification, as the ideological realignment hypothesis suggests, or whether party identification was influencing ideology, as Green, Palmquist, and Schickler (2002) suggest.

It is possible that the increasing clarity of ideological differences between the parties during the 1980s and 1990s caused Democratic and Republican partisans to adopt ideological positions consistent with their existing party loyalties in a process that might be termed *partisan persuasion*. However, partisan persuasion cannot explain increasing Republican identification among major subgroups within the electorate. Moreover, evidence from NES surveys indicates that for white Southerners and Catholics—two subgroups within the white electorate that experienced substantial increases in Republican identification between 1972 and 2004—ideological realignment rather than partisan persuasion was the primary mechanism of change.

If partisan persuasion was at work, increases in Republican identification among white Southerners and Catholics between 1972 and 2004 should have led to substantial increases in conservatism in these groups as the growing ranks of Republican identifiers adopted the conservative ideology of their new party. But in the survey data, there was no increase in conservatism among either white Southerners or white Catholics. Throughout the period from 1972 though 2004, the mean conservatism score of white Southerners hovered around 4.5, while that of white Catholics remained in the vicinity of 4.2.

Contrary to the partisan persuasion hypothesis, white Southerners and Catholics did not become much more conservative between 1972 and 2004; however, conservative white Southerners and Catholics did become much more Republican. Between 1972 and 2004, the proportion of conservative Southern whites identifying with the Republican Party increased from 39 percent to 80 percent and the mean score of conservative Southerners on the seven-point party identification scale rose from 3.7 to 5.5. During the same period, the proportion of conservative Catholics identifying with the Republican Party increased from 48 percent to 82 percent and the mean score of conservative Catholics on the seven-point party identification scale rose from 4.1 to 5.7. This evidence clearly indicates that ideological realignment rather than partisan persuasion was responsible for the increasing correlation between ideology and party identification among white Southerners and Catholics.

Evidence from the 1992–1996 NES Panel Survey

Additional evidence concerning the relative importance of ideological realignment and partisan persuasion can be obtained from the only major long-term panel study conducted by the NES between 1976 and 2000: the

1992–1996 panel survey. Although the study covers only a four-year period and the sample is fairly small (only 597 respondents were interviewed in both 1992 and 1996), the panel design of the study allows us to estimate the influence of ideology on party identification, as well as the influence of party identification on ideology.

Figure 18.1 presents the results of a path analysis of ideology and party identification among white respondents in the survey. These results indicate that there was a high degree of stability in both ideological orientations and party identification among survey respondents. In fact, ideological orientations were even more stable than party identification over the four years of the panel. Despite the high degree of stability of party identification, however, the results of the path analysis provide strong support for the ideological realignment hypothesis. Twenty-seven percent of conservative Democrats and liberal Republicans switched parties between 1992 and 1996. In contrast, only 5 percent of conservative Republicans and liberal Democrats switched parties between 1992 and 1996. Even after controlling for 1992 party identification and a wide variety of social background characteristics, 1992 ideological orientations had a significant impact on 1996 party identification.

Figure 18.1 Path Analysis of Ideology and Party Identification for White Respondents in 1992–1996 NES Panel Survey

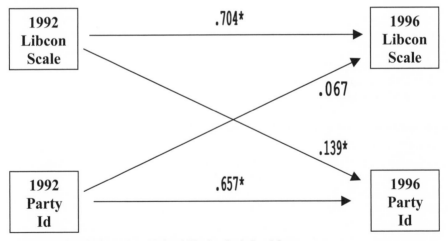

Source: 1992–1996 American National Election Study Panel Survey.

Note: Party identification measured by standard seven-point scale. Ideological orientation measured by eleven-item scale. Figures shown are standardized regression coefficients. Control variables included in regression analyses are age, church attendance, religion, region, gender, marital status, education, family income, and household union membership. Coefficients marked with asterisk are statistically significant at $p < .001$.

Social Identity, Ideology, and Party Identification

According to the social identity theory, party identification is based largely on membership in social groups—citizens choose a party identification based on their perception of the fit between their own social characteristics and the social characteristics of supporters of the two major parties. Since the New Deal, the Democrats have generally been viewed as the party of the poor, the working class, union members, urban dwellers, racial and ethnic minorities, Catholics, and Jews, while the Republicans have more often been seen as the party of the wealthy, business executives, smalltown and rural residents, and white Protestants outside of the South. However, the social images of the Democratic and Republican parties have undergone considerable change in recent years. As Green, Palmquist, and Schickler (2002) point out, Southern whites, who were once a key component of the Democratic coalition, have been moving into the Republican camp since the 1950s. More recently, gender, marital status, sexual orientation, and religious beliefs have emerged as important correlates of party affiliation: members of traditional families and those with strong religious convictions tend to be Republicans, while singles, gays, and less-religious voters tend to be Democrats.

The changing relationship between social groups and the parties raises the question of whether membership in social groups has a direct impact on party identification, as the social identity theory proposes, or whether partisan differences between social groups are simply a result of the policy preferences of group members. According to the latter ideological differences hypothesis, the reason some groups, such as white evangelicals, have become increasingly Republican in recent years while other groups such as gays and lesbians have become increasingly Democratic is because of the policy preferences of their members.

As a first test of the social identity and ideological differences hypotheses, table 18.7 presents data from the 2004 national exit poll on net party identification among members of a number of groups that are closely aligned with either the Democratic or the Republican party, controlling for ideological orientation. We measured the ideological orientations of respondents in the exit poll with the three-point liberal-conservative identification question because this question was included in all three versions of the exit poll questionnaire.[4]

The results in table 18.7 show that, except for African Americans, the differences between white liberals and conservatives within each social group were much larger than the differences between social groups. African Americans, regardless of their ideological orientation, strongly favored the Democratic Party. Otherwise, across all social groups, white liberals strongly preferred the Democratic Party and white conservatives strongly

Table 18.7 Net Party Identification by Social Identity and Ideological Identification, 2004

	Liberal	Moderate	Conservative
African Americans	+76	+71	+44
Hispanics	+44	+16	−42
Whites	+52	−4	−70
Income < $15,000	+50	+33	−47
Income $200,000+	+73	−21	−88
Union members	+65	+24	−53
Northeast	+53	+1	−61
South	+38	−6	−75
Big city dwellers	+61	+8	−83
Small town, rural residents	+30	−2	−62
Protestant	+46	−6	−74
Catholic	+49	−4	−61
Jewish	+87	+27	−50
Most observant	+39	−9	−75
Least observant	+53	−2	−55
Born again/Evangelical	+22	−11	−73
Male	+29	−19	−57
Female	+45	−1	−46
Married	+53	−6	−73
Single	+52	+2	−60
Gun owners	+43	−8	−71
Gay, lesbian, bisexual	+45	+24	−28

Source: 2004 National Exit Poll.

Note: Net party identification = percentage of Democratic identifiers minus percentage of Republican identifiers.

preferred the Republican Party. While the large majority of Hispanics identified with the Democratic Party, most conservative Hispanics identified with the Republican Party. Jews overwhelmingly identified with the Democratic Party, but conservative Jews strongly identified with the Republican Party. Wealthy liberals favored the Democrats, and poor conservatives favored the Republicans; conservative gays and lesbians preferred the Republican Party by a wide margin, while liberal evangelicals (yes, there were some) preferred the Democratic Party.

The results in table 18.7 provide only limited support for the social identity theory. It is true that the partisan orientations of certain groups cannot be completely explained by their policy preferences. For African Americans, in particular, social identity and party identification seem to be closely connected. African Americans, regardless of ideology, tend to be Democrats. For other groups, however, the connection between objective social identity and party identification is much weaker or nonexistent. Even for members of groups with very close ties to one party or the other, such as Jews or evangelical Christians, ideology trumps social identity. The reason most Jews identify with the Democratic Party and most evangelical Christians identify with the Republican Party is because of their policy preferences, not because of their social identity.

The data in table 18.7 show that there were some differences among groups even after controlling for ideology. Liberal and moderate Jews were much more likely to identify with the Democratic Party than liberal and moderate evangelicals. Similarly, wealthy moderates were much more likely to identify with the Republican Party than poor moderates. Moreover, these data do not allow us to examine the impact of group identification on political attitudes. Individuals who feel close to a group may hold views that are more typical of that group than individuals who do not feel close to a group. Nevertheless, the fact that the connection between objective group membership and political attitudes is relatively weak raises serious questions about the explanatory power of the social identity theory, because group membership is generally considered a prerequisite for the development of social identity (Gurin, Miller, and Gurin 1980; Miller et al. 1981; Tajfel 1981; Turner 1982; Gurin 1985; Tajfel and Turner 1986; Turner 1987).

Social Identity, Ideology, and Party Identification in 2004

In order to directly compare the effects of ideology and group membership on contemporary party identification, we performed a logistic regression analysis of party identification. Our dependent variable in this analysis was a dichotomous measure of party identification, by grouping strong, weak, and independent Democrats together as Democrats and by grouping strong, weak, and independent together as Republicans. Pure independents were excluded from the analysis.[5] Independent variables in the analysis included a sixteen-item liberal-conservative scale and a variety of social background characteristics including age, education, income, gender, marital status, religion, church attendance, and household union affiliation. The results of the logistic regression analysis are presented in table 18.8.

To facilitate comparisons of the effects of the independent variables on party identification, we converted each of the logistic regression coefficients into a change-in-probability score. This score can be interpreted as the change in the probability of identifying with the Republican Party associated with a change between categories of any of the dichotomous independent variables such as gender, union membership, or martial status, or the change

Table 18.8 Logistic Regression Analysis of Party Identification of White Respondents with Liberal-Conservative Policy Scale and Social Background Characteristics, 2004

Independent Variable	B	(S.E.)	z	Change in Probability	Sig.
Liberal-conservative scale	.313	(.025)	12.35	.63	.001
Age	−.010	(.006)	−1.57	−.06	NS
Education	.254	(.074)	3.43	.16	.001
Income	.005	(.021)	.26	.01	NS
Female	−.230	(.208)	−1.10	−.05	NS
Married	.342	(.222)	1.54	.08	NS
Nonunion	.116	(.064)	1.72	.10	.05
Religion					
Catholic	−.584	(.242)	−2.41	−.14	.01
Jewish	−.672	(.621)	−1.08	−.16	NS
No religion	−.024	(.323)	−.07	−.01	NS
Church frequency	.031	(.076)	.41	.02	NS
Constant	−1.068	(.745)	−1.43		NS

Pseudo R^2 = .38
N = 706

Source: American National Election Study 2004.
Note: Dependent variable is dichotomous party identification (strong, weak, and independent Republican vs. strong, weak, and independent Democrat). Change in probability is the estimated difference in probability of Republican identification between categories of dichotomous variables (nonunion vs. union household; female vs. male; Catholic, Jewish, or no religion vs. Protestant; married vs. not married) or between 25th and 75th percentiles of continuous variables and scales (age, education, church frequency, liberal-conservative).

in probability associated with a change between the 25th percentile and the 75th percentile on any of the continuous independent variables such as age, education, or ideology.

The major conclusion that emerges from table 18.8 is that the impact of ideology on party identification was much stronger than that of any of the social background variables. Most of the estimated coefficients for the social background variables are not statistically significant. In addition, the change-in-probability scores for most of the social background variables are generally small, with the largest effect (.16) being for education. Many social characteristics, including age, income, gender, martial status, and church attendance, had little or no impact on party identification after controlling for ideology. In contrast, the estimated coefficient for the ideology scale is statistically significant and its change-in-probability score is almost four times larger than that for education. Even after controlling for social background characteristics, the probability of identifying with the Republican Party was sixty-three percentage points higher for a voter at the 75th percentile of the liberal-conservative scale than it was for a voter at the 25th percentile.

According to Green, Palmquist, and Schickler (2002), the questions most voters ask themselves in deciding which party to support are: "What kinds of social groups come to mind as I think about Democrats, Republicans, and independents?" and "Which assemblage of groups (if any) best describes me?" Based on our evidence, however, it appears that the questions most voters ask themselves in deciding which party to support are actually: "What do Democrats and Republicans stand for?" and "Which party's positions are closer to mine?"

The Consequences of Ideological Realignment for Voting Behavior

The growing consistency between ideology and party identification has important consequences for voting behavior, because voters whose party identification and ideological orientation are consistent are much more loyal to their party than voters whose party identification and ideological orientation are inconsistent. In the 2004 presidential election, according to data from the national exit poll, 96 percent of liberal white Democrats voted for John Kerry, compared with only 62 percent of conservative white Democrats. Similarly, 97 percent of conservative white Republicans voted for George W. Bush, compared with only 58 percent of liberal white Republicans.

Overall, according to both national exit polls and the NES postelection surveys, more than 90 percent of Republican identifiers and almost 90 percent of Democratic identifiers voted for their own party's presidential candidates in the 2000 and 2004 elections. These two elections produced the highest levels of party voting in the history of the National Election Studies. Party voting was also very prevalent in recent congressional elections, especially in competitive races (Abramowitz and Alexander 2004).

The high level of partisan voting in recent presidential and congressional elections is due largely to the fact that an ideological realignment has taken place among white voters in both the South and the North since the 1970s. As a result of this realignment, voters' party affiliations are now more consistent with their ideological orientations than in the past. According to data from the American National Election Studies, liberal Democrats and conservative Republicans made up only 42 percent of all white party identifiers in 1972, while conservative Democrats and liberal Republicans accounted for 20 percent. By 2004, liberal Democrats and conservative Republicans made up 59 percent of all white party identifiers, while conservative Democrats and liberal Republicans were down to 9 percent. Because of this growing consistency, the outlook for the 2006 and 2008 elections is for a continuation of high levels of partisan voting.

Notes

1. We have grouped the data by decade in order to minimize fluctuations due to short-term forces or sampling variation. The measure presented here is simply the difference between the percentage of Democratic identifiers and leaners and the percentage of Republican identifiers and leaners in the overall electorate. Excluding leaning independents and calculating net party identification based on the difference between the percentage of Democratic identifiers and the percentage of Republican identifiers produces almost identical results.

2. Data from national exit polls also show a substantial increase in Republican identification among non-Southern whites since the 1970s. Between 1976 and 2004, the percentage of non-Southern whites identifying with the Republican Party in national exit polls increased from 28 percent to 43 percent. Moreover, contrary to the claim by Green, Palmquist, and Schickler (2002) that the party loyalties of white Southerners have stabilized in recent years, the national exit poll data show a continuing movement toward the Republican Party in this group: the Republican advantage in party identification among white Southerners increased from seventeen points in 2000 to thirty-one points in 2004.

3. In testing the ideological realignment hypothesis, we use different measures of ideology with different data sets. We use the seven-point ideological identification scale to classify respondents in NES surveys as liberal (1–3), moderate (4), or conservative (5–7) because this question is correlated with preferences on a wide range of policy issues and has been included in every survey since 1972. We use a similar ideological identification question with three response categories—liberal, moderate, and conservative—in our analysis of 2004 national exit poll data because the split-sample procedures used in the exit poll make it impossible to create a multiple-item scale for the entire sample. However, in our analyses of the 1992–1996 NES panel survey and the 2004 NES survey, we measure ideological orientations with multiple-item scales that include the seven-point ideological identification question along with a number of questions about specific policy issues.

The 1992–1996 ideology scale is based on eleven items included in both the 1992 and 1996 waves of the panel: liberal-conservative identification, abortion, government aid to blacks, defense spending, the death penalty, laws barring discrimination against gays and lesbians, allowing gays and lesbians to serve in the military, government vs. personal responsibility for jobs and living standards, government vs. private responsibility for health insurance, government spending and services, and the role of women in society. Because of the small number of respondents interviewed in both waves of the panel, we recoded all of the seven-point issue scales to place respondents with no opinion in the middle position (4) in order to avoid losing cases due to missing data. The 1992 scale has a reliability coefficient (Cronbach's alpha) of .70. The 1996 scale has a reliability coefficient of .75.

The 2004 ideology scale is based on sixteen items: liberal-conservative identification, abortion, abortion funding, partial-birth abortion, gay marriage, government vs. private responsibility for health insurance, government vs. personal responsibility for jobs and living standards, government services and spending, gun control, the death penalty, government aid to blacks, government aid to Hispanics, environmental protection vs. job creation, defense spending, use of diplomacy vs. military force, and the role of women in society. This scale has a reliability coefficient (Cronbach's alpha) of .77.

4. However, responses to this question were strongly related to opinions on three policy questions that were included in different versions of the questionnaire: abortion ($r = .40$), gay marriage ($r = .42$), and the role of the federal government ($r = .31$).

5. An OLS regression analysis using the seven-point party identification scale as the dependent variable produced almost identical results.

19

The Rise of the Right

More Conservatives or More Concentrated Conservatism?

Jeffrey M. Stonecash

By many accounts, America has become a more conservative nation in recent decades (Frank 2004; Micklethwait and Woolridge 2004). Republicans, long in the minority in the House, won a majority in 1994 with a conservative antigovernment agenda. Entitlement rights in the federal welfare programs were significantly curtailed by Republicans in 1996. George W. Bush was able to secure the enactment of large tax cuts in 2001, 2002, and 2003, with most of the benefits going to the most affluent. He cut environmental regulations, worker safety inspections, and regulations imposed on businesses.[1] He opposed same-sex marriages and sought to further limit abortion rights. Perhaps most important, he pursued this conservative agenda with full support from the Republican majority in Congress. Moreover, Bush and his congressional party allies were retained in office by the American electorate in the 2004 elections. It is not difficult to conclude that the country has become more conservative.

While that conclusion is plausible, it remains asserted more than examined—and another explanation is equally plausible. It may well be that the apparent increase in support for conservative policies reflects an increase not in conservatives themselves but in their "organization" and framing of issues. Over the last several decades, conservatives have increasingly moved to identify with the Republican Party, making them a significant and dominant presence within the party. The electoral base of conservatives that was split between two parties became much more unified within the one party. That created a cohesive ideological group within that party and provided a basis for a more forceful argument for conservative views. As V. O. Key argued in *Southern Politics* (1949), the crucial matter in politics is whether those advocating a set of positions can create a coherent coalition with continuity of an electoral base and positions to create pressure on opponents. It may be that the important matter is the consolidation of conservatives within the Republican Party, not the general drift of opinion in society.

Further, the ability of conservatives to capitalize on their concentration within the Republican Party was helped along by the efforts of conservative scholars and think tanks to represent the argument for less government. That allowed the party to frame issues in a way more conducive to American political culture with its emphasis on individualism. The combination of a more coherent conservative base and a more aggressive critique of liberalism focused the conservative argument and gave it more force within the political process. Voices scattered across the political landscape became more organized, focused, and prominent within the process.

This analysis will explore these alternative explanations. First, the general trends in public opinion over the last several decades will be reviewed to assess whether there has been an increase in support for conservative positions. Then the mobilization of conservatives into the Republican Party in recent decades will be examined, using both individual and aggregate-level results.

Trends in the Presence of Conservative Views

If the nation has become more conservative, then presumably there should have been an increase within the electorate in the percentage of those who hold conservative views or say they are conservative. Figure 19.1 presents time series of the percentages of National Election Study (NES) respondents reporting that they hold conservative views. The responses reported involve whether the respondent:

Figure 19.1 Trends in Conservative Positions, 1970–2004

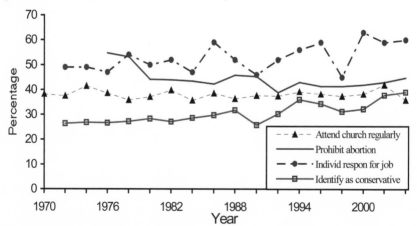

Source: American National Election Studies.

- attends church weekly or more often
- believes abortion should be prohibited
- believes individuals, rather than government, are responsible for finding a job
- identifies as a conservative when asked his or her position

The trends do not suggest any sort of consistent drift toward conservative views over the last thirty years. The percentage of respondents opposed to abortion has declined, as has the percentage saying they rely heavily on religion in daily life and the percentage who report they are "cool" to gays.[2] One of the important indicators of support for traditional patterns of living—whether someone attends church weekly or more often—has not increased in thirty years. However, the percentage who identify themselves as conservative has increased from about 26 percent to the upper 30s over thirty years, and there is an erratic increase in support for the idea that individuals should be responsible for finding their own jobs.

These trends indicate that we might accept the idea that some indicators suggest a more conservative society, while others do not. Perhaps most interesting is that the ones often presented as embodying the conservative movement—abortion opinions and attendance at church—do not follow a pattern of becoming more prevalent. While some indicators could be selectively pointed to, these data do not provide strong support for the idea that America is moving toward more conservativism.

Greater Support for Republicans

While there is not much evidence that the electorate as a whole has become more conservative, there is clear evidence that the Republican Party has developed a more conservative record and that a higher percentage of the electorate now identifies with the party and fewer identify with a Democratic Party that is becoming more liberal. The drift in party positions is evident from the voting record of members of Congress. While the average voting record of all members has not changed much in the last fifty years, Republicans have become more conservative. Since the 1970s there has been a steady drift of Republicans to more conservative positions and of Democrats to more liberal ones (Stonecash 2006).

While the congressional Republican Party has grown more conservative (and the Democrats more liberal), there has been a general, if erratic, drift toward greater identification with the Republican Party. Democrats fluctuated around the 55 percent level for much of the 1960s and 1970s and since then have ranged around 50 percent. Republicans varied around the 35 percent level during the 1960s and 1970s and have been between 40 and 45 percent since then (see chapter 16).

The trends present an important puzzle. The Republican Party has gained seats in Congress and held those seats. The party has compiled a more conservative voting record in Congress, and as that has happened, identification with the party has increased, while identification with the Democratic Party has declined. Yet, a review of survey data does not provide any clear indication that the electorate has become any more conservative. Thus, while the country does not appear to have become more conservative, the Republican Party has, and it has maintained its majority status.

Explaining the Rise of Republicans: Mobilizing Conservatives

How have Republicans been able to emerge as the majority party while becoming more conservative in a country that is not changing ideologically? The answer is secular realignment. For much of the last fifty years, conservatives (both fiscal and social) were distributed, if unevenly, between the two parties. Beginning in the 1960s (Hodgson 1996; Frank 2004; Micklethwait and Woolridge 2004), conservatives began a steady effort to mobilize conservatives and bring them into the Republican Party. In other words, the presence of conservatives has not increased, but they have been mobilized into the Republican Party. As they have become a larger portion of the party, they have become a more forceful presence in American politics.

The first matter to be documented below is the mobilization of conservatives into the Republican Party. Then their role as articulators of the conservative cause will be addressed.

Presidential Changes

Presidential elections often lead change in American politics, and that appears to have occurred in the attraction of conservatives to the Republican Party (Abramowitz 1994; Abramowitz and Saunders 1998). The NES survey does not ask many questions about ideological or policy positioning, but responses to several questions show that those who hold conservative positions were voting for the Republican presidential candidates at least as far back as the early 1970s.

While Republican presidential candidates have been attracting conservatives for several decades, the ability of the party as a whole to attract them has taken longer. Figure 19.2 tracks these patterns. While there have been erratic movements, the general pattern is of a gradual movement of conservatives to broader support for the Republican Party. With some lag, congres-

Figure 19.2   Percentage with Conservative Position Identifying with Republican Party, 1970–2004

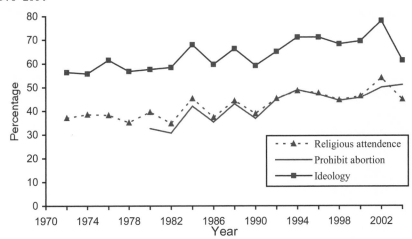

Source: American National Election Studies.

sional candidates and the party itself have also developed conservative support. It is likely that the presence of incumbents in office delayed the development of conservative support for Republicans, but the transition has gradually occurred.

The consequence of this development is that Republican House and presidential candidates and the party in general all have consistently high levels of support from those with conservative views. Thirty years ago, only presidential candidates received such support, but it is now more consistent, as figure 19.3 indicates. What has changed over time is that Republicans have been able to mobilize existing conservatives to support their party.

The result is that a much larger percentage of the Republican Party is now comprised of those with conservative views. Figure 19.4 indicates the percentage of self-identified conservatives that say they identify with the Republican Party and the percentage of the party comprised of conservatives. Over the last thirty years, conservatives have gradually come to align themselves more with the Republican Party and less with the Democrats. This transition has made them more dominant within the party. In 1972, the first year the question about self-defined ideology was asked, 53 percent of the Republican Party was conservative, 33 percent were moderates, and 13 percent were liberals. In 2002 and 2004, averaging the two years, 76 percent were conservative, 13 percent were moderate and 11 percent were liberal.

Figure 19.3   Percentage of Those with Conservative Views Voting for Republican Presidential and House Candidates, 1976–2004

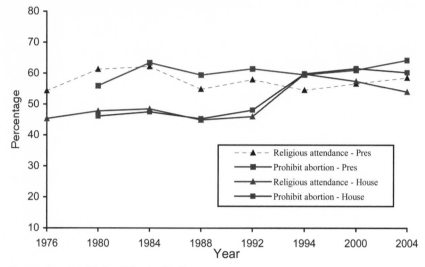

Source: American National Election Studies.

Figure 19.4   Percentage of Those with Conservative Views Identifying with the Republican Party and Percentage of Party from Conservatives, 1976–2004

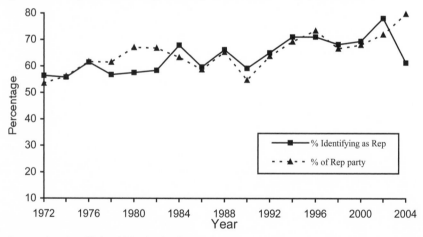

Source: American National Election Studies.

The Congressional Shift

While the party was attracting more conservatives at the individual level, it was also experiencing a change in the composition of its congressional party. The DW-Nominate scores provide a means to assess how the party's composition has changed.[3] The scores, on a scale of -1 to 1, can be (somewhat arbitrarily) grouped as follows: liberals are those with scores of less than -0.2, moderates are -0.2 to 0.2, and conservatives are greater than 0.2. As figure 19.5 indicates, the Republican Party, conservative for much of the early part of the century, experienced a rise in the presence of moderates in the 1950s–1970s. The party then began to again attract more conservatives, and by the 1990s conservatives once again dominated within the party.

Over the last forty years, the Republican Party has increasingly become comprised of conservatives. As figure 19.6 indicates, conservatives are now more concentrated within the Republican Party. As the transition in party bases occurred beginning in the 1930s (Stonecash 2006), conservatives were present in both parties, but by the 1960s, 30 percent of all conservative House members were in the Democratic Party. The rise of conservatives in the Republican Party is in many ways a resurgence of their presence within the party. If we adopt a longer time frame, the last several decades are a return to a prior situation. Nonetheless, it is clear that it is correct to see the Republican Party as becoming more conservative over the last several decades. The party has become a more coherent representative of the conservative views that exist within the nation.

Figure 19.5   Distribution of House Republican Members' Voting Records, 1900–2000

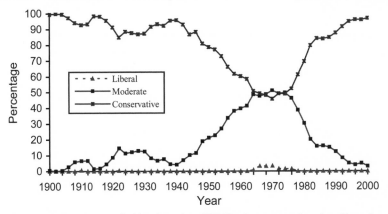

Source: Election results compiled by the author; DW-Nominate scores from http://voteview.com/dwnl.htm.

Figure 19.6   Percentage of House Conservatives within the Republican Party, 1900–2000

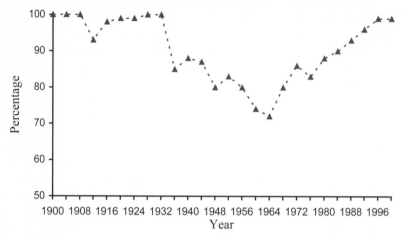

Source: Election results compiled by the author; DW-Nominate scores from http://voteview.com/ dwnl.htm.

Concentration and Clarity of Argument

The attraction of conservatives to the Republican Party did not occur by accident. By the mid-1960s, conservatives within the Republican Party were troubled by the expansion of the role of the federal government. The conservative wing of the party sought to reassert the conservative argument that government should be restrained (Rae 1989). It set out to attract fiscal conservatives in the South to the Republican Party (Phillips 1970) and eventually succeeded (Black and Black 1987).

This appeal on fiscal issues was combined during the 1970s and 1980s with initially tentative and then more focused efforts to attract social conservatives (Dionne 1997). There were troubling trends in American society, and Republicans thought they could attract social conservatives by focusing on those problems. Beginning in the 1960s there were substantial increases in the number of people on welfare (until welfare reform of 1996), divorce, the percentage of births that are illegitimate, single-parent families, sex on television, and the availability of pornography on the Internet, among other trends (Brewer and Stonecash 2006). Conservatives saw a society heading in the wrong direction and believed there was an urgent need to restore appropriate values and reduce the fiscal size of government and taxes on those more successful.

The ability to frame issues in a way that appealed to conservatives was supported by a significant increase in the presence of conservative think tanks, which have generated studies and position papers to help present conservative arguments. These think tanks have developed analyses of disturbing trends, provided explanations of what has gone wrong, commissioned focus groups and polls to help frame and focus arguments in appealing ways, and then provided lobbying support to present all this to members of Congress (Micklethwait and Woolridge 2004).

The framing of conservative critiques has been particularly important. Welfare has been opposed not on the grounds that welfare recipients are just lazy and undeserving but rather because it reduces individual accountability and responsibility and ultimately encourages behavioral patterns that prevent people from succeeding and being independent (Murray 1984); that argument appeals to American notions of individualism and personal responsibility. Abortion has been opposed as morally wrong. That argument has some appeal because many people are pro-choice but still uneasy about supporting this activity. The estate tax—labeled the "death tax"—is opposed on the grounds that it taxes people at death and is double taxation (Graetz and Shapiro 2005). Each of these frames appeals to pervasive views in the electorate and makes the conservative argument more compelling. All this has helped increase the impact of conservative arguments within the political process.

Conservatives in the "Right" Party

All these efforts helped move conservatives out of the Democratic Party and into the Republican Party, and the result has been a much more coherently conservative Republican Party. The party encompasses more and more of the conservatives in the nation, and this greater—though not complete—uniformity within the party provides the basis to make a more sustained and aggressive presentation of conservative principles. A set of views that was previously distributed between two parties is now concentrated in one.

The result is a twist on the V. O. Key argument that the less affluent fare better when there is a cohesive party based on the less affluent (1949). His argument was that a party that mobilized and consistently derived its electoral base from the less affluent was able to more effectively make its case in the political arena. This pattern was particularly likely if party leaders were in agreement on policy concerns within and across elections and were able to present a sustained argument for their cause. If these conditions prevailed, then it would be possible for a group advocating a set of positions to produce a coherent argument to create pressure on opponents.

A similar situation has developed for Republicans. Presidential and House candidates draw on the same electoral base, and the partisan vote within districts is increasingly similar. Figure 19.7 presents the correlation of House and presidential results across districts for the last century. Since

Figure 19.7   Correlation of House and Presidential Vote Results, 1900–2004

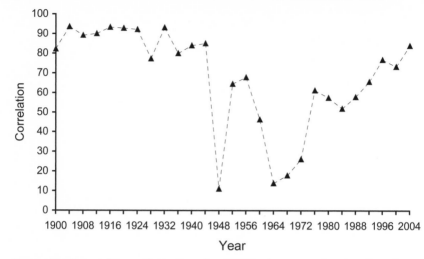

Source: Election results compiled by the author; DW-Nominate scores from http://voteview.com/
dwnl.htm.

1964, the low point for this association, this correlation has steadily increased, and after 1996 it reached its highest levels since the 1940s. This
consistency of results means that the presidential and congressional (at least
as represented by the House) wings of the party have the same electoral base,
which has become more predictably supportive of Republican candidates. At
the individual level, the association between party identification and presidential and House voting has also increased (Bartels 2000). As George W.
Bush's approval ratings have declined since 9/11, Republicans have remained loyal and inclined to support his various initiatives (Jacobson 2003).
The results have been a stable, cohesive, and a more forceful expression of
conservative views, more polarized political parties, and much less inclination to be tentative about presenting conservative positions.

This strenuous advocacy of conservative positions is unlikely to decline.
The Republican Party electoral base has been stable for some time. Republicans have improved their percentage of seats in the House and the Senate.
Unless they suffer a serious setback in the future, conservatives are likely to
continue to believe that political events are moving in directions favorable to
their position. The stability of their success has allowed conservatives to
make their views more central to American politics. The presence of conservatives in American society is not necessarily greater, but they are more concentrated in politically relevant ways.

Notes

1. Joel Brinkley, "Out of Spotlight, Bush Overhauls U.S. Regulations," *New York Times*, August 14, 2004.
2. The NES surveys ask respondents to indicate if they have a "cool" or "warm" reaction to gays. Each respondent is presented with a scale, with 0–49 cool and 50–100 warm. In the 1980s, 62 percent were cool. In the 2000, 2002, and 2004 surveys only about 32 percent were below 50 on this scale.
3. These data have been developed by Keith Poole. The data are available at http://voteview.com/dwnl.htm. The method is explained in "A Spatial Model for Legislative Roll Call Analysis," *American Journal of Political Science,* May 1985, 357–84, (with Howard Rosenthal), and "The Polarization of American Politics," *Journal of Politics,* December 1984, 1061–79 (with Howard Rosenthal).

Part VI

Party in Government

20

The Partisan Presidency

Richard M. Skinner

Traditionally, political scientists have tended to see the modern presidency of the twentieth and twenty-first centuries as the enemy of strong parties (see Davis 1992; Greenstein 1978; Jones 2002; Milkis 1993, 1999). Through an "objective" media, modern presidents appeal directly to voters, over the heads of party leaders, seeking to project a nonpartisan image. They build ad hoc coalitions of support in Congress without regard to party lines. They preside over an executive branch staffed by nonpartisan experts, more interested in policy than politics. Modern presidents show little interest in their party's performance in down-ballot races, let alone its long-term fate.

All of these propositions held true for presidents of the 1950s, 1960s and 1970s, especially Dwight Eisenhower, Lyndon Johnson, and Jimmy Carter. But since 1980, we have seen the rise of a new kind of presidency—a "partisan presidency."

Partisan presidents (see table 20.1) have polarized the electorate along partisan lines to an extent unimaginable a generation ago, often experiencing an "approval gap" of forty points or more (the "approval gap" is the difference between the approval given to a president by his own partisans and by members of the other party). Relatively few members of the other party have voted for them. Partisan presidents have received overwhelming support in Congress from their own party. More notably, they have confronted strong—sometimes near-unanimous—opposition from the other party. They have often relied heavily on their party's leadership to deliver votes on Capitol Hill, and they have been unable to enjoy the cozy relationship that earlier presidents had with the opposition (e.g., Eisenhower and Sam Rayburn, Johnson and Everett Dirksen). In recent decades, even a president predisposed to such a friendly relationship—George H. W. Bush—was unable to have one.

Partisan presidents have sought to put a stronger partisan imprint upon the executive branch, centralizing personnel decisions and favoring ideological loyalists or spinmeisters over career civil servants or nonpartisan experts.

Table 20.1   The "Modern Presidency" and the "Partisan Presidency"

Subject	*"Modern Presidency"*	*"Partisan Presidency"*
Congressional relations	President's party often divided; works across party lines	Partisan polarization: works closely with own party, but has difficult relations with opposition
Executive administration	Relies on nonpartisan experts and civil servants; patronage in decline	"Administrative presidency" for partisan/ideological ends
Policy advice	Nonpartisan experts	Political consultants, ideological think tanks
Public opinion	Gains support across party lines	Polarized public
Media relations	Cooperative; uses broadcasting to reach mass public	Antagonistic; uses "alternative media" or "partisan press" to reach niche publics
Electoral politics	Candidate-centered politics; plays down party affiliation; wins support across party lines	Increasing polarization; revival of party organizations

It's hard to imagine presidents less interested in "neutral competence" than Ronald Reagan or George W. Bush. Partisan presidents, those two in particular, have actively campaigned for their party's candidates and sought to use the national party committees as tools of governance. This behavior contrasts sharply with Eisenhower's apathy toward the GOP, or Johnson's and Richard Nixon's distrust of their national party committees. Reagan, Bill Clinton, and George W. Bush have all shown more interest in their party's long-term fortunes than, say, Carter. George W. Bush, perhaps the exemplar of a partisan president, has shown limited interest in wooing the conventional, "objective" media. Instead he has sought to get his message out through arguably more partisan outlets—Fox News, conservative talk radio, and "Christian" media.

We need to move beyond outdated notions that presidents are above party politics and instead understand that there are presidents who are passionately engaged with their parties and seek to use their parties as tools of governance. This chapter begins a project examining the changing relationship between presidents and their political parties, with special emphasis on George W. Bush.

The Presidency and Political Parties

Most scholars of the presidency agree that a distinctive "modern presidency" emerged in the first half of the twentieth century, first under Woodrow Wilson and Theodore Roosevelt, and then most fully under Franklin D. Roosevelt (Greenstein 1978).

Generally speaking, the heyday of the modern presidency—roughly from the presidency of Franklin D. Roosevelt through those of Lyndon Johnson and Richard Nixon—saw political parties in decline in the electorate, in government, and as organizations. Milkis (1993, 1999) identifies 1937–1938 as the key period of change in the relationship between presidents and their parties. Roosevelt alienated Southern Democrats through his wages-and-hours bill and his attempt to "pack" the Supreme Court; increasingly, these Southerners aligned with Republicans as part of a "conservative coalition" opposed to expansion of the New Deal. This split grew over the next generation, making it difficult for Democratic presidents to look to their party to serve as a base of support in Congress and elsewhere. Roosevelt attempted to diminish conservative influence within the Democratic Party through his "purge" of 1938; after he failed to defeat New Deal opponents in primaries, Roosevelt abandoned his goal of a more nationalized, programmatic party. Instead, he turned to the politics of administration, seeking to accomplish his liberal policies through executive action (Milkis 1993, 1999).[1]

The past quarter-century has seen a reversal of the trend toward weaker relationships between presidents and their parties. Beginning with Ronald Reagan, recent presidents have increasingly relied upon their parties for support both in the electorate and in the Congress. They have presented a more distinctively partisan image to voters and have found it difficult to cultivate support from the opposition. They have sought to lead their parties, using the national committees to garner support for their policies, campaigning extensively for their parties' candidates, and even seeking to mold their parties' futures.

This presidency is partisan in more ways than one. Most obviously, such presidents are partisan through the close ties binding them to their parties. But they are also partisan in that the executive branch is used as a tool to support the president's agenda, and expert advice is valued to the extent that it promotes the party's platform and the president's political future, rather than how it fulfills the ideals of "neutral competence." Finally, this presidency is partisan because the president performs as a partisan in the combat of the "permanent campaign." The president, rather than floating above the political system as "leader of all the people," leads the battalions of a partisan army into the battlefield of contemporary Washington. The parties that these presidents lead are not the decentralized, nonideological federations of the nineteenth century. They are nationalized, ideologically coherent, and headquartered in Washington—ultimately in the Oval Office (Aldrich 1995).

While some of the elements of the partisan presidency emerged under Nixon, it was Reagan that defined the partisan presidency as surely as Franklin Roosevelt did the modern presidency. Reagan sought to remake the Republican Party in his own conservative image and to vault it into majority status. To this end, he repeatedly campaigned for Republican candidates. He used the Republican National Committee (RNC) to win support for his programs, and he worked closely with Republican leaders in Congress, especially Senate Majority Leader Howard Baker. He polarized the electorate more than any of his predecessors—even Nixon. Through centralization of policy decisions and appointment of ideological loyalists, Reagan managed to make the executive branch a tool of conservative governance. Even a skeptic of presidential partisan leadership such as Sidney Milkis admits that the Reagan era may have "marked the watershed . . . for a renewed link between presidents and the party system" (1993, 270).

Despite his previous service as chairman of the RNC, George H. W. Bush harkened back to a less partisan style of leadership with his willingness to work with a Democratic Congress. But the era of détente did not last. Conservative Republicans angrily opposed Bush's agreement to raise taxes in the 1990 budget agreement; Bush found himself desperately tacking to the right to win back his base as the 1992 election approached. Meanwhile, congressional Democrats increasingly blocked his legislative proposals in anticipation of a Democratic win in November.

Bill Clinton was not as relentlessly partisan as his successor, but he still fits into the partisan mold. While he had his own brief period of détente with congressional Republicans beginning in late 1996 and climaxing with the 1997 budget agreement, he usually faced a remarkably united and determined opposition. In 1993–1994, Republicans almost unanimously opposed Clinton's budget and health care plan; in 1995–1996, an empowered GOP sought to impose its own agenda, attempting to overturn one of the defining characteristics of the modern presidency; and in 1998–1999, congressional Republicans attempted to remove Clinton from office, despite widespread public opposition. Clinton deeply polarized the electorate, experiencing an "approval gap" even larger than Reagan's. Even during his second term, when his overall popularity often soared above 60 percent, he continued to inspire intense loathing among evangelicals and conservative Republicans (Guth 2000; Harvey 2000; Rae 2000).

But George W. Bush has set a new standard for partisanship by a president. If Reagan was the Franklin Roosevelt of the partisan presidency, Bush has been the Lyndon Johnson, building upon his predecessor's legacy to an amazing extent. Unlike Reagan, Bush has been able to work with mostly Republican Congresses, freeing him of the need to win over Democrats.

With the exception of the rally-around-the-flag period after 9/11, Bush has been intensely unpopular with Democrats. Now that his support among independents has fallen to about one in three, Bush is forced to rely almost exclusively on his GOP base.

The President as Party Leader

Modern presidents placed little priority on leading their party and often found allies across the aisle. Lyndon Johnson and Richard Nixon showed scant interest in their national party committees; Dwight Eisenhower avoided partisan appeals and distributed patronage to "Citizens for Eisenhower" activists as well as to traditional Republicans. By contrast, partisan presidents have served as active party leaders, campaigning for candidates, working with party committees, and even trying to mold their party's future. Ronald Reagan and George W. Bush both sought to make the Republican Party both a majority and a more clearly conservative party. Bush set a new standard for presidential campaigning through his involvement in the 2002 and 2004 congressional elections, which included calling for the defeat even of moderate Democrats who had often supported Bush's policies (Bass 2004; Nelson 2004). Bill Clinton, while less disciplined in his commitment, tirelessly raised money for the Democratic Party and outlined a "New Democrat" vision to appeal to the center (Rae 2000). Partisan presidents have not shown the apathy that Johnson and Jimmy Carter displayed toward their parties. If the "reformed" presidential process of the 1970s produced nominees such as Carter and George McGovern who had had little contact with their party establishments, the "post-reformed" process of the past quarter-century has produced nominees backed by party insiders during the "invisible primary" (Cohen et al. 2003; Rockman 2004).

A Partisan Public?

Operating in an environment of declining partisanship, modern presidents sought to win over voters across party lines. Dwight Eisenhower, Lyndon Johnson, and Richard Nixon all won substantial support from voters in the other party; all three downplayed partisan themes in their campaigns. Before 1980, presidents rarely experienced an approval gap of more than 40 points; Eisenhower and John F. Kennedy enjoyed popularity across party lines, while Gerald Ford and Jimmy Carter confronted significant opposition within their own parties. Partisan presidents have experienced much larger approval gaps than their predecessors. From Eisenhower through Carter, no president had an average approval gap of more than 41 points, and the approval gap never exceeded 48 points in any quarter. By contrast, Ronald Reagan had an average approval gap of 52.9 points; Bill Clinton's was 55 points, falling below 50 points in only two quarters (Jacobson 2002).

But again, George W. Bush has set new standards for approval gaps. He has experienced the largest approval gaps ever measured, the first president to ever exceed 70 points, which he did during most of the 2004 campaign (Dimock 2004; Jacobson 2005b). Bush has usually received more than 90 percent approval among Republicans, making him one of the most popular presidents ever with his own party—but during 2004, his support among Democrats was among the worst ever received for a president within the opposition party. Independents tended to be closer to Democrats in their view of Bush, forcing him to rely on his own partisans for support (Jacobson 2005b). Even before the campaign began, Bush campaign operatives were open in their belief that large numbers of voters would never back the president; instead they emphasized turning out loyal Republicans.

When polarization reaches such an extent, one wonders if the phrase "public opinion" has much meaning, at least as a singular noun. Certainly, with the divergence in electoral constituencies and the decline in "split-ticket" states and districts, Democratic and Republican officeholders are operating in radically different contexts (Jacobson 2002).

Partisan presidents are also operating in a political system in which public opinion has become much more polarized along party lines (Bartels 2000; Brewer 2004; Fleisher and Bond 2001; Hetherington 2001; Jacobson 2000; Lawrence 2001; Layman and Carsey 2002). Americans perceive far more ideological distance between themselves and presidents than they did in the 1950s and 1960s. Arguably, more and more citizens see an enemy, not a leader, in the White House (Hetherington and Globetti 2003). According to the National Election Studies, the 2004 elections showed the highest level of party loyalty ever measured.

Congressional Relations

Modern presidents often could not depend upon their congressional parties for legislative support. Those parties were usually divided; the North-South split within the Democratic Party was most notable, but there were divisions among Republicans as well, such as that between internationalists and isolationists after World War II, which forced Dwight Eisenhower to look to Democrats for support of his foreign policy (Davis 1992; Jones 2002; Milkis 1993). But the period of the partisan presidency coincides with the rise of polarization and party leadership in Congress (Bond and Fleisher 2000; Cox and McCubbins 1993; Rohde 1991). In an era of increased partisanship, presidents find it more difficult to win support across party lines in

Congress (Jacobson 2002; Sinclair 2000b). Opposition parties not only unite against the president's policies but may even adopt a "no" strategy, refusing to cooperate on virtually anything, as did Republicans during Bill Clinton's first two years. Fewer members are likely to support the policies of an opposition-party presidency, as Southern Democrats had done so frequently for Republican presidents (Fleisher and Bond 2000).

But it is also true that partisan presidents are better able to rely on their congressional party for support than their predecessors could. There is some evidence that united and divided control matter more in a polarized era than they did a generation ago (Sinclair 2000a, 2000b; Nelson 2004). Both George W. Bush and Clinton enjoyed close relationships with the congressional leadership of their own parties and both had deeply troubled relations with the leaders of the opposition (Owens 2004; Wayne 2004). Whereas John F. Kennedy had refused to campaign against Senate Minority Leader Everett Dirksen in 1962 even though the senator faced a tough race in a state that had voted for Kennedy, in a similar situation in 2004 Bush led a successful Republican drive to oust Senate Minority Leader Tom Daschle (Davis 1992).

In late 2002, the Bush White House, dissatisfied with Senator Trent Lott's leadership and dismayed by the uproar over his remarks at Strom Thurmond's 100th birthday party, helped engineer his removal as majority leader. Contrary to Jones (2002), not only are Vice President Dick Cheney and White House strategist Karl Rove familiar figures at meetings of Capitol Hill Republicans but representatives of the Bush White House also regularly attend the gatherings of conservative activists hosted by Grover Norquist. Given congressional Republicans' unwillingness to challenge Bush on virtually any issue, one wonders how "separated" the "powers" of the federal government are today.

But congressional partisanship, of course, goes far deeper than the personalities of particular presidents. The voting records and constituencies of congressional Democrats and Republicans increasingly diverge, and party leaders wield more clout than they once did (Jacobson 2002; Sinclair 2000a, 2000b, 2004). Clinton's brief period of détente with congressional Republicans ended not only because of the Lewinsky scandal but also because Speaker Newt Gingrich nearly lost his position in an uprising by conservatives angry that he had "sold out." Partisan presidents may have helped polarize the political system, but they also must operate within it.

Partisan Administration

Modern presidents led an executive branch where party politics played a diminishing role. Technocrats and personal loyalists replaced patronage hacks in key jobs, especially under John F. Kennedy and Lyndon Johnson, who centralized many personnel decisions in the White House. But even Franklin Roosevelt, after lavishing patronage on a starved Democratic Party during his first term, gradually evolved to favor career civil servants and New Dealers of questionable partisan background (Milkis 1993). Modern presidents preferred advisers from policy-oriented backgrounds, even when they came from the opposite party or from outside politics altogether. Harry Truman and Dwight Eisenhower relied heavily on the "neutral competence" of the Bureau of the Budget in shaping their domestic policies. Johnson had nonpartisan task forces, dominated by academics and other specialists, to formulate his leading policy proposals. Richard Nixon appointed as his first domestic policy adviser Daniel Patrick Moynihan, a Democrat and veteran of the two preceding administrations; in fact, his first cabinet was so ideologically diverse as to lack coherence (Milkis 1993; Moe 1985; Nathan 1983).

While Nixon's "administrative presidency" strategy was often interpreted as a means of a president "governing alone" without the support of a political party, it can also be a means of turning the executive branch into a tool of partisan governance, as both Ronald Reagan and George W. Bush have shown (Aberbach 2004; Moe 1985; Nathan 1983; Waterman 1989). The administrative strategy lends itself especially well to an era when party activists are motivated more by ideology than by patronage. Yet one cannot dismiss the role of material incentives entirely; today, a prominent government position can open the door to a lucrative lobbying career—perhaps a new kind of patronage.

Nixon set the pattern for presidents taking greater control of the executive branch. Frustrated by the tendency of appointees to "go native" and by the continuing power of civil servants and clientele groups, Nixon sought to remake his administration in 1972–1973 (Nathan 1983). He centralized power in the White House and in a handful of trusted aides, increased the power of the White House Personnel Office, appointed loyalists to cabinet and subcabinet positions, and tried to use the Office of Management and Budget (OMB) to rein in regulatory agencies (Nathan 1983). While Nixon's efforts were thwarted by the Watergate scandal, Reagan and George W. Bush showed that his methods could reorient government in a more conservative direction. Both presidents selected ideologically sympathetic subordinates, centralized policy and personnel decisions in the White House, and used the OMB to curb regulatory excess. Bush took the "administrative presidency" a step further by seeking to curb the power of public employee unions (Aberbach 2004; Bass 2004; Moe 1985, 2003). These administrations also sought to secure greater partisan/ideological control of the judiciary, using recruitment processes that emphasized philosophy as much as competence or political connections (McKeever 2004; O'Brien 2004; Yalof 2003).

Neither Reagan nor George W. Bush showed much regard for "neutral competence" or disinterested expertise. Both men pursued policies widely denounced by scientific "experts": supply-side tax cuts; opposition to efforts to curb environmental dangers such as acid rain and global warming; and support for socially conservative policies such as abstinence-based sex education, teaching "intelligent design," and opposition to the "morning-after" pill. During the preparation for the invasion of Iraq, Bush and his allies showed little interest in the concerns raised by career officials in the CIA, the Pentagon, or the State Department.

Partisan presidents are more likely to turn to political consultants or ideologically driven think tanks for policy ideas; this marks a sharp difference from Jimmy Carter's reliance on technocrats or Lyndon Johnson's task forces of academics. Unlike Eisenhower or Nixon, George W. Bush is little interested in hearing different views on policy questions and has not created procedures to ensure open policy discussion (Bowman 2000; Campbell 2003; Heclo 2000; Medvic and Dulio 2001; Milkis 1993). Several veterans of the Bush administration, from John DiIulio to Paul O'Neill, have noted the Bush White House's avoidance of domestic policy and the president's dislike for substantive debate. Even Bush loyalist David Frum (2003) has admitted that the "faith-based" initiative was pursued primarily to woo religious voters rather than to remedy social problems (C. Campbell 2003; Suskind 2004). The disdain for "neutral competence" has extended to judicial nominations, with the administration ending the practice of submitting nominees to the American Bar Administration for evaluation (O'Brien 2004).

Partisan Media

Many scholars of the presidency see as the model for presidential-press relations the amiable back-and-forth between reporters and Franklin D. Roosevelt or John F. Kennedy; they may also envision the reliance of Lyndon Johnson, Richard Nixon, and Ronald Reagan on televised addresses, presumably aimed at the nation as a whole. Neither paradigm fits the reality of media relations in this partisan era. Since Nixon, administrations have tried to actively manage the news through the White House Office of Communications (Kernell 1997; Maltese 1994). With the rise of the Internet and cable television, the audiences for presidential addresses, except in crisis situations, have been declining; there is some evidence, at least for George W. Bush, that those audiences have also become partisan.[2] Bush's efforts at "going public," whether on television or on the stump, have usually been aimed more at "rallying the base" than "reaching out" (Edwards 2004; Wayne 2004).

Both the Clinton and George W. Bush administrations have had notably testy relationships with the White House press corps. Both have sought to bypass the conventional media: Clinton by using the "alternative media" (such as the Internet and cable television), and Bush by using conservative media outlets such as Fox News and conservative talk radio (Maltese 1994; Kurtz 1998; West 2001).

While most media outlets have audiences that reflect the partisan diversity of the general public, a few have striking tilts in viewership. A 2004 survey by the Pew Research Center found that 35 percent of Republicans "regularly watch" Fox News, while only 21 percent of Democrats do. Twice as many viewers of Fox watched the Republican convention as watched the Democratic gathering (overall ratings for the two events were about equal; Project for Excellence in Journalism 2005). One in seven Republicans regularly listens to Rush Limbaugh's radio talk show, whereas only one in fifty Democrats do (Pew Research Center 2004). The Project for Excellence in Journalism (2005) notes the growth of a "journalism of affirmation" (e.g, Republicans watching Fox News) and a "journalism of assertion" (e.g., bloggers or talk show hosts making unsubstantiated charges). This contrasts sharply with the Progressive-era ideal of objective, scientific journalism conducted by experts (Lippmann 1922).

Implications of the Partisan Presidency

The partisan presidency may have some positive effects on national politics. Turnout has increased in the past two presidential elections, both of which featured strikingly polarized views of the candidates among voters. Voters report clearer images of the two parties, images with greater ideological coherence than in the past. The decline of the Progressive-era ideals of objectivity in journalism and neutral competence in administration may have undermined the credibility of the mass media and the authority of the federal government. An objective media, however, can also demobilize voters, turning citizens into spectators, while turning over government to unelected experts can undermine democratic control.

But citizens also report greater ideological distance between themselves and presidents, which may be associated with increased distrust (Hetherington and Globetti 2003). Both Bill Clinton and George W. Bush generated unusually intense support and opposition at the same time, often distorting the national debate. The relentlessness of the "permanent campaign" makes it difficult for politicians of opposite parties to work together. United government in this partisan era may lead to greater productivity, but also to the adoption of policies out of sync with public sentiment. Politicians may then respond more to ideological currents within their party than to public desires or to objective expertise. Divided government may lead to the gridlock of the first Bush administration or to the political warfare of the Clinton era.

Combining contemporary partisanship with a shouting-head media culture can make it impossible to develop solutions across ideological lines.

Even in this polarized era, the broader political system continues to restrain presidential partisanship. The separation of powers often produces conflict that does not follow party lines; it also allows for divided government that can force cross-partisan coalitions, although they have become more difficult to form in recent years. The numerous counter-majoritarian features of the federal system—ranging from the Supreme Court to the Senate filibuster—continue to limit the possibility of party government. Individual politicians concerned with their own political futures may choose to break with an unpopular president. Even the quintessential "partisan president," George W. Bush, has found congressional Republicans to be cool to his plan for Social Security private accounts.

Some potential 2008 presidential candidates, such as Arizona senator John McCain and Virginia governor Mark Warner, might govern in a less partisan fashion—although one should remember that George W. Bush campaigned in 2000 as a "uniter, not a divider." Party factionalism, dormant in recent years, could revive: perhaps the Iraq War will heighten divisions among Democratic hawks and doves, perhaps the long-awaited rupture between social and fiscal conservatives will finally split the GOP (Reiter 2005). But most of the factors contributing to the partisan presidency appear to be long-term, not short-term. Simply put, we are not likely to see a return to the above-the-fray style of the Eisenhower administration any time soon.

Notes

1. In the 1970s and 1980s, scholars discussed a "postmodern presidency," which could also be called a "postpartisan presidency." This concept most clearly applied to Gerald Ford and Jimmy Carter and, to a lesser extent, to Richard Nixon and Lyndon Johnson, particularly at their political nadirs. Presidents could no longer count on their party to provide them with a base in the electorate or in Congress. The weakening of parties and the decentralization of power on Capitol Hill left presidents with few allies able to deliver support. Due to the reform of the nomination process, an "outsider" like Carter was able to reach the presidency without gaining the support of traditional party leaders; presidents increasingly "went public" to appeal to voters directly. The executive branch was increasingly dominated by bureaucrats and issue activists detached from party politics. See Greenstein 1978; Kernell 1997; King 1978; Nathan 1983; Polsby 1983; Ranney 1975; Rose 1991.

2. For example, a Gallup poll found that the audience for Bush's address on June 27, 2005, in which he defended his Iraq policy, was 50 percent Republican, 27 percent independent, and 23 percent Democratic—a much more Republican group than the nation as a whole. Not surprisingly, three-quarters of viewers approved of the speech. A similar partisan pattern has prevailed for many Bush addresses (see E. J. Dionne, "Who's Listening to the President," *Washington Post*, July 1, 2005, and Kenneth Bazinet, "Bush Jumps in Polls After War Speech," *New York Daily News*, June 30, 2005). At the time, the most recent Gallup poll showed only 45 percent of Americans approved of Bush's performance as president, with just 42 percent approving of his handling of Iraq.

21

Party Leadership in the House of Representatives

R. Lawrence Butler

Party leadership exists in the House of Representatives to resolve a classic collective action problem. Congressional scholars have long held that individual members of Congress have three goals: reelection, policy making, and gaining power within the institution. However, all members need a successful party in order to advance these goals. Reelection becomes more problematic when one's party is unpopular. Creating new policy requires the development of a winning coalition of at least 217 other representatives. And House members' power is enhanced exponentially when their party is in the majority. Acting purely as individuals, members could not build the coalitions necessary to achieve their goals. Party leaders are chosen, therefore, to force the compromises necessary to enable individual members to work together for the good of the whole.

The traditional model of successful party leadership is the responsible party government model espoused by Wilson (1885), Schattschneider (1942), Ranney (1954), Chambers and Burnham (1975), and many others. Patterned after the party system in parliamentary democracies, responsible party government suggests that party members vote as a unit to advance a predetermined party platform. Since American political parties are not as tightly structured as their European brethren, this model requires party leaders to gain the maximum possible unity among members on roll-call votes.

A more recent model of party activity developed by Cox and McCubbins (2005) has party leaders using their agenda-setting powers to achieve party unity. Instead of using intensive pressure to whip party members into line, leaders allow votes on issues for which the party is unified and avoid those that split the party. No matter the approach, the result is that party members vote as a group to enact the party's policy agenda.

Rohde (1991) has argued that parties will be much more successful at solving the collective action problem when they are ideologically cohesive. When party members basically agree on policy issues, they will be more willing to empower party leadership to advance that agenda. However, they will insist on the creation of monitoring mechanisms to ensure that party leaders are acting as faithful agents. Consequently, the increased party polarization in the House of Representatives over the past forty years has led to heightened party activity.

Figure 21.1 presents a measure of polarization in the House of Representatives for each Congress since 1965.[1] The graph shows that ideological polarization in the House has indeed continued to rise over the past forty years. Because of this, we would anticipate party governance to have grown dramatically during the period.[2]

Much has been written on the structure of the Democratic Party leadership in the House during the post-reform era that began in 1975. However, less has been written on the structure of the Republican leadership in the House after their 1995 takeover. Now that that team has been in charge for a decade, it is time to examine its structure. The Republicans made numerous internal changes in the House upon assuming power, many of which related to the relationship between party leaders, committee chairs, subcommittee chairs, and rank-and-file members. This chapter contains a careful analysis of the relative balance of power between these levels of leadership in the Democratic and Republican post-reform House to examine the extent to which congressional party leadership structure really matters.

The Democratic Revolt

After decades in which committee chairs dominated the activities of Congress, liberal Democrats in 1975 instigated a series of reforms that overhauled the party structure in the House. Their frustration had boiled over because conservative Southern Democrats had been using the seniority system to keep a stranglehold on the most important committee chairmanships. They had used this power to block liberal legislation favored by a majority of the Democratic caucus. Finally, after the Watergate landslide election of 1974, young liberals gained enough of a majority that they were able to force through a series of changes that established a system later dubbed by Rohde (1991) "conditional party government."

The underlying principle of the reforms was to shift power away from the committee chairs. Instead, power would be vested in the party leadership and also distributed more broadly among caucus members. Rank-and-file members were willing to centralize authority in the party leadership because of the growing ideological homogeneity in the party and the increased polarization of the House. Since most caucus members wanted to move in the same policy direction, they were willing to give party leaders the tools needed to enact the party agenda. However, they also created mechanisms to ensure a larger role for all members in the development and implementation

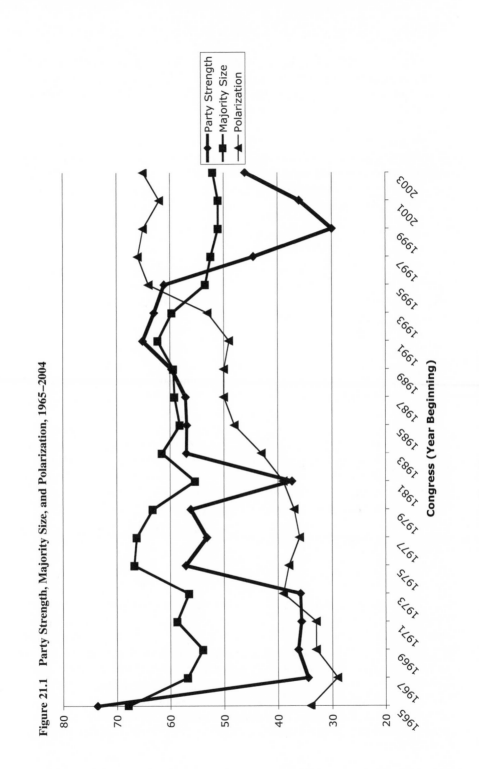

Figure 21.1   Party Strength, Majority Size, and Polarization, 1965–2004

of that policy. Thus, party leaders would have added power but they would be required to consult with the broad membership to ensure that they exercised it in accord with the party's wishes. In short, they allowed party leaders to act as the agent of the caucus with a consultation mechanism created to keep the leadership in line.

To analyze the structure of party leadership, it is helpful to look at it as if it were a four-level wedding cake. On top is the elected party leadership. Underneath that are the committee chairs and the subcommittee chairs. On the bottom are the backbenchers. Let us examine how power was shifted among the layers at the creation of conditional party government.

Party Leaders

A key ingredient of the reforms of 1975 was the creation of the Steering and Policy Committee. Half of its twenty-four members either were members of the elected party leadership or were handpicked by them. The remaining twelve members were each chosen to represent the interests of the members from a particular geographic region. The Steering and Policy Committee took over the task of making committee assignments and selecting committee chairs. Previously, the members of the Ways and Means Committee had made all committee selections, and seniority governed the choice of chairs. Additionally, the Steering and Policy Committee began making policy recommendations for consideration by the caucus.

Moreover, the Speaker was given additional tools to move legislation through the chamber in a manner designed to achieve the policy outcomes desired by the party. The Speaker was given the power to select members of the Rules Committee, the entity that had been so important to the conservative Democrats' success in bottling up legislation. The Speaker was also given more discretion in referring bills to committee. He was empowered to grant multiple referral to ensure that a single dissenting committee chair could not block the will of the caucus.

Committee Chairs

The major goal of the 1975 reforms was to take power away from the committee chairs. Speakers in previous years had to negotiate with the all-powerful chairs in order to advance the party's agenda. Now, committee chairs assumed those positions only with the consent of the caucus, potentially by secret ballot. Thus, a chair that was out of step with the party could be removed—and several were. Also, steps were taken to lessen the power of committee chairs over rank-and-file members during floor consideration of bills. In 1971, the Democrats changed the rules to allow for recorded votes in the Committee of the Whole, giving members added capacity to pass amendments. Similarly, the Rules Committee was required to make allowance for floor consideration of any amendment that was supported by at least fifty caucus members. Instead of being able to strong-arm caucus members, committee chairs would have to serve them.

Subcommittee Chairs

The 1975 reforms also weakened the committee chairs by granting greater power to the subcommittee chairs via the Subcommittee Bill of Rights. Subcommittee chairs obtained greater independence because they would be chosen by seniority, not by the head of the full committee. Also, they were guaranteed the right to hire their own staff. Finally, their jurisdictions were clarified to give them unquestioned authority over their specified policy area.

The Rank and File

Despite the ideological polarization of the House, caucus members were not willing simply to surrender power to the party leadership. While leaders were given greater authority, the new party structure created mechanisms that mandated consultation with the rank and file. This ensured that party leaders would be unable to use their powers in ways unacceptable to the liberal base of the caucus.

One of the mechanisms for drawing members closer to the leadership was to increase the number of positions of power. The 1975 reforms increased dramatically the number of subcommittees and mandated that no member could chair more than one. This created subcommittee chairmanships for many more members, thus spreading power to more members and making them a part of the leadership team. In a similar vein, the Democrats expanded the whip system. This created more leadership jobs, but it also gave party leaders the resources to consult more broadly and fully with members.

Finally, the 1975 reforms provided for the election of certain leaders who had previously been appointed. The whip and the chair of the Democratic Congressional Campaign Committee became elected positions no longer chosen by the Speaker. Similarly, committee chairs were to be nominated by the Steering and Policy Committee but voted on by the caucus. While Steering and Policy always nominated the most senior person to be the chair, the caucus rejected those it deemed to be ideologically out of step with the majority of members, selecting instead more junior members who would support the policy preferences of the caucus.

The 1975 reforms shifted power within the party in two important ways. Party leaders were empowered to set the policy agenda without having committee chairs block the will of the caucus. On the other hand, party members were brought more closely into the leadership structure by increasing the size of the leadership and allowing them a greater say in the choice of leaders. Conditional party government, therefore, centralized authority but made it so that the exercise of that power would be constrained by the will of the membership.

The Republican Revolution

In January 1995, Republicans organized the House of Representatives for the first time in forty years. On the first day of the session, they passed a new set of rules for the chamber that significantly altered, and in some cases repealed, many of the 1975 reforms that had established conditional party government. Scholars analyzing those first two years of the Republican regime described those reforms as having centralized power in the speakership (see, for example, Peters 1997 and Aldrich and Rohde 1997).

There can be no doubt that Republicans gave the Speaker a great deal of power. The caucus accepted the reform package that he and his lieutenants prepared almost without change. During his speakership, Newt Gingrich had virtual carte blanche authority to lead the caucus as he saw fit. However, the fact that a leader exercises unbridled power does not mean that the underlying system, designed to keep a rein on party leaders, has been abandoned. The first years of Republican rule were unusual in that the party had been out of power for so many decades. Republicans viewed Gingrich as the Moses who had brought them to the Promised Land. However, unlike in the biblical story, Gingrich continued as the party's leader after it took control. It is no surprise, then, that Republicans would grant him so much power. As the visionary who had brought them to power, they naturally trusted his leadership.

Ten years have passed now and Gingrich is no longer Speaker. We are now in a position to examine the leadership structure established by the Republican majority without Gingrich's shadow impairing our vision. Let us examine the changes in leadership structure as they have evolved over the ten years of Republican rule. Do they mark a return to the boss era of the late nineteenth and early twentieth centuries, or are they simply a variation on the Democratic theme of conditional party government?

Party Leaders

The Republican majority made very few changes in the powers of the party leaders. Democrats had strengthened these positions dramatically during their era of conditional party government, and Republicans essentially mimicked their rivals. In 1995, Republicans placed an eight-year term limit on the office of Speaker; they abandoned this reform in 2003, however. The only other structural change in the power of party leaders was the repeal of multiple referral of legislation. This had been instituted by the Democrats to keep a single hostile committee chair from blocking legislation desired by the caucus. The downside, however, was the "too many cooks" syndrome. One of the reasons why House Democrats were unable to bring the Clinton health care reform bill to the floor in 1993 was that it had been referred to three separate committees, each with its own idea of what a reformed system should look like. Merging those bills proved impossible. So while Republicans repealed the practice of multiple referral that Democrats had intended as a method of strengthening party leadership, they did so because it was unworkable, not as an effort to weaken the Speaker.

The most important difference between the two party leaderships was not the amount of power vested but the extent to which they were willing to exercise that authority. The Republican Committee on Committees, the counterpart to the Democratic Steering and Policy Committee, often went beyond seniority in recommending committee chairs to the caucus. While the caucus ultimately selected the committee chairs, Democratic Party leaders had automatically submitted the name of the most senior member for approval. Republican Party leaders often reached down into the committee ranks to pick their nominee. This gave the party leadership greater leverage over the committee chairs, who knew that they were beholden to the leaders for their position of power.

Committee and Subcommittee Chairs

The Republican majority in 1995 reserved its biggest changes for the powers and selection processes of committee and subcommittee chairs. Gingrich eliminated three committees that primarily served Democratic constituencies: Post Office and Civil Service, Merchant Marine and Fisheries, and the District of Columbia. He also capped the number of subcommittees per committee at six, with exceptions made for Appropriations and Government Reform. The overall effect of this streamlining was to eliminate twenty-five subcommittees along with one-third of the overall committee staff. Thus, fewer Republicans were made participants in leadership by being given a subcommittee to chair.

The Republicans also changed the balance of power between the full committee chair and the subcommittee chairs. They abolished the portions of the subcommittee bill of rights that had allowed subcommittee chairs to select their own staffs, and they also eliminated the seniority system for granting subcommittee chairmanships, granting the full committee chair more flexibility in the selection. The net effect of these reforms was to give the full committee chair greater authority and flexibility to shape the legislative agenda of the committee and to push bills to the floor.

However, additional changes were made to ensure that committee chairs used their expanded powers to advance the will of the caucus. Six-year term limits were established to keep chairs from building a fiefdom to advance their own agendas within the policy jurisdiction of their committee. This also encouraged chairs to push legislation aggressively, because they would have power for only a short period of time; at the end of six years, a new member of the committee would take over the reins.

At the same time, Republicans went well beyond the Democratic reforms of the seniority system. Violations of seniority in the selection of committee chairs became routine. Although the most senior member is more likely to be named chair than any other, there is usually an open competition for the slot. The Republican Committee on Committees sorts through the applicants and makes its recommendation to the caucus, which makes the final selection. Thus, any member who wants to chair a full committee will need to show his or her dedication to the party leaders and to advancing the party's agenda.

The Rank and File

The members of the Republican caucus have the final word in the selection of party leaders and committee chairs. As the data on party polarization show, there is far less ideological diversity in the caucus than in years past. Thus, the rank and file are in a position to demand that party leaders and committee chairs reflect their policy views. Because of term limits, chairmanship elections are a frequent occurrence. These elections, therefore, provide the opportunity for members to deliberate over the policies they wish each committee to pursue and to examine which candidate would be best at achieving that goal.

Candidates for committee chairs, as a result, have to make their appeals both to the party leaders and to the caucus members. Since party leaders have flexibility in deciding which member to recommend for the chairmanship, the caucus has the ability to influence that initial step in the process. Party leaders cannot hide behind seniority if they suggest a candidate who is not favored by the caucus. Brewer and Deering (2005) note that those seeking committee chairmanships curry favor by raising large amounts of money through their leadership political action committees and distributing it to members. Not only are they buying support but they are also showing their willingness to help the party retain its majority—and without majority status, every Republican would lose substantial power. Thus, the constant turnover of committee chairs has the added benefit of helping Republicans retain power, the highest goal of everyone in the party.

Chairmanships, however, are not merely fundraising contests. At the end of the process, chairmanship candidates have to make a presentation to the Committee on Committees explaining why they should lead the committee and how they would advance the party agenda. As Cohen (2005, 1681) reports, this presentation is merely the end of a two-year process of building support. He quotes a chairmanship candidate as saying that the four keys to victory are "demonstrated legislative leadership, political teamwork, a vision for the committee, and seniority." The choice is not purely ideological—it is based on who the party believes will best lead the committee to their desired outcome. Determining the nature of that outcome is ultimately a joint effort of the party leadership and the rank and file.

To summarize the reforms of 1995, it is clear that the relative balance of power among the four layers of the party has changed. Subcommittee chairs have been made subservient to committee chairs. Party leaders have gained greater influence over committee chairs through the selection process. Committee chairs have been given stronger tools to run their committees, but they must use those tools to advance the party's agenda rapidly. The rank and file are actively engaged in determining the direction of the party because of the constant elections for committee chairs.

Although they have rearranged power within the party, the overriding philosophy is that of conditional party government. An ideologically unified party empowers its leadership to achieve the members' policy goals. However, they also create mechanisms to ensure that that power is being exercised in a manner that serves the will of the members. Democrats achieved this by creating a participatory structure in which most members had a voice as subcommittee chairs. Republicans, by contrast, use competitive elections as a means of keeping party leaders and committee chairs in line. Both methods achieve the same goal; they just do it in different ways.

Effectiveness of Post-Reform Party Leaders

Measuring the relative success of party leadership is not as easy at it might seem. Scholars of party leadership in the House of Representatives have used a variety of indicators to measure the extent to which party leaders are serving effectively. Most indicators involve some combination of measures of party unity and partisanship. The logic behind them is to measure how well the majority party sticks together on votes where the two parties disagree.

Unfortunately, party unity and partisanship are not the same thing as party effectiveness and party strength. There are times when a party need not be unified to get its way. Furthermore, sometimes a very unified majority party can be defeated by an even more unified minority. We thus will assess the relative effectiveness of the two post-reform party leadership structures by using the Majority Party Strength index (Butler 2003). Inspired by the responsible party government literature, this indicator measures how frequently the majority party is able to guarantee itself victory by being so unified that minority party votes become irrelevant. In such instances, the majority party is acting like a responsible party in a parliamentary system.

Figure 21.1 shows the level of the Majority Party Strength index for Congresses from 1965 to 2004, along with two independent variables that significantly affect its value: ideological polarization and majority caucus size. Consistent with the conditional party government theory, party strength rises as polarization increases. Moreover, party strength rises as the caucus size grows. With a larger caucus, the majority party can guarantee victory even with a large number of defectors. An additional factor that increases party strength is the existence of unified government.

These relationships would suggest that party leadership structure has little impact on the majority's ability to act consistent with responsible party government. After all, party strength appears to be a function of a number of factors that are exogenous to the party leadership. However, Butler (2001) shows that the two structural efforts to strengthen majority party leadership—the Reed Rules of 1890 and the advent of conditional party government—also increased party strength in the House. Thus we can conclude that empowering party leaders has improved the majority's ability to act as a responsible party, but a small caucus, divided government, or a relatively heterogeneous caucus can hinder their capacity.

To illustrate this argument, we need only compare the Majority Party Strength index for the post-reform Democratic and Republican congresses. Throughout the period, Democrats appear to have had much greater success at acting like a responsible party. With the exception of the first Gingrich congress in 1995–1996, the index is consistently lower under Republican majorities than it is under Democratic ones. However, this comparison is somewhat misleading. Republicans have had to work with a much smaller majority than the Democrats did. The largest Republican majority was 54 percent, whereas the *smallest* Democratic majority in the post-reform era was 56 percent. Thus, even though Republicans have been remarkably unified in their voting, it has often not been enough to guarantee themselves victories on roll-call votes.

The study of leadership often resembles "chicken and egg" analysis. When party leadership is functioning perfectly, the caucus is in perfect accord with its leaders. In such cooperative circumstances, we cannot observe whether the caucus is following its leadership blindly or whether the leaders are perfectly mirroring the will of the caucus. Perhaps the truth is some combination of the two. It is only when conflict arises and the two are pulling in opposite directions that we can determine who is really calling the shots.

For that reason, it is hard to say definitively whether or not power in the Republican Congress has been centralized in its leadership or whether conditional party government still exists. To date, there has seldom been much difference between the wishes of the party leaders and the conservative base of the party. Nonetheless, two incidents stand out as examples in which the rank and file appear to have forced party leaders to respond.

During Gingrich's second term as Speaker, he was nearly removed from office by his lieutenants. Key members of the Republican leadership had become disenchanted by his leadership and plotted to remove him from the position. Gingrich discovered the plot, squashed it, and remained in power. At the end of that Congress, however, Gingrich found himself in even deeper trouble. Many conservative members of the caucus had grown weary of "caving in" to the Clinton administration on policy issues. Gingrich had told them that these compromises were necessary in order to maintain their congressional majority. Nonetheless, the Republicans lost seats in the House for the second consecutive cycle. When it became public in the wake of the Clinton impeachment that Gingrich had also been cheating with an intern, his support among the rank and file collapsed and he stepped down as Speaker. Where party leaders had failed, the caucus had succeeded.

More recently, conservative House members have grown dismayed over the lack of spending restraint by the Congress. House conservatives have formed the Republican Study Committee, an organization that now boasts nearly half the caucus as members. Early in 2005, conservatives forced Speaker Dennis Hastert to include mechanisms in the budget to reduce spending. In September of that year, conservatives brushed aside Hastert's selection to temporarily replace Tom DeLay as majority leader after the latter had stepped down to battle indictments related to campaign fundraising. Hastert recommended David Dreier of California for the position, but conservatives insisted that the whip, Roy Blunt of Missouri, who had worked cooperatively with the group in spending cuts, take over most of the majority leader's duties.[3] Hastert was forced to back down on his selection in the face of this rebellion.

After watching the Republican Study Committee dig in its heels, moderate Republicans began to do likewise. At the end of the year, they forced the leadership to reinstate some domestic spending before they would accept the annual appropriations bills. They also succeeded in stripping a provision to allow drilling in the Arctic National Wildlife Refuge from a package of reductions in entitlement programs. With Democrats united in opposition, the two wings of the party began to flex their muscles to push their own policy

R. Lawrence Butler

preferences at the expense of party unity. It is at such times that party leadership is put to the test.

Notes

1. As a measure of ideology, we use Poole and Rosenthal's DW-NOMINATE scores (for a complete description of DW-NOMINATE scores, see McCarty, Poole, and Rosenthal 1997). We then apply the formula

1 − [St.Dev.(Majority)]/[St.Dev.(All)],

where St.Dev.(Majority) is the standard deviation of the DW-NOMINATE scores for majority party members and St.Dev.(All) is the standard deviation for all House members. This measure of polarization was proposed by Aldrich, Berger, and Rohde (2002). As specified in this paper, the measure would take a value of 0 if both party caucuses were distributed identically across the ideological spectrum and would take a value of 1 if all majority-party members voted together on every roll call.

2. Aldrich, Berger, and Rohde (2002, 25) find a similar rise in party polarization in the Senate during the period. However, this would have a smaller impact on the strength of party leadership in that chamber because of the protections granted to the minority in Senate rules.

3. Ironically, Blunt lost the February 2006 contest to permanently replace DeLay as majority leader to Rep. John Boehner of Ohio. Boehner, the chair of the Committee on Education and the Workforce, had been part of Gringrich's original leadership team from 1995 through 1998.

22

Ten Years after the Revolution

1994 and Partisan Control of Government

Shannon Jenkins, Douglas D. Roscoe,
John P. Frendreis, and Alan R. Gitelson

The elections in 1994 produced a truly remarkable set of outcomes. Rarely in American history has one party so clearly dominated electoral contests across the country. Republicans gained fifty-four seats in the U.S. House of Representatives and eight seats in the U.S. Senate. Not one single Republican incumbent in the House was defeated, while thirty-four Democratic incumbents lost. The magnitude of this change is well illustrated by the remarkable transformation in the Washington State delegation, which went from eight Democrats and one Republican to seven Republicans and two Democrats. The Republicans picked up seats in thirty-three of forty-one state senates and forty-three of forty-six state lower chambers holding elections in 1994. Finally, Republican candidates defeated five incumbent Democratic governors and won fifteen open seat elections, while all Republican incumbent governors won their reelection bids. These sweeping events caught many of those who studied American politics by surprise. In fact, 1994 had seen the publication of *Congress' Permanent Minority? Republicans in the U.S. House* (Connelly and Pitney 1994). Clearly, there were few who predicted these sweeping gains and the return of the Republican Party to majority status after a long hiatus.

As a result, after the 1994 elections, there was a flurry of questions and research about what exactly had happened. Did "the elections reflect *only* a short-term rebellion against the Democratic Party in general and Bill Clinton in particular? Were the results due to *enduring* structural shifts in the parties' electoral coalitions? Was 1994 a 'critical election' indicating that a *realignment* has occurred?" inquired Tuchfarber and Rademacher (1995, 689). Abramowitz asked, "Can we explain the Republican victory? . . . Was it a temporary aberration caused by short-term forces or does it signal a long-term realignment of party strength in the United States?" (1995, 874).

Many of these studies developed (often conflicting) theories to explain the Republican gains of 1994, but almost all agreed that looking at this election with a short-term focus meant that many questions about 1994 had to remain unanswered. As Little (1998, 188) suggested, more time was needed to determine the degree to which the fruits of the Republicans' successful strategy in this election cycle were merely temporary or more durable.

But despite the near-universal agreement on the need for perspective, little research has been done that looks at the implications of the 1994 elections historically. Most research on the 1994 elections was published in 1998 or earlier, and 1994 is the last election included in those studies examining that election as part of electoral trends. This chapter returns to the questions surrounding the 1994 elections with the goal of developing more definitive answers now that we have the vantage point of time. Was 1994 a watershed election or simply the culmination of gradual processes of change? To what extent have the Republican gains of 1994 persisted through 2004? Are there regional variations to the national trends? Have these changes played out against a backdrop of change with respect to the nationalization of American electoral politics?

To begin answering these questions, we utilize data on the partisan balance in the U.S. Congress and state legislatures and control of the fifty governors' mansions from 1984 through 2004. Generally speaking, the results reveal that 1994 was indeed a revolutionary election; there was little evidence of Republican gains prior to and immediately after the 1994 elections. Furthermore, while the Republican gains of 1994 have for the most part persisted, there have not been additional gains. However, there are clear regional variations to these trends, particularly at the state level. Southern state legislatures, rather than being part of the revolution, were undergoing evolutionary change that predated 1994 and continued after. These changes, both nationally and in the South, suggest American politics became more nationalized, although in the period since 1994, Southern congressional delegations have become as distinctively Republican as they were Democratic for most of the twentieth century.

Early Explanations for the Republican Surge

On November 8, 1994, many politicians and political scientists alike were stunned by the results of the congressional and state elections. Even Republican congressional leaders were surprised—and unprepared for their new role as a majority. As one newly elected Republican U.S. representative noted, "I never dreamed I would serve in the majority. I expected a 20-seat gain. . . . I don't care what those leaders say, they didn't know we were going to win either. If they had, they would have known what to teach us in orientation" (Gimpel 1995, 16). Political scientists were caught off guard, too. Abramowitz described the election as a Republican "tidal wave" (1995, 873), while Gimpel used words such as "landmark," "spectacular," and "stunning" (1995, 1) to describe the turn of events. Almost immediately, researchers turned to the task of explaining what happened in these elections and why almost everyone failed to predict these results.

Some have argued that these Republican victories were a function of unique conditions in 1994. Tuchfarber and Rademacher conclude that the 1994 elections were both a rejection of Bill Clinton, the Democratic Party, and liberalism *and* an embrace of conservatism (1995, 694). Little (1998) argues state-level victories for the Republican Party were a function of unprecedented, coordinated national party activity that induced state-level parties to adopt state-specific Contracts with America.[1] The Republicans also efficiently targeted resources to those races where they would make the most difference, which had a noted impact in these races (Abramowitz 1995). According to these arguments, then, in the absence of these specific conditions in future elections, one would predict that Republican gains would not persist or, at the very least, that such gains would not continue.

But others argued that these victories were simply a part of larger trends or explanations of midterm elections generally. For example, Coleman (1997) argues that these victories were not altogether surprising due to a long-standing Republican advantage in midterm elections. The congressional parties have different fortunes in midterm elections where—even when controlling for factors such as presidential approval, economic growth, surge and decline, and safe seats—Republicans lose fewer seats than do Democrats. The Democrats lost so badly in 1994 because they were Democrats, serving under a Democratic president, the reasoning goes. Thus, if presidential party is incorporated into existing models of midterm elections, the results are almost entirely explicable.

Campbell (1997) argues that the results of the 1994 elections are consistent with a revised theory of surge and decline. The results of the election are due to a staggered realignment in the South, where the South had become solidly Republican in presidential elections in the 1980s but only became solidly Republican in congressional elections in the 1990s. The 1994 elections, he claims, mark the unification of the South into the Republican camp. Thus, Republican gains were so large because of two forces, the realignment of the South and midterm decline, both of which worked against the Democrats.

Some have argued that changes in the electorate led to the sweeping Republican gains (Abramowitz 1995). The electorate had grown less Democratic and more conservative since the 1980s. At the same time, ideology and party became far more important predictors of vote choice in 1994, particularly for Republicans and conservatives. From these findings, then, one could argue that the Republican gains should continue past the 1994 time period. While the changes in the 1994 election may have been large, they are explainable by minor revisions to existing models and are not a historical anomaly.

Additionally, there is disagreement over the extent to which these victories were driven by changes in the South. While Campbell (1997) attributes much of the observed change in congressional elections to changes in the South, Little (1998) finds state-level gains by the Republican Party are not related to region. Thus, it is not clear to what extent regional changes in the South were generally important or whether such changes were critical only at the congressional level.

Despite their disagreement over the causes of the 1994 Republican victories, all these findings seem to suggest congressional elections are increasingly responding to national-level forces. While previous research has shown congressional elections have not become nationalized and are more responsive to state and local forces (Vertz, Frendreis, and Gibson 1987; Claggett, Flanigan, and Zingale 1984), the widespread nature of the Republican gains in this election cycle suggests that voters have been responding to national forces when making choices in congressional elections. Was this nationalization of midterm elections a one-time event or have the midterm elections become more nationalized since the 1980s?

Finally, despite the contradictory claims about the nature of these victories, what all authors seems to agree upon is the fact that it is difficult to find definitive answers about the long-term significance of the 1994 elections from a short-term vantage point. For example, Tuchfarber and Rademacher (1995, 694) note that only future elections will allow us to tell if 1994 marks the beginning of a period of Republican dominance or a continuation of a period of electoral dealignment. Abramowitz (1995, 885) wonders whether the changes he identifies represent long-term changes in the electorate or short-term reactions to the perceived failures of the Clinton administration and the Democratic Congress. Without examining elections beyond these events, it is difficult to answer these questions or determine to what extent the Republicans continued to make gains in Congress and in the states beyond the 1994 election or even the extent to which the gains made in the 1994 elections persisted.

Reexamining the Revolution Ten Years After

In order to develop answers to questions surrounding the 1994 election results, we utilize data on the partisan balance in the U.S. Congress and state legislatures and control of the fifty governors' mansions from 1984 through

2004. This time frame was chosen to allow analysis of the data ten years before and ten years after the 1994 election.

At the national level, we collected data on the partisan balance of each state's delegation to the U.S. House and the U.S. Senate after each election cycle.[2] Data were coded so that any gains or losses from a given election were associated with the year of the election, not the year in which the winners actually served. So, for example, changes in a state delegation to Congress in the 1994 election year are reflected in the data for 1994, not 1995. Because the overall data set is yearly, the data for the odd years, when no elections were held, simply reflect the data for the previous year.

Data on state-level election returns came from Klarner (2003). For each state, the percentage of Republicans in the upper and lower chambers, as well as a variable indicating whether Republicans controlled each chamber, is included for each year.[3] Where there was a tie in a chamber, these cases were coded as non-Republican controlled. Finally, this data set contains a variable indicating the party of the governor. There are twenty-six cases where the party of the governor switched midyear or there was a minor-party governor. Once again, these cases were coded as non-Republican control of the gubernatorial post. Finally, in the state data, because different states hold elections in different years, the statistics reflect who actually served in that year, rather than gains/losses from elections that year. So, for example, gains in the 1994 election are reflected in the 1995 totals.

Because much of the speculation surrounding the changes in 1994 involves regional variation, the data have also been split into non-South and South, with the latter composed of the eleven ex-Confederate states (Alabama, Arkansas, Florida, Georgia, Louisiana, Mississippi, North Carolina, South Carolina, Tennessee, Texas, and Virginia).

The primary means of analysis is an examination of trends in the variables during the twenty-one-year period centered on 1994. In each figure, a vertical line indicates the first year reflecting the effects of the 1994 elections: for the congressional data, this is 1994; for the states, this is 1995, because these data record the numbers serving each year, rather than election returns. The analysis also includes an assessment of the trends before and after 1994. To measure these trends, the variable of interest was regressed on the time variable (year) separately for the early period (before the Republican revolution) and then again for the later period.[4] The slope from these regressions serves as a good measure of trend, capturing the average annual change in each period.

Two additional statistics are helpful in understanding the dynamics in the time series. First, the difference between the mean level of each variable in the early and later periods is calculated. This change, which we have termed the "bump," indicates the durable gains made by the GOP. A second statistic, termed the "jump," measures the specific increase in the variable as a result of the 1994 elections. For the congressional data, the jump is the gain from 1993 to 1994; for the state data, it is the difference between 1994 and 1995. If the 1994 election was truly a revolution, we would expect to see a large jump that is equal to or larger than the bump; in such situations, all of the change between the two periods would be explained by the jump in 1994. However, if 1994 were part of an evolutionary process, then we would expect to see a bump that is larger than the jump. This would suggest that while the Republicans made some gains in 1994, there were also gains that occurred outside this election.

The Nature of the Republican Revolution in Perspective

The 1994 election is often referred to as the "Republican revolution," but to what extent were the changes truly revolutionary? Did any of the outcomes reflect evolutionary processes that had been unfolding in the years prior? The story told by the data initially appears fairly clear: 1994 truly *was* a revolution. Consider first the Republican share of seats in the U.S. Congress. Figure 22.1 graphs the series for the House and Senate separately. The trend in the House prior to 1994 is essentially flat—the slope during this period is − 0.03. At this rate, it would have taken the Republicans more than thirty-three years to lose one percentage of their seats. The trend in the House prior to 1994, is essentially flat, going down a bit at first then trending up, the net result of which is a slope of − .03. As a result, almost all of the change in representation of Republicans in the House comes as a result of 1994. The *bump* in the Republican percentage—the increase from the mean level in the early period to the mean level in the later period—is 11.3 points, as Republicans went from controlling about 40 percent of the seats to having a bit over half. But most of this comes from the *jump* from 1992 to 1994— 10.5 points. Indeed, no one could have seen this revolution coming. And, moreover, once the revolution was over, equilibrium returned.

The story is similar in the Senate, although the first two years reflect the Republican majority during the Reagan era (see figure 22.1). As a result, the slope in the early period is negative and sizable (− 1.31). This also means the bump in the average percentage Republican, 7.0, is smaller than the jump in 1994, 11.0. In other words, although the Republicans picked up eleven Senate seats in 1994, their average in the post-1994 period was only seven seats greater than in the ten years prior to 1994. Despite this characteristic of the changes, there is certainly no evidence of secular gains prior to 1994 and equally little evidence of continuing progress after the revolution—in fact, the slope in the later period is slightly negative (− 0.28).

The national-level changes clearly fit the revolution mold, but what about the dynamics in the states? Figure 22.2 graphs the number of Republi-

Figure 22.1   Republican Percentage in the U.S. House and Senate

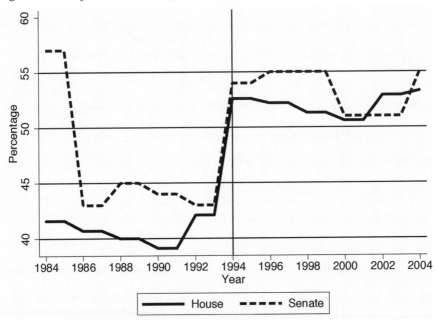

can governors, along with the number of state upper and lower houses controlled by Republicans. Here, too, the changes are much more revolutionary than evolutionary. The Republicans were gaining a governor at the rate of about one every five years in the period before 1994 (slope = 0.20). This was progress for the GOP, but it pales in comparison to the jump in 1994 of eleven gubernatorial positions. This completely accounts for the bump of 10.3 positions from the early to later period. Interestingly, the Republican Party has been handing back keys to a number of governors' mansions since 1994, losing one position every two years on average (slope = −0.56).[5]

The patterns in Republican control of state legislatures follow the same revolutionary mold (see figure 22.2). The trends in both upper and lower house control in the early period and later period are essentially flat, although the GOP is gaining one upper house every five years or so in the post-1994 period (slope = 0.22). The changes occur almost completely in the jump from 1994 to 1995—eight upper houses and ten lower houses move into the Republican column. Both of these jumps account for almost the entire bump in average number of chambers owned by the GOP—8.9 upper houses and 10.7 lower houses.

So far the conclusion about the nature of change is clear: 1994 was a

Figure 22.2   Number of Governorships and State Legislatures Controlled by Republicans

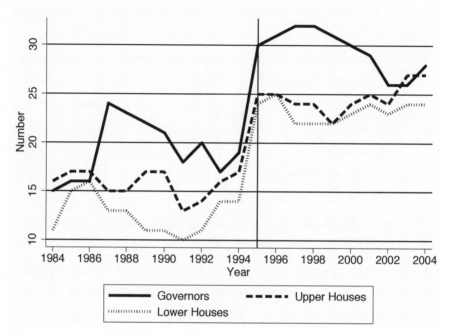

truly remarkable election, in which the Republicans made major gains that were not part of any gradual process of increasing electoral success. Similarly, little has happened since that revolution to alter the basic partisan balance in Congress and in the states. The gains have persisted. On the one hand, given the popular characterizations of the Republican revolution, this conclusion is not surprising. On the other hand, there are good reasons to expect *some* buildup to the "big bang" in 1994. For one, it has been known from survey data that the population has been trending Republican since the mid- to late 1970s. Second, a secular realignment in the South has been under way for some time and started to reach its maturity in the late 1980s and early 1990s. Republican identification in both the non-South and South increased dramatically from the late 1970s into the mid-1980s and then stabilized. The changes in the South were especially pronounced, as the percentage of Republicans roughly doubled in about a decade (Erikson, Mac-Kuen, and Stimson 2002). And all of the increases occurred well before the 1994 election.

Certainly, it is reasonable to speculate, these changes in mass partisanship must have had some effects on partisan control of government before

1994. Or did the disparity between macro partisanship and party control simply create increasing tension that was abruptly released in 1994? The answer
is that there were, in fact, signs of increasing Republican ascendancy before
1994, but only in the South and particularly in state legislatures.

This fact becomes apparent when the trends examined above are broken
down by region. Figure 22.3 displays the Republican percentage of the members in the U.S. House and Senate from non-Southern and Southern regions.[6]
The two House series are basically flat in the pre- and post-1994 periods—all
of the slopes are much less than 1 in magnitude. So, on average, gains in
each period were offset by losses. But the Southern House series rises consistently between 1990 and 1996. This suggests the Republican revolution in
the Southern congressional delegations played itself out over four election
cycles. A good indicator of this fact is that only 12.8 of the 21.8 percentage
points in the bump in average Republican House percentage in the South was
due to the jump from 1993 to 1994. In other words, just under half of the
durable Republican gains in the House over the last twenty years occurred in
elections besides 1994. In contrast, the 1993–1994 jump in non-Southern
states was 9.7 percentage points but resulted in a bump of only 7.5 points.
The much smaller, durable change outside the South was therefore clearly
limited to 1994.

Figure 22.3   Republican Percentage in the U.S. House and Senate, by Region

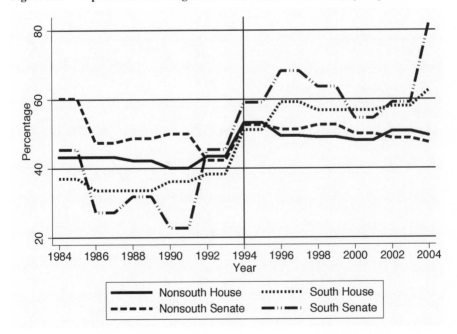

A similar story emerges for the Senate. The increases in the percentage of Southern Republican senators start in 1992 and continue through 1996. This is a shorter span than in the House, but it is still evidence of evolution. In contrast, the non-Southern series looks remarkably stable in both periods and exhibits only a minor jump in 1994 that really only served to make up ground lost in 1992.

Are signs of evolution equally apparent in Southern statehouses? Figure 22.4 shows the percentage of upper and lower chambers in each region under GOP control. The non-Southern series both show the expected jump, though there were some gains in the years prior. But in the South, there were *no* Republican-controlled chambers prior to 1995. After the 1994 elections, however, there is a notable trend upward in both upper and lower houses with GOP majorities. Unlike the congressional trends in the South, which seemed to suggest a series of years surrounding 1994 that were responsible for a Republican "evolution," the state legislative data portray 1994 as the push that started the ball rolling. Starting in 1995, the Republicans picked up 4.5 percent of Southern upper houses and 1.8 percent of Southern lower houses per year on average. The immediate post-1994 jump is clear in the lower chambers, but for the upper chambers it is not unusually large com-

Figure 22.4   Percentage of State Upper and Lower Houses Controlled by Republicans, by Region

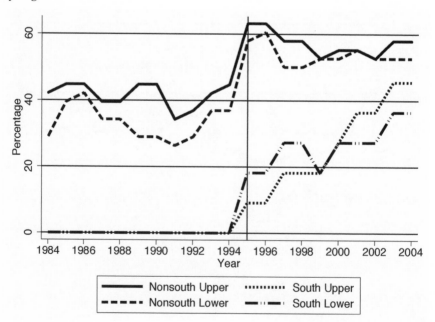

pared to change later in the period. It looks like something happened in Southern statehouses in 1994, but it was not the radical, instantaneous change evident in the rest of the country and in Washington.

In fact, what happened in 1994 was simply that long-standing increases in Republican membership in Southern state legislatures had finally led to majority status for the GOP. This is clear in figure 22.5, which displays the mean Republican percentage in upper and lower houses in the non-South and South. What is remarkable in these figures is the relatively smooth, unbroken trend upward in the South. In contrast to almost all of the previous figures, one would be hard-pressed to identify any particular point as a clear jump indicative of revolutionary change. Republicans were making steady progress in Southern statehouses long before 1994 and have continued to do so at mostly the same rate.[7] What happened in 1994 was simply that some of these increases started to create GOP majorities in some Southern states. As the GOP presence continued to increase in the South, more and more chambers fell into Republican hands, as figure 22.4 shows.

These patterns are the clearest evidence of evolutionary change. Southern state legislatures were simply not part of the Republican revolution. Iron-

Figure 22.5 Mean Republican Percentage in State Upper and Lower Houses, by Region

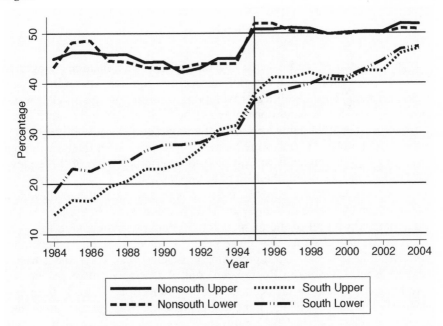

ically, though the Republican pickups in the South in 1994 are often presented as part of the evidence for a sweeping, critical realignment in 1994, the timing of the gains is purely accidental. They coincide with the other clear jumps in partisan control in 1994 not because they all share some common source but simply because that happened to be the year the secular realignment in the South yielded some GOP majorities.

One thing is relatively clear: both the sharp and gradual gains together have nationalized American politics. At the beginning of the time frame considered here, the South was clearly less Republican than the rest of the country. By the end of the period, the South was much less distinctive and in many instances had become even more Republican than the non-South. In the states, both Republican control and mean percentage in the Southern state legislatures had approached convergence with the non-South (figures 22.4 and 22.5). While the South has become as distinctly Republican as it was Democratic in the earlier era, this actually indicates the South and the non-South are both responding to similar forces. The South is becoming more Republican because the South is, generally speaking, more conservative than most of the rest of the country. Nationalization has led not to partisan homogeneity across regions but to similarity in how party control reflects the underlying ideological and demographic profile of each region's population. In the South, that means the Republicans have a natural edge.

Conclusion

On one hand, some previous analyses of the 1994 elections suggested the Republican gains were a function of specific conditions that were present in that election. The Republican revolution, according to this model, was a spectacular event that would probably not be replicated. On the other hand, some argued the 1994 gains were part of a larger process of political change in the United States and thus were more evolutionary, rather than revolutionary, in nature. Of course, it was difficult to determine which of these viewpoints was correct without the benefit of perspective.

When looking at the Republican surge ten years later, it becomes clear that these changes were in many ways truly revolutionary. In the U.S. House and Senate, almost all of the gains made by Republicans came in the 1994 elections, despite the fact that mass partisanship was gradually becoming more Republican in the period preceding those elections. The same is true at the state level. Changes in Republican control of the executive branch and state legislatures almost all occur in the 1994 election. There is little evidence of evolutionary change at the aggregate level. Clearly, something happened in the electorate in 1994. In the search for understanding what is going on in contemporary electoral politics, discovering exactly what happened in that election cycle is critical.

However, it is also true that the South had gradually tilted more Republican during this time period, and there is evidence to suggest that the changes in the South were happening much more gradually than in the rest of the country. Republican gains in non-Southern states—in congressional delegations, in governorships, and in state legislatures—were almost entirely confined to the 1994 election. Southern congressional delegations, in contrast, were becoming more Republican throughout the 1990s. This evolutionary process is even more clearly evident in Southern state legislatures, particularly when looking at the percentage of Republicans in these chambers. In these legislatures, Republican representation increased smoothly across the twenty-one years with little evidence of a surge at all.

So it seems clear that the 1994 Republican revolution was a remarkable confluence of events. A gradual process of evolutionary change in the South was reaching its culmination at the same time a number of conditions favoring the Republicans occurred. The Republicans were in an excellent position to capitalize on these two factors—and capitalize they did, making tremendous gains. However, while these gains have not evaporated, they also have not continued. There is a new equilibrium in congressional politics, much to the Democrats' disadvantage.

As a result of the 1994 elections, it appears that politics became more nationalized. In state legislatures, Southern Republican gains have brought that region to levels similar to those in the rest of the country, and their growth continues. If trends remain the same, in just a few years the typical Southern statehouse will be virtually indistinguishable from its Northern counterpart. A few years later, these legislatures are likely to be even more Republican than the non-South. At the national level, GOP gains in Southern congressional delegations have already made them look even more Republican than the rest of the country.

The shift of the South from solidly Democratic to staunchly Republican must surely be seen as a realignment of some sort, though it appears to have happened—and is still happening—in waves. The shift occurred in presidential elections earliest. The Republican "L" has been a staple of the electoral map for decades. Then, state legislatures started moving in a Republican direction. This change is still under way, but signs point toward Republican dominance in Southern statehouses soon. The element of these partisan shifts that most resembles the classic critical realignment was the change in Congress, which occurred primarily in 1994 but also extended over surrounding elections in the South. The Republican gains in the 1994 surge have persisted, giving the GOP a durable majority in Congress.

Many people, of course, have described the Republican surge in 1994 as a realignment. With a ten-year perspective on these events, it is now possible to better understand the complexity of this realignment process. In thinking about realignments, we normally look for nationwide change driven by intense, polarizing issues that is the result of interplay among party elites and party factions, leading to mass voter changes and enduring changes in election results. Some of this describes the elections of 1994. However, the changes unfolded with a unique regional dimension unlike any major realignment in the past. In addition, rather than mass partisanship realigning with newly defined parties, the changes in party identification seem to have preceded the shifts in partisan control. Furthermore, while the New Deal coalition may have faded, New Deal issues are still important and continue to define the major divisions between the parties. Of course, these issues have been joined by other issues of a more contemporary nature, but these issues are rarely cross-cutting.

If 1994 represented a realignment, it is not clear what the realigning issue was. This complexity only confirms what many students of realignment theory have believed for years: there is no *typical* realignment. Perhaps we should drop the term altogether and simply discuss *partisan change*. Either way, the 1994 election was part of a major transformation in American politics with lasting consequences for the two major political parties.

Notes

1. Of course, one must question the extent to which the Contract drove voting behavior in the states, given that exit polls showed few voters knew about the Contract at the national level, let alone the state level. However, Little (1998) argues the importance of these state contracts is that they gave Republicans issues to hang their hats on—issues that resonated with the voters.
2. Information on state delegations to Congress came from the official Biographical Directory of the U.S. Congress (http://bioguide.congress.gov) and was confirmed by the Clerk of the House (http://clerk.house.gov) and official Senate (http://www.senate.gov) websites.
3. Nebraska was excluded from our analysis as its state legislature is unicameral and nonpartisan.
4. For the congressional data, the early period is 1984–1993 and the later period is 1994–2004. For the state data, the early period is 1984–1994 and the later period is 1995–2004.
5. It is important to note the slope reflects the regression line that "fits" the data and provides a measure of the rise-over-run of this estimated line. Therefore, it may not reflect exactly the difference between the first and last time points, particularly when the actual trend itself is not very straight.
6. More specifically, it is the number of Republicans from each region divided by the total number of House seats in that region (not the average of each state's delegation).
7. The slopes are largely unchanged: for upper houses, 1.7 in the early period and 0.7 in the later period; for lower houses, 1.0 before 1995 and 1.2 after. These numbers do suggest the upward trend flattens a bit for upper houses.

23

The Courts and Party Systems in 2004

Representation without Competition?

David K. Ryden

> Hardly any issue concerning the institutions of governance or the conduct
> of elections is outside the reach of contemporary constitutional law.
>
> —Richard H. Pildes

The constitutionalizing of the American political process continues unabated. In recent years, the U.S. Supreme Court has weighed in on the most significant dimensions of elections—race-based redistricting, campaign finance reform, partisan gerrymandering, even regulating state judicial campaigns. The Court, unchastened by the controversy surrounding *Bush v. Gore*, is poised to extend its central role in shaping the rules of politics, democracy, and representation.

Yet the Court is no closer to a sound doctrine that might guide its election law jurisprudence. It has neither an "organizing principle" nor a generally defined political structure around which the expanding constitutional "law of politics" might cohere (Pildes 2004, 39). This is equally true of the Court's treatment of party organizations. It exhibits neither a normative understanding of parties nor an appreciation of their representative role and functions (Ryden 1999, 52).

The upshot is an ironic and prickly puzzle. The well-being of the political system rests in significant part on (1) an antimajoritarian, undemocratic institution (the Court) (2) assuming major responsibility for mediating the behavior of the institutions at the center of the representative system (the parties) but (3) lacking the doctrinal tools to do so effectively. It is pointless to argue that the Court ought not to be the guardian of representative principles as embodied in parties. It is, and it will continue to be. Hence it behooves political scientists to scrutinize those decisions that touch on parties, in hopes of informing the resolution of future election law issues.

This chapter parses two recent Supreme Court decisions, not to see if they adhere to some high-minded theoretical justification for parties but to discern their impact on party systems—in particular, on parties' functional capacity to meet the demands of representative democracy. *McConnell v. FEC* (2003) and *Vieth v. Jubelirer* (2004) involved two central facets of the contemporary campaign and election landscape: campaign finance practices and partisan redistricting. In each case, the Court struck a largely deferential pose. In *McConnell*, it upheld most of the Bipartisan Campaign Reform Act (BCRA), enacted by Congress in 2002. In *Vieth*, it let stand the party-based redistricting scheme imposed by the Pennsylvania State General Assembly.

These decisions intersect at the point of the Court's complicity in a congressional electoral system devoid of meaningful competition. The Court, particularly in its refusal to rein in blatant party gerrymandering, bears significant responsibility for a legal regime within which congressional parties are so entrenched and ossified that they do not approximate general shifts in public preferences. As such, they fail to satisfy basic representative criteria. Until the Court raises its consciousness of the functional attributes of parties—including circumstances where party systems break down—and gauges its decisions accordingly, it will continue to aid and abet in the erosion of basic representative government.

Party Functions and the Maintenance of Constitutional Values

> The more that scholars and courts recognize the unique constitutional position of political parties and the need to construct rules that account for their uniqueness, the richer the debate will become on which party functions, if any, judges ought to protect.
>
> —Nathaniel Persily

Vieth and *McConnell* reflect neither an embrace of any particular theoretical approach nor a recognition of parties as representative entities.[1] Both cases rest on judicial deference to the parties' policy-making role within government. As a result, they raise serious questions about the Court's role in the law of politics. A judicial predisposition favoring party autonomy makes sense in the context of party organizations engaged in campaign and election activities. But parties within government may not deserve the same deference.[2] They often fail to legally promote representative functions by partisan campaign organizations. On the contrary, parties (and party leaders) in Congress are motivated, and in turn motivate state party officials, to take action that undermines those functions parties ideally should carry out. Partisan self-interest that leads to entrenchment within government is deleterious to basic standards of representation and undercuts a standing policy of judicial deference.

This problem is most prominent when the Court is asked to review efforts to reform the political process. It has occasionally facilitated reforms, condoning broader rules regarding primary participation and rejecting further restrictions on the initiative process. More frequently, it has proven a significant obstacle to political reform. Until *McConnell*, its equating of money with political speech hindered reform of campaign finance rules. Its nullification of term limits for House and Senate in *U.S. Term Limits v. Thornton* (1995) effectively preempted a popular grassroots movement. In *Timmons v. Twin Cities Area New Party* (1997), it thwarted efforts by minor and new parties to crack the major parties' lock on electoral politics. In *California Democratic Party v. Jones* (2002), it sided with the major parties to stymie broadened participation through a blanket primary system.

It is the Court's role neither to provoke reform nor to stanch it—doing so would require that the Court buy into a particular, and likely contestable, political theory. A proper sense of judicial modesty should prevent the Court from substituting its notions of good government for those of legislatures. But at times, judicial intercession is the only means of preserving constitutional values. Hence, judicial deference in the redistricting context ensconces the parties in power, rigidifying partisan structures at the expense of maintaining constitutional fundamentals. A more assertive judicial role is not to impose reform by fiat, but to free up the system to allow for the possibility of reform.

This demands a constitutional law of democracy that is cognizant of parties and mindful of the consequences judicial decisions hold for them—a functionally derived, *party-conscious* standard of analysis. As Bruce Cain notes, "Political parties are part of the informal constitution—institutions that fill in the implied functions that arise out of the formal electoral structure" (2001, 806–7). The constitutional order should acknowledge that parties, even in imperfect form, are instrumental to the realization of crucial democratic values of competition, consent, responsiveness, equality, public choice, and accountability (Ryden 1999, 52; Maveety 1991, 66).[3]

This does not require a constitutional doctrine that squares neatly with party theories. It is beyond the judiciary's competency to resolve "deeply contested claims resting largely on normative theory" (Issacharoff 2001, 311). Nor would it necessarily be advantageous. Parties perform their representational tasks informally, without explicit legal intervention. They paper over contradictions in democratic theory and practice, in ways that vary with circumstances and defy categorization (Fitts 2002, 98). The adaptability of parties that makes them difficult to integrate into legal doctrine is what allows them to perform an array of functions effectively; doctrinally forcing them into a preferred theoretical box would only dampen that elasticity. In short, "[The parties] functional virtue is their doctrinal vice" (Fitts 2002, 98). A settled constitutional elucidation of rights is an ill fit for a constantly evolving system of parties and politics.

Instead, the parties' legal status, and the constitutional protections to which they are entitled, should mirror the degree to which they perform representative functions (Persily 2001, 815–24; Issacharoff 2001, 276). *McConnell* and *Vieth* illustrate how a nuanced functional approach to parties might guide courts through the conceptual maze of election law. A functional analysis leads to opposite conclusions as to the appropriateness of the deference exercised in each case. In *McConnell*, the uncertainties surrounding BCRA's likely ramifications necessitated giving Congress wide latitude to experiment. In contrast, viewing *Vieth* through a functional lens demanded a stronger judicial presence to safeguard against manipulation of the electoral rules for partisan advantage. The deeply ingrained self-interest of state legislators obligated the Court to police the composition of new districts to preserve the interests of fair and effective representation.

Considering the Impact of BCRA and *McConnell* on Party Systems

Congress passed BCRA in 2002 after years of repeated failure and hotly contested debate. The statute's thrust was threefold. First, it banned soft money contributions that had become so prominent in recent campaigns. Second, it constrained the practice of issue advocacy by corporations, unions, and interest groups. Finally, it increased the hard money caps on individual contributions to candidates, parties, and campaigns. These measures reshaped party financing to a greater extent than perhaps any reform in the last century (Corrado 2006, 1).

Invoking "responsible parties" rhetoric, BCRA opponents contended that the elimination of soft money would weaken the aims of responsible parties: accountability, competitive elections, and effective governance. They speculated that parties would be unable to fund serious challengers or make House and Senate races competitive. Some saw parties as becoming subordinated to unregulated private nonparty groups. Others argued that the reform would undermine party integration by discouraging cooperation between state and national committees and by making coordination between parties and their candidates more difficult. These fears foresaw enfeebled parties unable to run coherent, focused campaigns, leading to less effective and accountable governance.

These arguments failed to move the Court. It upheld virtually all of BCRA's main provisions, deferring to Congress's expertise in weighing constitutional interests surrounding campaign finance. The Court declined to second-guess Congress's finding of corruption resulting from large contributions to the national party organizations. The close relationship between candidates and parties, and the parties' willingness to trade on that relationship, rendered all soft money contributions to national parties suspect.[4]

Eying BCRA, as modified by *McConnell*, through a functional lens yields a fuzzy picture at best, and one that is decidedly incomplete. The litany of woes that campaign finance reform was to have visited upon political parties has not materialized, at least not after a single presidential election cycle. Indeed, the report card for party performance in 2004 shows high marks:

- Contrary to the predictions of BCRA opponents, the financing role of the national political party organizations did not flag. Parties proved adept in adapting to the statute, ultimately raising records sums of money (Corrado 2006, 13) and exceeding levels that even BCRA supporters had thought possible.
- The parties compensated for the loss of soft money through dramatic increases in hard money. They managed an unprecedented increase in party givers, particularly small donors of less than $200. Money from unitemized small donors rose from $59 million to $166 million for the Democratic National Committee and from $91 million to $157 million for the Republican National Committee between 2000 and 2004 (Malbin 2006), a "historic [increase] by any standard" (Corrado 2006, 8).
- At the same time, 527s surfaced as major finance players and potential competitors to parties vying for money and influence with candidates and voters.

At first glance, parties in the post-BCRA/*McConnell* era look as strong as they did prior to the reforms. Financing reforms have not seriously eroded party functions—and may actually have strengthened them in some regards. The 2004 campaigns confirmed the resilience and adaptability of partisan organizations in adjusting to, even thriving in, altered legal environs.

Consider the *democratizing* function that parties play in *mobilizing* political participation. The parties' success in raising hard money enabled them to sustain party-building activities that had previously been funded through soft money. Both parties waged intensive, highly sophisticated voter outreach and mobilization efforts (Corrado 2006, 13). Consequently, the Bush-Kerry match engendered as much popular interest and involvement as any recent presidential election. The 60 percent voter turnout testified to the parties' success as democratizing institutions responsible for engaging and activating the electorate.

Likewise, the increased numbers of small hard money donors arguably made parties *more representative* of the rank and file. The gains in grassroots organizational development could translate into parties being less wedded to wealthy voices and more attuned and responsive to their members in the electorate (Corrado 2006, 14).

Nor did the reforms come at the expense of the parties' *expressive func-*

tion. The 2004 presidential race was a relatively substantive and issue-oriented campaign, characterized by robust, widespread speech and debate. The rise of 527s meant that parties yielded some degree of control over the content of campaign speech, but this was minimized by party success in overlaying their identity on the 527s, with many in 527s' leadership positions having prior histories within the parties.

The impact on other party functions is more ambiguous and suggests a more guarded assessment. For example, the parties' *aggregation* and *governance* functions depend upon their standing relative to other political actors. Parties are thought to simultaneously give voice to groups and collective interests while modulating, controlling, and channeling them. As parties build coalitions and construct platforms in pursuit of electoral success, they soften and prioritize the interests within their coalition, thus aggregating group interests into the American political system (Persily 2001, 750). Likewise parties within government are distinct in coordinating action across levels and branches of government. They alone can work compromise, within and between partisan entities, to make formal action possible in a system of constitutionally fragmented and dispersed power.

Any appraisal of these functions must take into account the parallel universe of 527 fundraising and spending that sprang up in 2004. The extent to which parties aggregate and govern rests in part on their ability to control and diffuse group influence, so as to impose consensus and compromise on self-interested groups. Groups operating outside the party framework diminish these capabilities (Ryden 1996, 115–22). In this respect, the parties' functional capacity to mute and constrain outside voices was undoubtedly affected by BCRA. The magnitude of the harm could have been much greater, but for the high level of involvement of former party officials with 527s. The substantial overlap and shadowing of party identification produced more cooperation and coordination than otherwise might have been expected.

Moreover, the parties' governing capabilities are related to the leverage they can wield over officeholders to enforce party discipline. That leverage is a by-product of party support and benefits for candidates seeking election. As parties wane in their electoral usefulness to candidates, they will have less leverage and control over those candidates once they are in office.

Consequently, the impact of 527s is a largely unknown but potentially significant factor in the future of the parties' aggregation and governance functions. While parties proved versatile in adapting to BCRA, so too did nonprofits. They quickly stepped in as "willing conduits for . . . the flow of 'soft money' . . . that had previously gone to the national and state parties" (Holman and Claybrook 2004, 238). One observer describes 527s as the "genie[s] of huge contributions" that, having escaped the bottle in 2004, are unlikely to return (Weissman and Hassan 2006).

Whether 527s grow to more directly threaten the parties remains to be seen. It is not implausible that 527s might diminish in their financial commitment to elections. Wealthy individuals who spent millions in 2004 with little tangible payoff might be inclined to pull back or even out of campaign funding. The more ideologically driven motives of 527 donors could mean weaker long-term commitments compared to those that characterize parties. Indeed, some of the most aggressive Democratic-leaning 527s have faltered since November 2004, raising questions about their ongoing viability.[5]

On the other hand, if these groups follow through on their stated intentions of sustaining their efforts in future elections, it could further undermine the parties as countervailing dampers on rampant interest group politics (Maveety 1991, 172–73; Ryden 1999, 61). As independent sources of financial support, more influential 527s could substantially erode, if not replace outright, the parties' instrumental functions. More likely they would force parties to compete for dollars, thus moving parties in the direction of 527s to give donors the incentives to "invest in party politics, rather than the initiatives of more specialized organized groups" (Corrado 2006, 15). This could impact parties' representative nature. The 527s and those who fund them differ from the parties and donors who previously kept parties' soft money accounts filled. They are more idealist than pragmatic. They are driven by ideology more than partisan commitment. Unlike parties, they are not accountable to voters for their conduct. Parties seeking their contributions will need to reflect their donors' ideologically driven perspective. This could render parties more polarized and responsive to wealthy elites, favoring "millionaires over workers, and ideologues over pragmatists" (Bai 2005).[6]

Finally, the respective positions of parties and other groups will hinge on the likelihood and nature of additional reforms. *McConnell* paves the way for broader regulation of parties as perceived agents of corruption and special access, by essentially equating access to officeholders with corruption per se. But there is no move at present in Congress to follow that path. Indeed, the reforms currently under consideration would work to the competitive advantage of parties over 527s and other private groups. Still, none has ignited a groundswell of support, and ongoing reform efforts are becoming increasingly fragmented and contradictory. At this stage, imminent passage of additional reforms is unlikely.

In the end, it simply is too early to make definitive predictions regarding the long-term health of parties relative to other group competitors. A single election cycle is not a solid foundation upon which to base meaningful conclusions as to the effects of BCRA and *McConnell*. The 2004 elections took place in an environment framed by war and other important debates over the future of American domestic and foreign priorities. The energy and polarization of 2004 led to " 'a perfect storm' for party fundraising," with historic levels of party contributions, individual participation, and amounts raised (Corrado 2006, 6). Hence, one should be wary of extrapolating BCRA's effects from 2004. Too many fundamental questions remain over the future direction of campaign financing, what it might mean for party systems, and how parties will respond.

The mixed and open-ended legacy of BCRA after a single election cycle validates the Court's deference to Congress in *McConnell*. The divergent assessments of the impact of campaign finance reform rightly gave the Court pause. The 2004 elections gave us a marginally clearer view, but the complexities of the financing system render any analysis highly speculative. For the Court to have struck down the law based on hypothetical or empirically untested fears would have constituted judicial activism (see Fitts 2002, 111; Lowenstein 1995, 301). The Court rightly concluded that the effects of campaign finance laws are simply too complex to justify judicial superseding of congressional judgments (Pildes 2004, 146).

Vieth, Parties, and the Disappearance of Competition

> Functional principles of competition and representation form the core of . . . [what] distinguishes political parties from other organizations. . . . Constitutional analysis of parties' associational claims . . . must ground itself in the parties' role in interest group representation and electoral competition
>
> —Nathaniel Persily

Vieth involved a challenge to the Pennsylvania General Assembly's congressional redistricting plan subsequent to the 2000 census. That census cost Pennsylvania two congressional seats. Republicans, who controlled both houses of the state legislature and occupied the governor's mansion, took full advantage to redraw the districts to maximize the number of safe districts in their favor. The plan was challenged by Democratic voters as violating the equal protection clause.

The Court's fractured split decision failed to constitutionally resolve one of the most deep-seated American political pathologies: the practice of partisan-based gerrymandering (Pildes 2004, 56). Nearly two decades had elapsed since *Davis v. Bandemer* (1986); in that case, the Court determined that partisan gerrymandering could be found unconstitutional but required plaintiffs to demonstrate that they had effectively been shut out of the political process. *Bandemer* set the bar so high that a finding of unconstitutionality proved practically impossible. Meanwhile, enhanced computer sophistication and increasingly brazen line drawers left fewer and fewer congressional seats in the competitive column.

On the badly divided Court, a plurality of four justices argued that partisan gerrymandering was nonjusticiable, due to a lack of manageable standards or a workable approach. Opposing them were four dissenters who found the gerrymander in question to be unconstitutional but could not agree on a standard to apply. With four distinct dissents proffering four alternative standards, they actually lent credence to the plurality's claims of the unmanageablility of the entire enterprise.

Standing astride the two opposing blocs was Justice Anthony Kennedy's controlling but singularly unhelpful opinion. To Kennedy, partisan gerrymandering presented the potential for serious harm to "representational rights" by "burdening or penalizing citizens because of their . . . association with a political party" (*Davis v. Bandemer* at 1797). Kennedy acknowledged that similar burdens on voters and parties in other First Amendment contexts "are unconstitutional absent a compelling government interest" (at 1797), yet he made no attempt to articulate a compelling governmental interest that might justify the gerrymandering. Though there was little dispute over the burdensomeness of the redistricting plan to Pennsylvania Democrats, Kennedy refused to strike down the gerrymander. The constitutional challenge could not succeed without "clear, manageable, and politically neutral standards" by which to measure the effect of apportionment or the burdens imposed on the voters of a party (at 1793, 1797). Meanwhile, Kennedy held out a reed of hope that future partisan gerrymanders might be unconstitutional if a workable standard were to emerge (at 1795–96). The upshot of *Vieth* is that the constitutional constraints on partisan gerrymandering exist in theory, but are, for all practical purposes, absent in fact.

Unlike *McConnell*, the functional impact of the Court's deference to parties within government in *Vieth* is plain; the unconstrained redrawing of lines to maximize safe electoral seats has helped obliterate *competition* in the U.S. House of Representatives.

The dearth of competition, thanks in large part to partisan gerrymandering, is striking. Safe House seats rose from 281 in 1992 to 356 in 2002. By the close of the 2002 elections, only forty-five House seats were rated as competitive. Jacobson demonstrates how redistricting reduced competitive House seats by strengthening marginal incumbents. He concludes that "three-quarters of the marginal districts in the country were made safer through redistricting" (2006, 2). Consequently, only 4 of 382 incumbents seeking reelection in 2002 lost. The paucity of competition was even worse in 2004, dropping to its lowest levels ever (Jacobson 2006, 3). *Congressional Quarterly* ratings in the October before the vote listed thirty-seven House races, 9 percent, as competitive. Only 10 of 435 districts were decided by less than 5 percent. On the state level, not one of California's 173 House and state legislative races changed hands in 2004. In Florida, incumbents have won all but one of the last 140 races.

In short, the near-complete absence of competition is the defining trait of congressional elections, thanks largely to redistricting done without fear of judicial intervention. Highly sophisticated software in the hands of audaciously unrestrained and politically motivated line drawers has led to the virtual extinction of legitimate competition in the House of Representatives. In this context, the parties have abandoned the function of cultivating competition.

Competition is a core value of the constitutional structure and a prerequisite for representative government. Without legitimate choice, voting means little. This is why proponents of a party-friendly constitutional doctrine pin their arguments on parties' capacity for promoting competition (see Persily 2001, 752). But parties are as capable of frustrating competition as they are of engendering it.

The lack of competition caused by redistricting has a trickle-down effect, leading to the erosion of other functional attributes of parties. The parties' propensities for the mobilizing, democratizing, and expressive functions are maximized in the context of highly competitive elections because energized parties eager to win are motivated to pursue these functions vigorously. Conversely, party organizations provide little support for a challenger with little or no hope of winning. Uncompetitive races dampen enthusiasm. Without party volunteers for get-out-the-vote drives or money for an ad campaign, mobilization flags. The expressive element is muted. Turnout sinks.

Partisan gerrymandering impacts the parties' *governing capabilities* more subtly. It is credited with the widening ideological gulf between the parties in Congress. In this respect, *Vieth* and the redistricting dilemma reveal the shortcomings of a theoretically driven jurisprudential approach. Those who advocate a theoretical guide to election law doctrine usually invoke the "responsible party" model of government, which in this context is a justification for the indefensible.

At first glance, partisan gerrymandering does not necessarily offend— and may even advance—responsible party government. By maximizing safe seats, it leads to more conservative and liberal incumbents and respective party caucuses. The upshot is parties that are distinct and differentiated, more unified and disciplined (i.e., responsible), and that provide clear choices and competing programs. To responsible party adherents, this is a recipe for meaningful elections and decisive, accountable government.

But this is where neatly constructed theories of party government run headlong into the constitutional reality of fragmented, dispersed, and diffused power structures. A disciplined House majority party is inevitably stymied at countless other points, starting with the Senate's ample checks on majority rule. An ideologically polarized House is less effective in its purity than if it were forced to be more pragmatic, compromising, and centrist at the outset.

More importantly, blind pursuit of an abstract ideal of responsible parties loses sight of the most basic measure of party legitimacy: their promotion of representative democracy. Responsible parties should institutionalize public opinion rather than distorting it. They should discern and reflect majority sentiment, not obscure it. Responsible parties are desirable only as channels through which representative government is assured by public consent and accountability through competitive elections (Ryden 2003, 80–81). Party-based redistricting eviscerates this overarching objective, producing a false polarity grounded in the lack of meaningful electoral choices. Over time, congressional parties fail to reflect the broad electorate, resulting in less representative government.

This is especially true when party gerrymandering undermines majority rule. Parties legitimize government by converting majority sentiment into majority governance. When they frustrate that function instead, it compromises the integrity of the entire electoral system.

Realignment in a Noncompetitive Age?

The failure of congressional parties to engender more than token competition is the point at which campaign finance and redistricting practices converge. Together they produce a congressional party system that fails the threshold test of representativeness. Self-entrenchment has left the makeup and control of the House so resistant to changes in public preferences that party systems barely qualify as representative.

Consider again the 2004 elections, which yielded a positive picture only of the spirited and highly competitive presidential race. Any hope that BCRA would lead to more competitive elections in Congress was overwhelmed by more fundamental considerations favoring congressional incumbents. Campaign financing is still dictated by free market and cost-benefit considerations. Donors have little incentive to give to contests where the odds are long. The uncompetitiveness of congressional elections—due to redistricting and other incumbent advantages—is amplified by the habits of financial campaign supporters (see, for example, chapter 7 in this volume). No campaign finance rule could reverse these realities.

The functional shortcomings in terms of representation are apparent when looking for evidence of partisan realignment. Realignment is more than a parlor game to keep political scientists entertained; it is an important baseline for gauging deeper movements in the electorate's partisan attachments and how those movements translate into changes in government. Realignment presupposes party systems that are responsive to shifts in the public's partisan preferences. It assumes that legislatures are indeed "collectively responsive to the popular will" (*Reynolds v. Sims*, 377 at 565).

But the dearth of competition in the House defeats this presupposition by allowing a minority to entrench itself in power. It is ironic that so few competitive congressional seats exist in a political environment of relative parity between the major parties. The practical result is that such shifts in public sentiment, unless they rise to the level of the "tsunami" of 1994, fail to significantly impact the makeup of Congress. Despite near-parity in voters' party affiliation, the odds remain exceedingly slim that majority status will change hands in any given election. Incumbent entrenchment through redistricting makes it far more difficult for voters' displeasure with leadership to produce change in that leadership. In sum, it is difficult to have realignment in an era of noncompetitive House elections.[7]

Redistricting is so inimical to party structures as representative linkages that it compels policing. That policing must come from the courts, as the only institutions capable of "addressing the central structural problem of self-entrenchment" (Pildes 2004, 83). The Court simply cannot avoid responsibility for securing the necessary preconditions for genuine partisan competition. If it will not address the structural problems of self-entrenching laws, no one will (Pildes 2004, 54).

A functionally based constitutional treatment of political parties is rooted in "constitutional values of preventing incumbent entrenchment through manipulation of the rules of the game" (Persily 2001, 794). The gerrymandering of favorable electoral districts is such a manipulation. Democracy does not allow for those in power to wield that power in ways that freeze the status quo (Persily 2001, 795). Yet partisan line-drawing does exactly that, to the detriment of representative principles of accountability, responsiveness, and majority rule.

Conclusion

> The major role that constitutional law can justifiably assume in this area is that of ensuring that laws do not inappropriately undermine robust competition between political parties
>
> —Richard H. Pildes

The Supreme Court will continue to wield a central formative influence on key aspects of democratic structures and processes, including political parties. Despite the thorny nature of questions such as campaign finance and regulating partisan redistricting, the Court is unlikely to recede from the realm of election law. Rather, contemporary legal and political circumstances are certain to "spawn recurring challenges to existing democratic structures" (Pildes 2004, 39).

First among these are the potentially far-reaching implications of *Bush v. Gore* and its unbounded application of the equal protection clause (on this case, see Banks, Cohen, and Green 2005). The majority's reliance upon equal protection to bring the Florida recounts to an end stands as an open invitation to future litigation over campaign and election practices. A second factor is Congress's enactment of the Help America Vote Act (HAVA) in the wake of the Florida imbroglio in 2000. That legislation has further enriched the election soil out of which litigation is likely to sprout. Finally, the system is dominated by two polarized parties who are intensely motivated to pursue every avenue that might lead to majority status, including the way of litigation. This was evident in the flurry of preemptive litigation prior to the 2004 elections and the legal battalions each party recruited to dispatch to whatever hot spot might erupt on Election Day. Legal challenges to electoral practices are likely to increase, further ensnaring the Court and implicating the Constitution.

Given the complexity of forms, paths, and practices bound up in political representation, it is delusional to expect from the Court anything approximating an integrated jurisprudential theory of democratic governance. At most, one might hope for the Court to identify basic facets of representation implicated by various constitutional questions and to craft appropriate mediating principles. A doctrine that better captures the intricacies of political representation must begin with an acknowledgment that parties are essential to accommodating and arbitrating conflicting group interests in a pluralist system. It would functionally evaluate parties' legal status and in the process decide cases that implicate that status. A functional view of parties as channels of representation has them bringing a broader array of interests into the political arena, then providing a means of mediating and resolving those conflicts and differences to make governance possible. This implies judgments sympathetic to parties when they are serving to create a more inclusive political arena. Parties should receive more generous constitutional treatment when they are widening the interests involved in politics and subsequently working to effectively reconcile those interests.

With respect to campaign finance, this means that parties are distinguishable from, and in fact preferable to, interest groups in the realm of campaigns and elections. They are assembling majority coalitions consisting of a variety of interests and views. In the process, no single view or interest wields undue power or influence, but each is subordinated to the overarching party messages and goals. As decisions are made through intraparty primary contests, interparty competition, and majority-versus-minority party relations within government, the values of compromise, accommodation, and moderation are served.[8] Through party politics, interests are activated, then constrained. Outside of parties, the politics is win-or-lose, the interests polarized and unrestrained, and representation but a crude imitation of what it should be.

Notes

1. If there is a unifying theme in the Court's party jurisprudence, it is the Court's respect for organizational autonomy rather than a discernible theory of party-based representation (Maveety 2002, 31; see *California Democratic Party v. Jones* [2002]). For a contrary view, see Richard Hasen's claim that "the Supreme Court has proven itself quite enamored of the responsible party government position" and has even "adopted [the responsible party government scholars] viewpoint" (2001, 819, 820).

2. Hasen has argued against First Amendment protection for parties in the electoral process, asserting that, if anything, the parties' "pervasive control over the political process should militate toward lesser, rather than greater, judicial protection" (2001, 835). Likewise, Dan Lowenstein has remarked that the "parties are 'grown-ups' who should be expected to take care of themselves" (Hasen 2001, 835).

3. Parties are integral to building consensus across branches and levels of government, without which effective governance would be inconceivable. Party subsystems are crucial representational linkages, melding individuals, groups, and states into a representative pluralist democracy. They channel group influence while diffusing factions, balance majority rule and minority rights, and simultaneously pursue multiple democratic aims of aggregation, consensus, compromise, and civic education. By consolidating and accommodating the various strands of representation, party structures engender a richer, more effective system of representation (Ryden 1996, 115–22).

4. The Court did strike down a provision that required parties to choose, at the time a candidate is nominated, between coordinated or independent expenditures. This was found to breach the parties' constitutional right to engage in unlimited independent expenditures.

5. Chris Suellentrop, "Follow the Money," *Boston Globe*, June 26, 2005, available at http://www.boston.com/news/globe/ideas/articles/2005/06/26/follow_the_money?mode = PF.

6. Indeed, some have already suggested that we are in a "post-party world," with power moving out of party headquarters and into a "decentralized network of grass-roots groups, donors and Internet impresarios" (Bai 2005).

7. Another explanation for the decline of competition at the district level is that a realignment occurred in 1994 (see chapter 19). This pattern can be due to both redistricting (in which voters with similar demographic characterizes and voting patterns are packed into districts) and realignment (districts, especially in the South, are no longer cross-pressured to vote for candidates of different parties). Burnham (1981) argues that one of the hallmarks of the "System of 1896" was the decline in competition across congressional districts, especially in the North. This was due to both a realignment of citizen preferences favoring the GOP and institutional changes that increased the difficulty of voting for many citizens, reducing voter turnout and district competition.

8. This is not to say that the Court necessarily got it wrong in *McConnell* by not offering up more constitutional protection to the parties. But it does suggest that the Court's musing would be more reassuring if it grasped the functional differences between parties and other group actors, and the unique attributes of the former.

References

Abbe, Owen G., and Paul S. Herrnson. n.d. "Adversaries or Allies? Campaign Professionals and Political Parties in the States." Center for American Politics and Citizenship, University of Maryland.

Aberbach, Joel D. 2004. "The State of the Contemporary American Presidency." In Campbell and Rockman 2004.

Abramowitz, Alan I. 1994. "Issue Evolution Reconsidered: Racial Attitudes and Partisanship in the U.S. Electorate." *American Journal of Political Science* 38, no. 1 (February): 1–24.

———. 1995. "The End of the Democratic Era? 1994 and the Future of Congressional Election Research." *Political Research Quarterly* 48:873–89.

———. 1997. "The Cultural Divide in American Politics: Moral Issues and Presidential Voting." In Barbara Norrander and Clyde Wilcox, *Understanding Public Opinion.* Washington, D.C.: CQ Press.

———. 2004. "Terrorism, Gay Marriage, and Incumbency: Explaining the Republican Victory in the 2004 Election." *Forum* 2, no. 4.

Abramowitz, Alan I., and Brad Alexander. 2004. "Incumbency, Redistricting, and the Decline of Competition in Congressional Elections: Evidence from the 2002 Midterm Election." Paper presented at the annual meeting of the Western Political Science Association, Portland, Oregon.

Abramowitz, Alan I., John McGlennon, and Ronald B. Rapoport, eds. 1986. *The Life of the Parties: Activists in Presidential Politics.* Lexington: University of Kentucky Press.

Abramowitz, Alan I., and Kyle L. Saunders. 1998. "Ideological Realignment in the U.S. Electorate." *Journal of Politics* 60:634–52.

———. 2005. "Why Can't We All Just Get Along? The Reality of a Polarized America." *Forum* 3, no. 2: 1–22.

Agranoff, Robert. 1972. *The New Style in Election Campaigns.* Boston: Holbrook Press.

Aldrich, John H. 1995. *Why Parties? The Origin and Transformation of Political Parties in America.* Chicago: University of Chicago Press.

———. 2000. "Southern Parties in the State and Nation." *Journal of Politics* 62, no. 3: 643–70.

Aldrich, John H., and James S. Coleman Battista. 2002. "Conditional Party Government in the States." *American Journal of Political Science* 46:164–72.

Aldrich, John H., Mark M. Berger, and David W. Rohde. 2002. "The Historical Variability in Conditional Party Government, 1877–1994." In *Party, Process, and Political Change in Congress: New Perspectives on the History of Congress*, ed. David W. Brady and Mathew D. McCubbins. Stanford, Calif.: Stanford University Press.

Aldrich, John H., Brad Gomez, and John Griffin. 1999. "State Party Organizations Study, 1999; State Party Chair Questionnaire." Duke University.

Aldrich, John H., and David W. Rohde. 1997. "The Transition to Republican Rule in the House: Implications for Theories of Congressional Politics." *Political Science Quarterly* 112, no. 4.

Alford, Robert R. 1963. *Party and Society: The Anglo-American Democracies.* Chicago: Rand-McNally.

Almeida, Richard A. 2005. "Strange Bedfellows or the Usual Suspects? Spatial Models of Ideology and Interest Group Coalitions." Paper presented at the annual meeting of the Midwest Political Science Association.

American National Election Studies. Various years. Electronic resources from the National Election Studies (Center for Political Studies, University of Michigan) website, www.umich.edu/~nes.

American Political Science Association. 1950. "Toward a More Responsible Two-Party System." New York: Rinehart.

America Votes. 2003. "Largest Grassroots Political Groups in the Country Join to Form Historic Organization." Press release, July 15. Available at http://www.america votes.org/press/july-15-2003.cfm.

Andres, Gary. 2005. "Polarization and White House/Legislative Relations: Causes and Consequences of Elite Level Conflict." *Presidential Studies Quarterly* 35:761–70.

Ansolabehere, Stephen, Jonathan Rodden, and James M. Snyder Jr. 2005. "Purple America." *Journal of Economic Perspectives* 109: 465–90.

Appleman, Eric. 2004. "Ralph Nader." Democracy in Action. http://www.gwu.edu/~action/2004/nader.html.

Armendariz, Agustin, and Aron Pilhofer. 2005. "McCain-Feingold Changes State Party Spending." Center for Public Integrity *Party Lines*, May 26. Available at http://www.publicintegrity.org/partylines/report.aspx?aid=690.

Axelrod, Robert. 1967. "The Structure of Public Opinion on Policy Issues." *Public Opinion Quarterly* 31:51–60.

Bai, Matt. 2004a. "The Multilevel Marketing of the President." *New York Times Magazine*, April 25.

———. 2004b. "Wiring the Vast Left-Wing Conspiracy." *New York Times Magazine*, July 25.

———. 2005. "Machine Dreams." *New York Times Magazine*, August 21.

Ball, Terence. 1989. "Party." In *Political Innovation and Conceptual Change*, ed. Terence Ball, James Farr, and Russell L. Hanson. New York: Cambridge University Press.

Banks, Christopher P., David C. Cohen, and John C. Green, eds. 2005. *The Final Arbiter: The Consequences of Bush v. Gore for Law and Politics.* Albany: State University of New York Press.

Barber, Denise Roth. 2004. "A Changing Landscape: Life after McCain-Feingold for Florida's Political Parties." Institute on Money in State Politics, September 15. Available at http://www.followthemoney.org/press/reports/200409151.pdf.

Barker, David C. 2002. *Rushed to Judgment? Talk Radio, Persuasion, and American Political Behavior.* New York: Columbia University Press.

Barone, Michael. 2003. *The Almanac of American Politics, 2004.* Washington, D.C.: National Journal Group.

Bartels, Larry M. 2000. "Partisanship and Voting Behavior, 1952–1996." *American Journal of Political Science* 44:35–50.

————. 2002. "Beyond the Running Tally: Partisan Bias in Political Perceptions." *Political Behavior* 24:117–50.

Bartolini, Stefano, and Peter Mair. 1990. *Identity, Competition, and Electoral Availability: The Stabilization of European Electorates, 1885–1985.* Cambridge: Cambridge University Press.

Bass, Harold F. 2004. "George W. Bush: Presidential Party Leadership Extraordinaire?" *Forum* 2, no. 4.

Beck, Paul Allen. 1974. "Environment and Party: The Impact of Political and Demographic County Characteristics on Party Behavior." *American Political Science Review* 68 (December): 1229–44.

————. 2003. "A Tale of Two Electorates: The Changing American Party Coalitions, 1952–2000." In Green and Farmer 2003, 38–53.

Beller, Dennis C., and Frank P. Belloni. 1978. "Party and Faction." In *Faction Politics*, eds. Frank P. Belloni and Dennis C. Beller. Santa Barbara, Calif.: ABC-Clio.

Benson, Lee. 1961. *The Concept of Jacksonian Democracy.* Princeton, N.J.: Princeton University Press.

Berelson, Bernard R., Paul F. Lazarsfeld, and William N. McPhee. 1954. *Voting: A Study of Opinion Formation in a Presidential Campaign.* Chicago: University of Chicago Press.

Berry, Jeffrey M. 1999. *The New Liberalism: The Rising Power of Citizen Groups.* Washington, D.C.: Brookings.

Berry, Jeffrey M., and Deborah Schildkraut. 1998. "Citizen Groups, Political Parties, and Electoral Coalitions." In *Social Movements and American Political Institutions*, ed. Anne N. Costain and Andrew S. McFarland, 136–56. New York: Rowman & Littlefield.

Berry, William D., and Stanley Feldman. 1985. *Multiple Regression in Practice.* Beverly Hills, Calif.: Sage.

Berry, William D., Evan Ringquist, Richard C. Fording, and Russell L. Hanson. 1998. "Measuring Citizen and Government Ideology in the American States, 1960–1993." *American Journal of Political Science* 42:327–48.

Bibby, John F. 1990. "Party Organization at the State Level." In *The Parties Respond: Changes in the American Party System*, ed. L. Sandy Maisel. Boulder Colo.: Westview Press.

————. 1999. "Party Networks: National-State Integration, Allied Groups, and Issue Activists." In Green and Farmer 2003, 300–319.

Bibby, John F., and Thomas Holbrook. 1996. "Parties and Elections." In *Politics in the American States: A Comparative Analysis*, ed. Virginia Gray and Herbert Jacobs, 6th ed. Washington, D.C.: CQ Press.

————. 2004. "Parties and Elections." In *Politics in the American States: A Comparative Analysis*, ed. Virginia Gray and Russell L. Hanson, 8th ed. Washington, D.C.: CQ Press.

Bimber, Bruce, and Richard Davis. 2003. *Campaigning Online: The Internet in U.S. Elections.* New York: Oxford University Press.

Binning, William C., Melanie J. Blumberg, and John C. Green. 1996. "Change Comes to Youngstown: Local Political Parties as Instruments of Power." In Green and Shea 1996.

Bishop, George F., Robert W. Oldenick, Alfred J. Tuchfarber, and Stephen E. Bennett. 1978. "The Changing Structure of Mass Belief Systems: Fact or Artifact?" *Journal of Politics* 40:781–87.

Black, Earl, and Merle Black. 1987. *Politics and Society in the South.* Cambridge, Mass.: Harvard University Press.

Blumberg, Melanie J., William C. Binning, and John C. Green. 1999. "Do the Grassroots Matter? The Coordinated Campaign in a Battleground State." In Green and Shea 1999.

———. 2003. "No [Mo]mentum in Ohio: Local Parties and the 2000 Presidential Campaign." In Green and Farmer 2003.

Boatright, Robert G., Michael J. Malbin, Mark J. Rozell, and Clyde Wilcox. 2006. "Interest Groups and Advocacy Organizations after BCRA." In Malbin 2006.

Bolce, Louis, and Gerald De Maio. 1999. "Religious Outlook, Culture War Politics, and Antipathy toward Christian Fundamentalists." *Public Opinion Quarterly* 63:29–61.

Bond, Jon R., and Richard Fleisher. 2000. *Polarized Politics: Congress and the President in a Partisan Era.* Washington, D.C.: CQ Press.

Bowler, Kathleen. 2003. "State Party Activity and the BCRA." In Corrado, Mann, and Potter 2003.

Bowler, Shaun, David M. Farrell, and Richard S. Katz. 1999. "Party Cohesion, Party Discipline, and Parliaments." In *Party Discipline and Parliamentary Government,* ed. Shaun Bowler, David M. Farrell, and Richard S. Katz. Columbus: Ohio State University Press.

Bowman, Karlyn. 2000. "Polling to Campaign and to Govern." In Ornstein and Mann 2000.

Brewer, Mark D. 2004. "Stability or Change? Party Images in America." Paper delivered to the Northeastern Political Science Association, Boston.

Brewer, Mark D., and Jeffrey M. Stonecash. 2006. *Class and Culture in American Politics.* Washington, D.C.: CQ Press.

Brewer, Paul R., and Christopher J. Deering. 2005. "Musical Chairs: Interest Groups, Campaign Fund-Raising, and Selection of House Committee Chairs." In *The Interest Group Connection: Electioneering, Lobbying, and Policymaking in Washington,* ed. Paul S. Herrnson, Ronald G. Shaiko, and Clyde Wilcox, 2nd ed., 141–63. Washington, D.C.: CQ Press.

Broder, David. 1971. *The Party's Over: The Failure of Politics in America.* New York: Harper & Row.

Brody, Richard A. 1991. *Assessing the President: The Media, Elite Opinion, and Public Support.* Stanford, Calif.: Stanford University Press.

Brown, Robert D., Robert A. Jackson, and Gerald C. Wright. 1999. "Registration, Turnout, and State Party Systems." *Political Research Quarterly* 52:463–79.

Burden, Barry C. 2004. "Minor Parties in the 2000 Presidential Election." In Weisberg and Wilcox 2004.

———. 2005. "The Nominations." In Nelson 2005.

Burden, Barry C., and David C. Kimball. 2002. *Why Americans Split Their Tickets: Campaigns, Competition, and Divided Government.* Ann Arbor: University of Michigan Press.

Burke, Edmund. 1971. *Works.* Boston: Little, Brown.

Burnham, Walter Dean. 1970. *Critical Elections and the Mainsprings of American Politics.* New York: Norton.

———. 1981. "The System of 1896: An Analysis." In *The Evolution of American Electoral Systems,* ed. Paul Kleppner. Westport, Conn.: Greenwood Press.

———. 1982. *The Current Crisis in American Politics.* New York: Oxford University Press.

Burns, James McGregor. 1973. *The Deadlock in American Politics.* New York: Prentice-Hall.

Butler, R. Lawrence. 2001. "Explaining Party Strength in the House of Representatives, 1789–1998." Paper presented at the annual meeting of the Midwest Political Science Association, Chicago.

———. 2003. "Taking Responsibility Seriously: Assessing Party Strength in the House of Representatives." In Green and Farmer 2003, 254–63.

Cain, Bruce E. 2001. "Party Autonomy and Two-Party Electoral Competition." *University of Pennsylvania Law Review* 149:793–814.

Camejo, Peter. 2005. "The Crisis in the Green Party." *Counterpunch,* April 6.

Campbell, Angus, Philip E. Converse, Warren E. Miller, and Donald E. Stokes. 1960. *The American Voter.* New York: John Wiley & Sons.

Campbell, Angus, Gerald Gurin, and Warren E. Miller. 1954. *The Voter Decides.* Evanston, Ill.: Row, Peterson, and Co.

Campbell, Colin. 2003. "Unrestrained Ideological Entrepreneurship in the Bush II Advisory System." In Campbell and Rockman 2004.

Campbell, Colin, and Bert A. Rockman. 2004. *The George W. Bush Presidency: Appraisals and Prospects.* Washington, D.C.: CQ Press.

Campbell, James E. 1997. "The Presidential Pulse and the 1994 Midterm Congressional Elections." *Journal of Politics* 59:830–57.

———. 2003. "The Stagnation of Congressional Elections." In Malbin 2003.

Carmines, Edward G., John P. McIver, and James A. Stimson. 1987. "Unrealized Partisanship: A Theory of Dealignment." *Journal of Politics* 49:376–400.

Carmines, Edward G., and James A. Stimson. 1989. *Issue Evolution: Race and the Transformation of American Politics.* Princeton, N.J.: Princeton University Press.

Carney, Eliza Newlin. 2004. "In the Money." *National Journal,* July 10.

Carsey, Thomas, and Geoffrey Layman. 2002. "Party Polarization and 'Conflict Extension' in the American Electorate." *American Journal of Political Science* 46:786–802.

Carty, R. Kenneth. 2004. "Parties as Franchise Systems: The Stratarchical Organizational Imperative." In *Party Politics* 10, no. 1: 5–24.

Ceaser, James W., and Andrew E. Busch. 2001. *The Perfect Tie: The True Story of the 2000 Presidential Election.* Lanham, Md.: Rowman & Littlefield.

———. 2005. *Red over Blue: The 2004 Elections and American Politics.* Lanham, Md.: Rowman & Littlefield.

Center for Responsive Politics. 2004. "527 Committee Activity: Top 50 Federally Focused Organizations." http://www.opensecrets.org/527s/527cmtes.asp?level = C& cycle = 2004.

Chambers, William Nisbet, and Walter Dean Burnham, eds. 1975. *The American Party Systems: Stages of Development.* 2nd ed. London: Oxford University Press.

Chubb, John E., and Paul E. Peterson, eds. 1985. *The New Direction in American Politics*. Washington D.C.: Brookings.

Cigler, Allan J. 2002. "Interest Groups and Financing the 2000 Elections." In Magleby 2002.

———. 2006. "Interest Groups and the Financing of the 2004 Elections." In *Financing the 2004 Elections*, ed. David B. Magleby, Kelly Patterson, and Anthony Corrado. Washington, D.C.: Brookings.

Claggett, William, William Flanigan, and Nancy Zingale. 1984. "Nationalization of the American Electorate." *American Political Science Review* 78:77–91.

Clark, John A., and Charles Prysby, eds. 2004. *Southern Political Party Activists: Patterns of Conflict and Change, 1991–2001*. Lexington: University Press of Kentucky.

Clark, Peter B., and James Q. Wilson. 1961. "Incentive Systems: A Theory of Organizations." *Administrative Science Quarterly* 6 (September): 219–66.

Coffey, Daniel J. 2005. "Measuring Gubernatorial Ideology: A Content Analysis of U.S. Governors' Annual State of the State Speeches." *State Politics and Policy Quarterly* 5:88–103.

Cohen, Jeffrey E., Richard Fleisher, and Paul Kantor, eds. 2001. *American Political Parties: Decline or Resurgence?* Washington, D.C.: CQ Press.

Cohen, Marty, David Karol, Hans Noel, and John Zaller. 2001. "Beating Reform: The Resurgence of Parties in Presidential Nominations, 1980–2000." Paper presented at the annual meeting of the American Political Science Association, San Francisco.

———. 2003. "What Drives Presidential Nominations: Pols or Polls?" *Brookings Review*. Summer.

Cohen, Richard E. 2005. "Gavel Envy." *National Journal*, June 4.

Coleman, John J. 1996. "Resurgent or Just Busy? Party Organizations in Contemporary America." In Green and Shea 1996, 367–84.

———. 1997. "The Importance of Being Republican: Forecasting Party Fortunes in House Midterm Elections." *Journal of Politics* 59:497–519.

Collet, Christian. 2002. "Openness Begets Opportunity: Minor Parties and the Blanket Primary in California." In Bruce E. Cain and Elizabeth Gerber, eds. *Voting at the Political Faultline*. Berkeley: University of California/Institute of Governmental Studies Press.

Collet, Christian, and Jerrold Hansen. 2002. "Sharing the Spoils: Ralph Nader, the Green Party and the Elections of 2000." In Herrnson and Green 2002.

Connelly, William F., and John J. Pitney Jr. 1994. *Congress' Permanent Minority? Republicans in the U.S. House*. Lanham, Md.: Rowman & Littlefield.

Conover, Pamela J., and Stanley Feldman. 1981. "The Origins and Meaning of Liberal/Conservative Self-Identification." *American Political Science Review* 25:617–45.

Converse, Philip E. 1964. "The Nature of Belief Systems in Mass Publics." In *Ideology and Discontent*, ed. David Apter. Glencoe, Ill.: Free Press.

———. 1966. "The Concept of a Normal Vote." In *Elections and the Political Order*. Angus Campbell et al., New York: Wiley.

———. 1974. "Priority Variables in Comparative Research." In *Electoral Behavior*, ed. Richard Rose. New York: Free Press.

Corrado, Anthony. 1996. "The Politics of Cohesion: The Role of the National Party Committees in the 1992 Election." In Green and Shea 1996.

————. 2006. "Party Finance in the Wake of BCRA: An Overview." In Malbin 2006.

Corrado, Anthony, Sarah Barclay, and Heitor Gouvea. 2003. "The Parties Take the Lead: Political Parties and the Financing of the 2000 Presidential Election." In Green and Farmer 2003.

Corrado, Anthony, Thomas Mann, and Trevor Potter, eds. 2003. *Inside the Campaign Finance Battle: Court Testimony on the New Reforms.* Washington, D.C.: Brookings.

Cotter, Cornelius P., James L. Gibson, John F. Bibby, and Robert J. Huckshorn. 1984. *Party Organizations in American Politics.* New York: Eagleton Institute of Politics, Rutgers University.

Cotter, Patrick R., and Samuel H. Fisher III. 2004. "A Growing Divide: Issue Opinions of Southern Party Activists." In Clark and Prysby 2004.

Cox, Gary W., and Mathew D. McCubbins. 1993. *Legislative Leviathan: Party Government in the House.* Berkeley: University of California Press.

————. 2005. *Setting the Agenda: Responsible Party Government in the U.S. House of Representatives.* New York: Cambridge University Press.

CQ Weekly. 2004a. "Party Unity." December 11: 2952–56.

————. 2004b. "Presidential Support." December 11: 2946–51.

Craig, Stephen C., and Thomas L. Hurley. 1984. "Political Rhetoric and the Structure of Political Opinion: Some Experimental Findings." *Western Political Quarterly* 37:632–40.

Curriander, Marian. 2005. "Campaign Finance: Funding Presidential and Congressional Elections." In Nelson 2005.

Damore, David F., and Thomas G. Hansford. 1999. "The Allocation of Party Controlled Campaign Resources in the House of Representatives, 1989–1996." *Political Research Quarterly* 52:371–85.

D'arcy, Janice. 2004. "Weay Nader Ends Quest in Near Isolation." *Hartford Courant.* (November 3).

David, Paul T., Ralph M. Goldman, and Richard C. Bain. 1960. *The Politics of National Party Conventions.* Washington, D.C.: Brookings.

Davis, James W. 1992. *The President as Party Leader.* Westport, Conn.: Greenwood Press.

Day, Christine L., Charles D. Hadley, and Harold W. Stanley. 2005. "The Inevitable Unanticipated Consequences of Political Reform: The 2004 Presidential Nominating Process." In *A Defining Moment: The Presidential Election of 2004*, ed. William Crotty. Armonk, N.Y.: M. E. Sharpe.

Democracy Corps. 2005. "The Cultural Divide and the Challenge of Winning Back Rural and Red State Voters." http://www.democracycorps.com/focus/Democracy _Corps_August_2005_Focus_Group_Report.pdf.

Democratic National Committee Voting Rights Institute. 2005. "Democracy at Risk: The 2004 Election in Ohio: Section II Executive Summary." Washington, D.C.: DNC Services.

DiMaggio, Paul, John Evans, and Bethany Bryson. 1996. "Have Americans' Social Attitudes Become More Polarized?" *American Journal of Sociology* 102:690–775.

Dimock, Michael. 2004. "Bush and Public Opinion." In Gregg and Rozell 2004.

Dionne, E. J. 1997. *They Only Look Dead.* New York: Touchstone.

Donovan, Todd, Caroline Tolbert, Daniel Smith, and Janine Parry. 2005. "Did Gay Marriage Elect George W. Bush?" Paper prepared for the State Politics and Policy Conference, East Lansing, Michigan, May 14–15.

Downs, Anthony. 1957. *An Economic Theory of Democracy.* New York: Harper & Row.

Dulio, David A. 2004. *For Better or Worse? How Political Consultants Are Changing Elections in the United States.* Albany: State University of New York Press.

Dulio, David A., and Candice J. Nelson. 2005. *Vital Signs: Perspectives on the Health of American Campaigning.* Washington, D.C.: Brookings.

Dulio, David A., and James A. Thurber. 2003. "The Symbiotic Relationship between Political Parties and Political Consultants: Partners Past, Present, and Future." In Green and Farmer 2003.

Dunbar, John. 2002. "National GOP Exchanges Soft Money for Hard in Florida." Center for Public Integrity *Party Lines*, October 24. Available at http://www.public integrity.org/partylines/report.aspx?aid = 178.

Duverger, Maurice. 1954. *Political Parties: Their Organization and Activity in the Modern State.* Trans. Barbara North and Robert North. London: Methuen. (Orig. pub. 1951.)

Dwyre, Diana. 1994. "Party Strategy and Political Reality: The Distribution of Congressional Campaign Committee Resources." In Shea and Green 1994.

Dwyre, Diane, and Robin Kolodny. 2002. "Throwing Out the Rule Book: Party Financing of the 2000 Elections." In Magleby 2002.

———. 2006. "The Parties' Congressional Campaign Committees in 2004." In Malbin 2006.

East, Pauline. 2004. "Notes from the Campaign Chair." *RWLC Blog* www.rwlc.net (4 October).

Edwards, George C., III. 2004. "Riding High in the Polls: George W. Bush and Public Opinion." In Campbell and Rockman 2004.

Edwards, George C., III, and Philip J. Davies, eds. 2004. *New Challenges for the American Presidency.* New York: Longman.

Elazar, Daniel. 1972. *American Federalism: A View from the States.* New York: Cromwell.

Eldersveld, Samuel J. 1956. "Experimental Propaganda Techniques and Voting Behavior." *American Political Science Review* 50 (March): 154–65.

———. 1964. *Political Parties: A Behavioral Analysis.* Chicago: Rand-McNally.

Elling, Richard C. 1979. "State-Party Platforms and State Legislative Performance: A Comparative Analysis." *American Journal of Political Science* 23:383–405.

Epstein, Leon. 1986. *Political Parties in the American Mold.* Madison: University of Wisconsin Press.

Erikson, Robert S., Michael B. MacKuen, and James A. Stimson. 2002. *The Macro Polity.* New York: Cambridge University Press.

Erikson, Robert S., Gerald C. Wright, and John McIver. 1993. *Statehouse Democracy: Public Opinion and Policy in the American States.* New York: Cambridge University Press.

Evans, Geoffrey, and Stephen Whitefield. 1993. "Identifying the Bases of Party Competition in Eastern Europe." *British Journal of Political Science* 23:521–48.

Evans, John H. 2003. "Have Americans' Social Attitudes Become More Polarized? An Update." *Social Science Quarterly* 84:71–90.

Federal Election Commission. 2005a. "Party Committees Raise Nearly $1.5 Billion." *Record* 31, no. 5 (May): 5–7.

———. 2005b. "Party Financial Activity Summarized for 2004 Election Cycle." News release, March 14.

———. n.d. "Campaign Finance Law Quick Reference for Reporters." Available at http://www.fec.gov/press/bkgnd/bcra_overview.shtml#Contribution%20Limitations%20and%20Prohibitions.

Field, John O., and Ronald E. Anderson. 1969. "Ideology in the Public's Conceptualization of the 1964 Election." *Public Opinion Quarterly* 33:380–98.

Fiorina, Morris P. 1981. *Retrospective Voting in American National Elections*. New Haven, Conn.: Yale University Press.

———. 1996. *Divided Government*. 2nd ed. Needham Heights, Mass.: Allyn & Bacon.

———. 2005. *Culture War? The Myth of a Polarized America*. With Samuel C. Abrams and Jeremy C. Pope. New York: Pearson Longman.

Fischle, Mark. 2000. "Mass Response to the Lewinsky Scandal: Motivated Reasoning or Bayesian Updating?" *Political Psychology* 21:135–59.

Fitts, Michael A. 2002. "Back to the Future: The Enduring Dilemmas Revealed in the Supreme Court's Treatment of Political Parties." In Ryden 2002, 97–111.

Fleisher, Richard, and Jon R. Bond. 2000. "Congress and the President in a Partisan Era." In Bond and Fleisher 2000.

———. 2001. "Evidence of Increasing Polarization among Ordinary Citizens." In Cohen, Fleisher, and Kantor 2001.

Francia, Peter L., John C. Green, Paul S. Herrnson, Lynda W. Powell, and Clyde Wilcox. 2003. *The Financiers of Congressional Elections: Investors, Ideologues, and Intimates*. New York: Columbia University Press.

Frank, Thomas. 2004. *What's the Matter with Kansas? How Conservatives Won the Heart of America*. New York: Metropolitan Books.

Franke-Ruta, Garance, and Harold Meyerson. 2004. "The GOP Deploys." *American Prospect* 15, no. 2 (February), http://www.prospect.org/print/V15/2/franke-ruta-g.html.

Franklin, Charles H. 1992. "Measurement and the Dynamics of Party Identification." *Political Behavior* 14:297–309.

Franklin, Charles H., and John E. Jackson. 1983. "The Dynamics of Party Identification." *American Political Science Review* 77:957–73.

Frendreis, John P., James L. Gibson, and Laura L. Vertz. 1990. "The Electoral Relevance of Local Party Organizations." *American Political Science Review* 84:225–35.

Frendreis, John P., and Alan R. Gitelson. 1993. "Local Political Parties in an Age of Change." *American Review of Politics* 14:533–47.

———. 1999. "Local Parties in the 1990s: Spokes in a Candidate-Centered Wheel." In Green and Shea 1999.

Frendreis, John P., Alan R. Gitelson, Gregory Flemming, and Anne Layzell. 1996. "Local Political Parties and Legislative Races in 1992 and 1994." In Green and Shea 1996, 149–62.

Frum, David. 2003. *The Right Man: An Inside Account of the Bush White House*. New York: Random House.

Gallup. 2005a. "Bush Ratings Reach Low Point of Presidency." September 20.

————. 2005b. "Hillary Clinton Easily Paces Democratic Field." August 11.

Galston, William A. 2001. "Political Knowledge, Political Engagement, and Civic Education." *Annual Review of Political Science* 4 (June): 217–34.

Garrett, R. Sam. 2005. "'Adrenalized Fear': Crisis-Management in U.S. House and Senate Campaigns." Ph.D. diss., American University.

Garson, Robert A. 1974. *The Democratic Party and the Politics of Sectionalism, 1941–1948.* Baton Rouge: Louisiana State University Press.

Gerber, Alan, and Donald P. Green. 2000. "The Effects of Canvassing, Telephone Calls, and Direct Mail on Voter Turnout: A Field Experiment." *American Political Science Review* 94 (September): 653–63.

Gerring, John. 1997. "Ideology: A Definitional Analysis." *Political Research Quarterly* 50:957–94.

————. 1998. *Party Ideologies in America, 1828–1996.* New York: Cambridge University Press.

Gibson, James L., Cornelius P. Cotter, John F. Bibby, and Robert J. Huckshorn. 1983. "Assessing Party Organizational Strength." *American Journal of Political Science* 27, no. 2: 193–222.

Gilbert, Christopher P. 1993. *The Impact of Churches on Political Behavior.* Westport, Conn.: Greenwood Press.

Gimpel, James G. 1995. *Fulfilling the Contract: The First 100 Days.* New York: Longman.

Graetz, Michael J., and Ian Shapiro. 2005. *Death by a Thousand Cuts: The Fight over Taxing Inherited Wealth.* Princeton, N.J.: Princeton University Press.

Gray, Virginia. 1976. "Models of Comparative State Politics: A Comparison of Cross-Sectional and Time Series Analyses." *American Journal of Political Science* 20:235–56.

Green, Donald. 1988. "On the Dimensionality of Public Sentiment toward Partisan and Ideological Groups." *American Journal of Political Science* 32:758–80.

Green, Donald, Bradley Palmquist, and Eric Schickler. 2002. *Partisan Hearts and Minds: Political Parties and the Social Identities of Voters.* New Haven, Conn.: Yale University Press.

Green, John C. 2004. "Ohio: The Heart of It All." *The Forum* 2, no. 3. http://www.bepress.com/forum/vol2/iss3/art3.

Green, John C., and William Binning. 2002. "The Rise and Decline of the Reform Party, 1992–2000." In Herrnson and Green 2002.

Green, John C., and Rick Farmer, eds. 2003. *The State of the Parties: The Changing Role of Contemporary American Parties.* 4th ed. Lanham, Md.: Rowman & Littlefield.

Green, John C., and James L. Guth. 1991. "Religion, Representatives, and Roll Calls: A Research Note." *Legislative Politics Quarterly* 16:571–84.

Green, John C., James L. Guth, Corwin E. Schmidt, and Lyman A. Kellstedt. 1996. *Religion and the Culture Wars.* Lanham, Md.: Rowman & Littlefield.

Green, John C., and Paul S. Herrnson. 2002. *Responsible Partisanship? The Evolution of American Political Parties since 1950.* Lawrence: University Press of Kansas.

Green, John C., John S. Jackson, and Nancy L. Clayton. 1999. "Issue Networks and Party Elites in 1996." In Green and Shea 1999, 105–19.

Green, John C., Mark D. Rozell, and Clyde Wilcox, eds. 2000. *Prayers in the Precincts:*

The Christian Right in the 1998 Elections. Washington, D.C.: Georgetown University Press.

Green, John C., and Daniel M. Shea, eds. 1996. *The State of the Parties: The Changing Role of Contemporary American Parties.* 2nd ed. Lanham, Md.: Rowman & Littlefield.

———. eds. 1999. *The State of the Parties: The Changing Role of Contemporary American Parties.* 3rd ed. Lanham, Md.: Rowman & Littlefield.

Green, John C., Corwin E. Smidt, James L. Guth, and Lyman A. Kellstedt. 2005. "The American Religious Landscape and the 2004 Presidential Vote: Increased Polarization." Bliss Institute, University of Akron, Ohio.

Greenberg, Stanley B. 2004. *The Two Americas: Our Current Political Deadlock and How to Break It.* New York: St. Martin's.

Greene, Steven. 2004. "Social Identity Theory and Party Identification." *Social Science Quarterly* 85:136–53.

Greenstein, Fred I. 1978. "Change and Continuity in the Modern Presidency." In *The New American Political System*, ed. Anthony King. Washington, D.C.: American Enterprise Institute.

Gregg, Gary L., II, and Mark J. Rozell, eds. 2004. *Considering the Bush Presidency.* New York: Oxford University Press.

Gulati, Girish J. 2004. "Revisiting the Link between Electoral Competition and Policy Extremism in the U.S. Congress." *American Politics Research* 32:495–520.

Gurin, Patricia. 1985. "Women's Gender Consciousness." *Public Opinion Quarterly* 49:143–63.

Gurin, Patricia, Arthur H. Miller, and Gerald Gurin. 1980. "Stratum Identification and Consciousness." *Social Psychology Quarterly* 43:30–47.

Guth, James L. 2000. "Clinton, Impeachment, and the Culture Wars." In Schier 2000.

Guth, James L., and John C. Green. 1990. "Politics in a New Key: Religiosity and Participation among Political Activists." *Western Political Quarterly* 43:153–79.

———. 1992. The *Bible and the Ballot.* Boulder, Colo.: Westview Press.

Guth, James L., Lyman A. Kellstedt, Corwin E. Smidt, and John C. Green. 2005. "Religious Mobilization and the 2004 Presidential Election." Paper presented at the annual meeting of the American Political Science Association, Washington, D.C.

Gwynne, Sam C. 2004. "The Daughter Also Rises." *Texas Monthly* 32 (August): 112–18.

Hacker, Jacob S., and Paul Pierson. 2005. "Abandoning the Middle: The Bush Tax Cuts and the Limits of Democratic Control." *Perspectives on Politics* 3:33–53.

Hammond, Susan Webb. 1997. "Congressional Caucuses in the 104th Congress." In *Congress Reconsidered*, ed. Lawrence C. Dodd and Bruce I. Oppenheimer, 6th ed. Washington, D.C.: CQ Press.

Harris Interactive. 2005. "Party Affiliation and Political Philosophy Show Little Change, According to National Harris Poll." Harris Poll no. 19, March 9. Available at http://www.harrisinteractive.com/harris_poll/index.asp?PID = 548.

Harvey, Diane Hollern. 2000. "The Public's View of Clinton." In Schier 2000.

Hasen, Richard L. 2001. "Do the Parties or the People Own the Electoral Process?" *University of Pennsylvania Law Review* 149:815–41.

———. 2003. "Looking for Standards (in All the Wrong Places): Partisan Gerrymandering Claims after *Vieth.*" *Election Law Journal* 3, no. 4: 626–42.

Hays, Samuel. 1975. "Political Parties and the Community-Society Continuum." In Chambers and Burnham 1975.

Heberlig, Eric S., and Bruce A. Larson. 2005. "Redistributing Campaign Contributions by Members of Congress: The Spiraling Costs of the Permanent Campaign." *Legislative Studies Quarterly* 30:597–624.

Heclo, Hugh. 2000. "Campaigning and Governing: A Conspectus." In Ornstein and Mann 2000.

Heldman, Caroline E. 1996. "The Coordinated Campaign: Party Builder or Stumbling Block?" Paper presented at the annual meeting of the Midwest Political Science Association, Chicago.

Herrera, Richard. 1995. "The Crosswinds of Change: Sources of Change in the Democratic and Republican Parties." *Political Research Quarterly* 48:291–312.

Herrnson, Paul S. 1988. *Party Campaigning in the 1980s*. Cambridge, Mass.: Harvard University Press.

———. 2004. *Congressional Elections: Campaigning and at Home in Washington*. 4th ed. Washington, D.C.: CQ Press.

Herrnson, Paul S., and John C. Green, eds. 2002. *Multi-Party Politics and American Democracy*. 2nd ed. Lanham, Md.: Rowman & Littlefield.

Herron, Michael C., and Jeffrey B. Lewis. 2004. "Was Ralph Nader a Spoiler? A Study of Green and Reform Party Voters in the 2000 Presidential Election." Paper presented at the annual meeting of the American Political Science Association, Chicago.

Hershey, Marjorie Randon. 2005. *Party Politics in America*. 11th ed. New York: Longman.

Hetherington, Marc J. 2001. "Resurgent Mass Partisanship: The Role of Elite Polarization." *American Political Science Review* 95:619–31.

Hetherington, Marc J., and Suzanne Globetti. 2003. "The Presidency and Political Trust." In Nelson 2003.

Hill, Kim Quaile, and Jan E. Leighley. 1993. "Party Ideology, Organization, and Competitiveness as Mobilizing Forces in American Democracy." *American Journal of Political Science* 37:1158–78.

Hodgson, Godfrey. 1996. *The World Turned Right Side Up: A History of the Conservative Ascendancy in America*. Boston: Houghton Mifflin.

Holbrook, Thomas M., and Scott D. McClurg. 2005. "The Mobilization of Core Supporters: Campaigns, Turnout, and Electoral Composition." *American Journal of Political Science* 49:689–703.

Holman, Craig, and Joan Claybrook. 2004. "Outside Groups in the New Campaign Finance Environment: The Meaning of BCRA and the McConnell Decision." *Yale Law and Policy Review* 22 (Spring): 235–53.

Hout, Michael, Clem Brooks, and Jeff Manza. 1995. "The Democratic Class Struggle in the United States." *American Sociological Review* 60:805–28.

Huckfeldt, Robert, and Carol Weitzel Kohfeld. 1989. *Race and the Decline of Class in American Politics*. Urbana: University of Illinois Press.

Hula, Kevin. 1995. "Rounding Up the Usual Suspects: Forging Interest Group Coalitions in Washington." In *Interest Group Politics*, ed. Allan J. Cigler and Burdett A. Loomis, 4th ed. Washington, D.C.: CQ Press.

————. 1999. *Lobbying Together: Interest Group Coalitions in Legislative Politics.* Washington D.C.: Georgetown University Press.

Hunter, James Davison. 1994. *Before the Shooting Begins: Searching for Democracy in America's Culture War.* New York: Free Press.

Institute of Politics, John F. Kennedy School of Government, Harvard University. 2006. *Campaign for President: The Managers Look at 2004.* Lanham, Md.: Rowman & Littlefield.

Irwin, Galen. 1984. "And the Walls Came Tumbling Down: Party Dealignment in The Netherlands." In *Electoral Change in Advanced Industrial Democracies: Realignment or Dealignment?* ed. Russell Dalton, Scott C. Flanigan, and Paul Allen Beck. Princeton, N.J.: Princeton University Press.

Issacharoff, Samuel. 2001. "Private Parties with Public Purposes: Political Parties, Associational Freedoms, and Partisan Competition." *Columbia Law Review* 101:274.

Jackson, John S., III, Nathan S. Bigelow, and John C. Green. 2003. "The State of Party Elites: National Convention Delegates, 1992–2000." In Green and Farmer 2003, 54–78.

Jackson, John S., Barbara L. Brown, and David Bositis. 1982. "Herbert McClosky and Friends Revisited." *American Politics Quarterly* 10:158–80.

Jackson, John S., and Nancy Clayton. 1996. "Leaders and Followers: Major Party Elites, Identifiers and Issues, 1980–1992." In Green and Shea 1996, 328–51.

Jacobson, Gary C. 2000. "Party Polarization in National Politics: The Electoral Connection." In Bond and Fleisher 2000.

————. 2002. "Partisan Polarization in Presidential Support: The Electoral Connection." Paper presented at the 2002 annual meeting of the American Political Science Association, Boston.

————. 2003. "Partisan Polarization in Presidential Support: The Electoral Connection." *Congress and the Presidency* 30:1–36.

————. 2005a. "The Congress: The Structural Basis of Republican Success." In Nelson 2005.

————. 2005b. "The Public, the President and the War in Iraq." Paper presented at the annual meeting of the Midwest Political Science Association, Chicago.

————. 2006. "The First Congressional Elections after BCRA." In Malbin 2006.

Jacobson, Gary C., Samuel Kernell, and Jeffrey Lazarus. 2004. "Assessing the President's Role as Party Agent in Congressional Elections: The Case of Bill Clinton in 2000." *Legislative Studies Quarterly* 29:159–84.

Jacoby, William G. 1995. "The Structure of Ideological Thinking in the American Electorate." *American Journal of Political Science* 39:314–35.

Jelen, Ted G. 1991. *The Political Mobilization of Religious Belief.* Westport, Conn.: Praeger.

Jennings, M. Kent. 1992. "Ideological Thinking among Mass Publics and Political Elites." *Public Opinion Quarterly* 56:419–41.

Jewell, Malcolm E. 1984. *Parties and Primaries: Nominating State Governors.* New York: Praeger.

Jewell, Malcolm E., and Sarah M. Morehouse. 2000. *Political Parties and Elections in American States.* 4th ed. Washington, D.C.: CQ Press.

Johnson, Dennis W. 2001. *No Place for Amateurs: How Political Consultants Are Reshaping American Democracy.* New York: Routledge.

Jones, Charles O. 2002. "Presidential Leadership in a Government of Parties: An Unrealized Perspective." In Green and Herrnson 2002.

Jones, E. Terrence, Martha Kropf, Laura Wiedlocher, and Lindsay Battles. 2005. "The 2004 Missouri U.S. Presidential Race." In Magleby, Monson, and Patterson 2005.

Judis, John, and Ruy Teixeira. 2002. *The Emerging Democratic Majority.* New York: Scribner.

Katz, Daniel, and Samuel J. Eldersveld. 1961. "The Impact of Local Party Activities on the Electorate." *Public Opinion Quarterly* 25:1–24.

Kaufmann, Karen M., and John R. Petrocik. 1999. "The Changing Politics of American Men: Understanding the Sources of the Gender Gap." *American Journal of Political Science* 43:864–87.

Keefe, William. 1988. *Parties, Politics, and Public Policy in America.* Washington, D.C.: CQ Press.

Keeter, Scott, Cary Funk, and Courtney Kennedy. 2005. "Campaign Involvement and the Internet: A Survey of Howard Dean's Campaign Activists." Paper presented at the annual meeting of the American Association for Public Opinion Research, Miami Beach, Florida, May 12–15.

Keith, Bruce E., David B. Magleby, Candice J. Nelson, Elizabeth A. Orr, Mark C. Westlye, and Raymond E. Wolfinger. 1992. *The Myth of the Independent Voter.* Berkeley: University of California Press.

Kelley, Robert. 1979. *The Cultural Pattern in American Politics: The First Century.* New York: Knopf.

Kernell, Samuel. 1997. *Going Public: New Strategies of Presidential Leadership.* 3rd ed. Washington, D.C.: CQ Press.

Key, V. O. 1949. *Southern Politics in State and Nation.* New York: Vintage Books.

———. 1955. "A Theory of Critical Elections." *Journal of Politics* 21:198–210.

———. 1956. *American State Politics: An Introduction.* New York: Knopf.

———. 1967. *Politics, Parties, and Pressure Groups.* 5th ed. New York: Thomas Y. Crowell.

Kimball, David C. 2005. "Priming Partisan Evaluations of Congress." *Legislative Studies Quarterly* 30:63–84.

King, Anthony. 1978. "The American Polity in the Late 1970s: Building Coalitions in the Sand." In *The New American Political System*, ed. Anthony King. Washington, D.C.: American Enterprise Institute.

Kirkpatrick, Jeane. 1976. *The New Presidential Elite.* New York: Russell Sage Foundation and Twentieth Century Fund.

Klarner, Carl. 2003. "The Measurement of Partisan Balance in State Government." *State Politics and Policy Quarterly* 3:309–19.

Kleppner, Paul J. 1970. *The Cross of Culture.* New York: Free Press.

Klingemann, Hans-Dieter, Richard I. Hofferbert, and Ian Budge. 1994. *Parties, Policies, and Democracy.* Boulder, Colo.: Westview Press.

Knight, Kathleen. 1985. "Ideology in the 1980 Election: Ideological Sophistication Does Matter." *Journal of Politics* 47:828–53.

Kolodny, Robin. 1998. *Pursuing Majorities: Congressional Campaign Committees in American Politics.* Norman: University of Oklahoma Press.

———. 1999. "Moderate Party Factions in the U.S. House of Representatives." In Green and Shea 1999.

———. 2000. "Electoral Partnerships: Political Consultants and Political Parties." In Thurber and Nelson 2000.

Kolodny, Robin, and Diana Dwyre. 1998. "Party-Orchestrated Activities for Legislative Party Goals." *Party Politics* 4:275–95.

Kolodny, Robin, and Angela Logan. 1998. "Political Consultants and the Extension of Party Goals." *PS: Political Science and Politics* 31, no. 2: 155–59.

Kurtz, Howard. 1998. *Spin Cycle: Inside the Clinton Propaganda Machine*. New York: Free Press.

Ladd, Everett C. 1970. *American Political Parties: Social Change and Political Response*. New York: W. W. Norton.

———. 1991. "On the Uselessness of Realignment." In Shafer 1991.

LaPalombara, Joseph, and Myron Weiner. 1966. "The Origin and Development of Political Parties." In *Political Parties and Political Development*, ed. Joseph LaPalombara and Myron Weiner. Princeton, N.J.: Princeton University Press.

La Raja, Ray. 2002. "Political Parties in the Era of Soft Money." In *The Parties Respond*, ed. L. Sandy Maisel, 4th ed. Boulder, Colo.: Westview Press.

———. 2003a. "State Parties and Soft Money: How Much Party Building?" In Green and Farmer 2003.

———. 2003b. "State Political Parties after BCRA." In Malbin 2003.

———. 2003c. "Why Soft Money Has Strengthened Parties." In Corrado, Mann, and Potter 2003.

———. 2006. "State and Local Political Parties." In Malbin 2006.

Laver, Michael, and John Garry. 2000. "Estimating Policy Positions from Political Texts." *American Journal of Political Science* 44:619–34.

Lawrence, David G. 2001. "On the Resurgence of Party Identification in the 1990s." In Cohen, Fleisher, and Kantor 2001.

Layman, Geoffrey C. 2001. *The Great Divide: Religious and Cultural Conflict in American Party Politics*. New York: Columbia University Press.

Layman, Geoffrey C., and Edward G. Carmines. 1997. "Cultural Conflict in American Politics: Religious Traditionalism, Postmaterialism, and U.S. Political Behavior." *Journal of Politics* 59:751–77.

Layman, Geoffrey C., and Thomas M. Carsey. 2002. "Party Polarization and 'Conflict Extension' in the American Electorate." *American Journal of Political Science* 46:786–802.

Layman, Geoffrey C., Thomas Carsey, John Green, and Richard Herrera. 2005. "Party Polarization and 'Conflict Extension' in the United States: The Case of Party Activists." Paper presented at the annual meeting of the Southern Political Science Association, New Orleans.

Lazarsfeld, Paul F., Bernard Berelson, and Hazel Gaudet. 1944. *The People's Choice: How the Voter Makes Up His Mind in a Presidential Campaign*. New York: Columbia University Press.

Leal, David L., Matt A. Barreto, Jangho Lee, and Rodolfo O. de la Garza. 2005. "The Latino Vote in the 2004 Election." *PS: Political Science and Politics* 38, no. 1.

Leege, David C., and Lymann A. Kellstedt, eds. 1993. *Rediscovering the Religious Factor in American Politics*. Armonk, N.Y.: M. E. Sharpe.

Lenski, G. 1961. *The Religious Factor*. New York: Doubleday.

Lewis, Gregory B. 2005. "Same-Sex Marriage and the 2004 Presidential Election." *PS: Political Science and Politics* 38, no. 2.

Lijphart, Arend. 1968. *The Politics of Accommodation*. Berkeley: University of California Press.

———. 1977. *Democracy in Plural Societies: A Comparative Exploration*. New Haven, Conn.: Yale University Press.

———. 1979. "Religious vs. Linguistic vs. Class Voting: The 'Crucial Experiment' in Comparing Belgium, Canada, South Africa, and Switzerland." *American Political Science Review* 73 (June): 442–58.

———. 1989. "The Cleavage Model and Electoral Geography: A Review." In *Developments in Electoral Geography*, ed. R. J. Johnston, F. M. Shelley, and P. J. Taylor. London: Routledge.

Lippmann, Walter. 1922. *Public Opinion*. New York: Harcourt, Brace. Reprint, New York: Free Press, 1997.

Lipset, Seymour M. 1960. *Political Man: The Social Basis of Politics*. Garden City, N.Y.: Doubleday.

———. 1970. "Political Cleavages in 'Developed' and 'Emerging' Polities." In *Mass Politics: Studies in Political Sociology*, ed. Erik Allardt and Stein Rokkan. New York: Free Press.

Lipset, Seymour M. and Stein Rokkan. 1967. "Cleavage Structures, Party Systems, and Voter Alignments: An Introduction." In *Party Systems and Voter Alignments*, ed. Seymour M. Lipset and Stein Rokkan. New York: Free Press.

Little, Thomas H. 1998. "On the Coattails of a Contract: RNC Activities and Republican Gains in the 1994 State Legislative Elections." *Political Research Quarterly* 51:173–90.

Lowenstein, Daniel Hayes. 1995. *Election Laws: Cases and Materials*. Durham, N.C.: Carolina Academic Press.

Lowi, Theodore J. 1995. *The End of the Republican Era*. Norman: University of Oklahoma Press.

Lubell, Samuel. 1952. *The Future of American Politics*. New York: Harper & Row.

Luskin, Robert C., John P. McIver, and Edward G. Carmines. 1989. "Issues and the Transmission of Partisanship." *American Journal of Political Science* 33:440–58.

Maggiotto, Michael A., and Gary D. Wekkin. 2000. *Partisan Linkages in Southern Politics: Elites, Voters, and Identifiers*. Knoxville: University of Tennessee Press.

Magleby, David B. 1984. *Direct Legislation: Voting on Ballot Propositions in the United States*. Baltimore: Johns Hopkins University Press.

———. 2000. *Outside Money: Soft Money and Issue Advocacy in the 1998 Congressional Elections*. Lanham, Md.: Rowman & Littlefield.

———, ed. 2002. *Financing the 2000 Election*. Washington, D.C.: Brookings.

———, ed. 2003. *The Other Campaign: Soft Money and Issue Advocacy in the 2000 Congressional Elections*. Lanham, Md.: Rowman & Littlefield.

Magleby, David B., and J. Quin Monson, eds. 2004. *The Last Hurrah? Soft Money and Issue Advocacy in the 2002 Congressional Elections*. Washington, D.C.: Brookings.

Magleby, David B., J. Quin Monson, and Kelly D. Patterson, eds. 2005. *Dancing without Partners: How Candidates, Parties, and Interest Groups Interact in the New Campaign Finance Environment*. Provo, Utah: Center for the Study of Elections and Democracy.

Magleby, David B., Kelly D. Patterson, and James A. Thurber. 2002. "Campaign Consultants and Responsible Party Government." In Green and Herrnson 2002.

Maguire, Maria. 1983. "Is There Still Persistence? Electoral Change in Western Europe, 1948–1979." In *Western European Party Systems: Continuity and Change*, ed. Hans Daalder and Peter Maier. Beverly Hills, Calif.: Sage.

Maisel, L. Sandy. 1999. *Parties and Elections in America*. Lanham, Md.: Rowman & Littlefield.

Malbin, Michael J., ed. 2003. *Life after Reform: When the Bipartisan Campaign Reform Act Meets Politics*. Lanham, Md.: Rowman & Littlefield.

————. 2004. "Political Parties under the Post-*McConnell* Bipartisan Campaign Reform Act." *Election Law Journal* 3, no. 2: 177–91.

————. 2006. *The Election after Reform: Money, Politics, and the Bipartisan Campaign Reform Act*. Lanham, Md.: Rowman & Littlefield.

Maltese, John Anthony. 1994. *Spin Control: The White House Office of Communications and Management of Presidential News*. 2nd ed., rev. Chapel Hill: University of North Carolina Press.

Mann, Thomas. 2003. "The Rise of Soft Money." In Corrado, Mann, and Potter 2003.

Margolis, Michael, and John C. Green. 1993. *Machine Politics, Sound Bites, and Nostalgia*. Lanham, Md.: University Press of America.

Martin, Patrick. 2005. "On Eve of Milwaukee Convention: Green Party Divided over Nader Campaign." World Socialist Web Site. http://www.wsws.org/articles/2004/jun2004/gree-j26.shtml. June 26.

Maveety, Nancy. 1991. *Representation Rights and the Burger Years*. Ann Arbor: University of Michigan Press.

————. 2002. "Representation Rights and the Rehnquist Years: The Viability of the 'Community of Interests' Approach." In Ryden 2002, 29–41.

Mayer, William G. 2001. "The Presidential Nominations." In Gerald M. Pomper et al., *The Election of 2000: Reports and Interpretations*. New York: Chatham House.

Mayhew, David R. 1986. *Placing Parties in American Politics: Organization, Electoral Settings, and Government Activity in the Twentieth Century*. Princeton, N.J.: Princeton University Press.

————. 2002. *Electoral Realignments: A Critique of an American Genre*. New Haven, Conn.: Yale University Press.

Mazmanian, Daniel A. 1974. *Third Parties in Presidential Elections*. Washington, D.C.: Brookings.

McCarty, Nolan M., Keith T. Poole, and Howard Rosenthal. 1997. *Income Redistribution and the Realignment of American Politics*. Washington, D.C.: American Enterprise Institute.

McClosky, Herbert, Paul J. Hoffman, and Rosemary O'Hara. 1960. "Issue Conflict and Consensus among Party Leaders and Followers." *American Political Science Review* 54 (September): 406–27.

McGlennon, John. 2004. "Factional Transformation in the Two-Party South: It's Getting Harder to Pick a Fight." In Clark and Prysby 2004.

McKeever, Robert J. 2004. "Presidential Strategies in the New Politics of Supreme Court Appointments." In Edwards and Davies 2004.

Medvic, Stephen K., and David Dulio. 2001. "Staffing the Permanent Campaign: Political Consultants in the White House." Paper delivered at the annual meeting of the Southern Political Science Association, Atlanta.

Mercurio, John. 2003. "Democrats Unveil Comprehensive Voter Turnout Project."

CNN.com. February 20. http://www.cnn.com/2003/ALLPOLITICS/02/20/dnc .meeting/index.html.

Meyers, Marvin. 1957. *The Jacksonian Persuasion: Politics and Belief.* Stanford, Calif.: Stanford University Press.

Micklethwait, John, and Adrian Woolridge. 2004. *The Right Nation: Conservative Power in America.* New York: Penguin.

Mileur, Jerome M. 1992. "Legislating Responsibility: American Political Parties and the Law." In *Challenges to Party Government,* John Kenneth White and Jerome Mileur, 167–89. Carbondale: Southern Illinois University Press.

Milkis, Sidney. 1993. *The President and the Parties: The Transformation of the American Party System since the New Deal.* New York: Oxford University Press.

———. 1999. *Political Parties and Constitutional Government: Remaking American Democracy.* Baltimore: Johns Hopkins University Press.

Milkis, Sidney, and Jesse Rhodes. 2005. "George W. Bush, the Republican Party, and the New American Party System." Paper presented at the annual meeting of the American Political Science Association, Washington, D.C.

Miller, Arthur H., Patricia Gurin, Gerald Gurin, and Oksana Malanchuk. 1981. "Group Consciousness and Political Participation." *American Journal of Political Science* 25:494–511.

Miller, Gary, and Norman Schofield. 2003. "Activists and Partisan Realignment in the United States." *American Political Science Review* 97, no. 2: 245–60.

Miller, Warren E. 1991. "Party Identification, Realignment, and Party Voting: Back to Basics." *American Political Science Review* 85:557–68.

Miller, Warren E., and M. Kent Jennings. 1986. *Parties in Transition.* New York: Russell Sage.

Miller, Warren E., and J. Merrill Shanks. 1996. *The New American Voter.* Cambridge, Mass.: Harvard University Press.

Miller, Warren E., and Donald E. Stokes. 1963. "Constituency Influence in Congress." *American Political Science Review* 57:45–56.

Mockabee, Stephen T., Michael Margolis, Stephen Brooks, Rick Farmer, and John C. Green. 2005. "The Battle for Ohio: The 2004 Presidential Campaign" In Magleby, Monson, and Patterson 2005.

Moe, Terry M. 1985. "The Politicized Presidency." In Chubb and Peterson 1985.

———. 2003. "The Presidency and the Bureaucracy: The Presidential Advantage." In Nelson 2003.

Morehouse, Sarah, and Malcolm Jewell. 2003a. "State Parties: Independent Partners in the Money Relationship." In Green and Farmer 2003.

———. 2003b. *State Politics, Parties, and Policy.* 2nd ed. Lanham, Md.: Rowman & Littlefield.

Mouw, Ted, and Michael E. Sobel. 2001. "Culture Wars and Opinion Polarization: The Case of Abortion." *American Journal of Sociology* 106:913–43.

Murray, Charles. 1984. *Losing Ground.* New York: Basic Books.

Nathan, Richard P. 1983. *The Administrative Presidency.* New York: John Wiley & Sons.

National Conference of State Legislatures. 2004. "Perfect Parity in Nation's State Legislatures." http://www.ncsl.org/programs/press/2004/pr041103a.htm.

Nelson, Michael, ed. 2003. *The Presidency and the Political System.* 7th ed. Washington, D.C.: CQ Press.

————. 2004. "George W. Bush and Congress." In Gregg and Rozell 2004.

————, ed. 2005. *The Elections of 2004*. Washington, D.C.: CQ Press.

Newman, Bruce. 1994. *The Marketing of the President: Political Marketing as Campaign Strategy*. Thousand Oaks, Calif.: Sage.

Nie, Norman H., and Kristi Anderson. 1974. "Mass Belief Systems Revisited: Political Change and Attitude Structure." *Journal of Politics* 36:540–91.

Nie, Norman H., and James N. Rabjohn. 1979. "Revisiting Mass Beliefs Systems Revisited; or, Doing Research Is Like Watching a Tennis Match." *American Journal of Political Science* 23:139–75.

Nie, Norman H., Sidney Verba, and John R. Petrocik. 1979. "The Changing American Voter." Cambridge, Mass.: Harvard University Press.

Norpoth, Helmut, and Jerrold G. Rusk. 2005. "The Focus of Electoral Realignments." Paper presented at the annual meeting of the American Political Science Association, Washington, D.C.

O'Brien, David M. 2004. "Ironies and Disappointments: Bush and Federal Judgeships." In Campbell and Rockman 2004.

Olson, Mancur. 1965. *The Logic of Collective Action*. Cambridge, Mass.: Harvard University Press.

Ornstein, Norman J., and Thomas E. Mann, eds. 2000. *The Permanent Campaign and Its Future*. Washington, D.C.: American Enterprise Institute.

Owens, John E. 2004. "Challenging (and Acting for) the President: Congressional Leadership in an Era of Partisan Polarization." In Edwards and Davies 2004.

P., Andrew. 2004. "Techniques of Persuasion in MLM or Network Marketing Companies." *EnergyGrid* (March). http://www.energygrid.com/business/2004/03ap-mlm.html.

Paddock, Joel. 1992. "Inter-Party Ideological Differences in Eleven State Parties, 1956–1980." *Western Political Quarterly* 45:751–60.

————. 1998. "Explaining State Variation in Interparty Ideological Differences." *Political Research Quarterly* 51:765–80.

Page, Benjamin I., and Calvin C. Jones. 1979. "Reciprocal Effects of Policy Preferences, Party Loyalties, and the Vote." *American Political Science Review* 73:1071–89.

Page, Benjamin I., and Robert Y. Shapiro. 1992. *The Rational Public: Fifty Years of Trends in Americans' Policy Preferences*. Chicago: University of Chicago Press.

Patterson, James T. 1967. *Congressional Conservatism and the New Deal: The Growth of the Conservative Coalition in Congress, 1933–1939*. Lexington: University of Kentucky Press.

Patterson, Kelly D., and Matthew Singer. 2002. "The National Rifle Association in the Face of the Clinton Challenge." In *Interest Group Politics*, ed. Allan J. Cigler and Burdett Loomis, 6th ed. Washington, D.C.: CQ Press.

Patterson, Thomas E. 2003. *The Vanishing Voter: Public Involvement in an Age of Uncertainty*. New York: Knopf.

Peck, Don. 2002. "The Shrinking Electorate." *Atlantic Monthly*, November: 48.

Peffley, Mark A., and Jon Hurwitz. 1985. "A Hierarchical Model of Attitude Constraint." *American Journal of Political Science* 29:871–90.

Persily, Nathaniel. 2001. "Toward a Functional Defense of Political Party Autonomy." *New York University Law Review* 76:750–824.

Peters, Ronald M. 1997. *The American Speakership: The Office in Historical Perspective.* 2nd ed. Baltimore: Johns Hopkins University Press.

Petracca, Mark P. 1989. "Political Consultants and Democratic Governance." *PS: Political Science and Politics* 22, no. 1: 11–14.

Petrocik, John R. 1981. *Party Coalitions: Realignments and the Decline of the New Deal Party System.* Chicago: University of Chicago Press.

———. 1987. "Realignment: New Party Coalitions and the Nationalization of the South." *Journal of Politics* 49 (May): 347–75.

———. 1989. "An Expected Party Vote: Some New Data for an Old Concept, with Applications." *American Journal of Political Science* 33 (February).

———. 1998. "Reformulating the Party Coalitions: The Christian Democratic Republicans." Paper presented at the annual meeting of the American Political Science Association, Boston, September 3–6.

Petrocik, John R., William L. Benoit, and Glen Hansen. 2003–2004. "Issue Ownership and Presidential Campaigning, 1952–2000." *Political Science Quarterly.* 118: 599–626.

Pew Research Center. 2004. "Online News Audience Larger, More Diverse; News Audiences Increasingly Politicized." June 8. http://people-press.org/reports/display .php3?PageID=833.

———. 2005a. "GOP Makes Gains among the Working Class." August 2. http://people-press.org/commentary/display.php3?AnalysisID=114.

———. 2005b. "Religion a Strength and Weakness for Both Parties." August 30. http:// people-press.org/reports/display.php3?ReportID=254.

Phillips, Kevin. 1970. *The Emerging Republican Majority.* Garden City, N.Y.: Anchor.

Pildes, Richard H. 2004. "The Constitutionalization of Democratic Politics." *Harvard Law Review* 118:28–154.

Polsby, Nelson W.. 1983. *Consequences of Party Reform.* Berkeley, Calif.: Institute of Governmental Studies Press.

Polsby, Nelson W., and Aaron Wildavsky. 1988. *Presidential Elections.* New York: Free Press.

Pomper, Gerald. 1970. *Elections in America.* New York: Dodd, Mead.

———. 2003. "Parliamentary Government in the United States: A New Regime for a New Century?" In Green and Farmer 2003.

Poole, Keith T., and Howard Rosenthal. 1991. "Patterns of Congressional Voting." *American Journal of Political Science* 35:228–78.

———. 1997. *Congress: A Political-Economic History of Roll Call Voting.* New York: Oxford University Press.

Powell, G. Bingham, Jr. 1982. *Contemporary Democracies: Participation, Stability, and Violence.* Cambridge, Mass.: Harvard University Press.

Project for Excellence in Journalism. 2005. "State of the News Media 2005." Available at http://www.stateofthemedia.org/2005.

Putnam, Robert D. 2000. *Bowling Alone: The Collapse and Revival of American Community.* New York: Simon & Schuster.

Racheter, Donald P., Lyman A. Kellstedt, and John C. Green. 2003. "Iowa: Crucible of the Christian Right." In *The Christian Right in American Politics: Marching to the Millennium,* ed. John C. Green, Mark J. Rozell, and Clyde Wilcox, 121–44. Washington, D.C.: Georgetown University Press.

Racicot, Marc. 2004. "New Voters Are the Key to Victory in 2004." Available at http://www.gop.org/news/risingtideread.aspx?id=12.

Rae, Nicol C. 1989. *The Decline and Fall of the Liberal Republicans from 1952 to the Present.* New York: Oxford University Press.

———. 2000. "Clinton and the Democratic Party." In Schier 2000.

Ranney, Austin. 1954. *The Doctrine of Responsible Party Government.* Urbana: University of Illinois Press.

———. 1975. *Curing the Mischiefs of Faction: Party Reform in America.* Berkeley: University of California Press.

Rapoport, Ronald B., and Walter J. Stone. 2005. *Three's a Crowd: The Dynamic of Third Parties, Ross Perot, and Republican Resurgence.* Ann Arbor: University of Michigan Press.

Reich, Brian. 2005. "Please Standby . . . The DNC Is Still Experiencing Technical Difficulties." Personal Democracy Forum. April 18. http://www.personaldemocracy.com/node/536.

Reichley, A. James. 2000. *The Life of the Parties: A History of American Political Parties.* Rev. ed. Lanham, Md.: Rowman & Littlefield.

Reiter, Howard L. 1981. "Intra-Party Cleavages in the United States Today." *Western Political Quarterly* 34:287–300.

———. 1996. "Why Did the Whigs Die (and Why Didn't the Democrats)? Evidence from National Nominating Conventions." *Studies in American Political Development* 10:185–222.

———. 1998. "The Bases of Progressivism within the Major Parties: Evidence from the National Conventions." *Social Science History* 22:83–116.

———. 2001a. "The Building of a Bifactional Structure: The Democrats in the 1940s." *Political Science Quarterly* 116:107–29.

———. 2001b. "Democratic and Republican Factionalism in the Age of Divided Government." Paper presented at the annual meeting of the American Political Science Association, San Francisco.

———. 2005. "Party Factions in 2004." Paper presented at the State of the Parties Conference, Akron, Ohio.

Rochon, Thomas R. 1999. "Adaption in the Dutch Party System: Social Change and Party Response." In *Comparative Political Parties and Party Elites: Essays in Honor of Samuel J. Eldersveld*, ed. Birol Yesilada. Ann Arbor: University of Michigan Press.

Rockman, Bert A. 2004. "Presidential Leadership in a Time of Party Polarization: The George W. Bush Presidency." In Campbell and Rockman 2004.

Rohde, David W. 1991. *Parties and Leaders in the Postreform House.* Chicago: University of Chicago Press.

Rokkan, Stein. 1970. *Citizens, Elections, Parties.* New York: David McKay.

Rose, Richard. 1974. *Electoral Behavior.* New York: Free Press.

———. 1991. *The Postmodern Presidency.* 2nd ed. Chatham, N.J.: Chatham House.

Rose, Richard, and Derek W. Urwin. 1969. "Social Cohesion, Political Parties, and Strains on Regimes." *Comparative Political Studies* 2:7–67.

———. 1970. "Persistence and Change in Party Systems." *Political Studies* 10:287–319.

Rosenbloom, David Lee. 1973. *The Election Men: Professional Campaign Managers and American Democracy.* New York: Quadrangle Books.

Rosenstone, Steven J., Roy L. Behr, and Edward R. Lazarus. 1996. *Third Parties in America.* 2nd ed. Princeton, N.J.: Princeton University Press.

Rosenstone, Steven J., and John Mark Hansen. 1993. *Mobilization, Participation and Democracy in America.* New York: Macmillan.

Rosenthal, Alan. 1990. *Governors and Legislatures: Contending Powers.* Washington, D.C.: CQ Press.

Ryden, David K. 1996. *Representation in Crisis: The Constitution, Interest Groups, and Political Parties.* Albany: State University of New York Press.

———. 1999. "'The Good, the Bad, and the Ugly': The Judicial Shaping of Party Activities." In Green and Shea 1999.

———, ed. 2002. *The U.S. Supreme Court and the Electoral Process.* 2nd ed., rev. and updated. Washington, D.C.: Georgetown University Press.

———. 2003. "Out of the Shadows but Still in the Dark? The Courts and Political Parties." In Green and Farmer 2003.

Sabato, Larry J. 1981. *The Rise of Political Consultants: New Ways of Winning Elections.* New York: Basic Books.

Salisbury, Robert H. 1969. "An Exchange Theory of Interest Groups." *Midwest Journal of Political Science* 13:1–32.

Saunders, Kyle L., and Alan I. Abramowitz. 2004. "Ideological Realignment and Active Partisans in the American Electorate." *American Politics Research* 32:285–309.

Schattschneider, E. E. 1942. *Party Government.* New York: Farrar and Rinehart.

———. 1975. *The Semisovereign People.* Hinsdale, Ill.: Dryden.

Schier, Steven E., ed. 2000. *The Postmodern Presidency: Bill Clinton's Legacy in U.S. Politics.* Pittsburgh, Pa.: University of Pittsburgh Press.

Schlesinger, Arthur M., Jr. 1986. *The Cycles of American History.* Boston: Houghton Mifflin.

Schlesinger, Joseph A. 1994. *Political Parties and the Winning of Office.* Ann Arbor: University of Michigan Press.

Shafer, Byron E. 1991. *The End of Realignment? Interpreting American Electoral Eras.* Madison: University Press of Wisconsin.

———. 2003. *The Two Major Parties and the Puzzle of American Politics.* Lawrence: University Press of Kansas.

Shanks, J. Merrill, Douglas Strand, Edward Carmines, and Henry E. Brady. 2005. "Issue Importance in the 2000 Election." Paper presented at the annual meeting of the American Political Science Association, Washington, D.C.

Shaw, Daron R. 2004. "Door-to-Door with the GOP." *Hoover Digest* (Fall). Available at http://www.hooverdigest.org/044/shaw.html.

Shea, Daniel M. 2003. "Schattschneider's Dismay: Strong Parties and Alienated Voters." In Green and Farmer 2003, 287–99.

Shea, Daniel M., and John C. Green, eds. 1994. *The State of the Parties: The Changing Role of Contemporary American Parties.* Lanham, Md.: Rowman & Littlefield.

———. 2004. "The Fountain of Youth: Political Parties and the Mobilization of Young Americans." Center for Political Participation, Allegheny College. Available at http://www.civicyouth.org/PopUps/WorkingPapers/Fountain%20Youth_CPP.pdf.

————. 2006. *Fountain of Youth: Strategies for Mobilizing America's Young Voters*. Lanham, Md.: Rowman & Littlefield.

Sidanius, James, and Felicia F. Pratto. 2001. *Social Dominance: An Intergroup Theory of Social Hierarchy and Oppression*. New York: Cambridge University Press.

Sinclair, Barbara. 1996. "Trying to Govern Positively in a Negative Era: Clinton and the 103rd Congress." In Campbell and Rockman, eds., *The Clinton Presidency: First Appraisals*. Chatam, NJ: Chatam House.

————. 2000a. "Hostile Partners: The President, Congress, and Lawmaking in the Partisan 1990s." In Bond and Fleisher 2000.

————. 2000b. *Unorthodox Lawmaking: New Legislative Processes in the U.S. Congress*. 2nd ed. Washington, D.C.: CQ Press.

————. 2002. "The Dream Fulfilled? Party Development in Congress, 1950–2000." In Green and Herrnson 2002.

————. 2004. "Leading and Competing: The President and the Polarized Congress." In Edwards and Davies 2004.

Skinner, Delacey. 2004. "America Votes Launched Fall Days of Political Action with National Women's Election Action Day." America Coming Together press release, September 15.

Skinner, Richard M. 2005. "Do 527's Add Up to a Party? Thinking about the 'Shadows' of Politics." *The Forum* 3, no. 3. http://www.bepress.com/forum/vol3/iss3/art5.

Smidt, Corwin E. 1993. "Evangelical Voting Patterns, 1976–1988." In *No Longer Exiles*, ed. Michael Cromartie. Washington, D.C.: Ethics and Public Policy Center.

Smith, Daniel A. 2004. "Strings Attached: Outside Money in Colorado's Seventh District." In Magleby and Monson 2004.

Smith, Devlin. 2005. "7 Tips for Network Marketing Success." *Entrepreneur.com*, May 5. http://www.entrepreneur.com/article/0,4621,321283,00.html.

Sonquist, John A., Elizabeth Lauh Baker, and James N. Morgan. 1973. *Searching for Structure*. Ann Arbor: Survey Research Center, University of Michigan.

Stanley, Harold M., and Richard G. Niemi. 2005. "Change in the Party Coalitions: Partisan and Group Support." Paper presented at the annual meeting of the American Political Science Association, Washington, D.C.

Stoltz, Gail. 2003. "Mobilizing Voters: The Coordinated Campaign." In Corrado, Mann, and Potter 2003.

Stonecash, Jeffrey M. 2000. *Class and Party in American Politics*. Boulder, Colo.: Westview Press.

————. 2006. *Political Parties Matter: Realignment and the Return of Partisan Voting*. Boulder, Colo.: Lynne Rienner.

Stonecash, Jeffrey M., Mark D. Brewer, and Mack D. Mariani. 2003. *Diverging Parties: Social Change, Realignment, and Party Polarization*. Boulder, Colo.: Westview Press.

Sullivan, John L., James E. Piereson, and George E. Marcus. 1978. "Ideological Constraint in the Mass Public: A Methodological Critique and Some New Findings." *American Journal of Political Science* 22:233–49.

Sundquist, James L. 1983. *Dynamics of the Party System*. Rev. ed. Washington, D.C.: Brookings.

Sunstein, Cass. 2001. *Republic.com*. Princeton, N.J.: Princeton University Press.

Suskind, Ron. 2004. *The Price of Loyalty: George W. Bush, the White House, and the Education of Paul O'Neill.* New York: Simon & Schuster.

Tajfel, Henri. 1981. *Human Groups and Social Categories: Studies in Social Psychology.* Cambridge: Cambridge University Press.

Tajfel, Henri, and John C. Turner. 1986. "The Social Identity Theory of Intergroup Behavior." In *Psychology of Intergroup Relations*, ed. S. Worchel and W. G. Austin. Chicago: Nelson-Hall.

Teixeira, Ruy. 2003. "Deciphering the Democrats' Debacle." *Washington Monthly* (May), http://www.washingtonmonthly.com/features/2003/0305.Teixeira.html.

Thurber, James A., and Candice J. Nelson, eds. 2000. *Campaign Warriors: Political Consultants in Elections.* Washington, D.C.: Brookings.

Thurber, James A., Candice J. Nelson, and David A. Dulio. 2000. "Portrait of Campaign Consultants." In Thurber and Nelson 2000.

Trippi, Joe. 2004. *The Revolution Will Not Be Televised.* New York: HarperCollins.

Trish, Barbara. 1994. "Party Integration in Indiana and Ohio: The 1988 and 1992 Presidential Contests." *American Review of Politics* 15:235–56.

Tuchfarber, Alfred J., and Eric W. Rademacher. 1995. "The Republican Tidal Wave of 1994: Testing Hypotheses about Realignment, Restructuring and Rebellion." *PS: Political Science and Politics* 28, no. 4: 689–96.

Turner, John C. 1982. "Toward a Cognitive Redefinition of the Social Group." In *Social Identity and Intergroup Relations*, ed. Henri Tajfel. Cambridge: Cambridge University Press.

———. 1987. *Rediscovering the Social Group: A Self-Categorization Theory.* Oxford, England: Basil Blackwell.

Usher, Douglas. 2000. "Strategy, Rules, and Participation: Issue Activists in Republican National Convention Delegations, 1976–1996." *Political Research Quarterly* 53:887–903.

Van Buren, Martin. 1967. *Inquiry into the Origins and Course of Political Parties in the United States.* New York: Kelley.

Verba, Sidney, and Kay Lehnan Schlozman. 2005. "Mobilization, Moral Values, and Political Equality: The 2004 Election and Citizen Participation." Paper presented at the annual meeting of the American Political Science Association, Washington, D.C.

Vertz, Laura L., John P. Frendreis, and James L. Gibson. 1987. "Nationalization of the Electorate in the United States." *American Political Science Review* 81:961–66.

Ware, Alan. 1996. *Political Parties and Party Systems.* New York: Oxford University Press.

Waterman, Richard. 1989. *Presidential Influence and the Administrative State.* Knoxville: University of Tennessee Press.

Wattenberg, Martin P. 1984. *The Decline of American Political Parties, 1952–1980.* Cambridge, Mass.: Harvard University Press.

———. 1998. *The Decline of American Political Parties, 1952–1998.* Cambridge, Mass.: Harvard University Press.

Wayne, Stephen. 2004. "Bush and Congress: Old Problems and New Challenges." In Edwards and Davies 2004.

Weisberg, Herbert F. 1987. "The Demographics of a New Voting Gap: Marital Differences in American Voting." *Public Opinion Quarterly* 51:335–43.

————, ed. 1995. *Democracy's Feast*. Chatham, N.J.: Chatham House.

Weisberg, Herbert F., and Dino Christenson. 2005. "Changing Horse in Wartime? The 2004 Presidential Election." Paper presented at the annual meeting of the American Political Science Association, Washington, D.C.

Weisberg, Herbert F., Audrey A. Haynes, and Jon A. Krosnick. 1995. "Social-Group Polarization in 1992." In Weisberg 1995.

Weisberg, Herbert F., and Timothy C. Hill. 2004. "The Succession Presidential Election of 2000: The Battle of the Legacies." In Weisberg and Wilcox 2004.

Weisberg, Herbert F., and David C. Kimball. 1995. "Attitudinal Correlates of the 1992 Presidential Vote: Party Identification and Beyond." In Weisberg 1995.

Weisberg, Herbert F., and Clyde Wilcox, eds. 2004. *Models of Voting in Presidential Elections: The 2000 Election*. Stanford, Calif.: Stanford University Press.

Weissman, Steve, and Ruth Hassan. 2006. "BCRA and the 527 Groups." In Malbin 2006.

West, Darrell M. 2001. *The Rise and Fall of the Media Establishment*. New York: Palgrave Macmillan.

White, John Kenneth. 2003. *The Values Divide*. Chatham, N.J.: Chatham House.

————. 2004. "Two Stable and Partisan Coalitions." Catholic University of America, Washington, D.C.

————. 2005. "Choosing the Candidates." In Kevin J. McMahon, David M. Rankin, Donald W. Beachler, and John Kenneth White, *Winning the White House, 2004: Region by Region, Vote by Vote*. New York: Palgrave Macmillan.

White, John Kenneth, and Daniel M. Shea. 2000. *New Party Politics: From Jefferson and Hamilton to the Information Age*. Boston: Bedford/St. Martin's.

————. 2004. *New Party Politics: From Jefferson and Hamilton to the Information Age*. 2nd ed. Belmont, Calif.: Wadsworth-Thomson.

Wilcox, Clyde, Lee Sigelman, and Elizabeth Cook. 1989. "Some Like It Hot: Individual Difference in Responses to Group Feeling Thermometers." *Public Opinion Quarterly* 53:246–57.

Williams, Rhys H., ed. 1997. *Cultural Wars in American Politics: Critical Reviews of a Popular Myth*. New York: De Gruyter.

Wilson, Woodrow. 1885. *Congressional Government*. Boston: Houghton-Mifflin.

Winger, Richard. 2005. "An Analysis of the 2004 Nader Ballot Access Court Cases." *Fordham Law Review* 32, no. 3: 567–87.

Wirls, Daniel. 1986. "Reinterpreting the Gender Gap." *Public Opinion Quarterly* 50:316–30.

Wolbrecht, Christina. 2002. "Explaining Women's Rights Realignment: Convention Delegates, 1972–1992." *Political Behavior* 24:237–82.

Wolfinger, Raymond E. 1965. "The Development and Persistence of Ethnic Voting." *American Political Science Review* 59:896–908.

Yalof, David A. 2003. "The Presidency and the Judiciary." In Nelson 2003.

York, Byron. 2005. *The Vast Left-Wing Conspiracy*. New York: Crown Forum.

Zaller, John R. 1992. *The Nature and Origins of Mass Opinion*. New York: Cambridge University Press.

Index

abortion: absent from "Contract with America," 238; American National Election Study on, 319; conservatives on, 325; Dean supporters on, 156; party elites on, 60–61, 63–65, 72

Abramowitz, Alan I., 10, 75, 355, 357, 358

Achelpohl, Steve, 215

Adams, John Quincy, 22

advertising: advocacy advertising, 105, 106; arranged by political consultants, 208; bought by America Votes, 145–47; spending on, by state parties, 115

advocacy advertising, 105, 106

affirmative action programs, 57–58

Afghanistan, 242

African Americans, 29, 57; in current party coalitions, 285; among Dean supporters, 156; Dean supporters on discrimination against, 162; in election of 2004, 26; identification with Democratic Party by, 310–12; Kerry campaign and, 193; in New Deal party coalitions, 282–83;

Aldrich, John H., 88, 199, 201–3, 354n2

Alito, Samuel, 277

Allen, Mike, 183

Alticor (firm), 174

Amendment 27 (Colorado), 122

American for Democratic Action (ADA), 41

American National Election Study (ANES; NES), 296n9; on conservatives, 318–19; on election of 2004, 314, 336; "feeling thermometer" ratings used by, 265; on identification with Republican Party, 301; on ideological identification and party preferences, 303–4; ideological identification scale used by, 315n3; on ideological realignment, 308–9; Perot voters in, 247n2; on political polarization, 267–70, 272–74; on Republican Party in presidential elections, 320–21; on withdrawal from politics, 218

American Political Science Association (APSA), 16, 90, 173, 185

Americans Coming Together (ACT; organization), 4, 118, 182; in America Votes coalition, 135, 140; after election of 2004, 149; in Mahoning County (Ohio), 188–90, 197; polls commissioned by, 143

America Votes (AV; organization), 4, 7, 149–50, 186; creation of, 135; electoral work of, 144–49; formation of, 139–41; incentives to join, 141–44; in Ohio, 188

Amway (firm), 174

Anderson, John, 259

Antonini, Lisa, 191–94

Bai, Matt, 149, 173, 177–78, 184–85, 375

Baker, Elizabeth Lauh, 296n4

Baker, Howard, 334

Ball, Terence, 36

Balz, Dan, 176, 177, 183

Barga, Rick, 192–94

Bartels, Larry M., 75

Battista, James S. Coleman, 88

battleground states: multilevel marketing techniques used by Republican Party in, 182–83; party polarization in, 275; spending by America Votes in, 145–47; state party spending in, 119–20, 132. See also Florida; Ohio

Bauer, Bob, 150n1

Beauprez, Bob, 177

Beck, Paul Allen, 89, 90

Bednarik, Michael, 255

Behr, Roy L., 232

Belcher, Cornell, 143

Beller, Dennis C., 36

Belloni, Frank P., 36

Bennet, Barry, 184

Berger, Mark M., 354n2

Berry, Jeffrey M., 82

Bibby, John F., 76
Bigelow, Nathan S., 6
Bindas, Debbie, 190
Bing, Stephen, 169n4
Binning, William C., 8
Bipartisan Campaign Finance Reform Act of
   2002 (BCRA; U.S.), 97–98, 110–11,
   223–24; candidates as donors under,
   100–101; election of 2004 under, 4, 16,
   95; express advocacy by organizations
   banned by, 141; hard money under, 120;
   impact in Mahoning County (Ohio) of,
   197; impact on state parties of, 113, 114,
   121–34; interest groups under, 145, 149;
   Levin Amendment to, 117; soft money
   banned under, 189; Supreme Court on,
   370, 372–76
blacks. *See* African Americans
Blagojevich, Rod, 20
Blumberg, Melanie J., 8
Blunt, Roy, 353
Bond, Jon R., 49
Bon Jovi, 195
Bowler, Kathleen, 114
Bradley, Bill, 40
Brewer, Paul R., 350
Broder, David, 15
Brown, A. Robert, 193
Brown, Jerry, 40
Bryan, William Jennings, 22
Buchanan, Pat, 53, 240
Buckley v. Vaelo (U.S., 1976), 107
Budge, Ian, 79
Burke, Edmund, 35
Burnham, Walter Dean, 15, 21; on decline in
   competition for House seats, 382n7; re-
   sponsible party government model of,
   343; on third parties, 232; thirty-year
   cycle theory of, 33
Burns, James McGregor, 15
Bush, George H. W., 44–45, 331, 334
Bush, George W.: administration posts filled
   by, 338–39; branding name of, 179–81;
   coalitions organized against, 138; coalitions supporting, in election of 2004,
   286–87; compassionate conservatism of,

55; conservative agenda of, 317; continued support of Republicans for, 326; donations to Republican Party by campaign
of, 104; in election of 2000, 21, 59, 135;
in election of 2004, 2–3, 5, 24–26, 44–
45, 215, 255; images of, in election of
2004, 289–95; involved in RNC fundraising, 99–100; Nader vote and, 249; as
partisan president, 10–11, 332, 334–36,
341; Perot supporters and, 246–47; polarization of public opinion on, 270; public
opinion on policies of, 267; relationship
with Congress of, 337; Republican
agenda under, 242–45; Republican voters
and, 45–48; response to Hurricane Katrina by, 265; Supreme Court appointments of, 61; voters opposed to, 163, 167;
White House press corps and, 339–40
Bush v. Gore (U.S., 2000), 369, 380–81
Butler, R. Lawrence, 11, 352

cable television, 339
Cain, Bruce, 371
California, 20
California Democratic Party v. Jones (U.S.,
   2002), 371, 382n1
Camejo, Peter Miguel, 251–52
campaign financing, 95–100; candidates as
   donors, 100–104; confusion over, in
   Ohio, 192; in election of 2004, 7, 16; independent expenditures in 2004, 108–9;
   professional fundraisers used for, 211,
   212, 214; reforms of, 243; spending in,
   104–6; Supreme Court on, 106–8, 370,
   372–76
Campbell, Angus, 267, 300
Campbell, James E., 357, 358
candidates: campaign donations by, 100–
   104; images of, in election of 2004,
   289–95; independent candidates, 231;
   political consultants and, 200, 209
candidates' personal campaign committees
   (PCCs), 101–2
Cannon, Joseph, 16
Carmines, Edward G., 88
Carney, Eliza Newlin, 100
Carsey, Thomas M., 272

About the Editors and Contributors

Alan I. Abramowitz is the Alben W. Barkley Professor of Political Science at Emory University. He has authored or coauthored four books, dozens of contributions to edited volumes, and more than forty articles in political science journals dealing with political parties, elections, and voting behavior in the United States. His most recent book is *Voice of the People: Elections and Voting Behavior in the United States* (2004).

Nathan S. Bigelow is assistant professor of political science at Austin College. His research and teaching interests include political campaigning, campaign finance, political parties, and interest group politics at both the national and state levels.

William C. Binning serves as chair and professor of political science at Youngstown State University. He has been active on Ohio politics for more than thirty years.

Melanie J. Blumberg is associate professor of political science at California University of Pennsylvania. She and her coauthors publish their work on the Coordinated Campaign in *The State of the Parties* series and their studies of Ohio and Pennsylvania congressional elections in *The Road to Congress* series.

R. Lawrence Butler is assistant professor of political science at Rowan University. He is the author of *Claiming the Mantle: How Presidential Nominations Are Won and Lost Before the Votes Are Cast* (2005).

Daniel J. Coffey is assistant professor of political science at the University of Akron and a fellow in the Ray C. Bliss Institute of Applied Politics. He studies political parties, public opinion, state and local politics, campaigns and elections, and research methods and has been published in *State Politics and Policy Quarterly*.

Christian Collet is associate professor of American politics at Doshisha University in Kyoto. His work on minor parties has appeared in *Public Opinion Quarterly* and several edited volumes.

David A. Dulio is assistant professor of political science at Oakland University. He is the author of *For Better or Worse? How Political Consultants are*

Changing Elections in the United States (2004) and *Vital Signs: Perspectives on the Health of American Campaigning* (2005, with Candice J. Nelson) and several articles and book chapters on political parties, professional political consultants, and campaigns and elections generally. He was also an American Political Science Association congressional fellow in 2001–2002 in the office of Rep. J. C. Watts Jr. (R-Okla.).

Diana Dwyre is professor and chair of the Political Science Department at California State University, Chico. She has published extensively on political parties and campaign finance, particularly in the context of congressional elections. She is coauthor, along with Victoria Farrar-Myers, of *Legislative Labyrinth: Congress and Campaign Finance Reform* (2001).

John P. Frendreis is professor of political science and the interim provost at Loyola University, Chicago. His publications include articles in the *American Political Science Review, American Journal of Political Science, Journal of Politics, Comparative Political Studies, Social Science Quarterly,* and *Journal of Urban Affairs,* and he is coauthor of *The Modern Presidency and Economic Policy* (1994) and *Professional Associations and Municipal Innovation* (1981).

Cary Funk is senior project director at the Pew Research Center in Washington, D.C., on leave from Virginia Commonwealth University, where she is associate professor. Her specialty in public opinion includes analysis of candidate evaluations, voting behavior, and the underpinnings of policy attitudes.

R. Sam Garrett is an analyst in American national government at the Congressional Research Service, Library of Congress. His dissertation at American University focused on crisis management in congressional campaigns. He also serves as a research fellow at American University's Center for Congressional and Presidential Studies and an adjunct faculty member in the Department of Government.

Alan R. Gitelson is professor of political science, assistant provost, and former chair of the Department of Political Science at Loyola University in Chicago. His books include *American Political Parties: Stability and Change, American Government* (7th ed., 2004), *Public Policy and Economic Institutions* (1991), and *American Elections: The Rules Matter* (2002). Gitelson has served as a member of the Executive Council of the American Political Science Association's Division on Political Organizations and Parties and the APSA Committee on Education and Professional Development.

John C. Green is distinguished professor of political science and director of the Ray C. Bliss Institute of Applied Politics at the University of Akron. His most recent publication is the edited volume *The Elections of 2000: Politics, Culture and Economics in North America* (2005).

Cassie A. Gross is a doctoral student in political science at the University of Missouri–St. Louis. Her research focuses on public policy and political participation.

Jerrold Hansen is regional coordinator of research and consulting, Asia-Pacific, with the Gallup Organization in Singapore.

Eric Heberlig is associate professor of political science at the University of North Carolina–Charlotte. He is coauthor of *American Labor Unions in the Electoral Arena* (2001), *Classics in Congressional Politics* (1999), and journal articles on congressional and interest group politics.

John S. Jackson III is a visiting professor at the Public Policy Institute at Southern Illinois University at Carbondale, where he was formerly interim chancellor and vice chancellor for academic affairs. His most recent book is *The Politics of Presidential Elections* (2000, with William Crotty).

Shannon Jenkins is assistant professor of political science at the University of Massachusetts, Dartmouth, specializing in state politics, urban politics, and public policy. Her research focuses on decision making in state legislatures, with a specific focus on the role of political organizations in these institutions. Her research has appeared in journals such as *Legislative Studies Quarterly*, *Urban Affairs Review*, and *Social Science Quarterly*.

Scott Keeter is director of survey research for the Pew Research Center in Washington, D.C. His published work focuses on public opinion, political participation, religion and politics, and survey research methods. He has held faculty positions at George Mason University, Virginia Commonwealth University, Rutgers University, and Union College.

Courtney Kennedy is a project director at the Pew Research Center in Washington, D.C., and a doctoral student in survey methodology at the University of Michigan. Her research interests include survey research methods and U.S. political behavior.

David C. Kimball is associate professor of political science at the University of Missouri–St. Louis. He is the coauthor of *Why Americans Split Their Tickets* (2002, with Barry Burden), and he has published articles in several academic journals. His research and teaching interests include voting behavior, interest groups, and election reform.

Robin Kolodny is associate professor of political science at Temple University. Her research focus is on political parties, campaign finance, and political consultants. She is the author of *Pursuing Majorities: Congressional Campaign Committees in American Politics* (1998).

Raymond J. La Raja is assistant professor of political science at the University of Massachusetts, Amherst, as well as an editor of *The Forum*, an electronic journal of applied research in contemporary politics. His research on American political parties, interest groups, and consequences of electoral reforms has appeared in numerous journals and edited volumes. He serves on the Academic Advisory Board of the Campaign Finance Institute in Washington, D.C.

Bruce Larson is assistant professor of political science at Gettysburg College. His current research interests are congressional parties and congressional campaign finance.

David B. Magleby is the dean of the College of Family, Home, and Social Sciences; a Distinguished Professor of Political Science; and a senior research fellow at the Center for the Study of Elections and Democracy at Brigham Young University. His recent work includes *Financing the 2004 Election* (2006) and *The Last Hurrah? Soft Money and Issue Advocacy in the 2002 Congressional Elections* (2004).

J. Quin Monson is assistant professor of political science and assistant director of the Center for the Study of Elections and Democracy at Brigham Young University. His interests include public opinion, voting behavior, religion, and politics, and his work has recently appeared in *Political Research Quarterly*, *Political Analysis*, and *Presidential Studies Quarterly*.

Susan E. Orr is a doctoral student in political science at the University of Florida. Her dissertation research explores the intersection of union organizing drives and political activity.

Kelly D. Patterson is associate professor of political science and the director of the Center for the Study of Elections and Democracy at Brigham Young University. His research interests include campaigns and elections and public opinion. His recent work includes *The Dawning of a New Day? Congressional Elections in the Wake of the Bipartisan Campaign Reform Act*.

John R. Petrocik is professor and chair of the Department of Political Science at the University of Missouri–Columbia. His teaching and research centers on mass attitudes and behavior, political parties, elections and campaigns, and survey research and analysis, and he has authored and coauthored books and research articles on these topics. His current projects are on issue ownership and conventional wisdoms about American public opinion and voting.

Ronald B. Rapoport is the John Marshall Professor of Government at the College of William and Mary. He is a coeditor of *The Life of the Parties: A Study of Presidential Activists* (1993) and coauthor of *Three's a Crowd: The Dynamic of Third Parties, Ross Perot, and Republican Resurgence* (2005, with Walter J. Stone).

A. James Reichley has written many books and articles on politics, including *The Life of the Parties* (2000), *The Values Connection* (2001), and *Faith in Politics* (2002). He has been political editor of *Fortune*, domestic policy assistant to President Gerald Ford, senior fellow at the Brookings Institution, and senior fellow in the Graduate Public Policy Institute at Georgetown University.

Howard L. Reiter is professor and chair of the Department of Political Science at the University of Connecticut. He is the author of *Selecting the President* (1985) and *Parties and Elections in Corporate America* (1987, 1993), and his writings on political parties have appeared in numerous journals. In 2001–2002, he was Fulbright Distinguished Professor at Uppsala University in Sweden.

Douglas D. Roscoe is assistant professor of political science at the University of Massachusetts, Dartmouth. His interests include Congress, the president, interest groups, and political parties. His research has been published in the *Journal of Politics, Social Science Quarterly, Legislative Studies Quarterly,* and *Congress and the Presidency.*

David K. Ryden is a professor of political science at Hope College and an attorney. One of his primary areas of scholarly work is the intersection between constitutional law and electoral politics. He has published and edited a number of books, including *Representation in Crisis: The Constitution, Interest Groups, and Political Parties* (1996) and *The U.S. Supreme Court and the Electoral Process* (2002).

Kyle L. Saunders is assistant professor of political science at Colorado State University. His research interests include political parties, public opinion, and political behavior. He is the author or coauthor of articles appearing in the *Journal of Politics, Comparative Political Studies, Political Research Quarterly, American Politics Research*, and other journals as well as contributions to several edited volumes.

Daniel M. Shea is associate professor of political science and director of the Center for Political Participation at Allegheny College. He has written widely on campaign strategy, political parties, Congress, and political participation.

Richard M. Skinner is visiting assistant professor of government at Bowdoin College. He previously served as a research analyst at the Campaign Finance Institute. He has authored or coauthored several scholarly articles and book chapters on political parties, interest groups, and campaign finance reform.

Daniel A. Smith is associate professor of political science at the University of Florida. He is the author of *Tax Crusaders and the Politics of Direct Democracy* (1998) and coauthor of *Educated by Initiative: The Effects of Direct Democracy on Citizens and Political Organizations in the American States* (2004). He serves on the Board of Directors of the Ballot Initiative Strategy Center Foundation.

Walter J. Stone is professor and chair of political science at the University of California, Davis. He is a coauthor of *Three's a Crowd: The Dynamic of Third Parties, Ross Perot, and Republican Resurgence* (2005, with Ronald B. Rapoport).

Jeffrey M. Stonecash is professor and chair of political science at the Maxwell School at Syracuse University. His research focuses on political parties, their electoral bases, and how these bases shape public policy debates. His most recent books are *Class and Party in American Politics* (2000), *Diverging Parties* (2003), and *Political Parties Matters: Realignment and the Return of Partisan Voting* (2006).

Peter Ubertaccio is assistant professor of political science at Stonehill College. He is the author of *Learned in the Law and Politics: The Office of the Solicitor General and Executive Power* (2005).